THE NORTHERN YELLOWSTONE ELK

THE NORTHERN YELLOWSTONE ELK

Ecology and Management

DOUGLAS B. HOUSTON

Macmillan Publishing Co., Inc.
NEW YORK
Collier Macmillan
LONDON

Macmillan Publishing Co., Inc.
866 Third Avenue, New York, N.Y. 10022

Collier Macmillan Canada, Inc.

Printed in the United States of America

printing number

1 2 3 4 5 6 7 8 9 10

Library of Congress Cataloging in Publication Data

Houston, Douglas B.
  The northern Yellowstone elk.

  Includes bibliographical references and index.
    1. Elk—Yellowstone National Park—Ecology.
2. Wildlife Management—Yellowstone National
Park. 3. Mammals—Ecology. 4. Mammals—Yellowstone
National Park—Ecology. 5. Yellowstone National
Park I. Title.
QL737.U55H68 1982   599.73′57   82-70079
ISBN 0-02-949450-8   AACR2

Contents

List of Figures   *ix*

List of Tables   *xii*

Foreword   *xv*

Acknowledgments   *xviii*

Chapter 1   INTRODUCTION   **1**

Chapter 2   STUDY AREA   **3**

Administration•Geology and
Geography•Climate•Vegetation

Chapter 3   THE ELK POPULATION—HISTORY AND NUMBERS   **10**

Early Records to 1886•The 1886–1910 Period•The
1911–20 Period•The 1921–29 Period•The 1930–68
Period•The 1969–79 Period•Interpretation: History
and Numbers

**Chapter 4   THE ELK POPULATION—SEASONAL
DISTRIBUTION**   **26**

Winter Distribution•Spring, Summer, and Autumn
Distribution•Herd Segments•Interpretation: Seasonal
Distribution

Chapter 5   **THE ELK POPULATION—DYNAMICS**   **36**

Natality•Sex and Age Composition•Mortality•*Sex Ratios•Mortality of Young•Mortality Patterns and Adult Mortality•Annual Mortality•Dispersal•Carrying Capacities•*Interpretation: Population Dynamics•*Natality•Mortality and Recruitment of Young•Adult Mortality and Mortality Patterns•Annual Mortality•Dispersal•Carrying Capacities•Population Regulation*

Chapter 6   **PHYSIOLOGICAL ECOLOGY**   **69**

Nutrition•Growth•Condition•Interpretation

Chapter 7   **ELK BEHAVIOR**   **76**

Group Constancy and Associations Between Individuals•Social Dominance•Interpretation

Chapter 8   **THE VEGETATION—STATICS AND DYNAMICS**   **85**

The Present Vegetation•Past Vegetation•*Holocene Trends•Vegetation of the Historical Past•*Vegetation Measurements•*Herbaceous Vegetation•Trees and Shrubs•*Narrative Reports of Range Conditions•Abiotic Influences on the Vegetation•*Climatic Trends•Fire•Erosion•Human Developments and Activities•*Interpretation: Vegetation•*Spring, Summer and Autumn Ranges•Winter Range•"Deterioration" of the Winter Range•*Ungulate Effects on the Vegetation

Chapter 9   **ELK–HABITAT RELATIONSHIPS**   **137**

Habitat Utilization•Food Habits•Forage Quality•Forage Utilization•Interpretation: Elk–Habitat Relationships•*The Food Supply and the Grazing System•Changes in Ecological Carrying Capacity Over Time•Herbivory in Perspective*

Chapter 10   **RELATIONSHIPS AMONG SPECIES OF HERBIVORES**   **156**

The Less Abundant Ungulates—History, Distribution, Numbers, and Dynamics•*Mule Deer•Bighorn Sheep•Bison•Pronghorn•Moose•*Resource Division•*Separation in Space•Food*

Preference•Effects of Elk Upon the Less Abundant
Ungulates•Other Herbivores•*White-Tailed
Deer*•*Beaver*•Interpretation: Interspecific
Relationships•*Ecological Separation and
Refugia*•*Interspecific Competition*•*Changes in* K_1
Over Time: The Less Abundant Ungulates

Chapter 11   ELK–CARNIVORE RELATIONSHIPS   186

The Carnivores•*Gray Wolf*•*Coyote*•*Cougar*•
Wolverine•*Grizzly Bear*•*Black Bear*•*Man*•Elk as
Food for Carnivores•Parasites and Diseases of Elk•
Interpretation: Carnivores and Elk•*Carnivore
Populations*•*The Effects of Predation*

Chapter 12   MANAGEMENT   196

Management Considerations and
Strategies•Management: Conflicts and
Recommendations•*The Vegetation*•*The
Herbivores*•*The Carnivores*•Monitoring and
Research•*Monitoring*•*Research*

**Appendix   I   Reports of Elk 1836–1886, Yellowstone Park and
                      Vicinity**   204

**Appendix   II   Reports of Elk 1886–1910, Yellowstone Park and
                      Vicinity**   212

**Appendix   III Reports of Elk 1911–1920, Yellowstone Park and
                      Vicinity**   219

Appendix   IV   Calculations and Analyses of Population Dynamics   238

Appendix   V   Comparative Photographs   248

Appendix   VI   Vegetation Measurements   353

Appendix   VII Narrative Reports of Range Conditions   421

Appendix   VIII Forage Consumption   432

Appendix   IX   Ungulates Other than Elk—Supporting Information   434

Appendix **X** **Common and Scientific Names of Animals and Plants** **444**

References *449*

Index *469*

LIST OF FIGURES

2.1.   Yellowstone Park showing study area.   4
2.2.   Climatic diagrams.   6
2.3.   Zonal distribution of annual precipitation.   7
2.4.   Hellroaring Creek area on the northern winter range.   8
3.1.   Elk numbers and removals, 1930–79.   18
3.2   Calculated winter and autumn elk numbers, 1930–79.   20
3.3.   Elk groups in the Lamar Valley, 21 December 1977.   22
4.1.   Elk distribution and density on the winter range during 1969, 1976, and 1978.   31
4.2.   Yellowstone region showing winter and summer ranges of nine different elk herds.   33
5.1.   Adult male elk wintering on the periphery of the northern range.   42
5.2.   The relationship between calf recruitment and population size.   45
5.3.   The relationship between recruitment of yearling males and population size.   46
5.4.   Standing age distributions of female elk, 1951–66.   52
5.5.   Changes over time in the proportion of standing age distributions of females.   53
5.6.   Standing age distributions of male elk, 1951 and 1965.   54
5.7.   Calculated age-specific mortality rates for male and female elk.   57
5.8.   Natural mortality of calves and of males 17 months and older.   58
5.9.   The $\hat{k}$-factors for calf mortality, 1969–75.   59
5.10.   Calf mortality, The $\hat{k}$-factors on log initial total population.   60
5.11.   The $\hat{k}$-factors for males, 1969–75.   60

7.1.   Social interaction—Female elk.   79
7.2.   Summary of agonistic interactions observed in 70 cow–calf groups.   80
7.3.   The relationship between the frequency of agonistic interaction and the relative ease of foraging.   82
8.1.   Annual and seasonal temperature trends at Mammoth Hot Springs.   103
8.2.   Annual and seasonal precipitation trends at Mammoth Hot Springs.   104
8.3.   Annual runoff for the Yellowstone River at Corwin Springs and snow–water equivalents from snow-course surveys.   106
8.4.   The Gardiner Airport burn of June 1961.   110
8.5.   The Blacktail Creek burn of 1963.   111
8.6.   Sagebrush steppe burn near Gardiner, Montana, 29 July 1974.   112
8.7.   Aspen regeneration on Bunsen Peak.   113
8.8.   Aspen regeneration in the Cinnabar Basin.   114
8.9.   Aspen regeneration in the Yankee Jim Canyon.   115
8.10.   A steep south slope showing erosion rills.   116
8.11.   Gardiner area view west along old park boundary, earlier interpreted as showing accelerated gully erosion.   117
8.12.   Percent occurrence of major vegetation types and influence of ungulate foraging.   126
8.13.   Willow stands on the northern winter range.   130
8.14.   Colonization of gravel bars by willows along the Gardner River.   132
8.15.   Willow stands on spring, summer, and autumn ranges of the northern Yellowstone elk.   133
9.1.   Observations of 59,784 feeding elk by vegetation type and seasonal periods, 1967–74.   138
9.2.   Observations of 45,541 feeding elk by slope and exposure classes, 1970–74.   139
9.3.   Elk counted during fixed-wing flights as percent of maximum count.   141
9.4.   Percent crude protein of grass and sedge species.   145
9.5.   A foraging female elk.   151
9.6.   Elk foraging activity in sage steppe.   153
10.1.   Mule deer feeding in a sagebrush steppe.   158
10.2.   Winter distribution of mule deer and bison.   159
10.3.   A wintering bighorn sheep.   160
10.4.   Winter distribution of bighorn sheep and pronghorn.   161
10.5.   Bighorn sheep observed during 33 aerial counts of the northern range, winter–spring, 1971–78.   162
10.6.   Relationship of the number of bighorn sheep observed during 33 aerial counts to mean daily temperature at Mammoth Hot Springs, 1971–78.   163
10.7.   Relationship of ln sheep numbers on time for 25 winter aerial counts, 1955–78.   164
10.8.   Relationship of ln sheep numbers on time for 32 adjusted winter–spring aerial counts, 1955–78.   165
10.9.   Bison foraging on a sedge meadow.   166
10.10.   Bison numbers on the northern range, Februrary aerial counts, 1966–80.   167
10.11.   Pronghorn numbers on the northern range, 1969–80.   168

10.12. Chest heights for six species of native ungulates. 171
10.13. Estimated foot loads of adult females for six species of native ungulates. 172
10.14. Observations of feeding mule deer, bighorn sheep, bison, pronghorn, and moose by vegetation type. 174
10.15. The relationship of relative narrowing of the face to female live weights for five species of grazers and mixed feeders. 176
10.16. The relationship of the angle of insertion of I_1 to female live weights for five species of grazers and mixed feeders. 177
10.17. The relationship of the percent of grasses in winter diets to female live weights for five species of grazers and mixed feeders. 178
10.18. The relationships between bison recruitment and elk and bison numbers on the northern range, 1970–79. 181
11.1. Remains of a male elk killed and eaten by a grizzly bear. 188
11.2. Coyotes and eagles counted on the northern range, 1971–78. 191
IV.1. Calf mortality. "Proof of density dependence" test for $\hat{k}_1$. 244
IV.2. Calf mortality. "Proof of density dependence" test for $\hat{k}_3$. 245
IV.3. Male mortality as k_2 on log initial total population. 247
V.1. Approximate camera point locations for Plates 1–21 on spring, summer, and autumn ranges of the northern Yellowstone elk. 249
V.2. Northern winter range showing approximate camera points of comparative photos. 352
VI.1. Northern winter range showing locations of 44 transects used. 354
VI.2. An *Idaho fescue/bearded wheatgrass ht.* on a deep loam soil. 361
VI.3. An example of the *Idaho fescue/bluebunch wheatgrass ht.*–xeric phase. 364
VI.4. Water year precipitation for Mammoth Hot Springs. A tree ring index and Palmer drought index are also shown. 370
VI.5. Autumn photos of bunchgrass plot 5-Y7 on Hellroaring slope. 378
VI.6. Autumn photos of swale grassland plot 5-Y6 on Hellroaring slope. 380
VI.7. Autumn photos of "spot plot" No. 6 in the BLA. 381
VI.8. Autumn photos of "spot plot" No. 7 in the BLA. 384
VI.9. Parker transect C1T1 inside the Blacktail exclosure and matching outside plot MC1T1. 387
VI.10. Summary of mean frequency of "hits" on vegetation and abiotic elements for 1957 and 1962 Parker transect exclosure studies. 391
VI.11. Parker transect Y1-1 on the open range at Geode Creek. 399
VI.12. Parker transect Y6-2 on the open range at Specimen Ridge. 400
VI.13. Summary of mean frequency of "hits" on vegetation and abiotic elements for Parker transects on the open range. 403
VI.14. Summary of mean frequency of "hits" on vegetation and abiotic elements for Parker transects in the BLA. 404
VI.15. Autumn photos of yd^2 plot NY4. 408
VI.16. Big sagebrush belt transect inside the Blacktail exclosure and matching outside transect. 417

LIST OF TABLES

3.1.   Elk census information, 1923–29.   15
3.2.   Elk numbers and removals, 1923–79.   16
4.1.   Distribution of northern Yellowstone elk during January–15 April periods, 1916–67.   27
4.2.   Human populations on the winter range of the northern Yellowstone elk outside Yellowstone National Park.   28
4.3.   Elk numbers, distribution, and density during winter, 1968–79.   29
5.1.   Pregnancy rates, northern Yellowstone elk, 1935–68.   37
5.2.   Schedules of pregnancy for elk two years and older, 1950–67.   39
5.3.   Sex and age composition of northern Yellowstone elk, autumn and winter, 1928–79.   43
5.4.   Sex ratios, northern Yellowstone elk.   47
5.5.   Elk mortality from birth to six to nine months.   48
5.6.   Age distributions of female elk, 1951–67.   50
5.7.   Age distributions of male elk, 1951–67.   50
5.8.   Life table for northern Yellowstone female elk.   55
5.9.   Life table for northern Yellowstone male elk.   55
8.1.   Vegetation on the northern winter range within Yellowstone National Park.   86
8.2.   Distribution and abundance of ridgetop and upper-slope vegetation with 40% or less canopy cover for vegetation.   88
8.3.   Summary of the types of vegetation measurements repeated over time on the northern winter range, 1930–78.   96
8.4.   Comparisons of canopy coverage and frequency of plant taxa on burned and unburned sage steppe.   108

8.5.   Livestock grazing, haycutting, winter feedgrounds, and other developments on the northern winter range.   120

9.1.   Winter utilization of grasses and grasslike plants on northern winter range, 1971–78.   147

9.2.   Winter utilization of willows and big sage on northern winter range, 1970– 78.   149

10.1.   Approximate winter numbers, biomass, and density of native ungulates on the northern range, 1978.   157

10.2.   Ungulate winter foods by forage class.   175

10.3.   Association of recuitment and numbers of the less abundant ungulates with elk and winter severity.   179

11.1.   Consumption of 1,084 elk carcasses by carnivores on the northern range in Yellowstone Park during 1975, 1976, and 1978.   190

11.2.   Parasites and diseases of elk in the Yellowstone National Park area.   192

IV.1.   Calculated elk numbers by sex and age class, 1968–76.   240

IV.2.   Calculated mortality of calves, 1969–75.   241

IV.3.   Calculated mortality of males 17 months and older, 1969–75.   242

IV.4.   Mortality of calves and $\hat{k}$-factors, 1969–75.   243

IV.5.   Mortality of males and k-factors, 1969–75.   246

VI.1.   Canopy cover and frequency of plant taxa at nine sagebrush grassland sites.   355

VI.2.   Canopy cover and frequency of plant taxa at five wet meadow sites.   357

VI.3.   Canopy cover and frequency of plant taxa at ten mesic grassland sites.   359

VI.4.   Canopy cover and frequency of plant taxa at eight xeric grassland sites.   362

VI.5.   Canopy cover and frequency of plant taxa on nine selected zootic climax sites.   365

VI.6.   Canopy cover and frequency of plant taxa on ridgetop grasslands of different types in the BLA.   367

VI.7.   Characteristics of soils from mudflows and alluvial deposits in the BLA.   369

VI.8.   Standing crop of herbage, 1935–50.   372

VI.9.   Plant area on protected and grazed m^2 quadrats, 1930–40.   375

VI.10.   Plant cover on 11 "square-foot-density" transects, 1938–42.   377

VI.11.   Analysis of variance for 1957 Parker transects of the Blacktail and Lamar exclosures, 1958–74.   390

VI.12.   Analysis of variance for 1962 Parker transects at the Blacktail, Junction Butte, and Lamar exclosures, 1962–74.   393

VI.13.   Comparisons of maximum leaf lengths of three bunchgrass species inside and outside of four exclosures established in 1962.   395

VI.14.   Analysis of variance for 1957 and 1962 Parker transects Gardiner exclosures, 1958–74.   397

VI.15.   Analysis of variance for open range Parker transects Y1 and Y5, 1954–74.   402

VI.16.   Analysis of variance for Parker transects on Specimen Ridge, 1956–74.   402

VI.17.   Analysis of variance for open-range Parker transects in the BLA, 1955–74.   405

VI.18. Summary of plant cover on nine "square-foot-density" transects, 1943 and 1947.   407

VI.19. Photo interpretation of vegetation on 17 yd^2 quadrats, 1948 or 1949 to 1973.   410

VI.20. Summary of plant basal intercept on 19 line transects, 1948 and 1952.   411

VI.21. Numbers of aspen inside and outside two exclosures, 1935–65.   413

VI.22. Aspen reproduction in 203 stands on the northern winter range, 1970.   414

VI.23. Big sagebrush belt transects on the northern range, 1958–74.   416

VI.24. Lamar exclosure, browse transect measurements, 1958–74.   419

VI.25. Willow belt transects on the northern range, 1958–74.   419

VI.26. Aspen belt transects on the northern range, 1958–74.   420

VIII.1. Estimates of mean autumn standing crop by vegetation type on the northern winter range.   433

IX.1. Sex and age composition for mule deer, 1971–79.   434

IX.2. Winter ground counts and reports of bighorn sheep on the northern winter range, 1922–50.   436

IX.3. Aerial counts of bighorn sheep, 1955–78.   439

IX.4. Sex and age composition for bighorn sheep, Mt. Everts and vicinity, 1971–79.   440

IX.5. Sex and age composition of "overall" bighorn sheep population, 1972–79.   441

IX.6. Sex and age composition for moose, 1972–78.   442

IX.7. Sex and age composition for pronghorn, 1971–79.   443

Foreword

It is the customary fate of new truths to begin as heresies and to end as superstitions.

T. H. Huxley

North America led the way during the first half of this century in developing the ideas and techniques of wildlife ecology, that branch of ecology concerned with larger mammals and birds and their habitats. In that period, observation and suggested explanations led to a comprehensive framework for how such ecosystems worked. Wildlife ecology is largely a practical subject, closely allied to management of populations for sport hunting purposes. Consequently, the framework of hypotheses on how such systems might work was translated into manuals and field guides for easy reference and application to real field problems.

The hypothesis became dogma. By the 1960s, many had long forgotten that the early observations, upon which much of the theoretical structure was based, were not as carefully evaluated and scrutinized as are similar data today. It was also forgotten that the early hypotheses were naive, as all early hypotheses are. But, above all, it was forgotten that the dogma was only hypothesis. Very little had been subjected to rigorous experimental testing for verification or rejection.

Wildlife ecology in the 1970s was therefore well behind related fields in ecology and ethology that were testing basic assumptions. "Wildlifers" are a skeptical lot; some are not given to ready acceptance of radically new ideas. And it was in this atmosphere that a small group of scientists and managers in the Yellowstone National Park during the late 1960s did a remarkable thing: they stopped killing animals. They decided to observe how the ecosystem returned to equilibrium following the major perturbation due to the continued shooting of elk and bison. Beginning in 1970, Doug Houston became concerned with elk, the most numerous ungulate species in the park. Elk had been shot and trapped for the previous forty years on the grounds that they were overgrazing, and hence damaging the ecosystem. The supposed evidence for overgrazing came from vegetation plots in which there was a low density of plants that were heavily grazed. Some plots showed an abundance of unpalatable invader plants—plants that have been traditionally used as indicators of overgrazing on rangeland. However, the vegetation did not respond to the elk removal, as was traditionally expected, even when elk numbers were only one quarter of the original number. Elk were also blamed for the disappearance of browse species such as aspen and willow. Through impressive detective work involving a series of photographs taken as early as 1871, Houston has been able to show that elk were not primarily responsible for the changes in woody vegetation and that rangeland sites, formerly thought to be overgrazed, had not changed in appearance in the past century. Could it be possible that some of the range manager's concepts are not relevant to natural grasslands at equilibrium with native grazers? Might invader species and heavily grazed plants be exactly what should be present in natural systems, contrary to traditional opinion? These are questions which now must be seriously addressed.

Part of Houston's work has been to document the elk population as it built up after the killing stopped. Another of the traditional dogmas is that herbivore populations cannot reach equilibrium once their predators, which originally regulated them, were removed. (Wolves were once present in Yellowstone but they have been exterminated.) Modern ecological theory has long surpassed such a naive view of life. Herbivores may be regulated by predators, but this is certainly not necessary—they may equally well be regulated by food supply. Two stable equilibria are possible. But this is just theory. The value of Houston's results is that they are the necessary experimental data to test the theory. The population has built up to, and leveled off at, approximately the same density they were before the removals. The results are consistent with a plant-herbivore equilibrium. Maybe predators are not necessary after all.

Dr. Houston and his colleagues persevered in their long-term work covering more than a decade, despite an atmosphere of disapproval from some of the traditionalists. As T. H. Huxley suggests, this is a good sign that new truths are on their way. This book is one of the first indications that an objective and experimental approach is entering the field of wildlife management.

There are several lessons to be learned from this work, but three are most important:

First, national parks and similar ecological reserves are special areas set aside for conservation. As such they require a different land-use philosophy from those areas used for sport hunting or other forms of exploitation. Ecological management criteria, developed for these latter areas, may not be appropriate for national parks. This work points to a new approach toward the protection of natural ecosystems.

Second, if there had not been rangeland vegetation plots set up and monitored, the evidence against overgrazing would not have been obtained, and inappropriate management may have continued. This is a clear example of the value of long-term monitoring; all national parks and reserves should be monitored systematically. This data base is the insurance policy against unforseen ecological problems of the future. All too often, when we become aware of a problem, we find there are no data from previous times with which to compare the present. Yet, few administrators of our natural reserves are aware of the need for long-term monitoring sites in the different habitats.

Third, although it is usually not necessary to interfere with natural or seminatural systems, when it does become necessary, management should be designed so that it becomes an experiment. Since we can never know all the facts about a situation, we can never be sure that management is necessary nor that its results will be what we predict: we must manage in an air of uncertainty. Consequently, management is experimental. It must treat some areas, while leaving other areas as controls, and, most important, follow-up monitoring of the experiment must be maintained. Monitoring of the elk population by Houston shows how much more was learned than if no follow-up had occurred. The ''principle of experimental management'' is one of the important themes brought out by Dr. Houston's studies.

A. R. E. SINCLAIR
Institute of Animal Resource Ecology
The University of British Columbia
Vancouver, Canada

Acknowledgments

I was employed as a Research Biologist by the National Park Service in Yellowstone Park during the 10 years of this study. It gives me great pleasure to acknowledge the generous help received from many people and organizations. W. J. Barmore, D. G. Despain, and M. M. Meagher, National Park Service; K. Constan, G. L. Erickson, and K. R. Greer, Montana Fish and Game Department; R. A. Dirks, University of Wyoming; G. E. Gruell, U.S. Forest Service; P. E. Farnes, U.S. Soil Conservation Service; R. H. McBee and D. C. Quimby, formerly of Montana State University; and W. H. Kittams former National Park Service Biologist, all permitted use of unpublished material. Additionally, the Montana Fish and Game Department and the Gallatin National Forest permitted access to their files on the elk population.

I was fortunate to be able to draw upon the previous work of many other persons in Yellowstone Park. This included studies of the vegetation and the ungulate populations initiated or continued by R. L. Grimm, W. H. Gammill, W. H. Kittams, R. E. Howe, W. J. Barmore, and other National Park Service personnel. Many of the records used in this study were gathered by the rangers of Yellowstone Park.

Former Yellowstone Superintendent J. K. Anderson, Superintendent J. A. Townsley, and Regional Chief Scientist N. J. Reid all generously supported this study. Former Yellowstone Superintendents L. A. Garrison and J. S. McLaughlin initiated and carried through, with great personal courage, the controversial elk population reductions of the 1960s from which so much biological information was gained.

I owe special thanks to the following individuals: Glen F. Cole, former Supervisory Biologist of Yellowstone Park, suggested the study and was a constant source of ideas, help, and encouragement. Mary Meagher, present Supervisory Biologist, located many of the historical reports and photos used in this study, generously permitted use of her extensive files of historical information, contributed many useful ideas, and helped in other ways too numerous to list. Glen and Mary took upon themselves many onerous administrative and "ceremonial" duties that left me free to pursue field work. W. J. Barmore, Park Service Biologist, permitted extensive citation of unpublished manuscripts containing analyses of vegetation measurements made from 1949 to 1968 and studies of ungulate–habitat relationships. Barmore developed computer programs for analysis of vegetation data and ungulate studies and gave freely of his time for overseeing computer tabulations and analysis of my vegetation studies. Dave Stradley, Gallatin Flying Service, skillfully piloted the flights made to determine ungulate numbers and distribution. Dave's ability to fly a Piper Supercub over difficult terrain during frigid winter mornings is coupled with a talent for counting wild critters that can make the observer in the rear seat feel quite superfluous.

National Park Service seasonal employees or volunteers M. Cohen, S. Fullerton, K. Goetz, A. Hohensee, C. Hunt, M. Nimir, M. Robinson, J. Rominger, and S. Sindt aided in field studies. Oregon State University graduate students D. Depree and H. Harvey aided in statistical analysis. E. E. Starkey, Leader, National Park Service Cooperative Studies Unit, provided administrative and clerical support during the period of writing at Oregon State University. R. Romancier, U.S. Forest Service, generously provided an office at the Forestry Sciences Laboratory during this period. D. R. Field, Associate Regional Director National Park Service, provided additional time and support to complete the final manuscript.

I thank M. M. Meagher and S. J. McNaughton for reviews of the entire manuscript. In addition, W. J. Barmore read Chapters 3–6 and 10; G. Caughley, Chapter 5; D. G. Despain, Chapters 8 and 9; V. Geist, Chapter 7; R. R. Knight, Chapter 11; R. F. Miller, Chapters 8 and 9; and C. T. Robbins, Chapter 6. A. R. E. Sinclair contributed many valuable ideas and suggestions during the analysis and kindly read Chapters 3–6, 8, and 9. R. A. Bryson reviewed the sections on present and past climates. W. F. Mueggler reviewed the description of the grasslands and shrub steppes of the winter range. E. T. Thorne and R. C. Bergstrom reviewed and contributed to a list of the parasites and diseases of elk. W. S. Overton suggested many useful statistical treatments and read parts of Chapters 3 and 5. An earlier report that contained much of the material here included in Chapters 3–5 benefited greatly from criticisms by G. Caughley, G. F. Cole, D. G. Despain, C. J. Martinka and M. M. Meagher. Similarly, another report containing some of the materials in Chapters 8 and 9 was critically reviewed by W. J. Barmore, G. F. Cole, D. G. Despain, G. E. Gruell, R. J. Mackie, M. M. Meagher, and F. J. Singer. J. Cone, V. Kurtz, J. Matthews, J. O'Neale, and S. Sindt greatly aided preparation of various manuscripts.

My wife, Jennifer, and our children, Janet and Steven, aided in various field studies and in the interminable proofing of manuscripts. Thank you all.

THE NORTHERN YELLOWSTONE ELK

CHAPTER 1

Introduction

ELK ARE THE MOST ABUNDANT UNGULATE SPECIES in Yellowstone National Park. Those wintering on the Yellowstone River drainage in and adjacent to the park have come to be known as the northern Yellowstone herd. The area occupied by these elk (*Cervus elaphus*)* during winter is often referred to simply as the "northern range." Elk occupy the northern range with mule deer, bighorn sheep, moose, pronghorn, bison, and a variety of smaller herbivores. Herbivores support a complement of predators and scavengers that includes the grizzly bear, black bear, coyote, cougar, wolverine, raven, bald eagle, and golden eagle. The system is, in short, an ecological gem unmatched for this assemblage of species.

The primary purpose of natural areas, such as Yellowstone, is to maintain ecosystems in as near pristine conditions as possible. This means that ecological processes, including plant succession and the natural regulation of animal numbers, should be permitted to proceed as under pristine conditions and that modern man should be restricted generally to nonconsumptive uses. The extent of management required to meet these objectives is of considerable practical interest. Few parks have a history of concern and debate surrounding the management of ungulates as does Yellowstone. Rarer still are controversies as intense as those surrounding management of the northern Yellowstone elk—the single largest ungulate population in the park. Recent concerns center upon the amount of human interference required, if any, to maintain vegetation–herbivore equilibria in the park. A laissez faire approach to park management represents one view, where natural regulatory processes are counted upon to produce acceptable equilibrium states. The contrasting view of park management is that pristine relationships have been destablized by modern man, and interference is required to impose vegetation–herbivore equilibria more in keeping with park objectives. In practice this interference has involved periodic reductions in ungulate numbers. Both approaches have been tried with the northern Yellowstone elk.

This study examines the nature of existing vegetation–ungulate relationships on

---

*Scientific names of animal and plant species are listed in Appendix X.

the northern range and attempts to determine if population reductions are necessary in the park. Field work was conducted from June 1970 to February 1979.

Even a partial answer to the question of population reductions required asking many others as interrelated research hypotheses subject to testing, modification, and rejection. The general hypothesis being tested was that vegetation–ungulate equilibria appropriate to the park were possible without cropping ungulates in the park. This was operationally difficult to test, so more specific hypotheses were developed. One such was that vegetation on ranges occupied by elk did not depart from pristine conditions because of grazing by the elk—i.e., progressive "range deterioration" was not occurring. This in turn required gaining considerable historical perspective on changes in elk numbers, in vegetation, and in the associated fauna—particularly large predators and other ungulate species. This led to studies of climate, fire history, and human activities in the park. The elk population was examined for evidence of density-dependent negative-feedback controls on population size and limitation through extrinsic forces such as human predation or resource levels.

From the outset it seemed that the objectives of maintaining pristine ecosystems, with generally nonconsumptive uses, might be only partially met, because the park does not contain the complete ecological unit for one "segment" of the population. Consumptive use of elk, as recreational hunting, is permitted outside the park on this segment. Another aspect of the study was an attempt to reconcile these two different, equally valid, uses.

Testing hypotheses in field studies is difficult at best, and doubly so in national parks where experimental manipulations are usually prohibited. Some hypotheses were tested using the method of successive approximations (Poore 1962). Others could be tested in a somewhat more experimental manner. For example, human predation had reduced elk numbers in the northern herd from around 12,000 to 4,000 between about 1955 and 1968. A moratorium on reductions went into effect in the park in 1969, and numbers increased again to around 12,000. These reductions are viewed here as experimental perturbations, potentially useful for testing research hypotheses and for providing insight into ecosystem dynamics.

The organization of this monograph requires explanation. Most chapters open with an outline of topics to be covered and the methods of study. Each closes with an interpretation of important points as they relate to the hypotheses under study. Appendixes are provided where the volume of data is very large.

CHAPTER 2

The Study Area

THE ADMINISTRATION, GEOLOGY, GEOGRAPHY, CLIMATE, AND VEGETATION of Yellowstone Park are described briefly in this section. Other aspects of the human history, climate, and vegetation are discussed in depth more conveniently elsewhere.

Administration

Yellowstone Park was established in 1872 and now occupies 8,995 km² in the northwest corner of Wyoming and adjacent parts of Montana and Idaho. The park was administered by civilian superintendents appointed by the Secretary of Interior from 1872 to 1886, by various detachments of the U.S. Army from 1886 to 1916, and by the National Park Service from 1916 to the present.

Geology and Geography

Geology of the park has been described by Keefer (1972). Much of the area is covered by Quaternary volcanic deposits that have undergone at least three extensive glaciations. General descriptions of physiography and soils are provided byMeagher (1973), Despain (1973), and Barmore (1980). Elevations in the park range from about 1,500 m to over 3,300 m, but much of the area is a series of forested rhyolite "plateaus" of 2,100–2,600 m. Most of the soils on the northern range are derived from glacial till deposited during the early and middle stades of the Pinedale glaciation.

The northern Yellowstone elk migrate seasonally between a high-elevation summer range and a lower-elevation winter range. The study area included all parts of the park used seasonally by these elk plus that portion of the winter range extending beyond park boundaries (Fig. 2.1).

Most work was conducted on the 100,000 ha northern winter range, which extends about 80 km down the Lamar, Yellowstone, and Gardner River drainages. About

3

FIGURE 2.1.

Yellowstone National Park and vicinity showing the study area (upper map, dotted line). The northern winter range is shaded. Important subdivisions of the northern range (lower map) include the "upper winter range" (A) and the "boundary line area" (BLA) within the park. The 1932 addition to the BLA is shown.

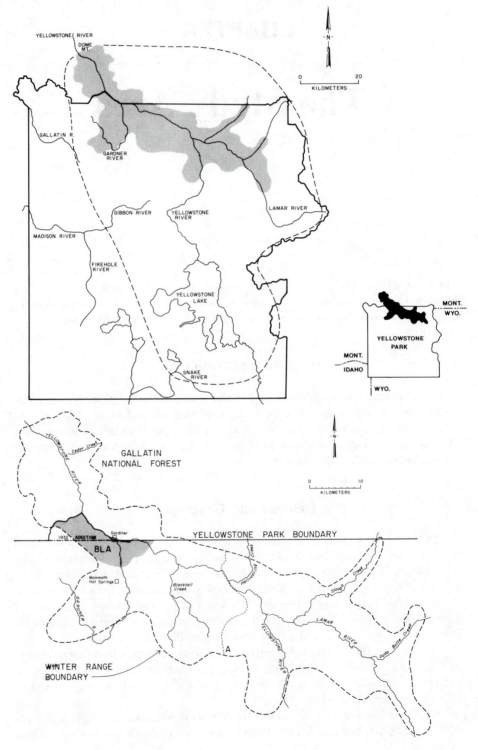

83% of the winter range is in the park; 17% is outside on Gallatin National Forest, State of Montana, and privately owned lands. No physiographic barrier blocks the downstream end of the winter range at Dome Mountain. This working definition of the boundary is based upon observations of seasonal distribution of the elk. Yellowstone Park was apparently beyond the seasonal ranges of other small groups of elk wintering farther down the Yellowstone River. This definition is subject to refinement as data accumulate on winter distribution and movements of elk.

The determination of winter range available outside the park is complicated because of the present interspersion of public and private lands and conflicting land use practices. Prior to settlement, about 23,000 ha of winter range would have been available. Currently, about 17,000 ha are considered to be available to wintering elk (about 13,600 ha on the Gallatin National Forest; 400 ha, Burlington Northern Railroad and State of Montana; 3,000 ha, private lands where conflicts with wintering elk are low). Most of these Forest Service lands west of the Yellowstone River and north of Cedar Creek are grazed by livestock (Fig. 2.1). This is a conservative estimate of the area actually utilized by elk outside the park. I consider the remaining 6,000 ha to be more or less unavailable to wintering elk because of conflicts with agriculture or high levels of development. However, the elk do not draw such fine distinctions in land ownership. These developed lands are occupied by elk some years; this use is not greeted with enthusiasm by some human residents.

The elevation of about 52% of the winter range within the park is between 1,500 and 2,100 m, 35% from 2,101 to 2,400 m, and 13% over 2,401 m. An "upper Yellowstone winter range" of about 46,000 ha has been designated in the park (Fig. 2.1). Additionally, a boundary line area (BLA) of about 4,900 ha is recognized in the park, 1,600 ha of which were added to the park in 1932. The BLA has been subjected to a wide variety of conflicting human uses. Artificial concentrations of elk have occurred there as a result of winter feeding and hunting outside the park.

Climate

The present climate of Yellowstone is generally characterized by long, cold winters and short, cool summers. The climate of the northern winter range is somewhat warmer and drier than the rest of the park. The temperature and precipitation "normals," mostly from 1941 to 1970 (from Dirks 1974), were used to construct climatic diagrams (Fig. 2.2) following the format of Walter (1973).

Although similar seasonal patterns of precipitation and temperature occur at each of the four stations on the winter range, the climates differ considerably. The Gardiner Station is by far the driest on a seasonal and annual basis, followed by Lamar, Tower, and Mammoth Hot Springs. Note especially that while Gardiner is only 6 km from Mammoth, it is 283 m lower and the annual precipitation is about 34% less. Gardiner is also the warmest station, followed by Mammoth, Tower, and Lamar. All four stations have dry seasons, with Mammoth and especially Gardiner showing extreme droughts.

The climates of Lake and Northeast Entrance were used to portray conditions on the higher elevation summer ranges occupied by the northern elk. The Lake climate is influenced by Yellowstone Lake (Dirks 1974). The effects may include a 0.6°–1.1°C reduction in summer temperature maxima. Summer minima may also be comparably higher. Temperature curves show the same pattern as the winter range, but mean and seasonal values are lower. Precipitation at both stations is greater, and curves differ

FIGURE 2.2.

Climatic diagrams for Gardiner, Mammoth, Tower, and Lamar on the northern range (shaded) and for Lake and Northeast Entrance on summer ranges.

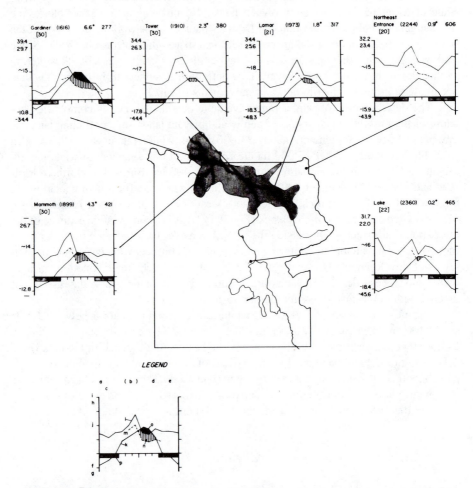

Key to Diagrams.
Abscissa = months from Jan. to Dec.;
Ordinates = one division = 10°C or 20 mm rain.
 a = station;
 b = height above sea level (m);
 c = duration of observation;
 d = mean annual temperature (C°);
 e = mean annual precipitation (mm);
 f = mean daily minimum of coldest month;
 g = lowest temperature recorded;
 h = mean daily maximum of warmest month;
 i = highest temperature recorded;
 j = mean daily temperature variation;
 k = curve of mean monthly temperature;
 l = curve of mean monthly precipitation;
 m = precipitation curve of 1:3; i.e., 10°C = 30 mm ppt.;
 n = relative period of drought;
 o = periods of extreme droughts or dry seasons;
 p = months with mean daily minimum below 0°C.

from those on the winter range by showing two definite seasonal peaks, June and winter. A short dry season occurs at Lake but not at Northeast.

In addition to these point descriptions of climate, Farnes (1975) calculated the approximate zonal distribution of annual precipitation for the entire park. Precipitation was calculated from snow-course data and elevation relationships to prepare this iso-hyetal map (Farnes 1970; Fig. 2.3). Summer ranges occupied by the northern elk are mostly in the 50- to 125-cm zones of annual precipitation; winter ranges, mostly 75 cm or less. The overall winter range has an annual snowfall of 500 cm or less (Farnes 1974).

These maps and climatic diagrams are still relatively crude expressions of climate

FIGURE 2.3.

Approximate zonal distribution of annual precipitation (cm) for Yellowstone Park and the northern winter range (shaded). Modified from Farnes 1975.

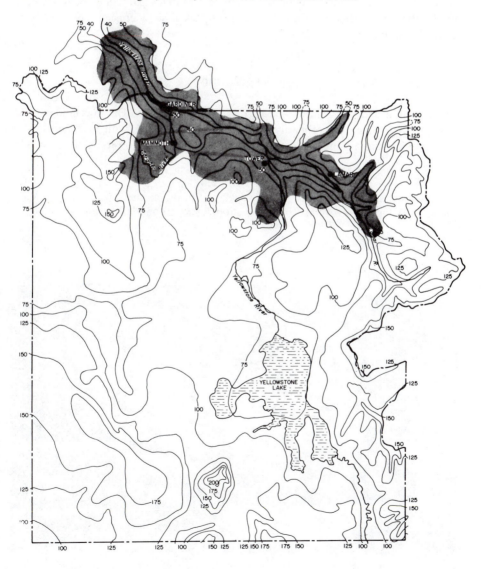

because of the great microclimatic differences that occur in mountainous country due to slope and exposure (Shreve 1924) and the further modification of microclimates by vegetation. Winter microclimates affect the availability of forage for ungulates. Frequent winter winds redistribute the snow cover, and windward slopes are sometimes blown snow free. Snow density and depth in forests are quite different from those of grasslands on similar slopes. On a smaller scale, pronounced depressions often occur in the snow cover at the bases of conifers and sagebrush plants. This apparently results from increased long-wave radiation from the plants (Janz and Storr 1977). Such sites become important foraging areas during severe winters.

Weather records, especially means, simply cannot convey the great variation in winter conditions that have occurred on the winter range of the northern Yellowstone elk since regular observations began around 1880. Narrative accounts showed that winters have varied from very ''open,'' with little snow and comparatively warm temperatures, to bitter cold, with prolonged deep snows lasting well into spring. Deep snows have been followed by periods of warm temperatures and rain, to be followed in turn by subzero conditions. These left the hard-packed snow crusted with ice, which severely restricted ungulate foraging.

Vegetation

The terrestrial area of Yellowstone park is mostly forested. The vegetation of the northern winter range is primarily a steppe or shrub steppe with interspersions of conifers occurring as single isolated trees or small stands at lower elevations and as

FIGURE 2.4.
Characteristic steppe and shrub steppe vegetation of the northern winter range. View north across the Yellowstone River (elevation 1,800 m) up Hellroaring Creek.

more continuous forests at high elevations or on north slopes (Fig. 2.4). The patterns of precipitation described above play an important role in delimiting broad vegetation zones in the park (Despain 1973). Further, the climate of the winter range varies in space and time so much that plant communities and succession both show great variation according to site. The vegetation of the park is discussed in detail in Chapter 8.

CHAPTER 3

The Elk Population: History and Numbers

THE HISTORY AND TRENDS in numbers of the northern Yellowstone elk are discussed by periods that are marked by changes in either the quality of the information available or in the management of the population. The effects of human predation on elk numbers and on rates of increase are discussed in some detail for 1930–79.

Yellowstone is fortunate in having available a wealth of records from which to reconstruct the history of the elk population. I have been able to draw from many first-person accounts and to compare accounts within and among the several agencies involved in the management of the northern herd. The original reference materials are on file in the Yellowstone Park archives and research library. Because my interpretations differ in many aspects from those made previously, I have included the supporting information in annotated appendixes. The data on elk numbers and removals for 1923–79 are mostly from unpublished files of the National Park Service and the Montana Fish and Game Department.

Early Records to 1886

Elk remains in glacial deposits of Illinoian age in Alaska indicate that ancestors of *C. elaphus* occurred in North America for more than 100,000 years before present (BP). However, the species may have first occupied central North America about 35,000 years BP or later (Péwé 1967, Hopkins 1967, Guthrie 1966). Subfossils of elk have been recovered from several sites of late Pleistocene age from Wyoming and Idaho (Anderson 1974). The species then was apparently associated with a much more diverse mammalian fauna. Elk could not have occupied most of the Yellowstone area until about 12,000 years BP following retreat of the Pinedale ice sheet (Keefer 1972, Richmond 1972). Remains of elk occur in archaeological sites from the Yellowstone area dated in excess of 9,000 years BP "continuously" to historic times (Lahren 1971, 1976).

The early historic period began with presettlement explorations from 1807 to 1871, which included a period of fur trapping from about 1826–40. Settlement near the park began during the early 1870s, and this brought more intense market hunting inside and outside the park through the mid-1880s. Osborne Russell (Haines 1965a) trapped and traveled the Yellowstone area from 1835 to 1842 and provided the earliest written accounts of abundant summering elk (Appendix I).

After the collapse of the fur trade, the Yellowstone area remained virtually unoccupied and poorly known by Euro-American man until transient mining and organized scientific exploration began in the 1860s and early 1870s (Haines 1977). Accounts from this period (Appendix I) indicate large elk populations during summer and autumn. Reports of abundant cast elk antlers (Blackmore 1972, Doane 1874 *in* Bonney 1970), accounts of extensive *winter* hunting of elk (Strong 1875, Ludlow 1876, Grinnell 1876, Norris 1877), and specific mention of wintering elk (Norris 1877, 1881; Yount 1881a,b) indicate that large numbers of elk occurred on the northern range in winter. Yount's (1881b) comment of only 400 elk spending the winter in the valleys of Soda Butte Creek and Lamar River during the severe winter of 1880–81 has been used to support the idea that the park was not historic winter range. My interpretation differs as a result of subsequent observations of wintering elk (see Chap. 4): only 400 animals remaining in this upper portion of the range during a severe winter is not unusual.

Accounts of elk numbers during 1882–86 are limited (Appendix I). Hunting in the park was prohibited in 1883 (Haines 1977), but considerable market hunting apparently continued until an ineffective and understaffed civilian administration was replaced by the U.S. Army in the summer of 1886.

The 1886–1910 Period

Market hunting and poaching continued at the beginning of this period, but illegal hunting was progressively suppressed within the park by the U.S. Army. A protectionist attitude developed toward native ungulates that included supplemental winter feeding and predator control. Human settlement increased on winter ranges outside the park.

The status of elk from 1886 to 1910 was determined from Annual Reports of the Acting Park Superintendents (all were U.S. Army officers, Appendix II), occasional observations by private citizens, and extensive observations by civilian scouts and army personnel.

Superintendents' reports usually contained generalized statements about elk that ranged from perceptive to occasionally inaccurate. Administrators reported that elk were abundant during this period. Numbers of elk in the park, or the park plus the adjacent 3760-km^2 Yellowstone Timber Reserve east and south of the park (considered a *de facto* part of the park, see Anderson 1891, Young 1897, Appendix II), were generally estimated at 15,000–40,000. Estimates sometimes showed an inverse relation to tenure as Superintendent, and in some cases were seemingly based on little more than the previous estimate. Officials customarily referred to elk and most other ungulates as increasing in numbers, although the individual chronological estimates do not support this interpretation. Accounts of elk migrations by Harris (1887), Anderson (1891), Lindsley (1897), Goode (1900), Pitcher (1905), Young (1908), and Benson

(1910) and specific accounts of wintering elk by Hofer (1887), Boutelle (1890), and Lindsley (1897) indicate that estimates for this period refer to the number of elk *summering* in the entire park (or park plus Timber Reserve). These estimates would have represented several major winter herds. This is an important distinction, because previous writers have sometimes interpreted these estimates of summer numbers to represent just those elk wintering in the northern herd; this is an erroneous interpretation. Pitcher's (1901) estimate of 25,000 elk wintering in the park was based upon the mistaken belief that the Yellowstone Timber Reserve was winter range for the southern Yellowstone or Jackson Hole herd. Reports of large-scale mortality of elk during the winters of 1892, 1897, 1899, and 1910 also may refer to aggregate summer herds. Recent work on distribution and history of elk in the Yellowstone area (see below, Cole 1969a, Gruell 1973, Lovaas 1970) suggests that estimates of 25,000–35,000 for park summer herds, or park plus Timber Reserve, were entirely reasonable. I estimate numbers now in the park by late summer to be over 20,000.

I analyzed the number and distribution of elk observed on 2,424 horseback and ski patrols of the northern range during January–15 April periods from 1898 to 1919 (Houston 1974, 1980). This information was recorded in diaries and patrol station log books by civilian scouts employed by the U.S. Army, by Army enlisted personnel stationed at outlying "soldier stations," and by Park Service rangers in 1918–19. These reports represented first-person accounts of winter elk distribution, free from administrative editing, gathered by covering the same areas over an extended period of time. Recognizing the limitations of this information, it appeared that the following was true. (1) Elk distribution and numbers reported for outlying areas of the northern range showed little change over the 22 years. Numbers were comparable to those reported during more recent censuses. (2) Large numbers of elk (very possibly 3,000–5,000) habitually occupied the upper range (Fig. 2.1) during mild to severe winters. No changes over the years could be detected. (3) Elk numbers on the lower winter range changed. The earliest patrols suggested that several thousand elk wintered in the park, but few occurred outside the boundary. Increasing numbers of elk were reported in the Mammoth-Gardiner area as feedgrounds were developed. This increase could have reflected mostly changes in winter distribution in response to feedgrounds rather than substantial changes in numbers. Increasing numbers of elk did, however, habitually winter outside the park after about 1905.

The 1911–20 Period

An increasingly intense protectionist attitude toward ungulate populations developed during this period. Conflicting reports of a population eruption followed by extensive winter mortality have resulted in an incredibly confused account of the status of the northern elk during the decade 1911–20. A review of the original reports (Appendix III) indicated how this confusion arose and suggested that the reported eruption and crash *did not* occur.

Elk were reported to occur by the "thousands" in the Superintendent's report of 1911 (Appendix III), and a migration north of the park into Montana is mentioned. Superintendent Brett reported 30,101, 32,967, and 35,308 elk in the northern herd for 1912, 1913, and 1914, respectively, from early censuses. An abstract of elk counts for these census attempts shows that the "northern herd" as defined during this period included elk wintering along the Gallatin River and the Madison River and its tributaries (see Fig. 4.2), in addition to those along the Yellowstone and Lamar Rivers (the current definition). Park authorities, however, were apparently claiming 25,000–30,000 elk for the Yellowstone River winter populations during this period.

A review of the procedures and computations used in these pioneer census attempts casts serious doubts upon their accuracy (Appendix III). Counts required three weeks or more to complete, were conducted in April and May by one to three scouts during the spring migrations of elk to higher elevations, and, most interestingly, were made while traveling in the same direction as the migrating elk. Numbers reported were "rounded" to the nearest hundred or thousand and represented general estimates rather than actual enumerations. The recorded itinerary of the individuals shows frequent overlap of counting units, and the computations used to derive totals are obscure, since individual estimates for 1912 exceed the total reported. Counts seem to have been largely independent estimates, obtained under difficult conditions, which were somehow summed to give an increase of about 10% per annum. No count was conducted during 1915 because of the mild winter; nevertheless the entire "northern herd" was assumed to have increased to over 37,000. An analysis of scout diaries and station log books for this period does not support increases of this magnitude (Houston 1974, 1980).

The status of the nation's elk was of general concern during this period. Herds in the Yellowstone area were investigated by U.S. Forest Service and Biological Survey personnel (Simpson and Bailey 1915; see Appendix III). The confusion in definitions of "northern" and "southern" herds was described (elk wintering on the Clarks Fork of the Yellowstone, Shoshone, and Greybull Rivers outside the east boundary of the park were also considered a part of the "northern" herd), and previous counts were considered to be highly questionable.

This investigation apparently led to a midwinter census of the Yellowstone River elk by Biological Survey and Forest Service personnel and park scouts from March 8 to 14, 1916. Counters worked down the drainages of the Lamar and Yellowstone Rivers from the upper margins of the winter range to the Dailey Lake basin 27 km north of the park boundary. They actually counted 9,564 elk and made a preliminary estimate of 11,564 for the total herd. Similar counts of the Madison and Gallatin River drainages combined with the Yellowstone River count gave 11,515 elk. An additional 940 elk counted on the Clarks Fork and Shoshone Rivers gave a grand total of 12,455, with the total "northern herd"—as defined during this period—estimated at 13,700, or 40% of previous estimates.

Another count of the Yellowstone River elk was ordered immediately by officials in Washington, D.C. This was conducted using procedures similar to those of the 1912–14 counts; a total of 25,000 elk was reported (Appendix III). Simpson, who directed counts of the "southern herd" and of elk in other areas of the intermountain west, witnessed this attempt. His account (Appendix III) supports my interpretation of the 1912–14 census procedures and indicates that similar problems plagued the April 1916 census and resulted in inflated estimates.

This great disparity in counts resulted in considerable controversy, and another census was conducted in 1917. Forest Service rangers were paired with park employees in several counting teams, with each member required to certify the correctness of the team's daily count. This count was conducted from May 26 to June 9 after the exceptionally severe winter of 1917. Counts were conducted down the drainages of the Yellowstone and Lamar Rivers to Stands Basin (24 km north of the park). Daily reports of counters (filed in the Yellowstone Park archives) suggest that counting was difficult.

The actual number of elk counted was 10,769, including 1,453 tallied outside the park. Counters sometimes recorded "calves"in totals, and it is often unclear if these were calves of the year. Although there are discrepancies among reports, nearly 1,900 dead elk were tallied—testimony to the severity of the previous winter. The number of elk present was estimated at 17,422 by adding nearly 7,000 to the total counted (accounts that give 19,000 or more for this census appear to include the Madison and Gallatin River elk).

The administration of Yellowstone changed from the military to the newly created National Park Service in 1916, and except for the censuses discussed above, first-person accounts of the northern elk are scarce and administrative reports very unclear from late 1916 through 1919 (Appendix III). This occurred because the transition from military to civilian authority was gradual and jurisdictions often overlapped, or were quite confused. Estimates of the total numbers of elk varied widely. Superintendents reported substantial elk migrations beyond park boundaries along the Yellowstone River, and hay was fed to many elk near Gardiner.

The epitome of confusion occurred during the winter of 1919–20 (Appendix III). By subtracting "known" removals and adding arbitrary estimates of increase to the 1917 census figures, the northern herd was assumed to have increased to over 25,000 by the autumn of 1919 (Appendix III). Unusually severe storms in late October and November caused many elk to leave the park and become available to hunters; extirpation of the northern herd was predicted. Reported hunter removals (legal harvests plus cripple losses) ranged from 3,000 to 8,000. However, the same storms that drove elk from the park blocked access to the area during the hunting season except by rail. A detailed tally of railway express receipts by time periods and point of embarkation showed 2,760 elk carcasses shipped. These, plus an estimated 405 animals killed by local residents (a reasonable estimate—see Table 4.2), gave a total harvest of 3,165. Actual counts made by Forest Service rangers conducting frequent patrols to determine winter range boundaries and to suppress illegal killing outside the park, and patrols by National Park Service rangers suggested that the number of elk crippled by hunters may have been 200–400.

Accounts by persons present during the winter indicated that the severe weather of autumn 1919 portending a disastrous winter for the elk became unseasonably mild from December to early March (Appendix III). (Note that the seemingly overstated accounts of this winter were by individuals who were not present.) March and April were considered to be "unfavorable" to wildlife, but spring growth of vegetation apparently began in April. Continued intensive patrols by forest rangers outside the park placed winter losses, i.e., malnutrition and illegal hunting for tusks (upper canine teeth of elk), at 350 elk. Apparently 600–700 elk, mostly calves, died on winter feedgrounds in the park. Descriptions of their physical condition suggested that artificial concentrations of elk that resulted from newly intensified winter feeding may have exacerbated mortality. Spring ranger patrols could account for 200–500 additional dead elk in the park. Estimates of overall winter mortality ranged from 700 to 1,500, depending upon the source. Reports indicated that other ungulate species sustained low winter mortality.

No attempt was made to census elk during the winter of 1919–20, and 10,000–12,000 were variously estimated to have "survived." This left a discrepancy of about 6,000 elk between calculated autumn herds and "survivors"—the difference being largely ignored (Shaw and Clark 1920) or the *suggestion* made that *if* there were

25,000 elk in the autumn herd, then these animals died during the winter (Albright 1920b).

My interpretation of these events is that the most acceptable data on hunter removals indicate legal harvests plus cripple losses of about 3,500. Documented winter mortality of elk was comparatively low, and much of that occurred among calves artificially concentrated by winter feeding. Weather records, accounts of the number of elk on feedgrounds, and accounts of the good condition and low mortality of other ungulate species support this interpretation of rather low elk mortality. The 1919 autumn herd was apparently overestimated by starting with an inflated 1917 census and adding arbitrary annual increases. This overestimate was apparently later recognized (Anon. 1920; see Appendix III).

Subsequent writers have either uncritically accepted or misinterpreted the *suggestion* of winter mortality offered to explain discrepancies between estimates of elk numbers, until, through repetition in the literature, a population crash is reported to have occurred during the winter of 1919–20, with 14,000 elk dying of malnutrition (Skinner 1928, Olsen 1938, Skinner 1950, National Park Service 1961, Pengelly 1963, Leopold et al. 1963, Craighead et al. 1972, and others). This is patently incorrect. Independent, first-person accounts do not support this interpretation, and no one present at the time ever suggested natural mortality of that magnitude. Evaluation of the census procedures and calculations used during this period suggests that the March 1916 count was possibly the only one that approximated the size of the population. Nothing resembling a population eruption and crash occurred at this or an earlier time.

The 1921–29 Period

A near-agricultural philosophy of stewardship of ungulates prevailed during this period. Winter feeding and predator control continued.

Results from five attempts at ground total counts of the northern Yellowstone elk from 1923–29 reported here differ from nearly all previous accounts, as earlier writers did not separate elk counted on the Madison and Gallatin Rivers from those on the Yellowstone and Lamar (Table 3.1). I have been unable to determine the techniques used in most of these counts, but there seems to have been concern that some were

TABLE 3.1
Elk Census Information, 1923–29

Date	Numbers Counted	Source[a]
May 1923[b]	11,648	June 1923
April 18–25, 1925	12,428	April 1925
February 1927	12,488	February 1927
April 1928[c,d]	8,959	April 1928
April 2–7, 1929	9,122	April 1929

[a]Superintendents Monthly Report for date given.
[b]Probably required 7–10 days.
[c]Cooperative counts involving U.S. Forest Service, Montana Fish and Game Department, and National Park Service.
[d]Probably included elk on Madison and Firehole Rivers.

poorly organized and totals possibly inflated (Albright 1926, Baggley 1930), and at best the counts represent first approximations of population size. Albright (1928) discusses an "apparent loss" or discrepancy of several thousand elk between counts in the late 1920s. This resulted from adding arbitrary increase rates to possibly inflated census figures—computations reminiscent of the previous decade that probably have little relevance to what actually happened to the population.

Elk were removed from the 1923–29 populations primarily by hunting outside the park (Table 3.2). Others were trapped in the park and shipped off to reestablish other populations. Estimates of hunting kills for this period show only the magnitude of removals. Park records of numbers trapped appear to be accurate. Total human predation may have averaged 470 per year from 1923–29, but ranged from 15 to 1,716. Although counts for this period are questionable, those from the 1930s suggest that late winter populations during the 1920s probably ranged from 10,000 to 15,000. Human predation probably averaged less than 5% of autumn populations; thus mortality from other sources must have been substantial.

TABLE 3.2
Elk Numbers and Removals, 1923–79

Winter Periods[a]	Winter Census	Removals		
		Hunter Kill	Park	Total
1923		33	49	82
1924		44	11	55
1925		366[b]	59	425
1926		88	80	168
1927		719	107	826
1928		1,529[c]	187	1,716
1929		15	0	15
1930	8,257	312	110	422
1931	7,696[d]	316	2	318
1932	10,624	290	37	327
1933	11,521	177	2	179
1934	10,042	136	11	147
1935	10,112[e]	2,598	667	3,265
1936	10,281	2,287	557	2,844
1937	8,794	257	574	831
1938	10,976	3,587	236	3,823
1939		2,971	307	3,278
1940		122	16	138
1941		275	12	287
1942		2,071	145	2,216
1943	8,235	6,539	691	7,230
1944		125	10	135
1945		403	0	403
1946	8,513	2,094	73	2,167
1947		3,069	76	3,145
1948	7,815	970	39	1,009
1949	9,496	2,837	49	2,886
1950		40	834	874
1951		1,265	818	2,083
1952		3,198	602	3,800
1953		110	172	282
1954		422	387	809

(continued)

TABLE 3.2 (*Continued*)

WINTER PERIODS[a]	WINTER CENSUS	REMOVALS		
		Hunter Kill	Park	Total
1955		763	598	1,361
1956	6,963[f]	3,900	2,635	6,535
1957		345	944	1,289
1958		50	536	586
1959	4,884[d,g]	372	1,334	1,706
1960		50	809	859
1961	8,150[f,g]	25	1,434	1,459
1962	5,725[f]	125	4,619	4,744
1963		530	1,290	1,820
1964		30	1,121	1,151
1965	4,865[f]	1,012	892	1,904
1966		30	1,240	1,270
1967	3,842[f]	1,108	1,540	2,648
1968	3,172[g]	116	984	1,100
1969	4,305[g]	50	0	50
1970	5,543[g,h]	50	0	50
1971	7,281[g]	45	0	45
1972	8,215[g]	75	0	75
1973	9,981[g]	154	0	154
1974	10,529[g]	210	0	210
1975	12,607[g]	147	0	147
1976	10,807[g]	1,547	0	1,547
1977	8,980[d,g]	219	0	219
1978	11,855[g]	1,086	0	1,086
1979	10,768[g]	340	0	340

[a]1923 = winter of 1922–23, etc.
[b]Total removal estimated at 1,000 including cripple losses.
[c]Contains estimates of cripple losses.
[d]Considered to be a very poor census.
[e]Combined ground and aerial; other census data are ground counts unless otherwise indicated.
[f]Helicopter.
[g]Fixed-wing aircraft.
[h]Maximum counts obtained in December or January from 1970 to 1979.

The 1930–68 Period

The stewardship of ungulates so characteristic of the 1920s continued into the early 1930s but changed to progressively more intense management (i.e., artificial regulation of elk numbers inside and outside the park) from 1935 to 1968. Better organized ground counts of elk began in 1930, and aerial counts began in 1956.

Ground total counts were attempted during 13 winters from 1930 to 1949 (Table 3.2, Fig. 3.1), usually during March or April (occasionally January and February). Four counts made from January to April 1930 ranged from 7,327 to 8,257. A 1931 count of 7,696 did not meet the accepted standards of the period and is not considered further here. Two counts in 1932 gave 8,566 in January and 10,624 in April—a range of 2,058 between attempts. A 1935 count of 10,112 resulted from a ground count of the major winter range plus an aerial count of peripheral areas. Numbers in 12 maximum annual counts from 1930 to 1949 averaged 9,556 (range, 7,815–11,521). Numbers prior to about 1935 also differ from some previous accounts because I omitted elk

FIGURE 3.1.

Elk numbers and removals, 1930–79. Ground total counts were made from 1930 to 1949 (○); single aerial total counts from 1956 to 1967 (●). Aerial total counts for 1968–79 (⊙) represent the maximum numbers observed in several attempts. Numbers of elk removed by human predation are shown for each year.

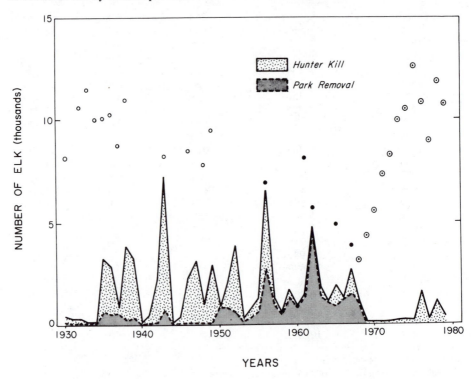

counted on the Madison and Gallatin Rivers and small numbers from southern portions of the park.

The bias errors associated with these ground total counts need to be explored before the trend in numbers can be determined. Errors occur:

1. When the animals actually observed are incorrectly counted.
2. When animals present are not observed.
3. When animals are counted more than once.

Errors are of consequence in any count, and given the circumstances of these counts, all sources of error could have been formidable. (This is not meant to be derogatory but simply to point out the reality of these data.) A review of the census reports suggest the following positive aspects of the counts:

1. The area occupied by elk was relatively small (± 500 km²) during many counts and was divided into easily recognized counting units.
2. Areas of high elk density were mostly open grasslands or shrublands and were reasonably accessible.
3. Snow cover was usually present.
4. Forests were somewhat less dense and less extensive than now.
5. Counters were often quite familiar with the area and with elk distribution.

6. Initially, elk may have been quite tolerant of the presence of counters (they likely became less tolerant as numbers removed by shooting increased).

Negative aspects included the following:

1. Elk occupancy of forests during late winter can be substantial.
2. Some counts were made with little snow cover or with snowfall during part of the count.
3. Some elk ranged in areas where access and observability were difficult.
4. Counters were often not in continual close contact, which could have caused large counting errors in forests or of elk moving within and between counting units.

In addition, counts were made at different times of the winter (into early spring). A comparison of a count made in January with one in April of the following year is difficult, because considerable natural mortality may occur during winter. Finally, the amount of disturbance of the population prior to counting varied considerably. Counts made following large-scale shooting are difficult to compare to others.

Comparisons of counts suggest that the net effect of these errors produced totals below the absolute numbers present. An estimate of a minimum net bias error was possible when consecutive counts were made about the same time of year. For example, a 1949 winter count of 9,496 was made after 2,886 were removed for a minimum autumn population of 12,382. Subtraction of calves of the year at 20% of the autumn population (see Sex and Age Composition, Chap. 5) left 9,906. Either the 1949 count was too high (less likely) or the 1948 count of 7,815 was low by 2,091 elk (27%). This is still a conservative estimate, because winter mortality following the 1948 count is not considered and the 1949 count was most likely also low. Similarly, the March counts of 1935, 1936, and 1938 were each compared to those of the previous year using a mean of 16% calves in winter herds during this period (April counts were too late to use such calculations). This suggested that the counts of 1934, 1935, and 1937 were low by 12, 9, and 41%, respectively. Accordingly, I increased all other ground total counts by 22%, the mean of the four comparisons, and considered this to represent a minimum bias error. This produced estimates of a high of 14,056 elk in 1933 and a low of 9,906 in 1948 (Fig. 3.2).

Aerial total counts were attempted during seven winters from 1956 to 1968 (Table 3.2, Fig. 3.1). The 1959 count of 4,884 made from fixed-wing aircraft was below accepted standards and was omitted. The five remaining counts made from 1956 to 1967 were mostly helicopter counts (the 1968 count was made by a different method considered in the next section). Counts were well organized and carefully executed. Negative aspects included: (1) only one count was made each winter, and some individuals had little opportunity to practice the art of counting elk from the air; (2) counts were often made following large-scale disturbance of the population by shooting or by trapping using helicopters. I did not witness these counts, but I have experienced the difficulty of counting elk outside the park in 1976 and 1978 after winter hunting began. Survivors were scattered widely throughout forests and were much more difficult to observe. Although park removals were far more efficient than hunting, counts made during 1956–68 were sometimes influenced by intense prior disturbance. Still, the errors were far less than for ground total counts. Calculations that compared the 1962 count with that of 1961 returned a minimum bias error of 8%. On these tenuous grounds, I increased the remaining aerial counts by this estimate.

FIGURE 3.2.

Calculated winter (●) and autumn (○) elk numbers, 1930–79. Trends are shown for 1930–67 winter populations (———) and for 1935–67 autumn populations (– –). Values for 1968–79 represent maximum winter counts (except 1977) and calculated minimum autumn numbers. Abrupt declines between 1942–43 and 1955–56 winter population (- - -) were estimated from levels of human predation. See text.

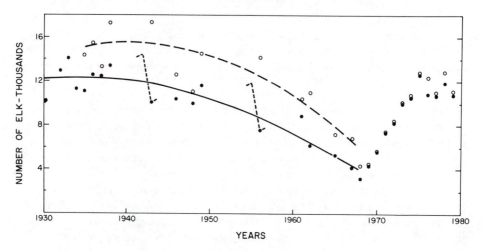

When the point estimates were converted to natural logarithms the regression of numbers on time returned an $\bar{r}$ (observed exponential rate of increase, Caughley 1977:53) of $-.013$ for the 1930–61 period, indicating a decline in numbers as human predation increased. The $\bar{r}$ for the 1961–68 period of more intense removals was $-.123$, and the winter population declined to a counted low of 3,172 elk in 1968. Estimates of population size were needed for occasional winters in which no count was made, so a quadratic regression was fitted to the adjusted counts (Fig. 3.2).

Estimates of minimum autumn (preremoval) populations required evaluation of the accuracy of the reported elk removals (Table 3.2). From 1930 to 1934, hunting removals were mostly crude estimates. Most of the larger hunting removals from 1935 were tabulated in the field at Montana Fish and Game Department hunter check stations; others were apparently determined by questionnaire that may have had a reporting bias (Cole pers. commun. 1973) and could be inflated. Park removals from 1930 to 1934 continued to represent elk trapped to reestablish herds in other areas. The 1935–68 removals (both trapping and shooting) were attempts to reduce herd size, and records are accurate. All removals are considered to be human predation, irrespective of the fates of trapped elk.

Human predation removed fewer than 300 elk/year from 1930 to 1934; about 88% by hunting, 12% by park removals (Fig. 3.1). Combined removals from 1935 to 1955 averaged 2,041 elk/year; 84% by hunting, 16% by the park. Human predation was not distributed evenly throughout the population. When attempts were initiated to reduce winter numbers through hunting, the frequency of large removals shows that large population segments were present that either habitually moved from the park during early winter storms or that summered in areas north of the park and moved onto winter ranges north of the park or both. Note that hunting removals exceeded 1,000 elk for 11 of the 21 years from 1935 to 1955, and that during the autumn and early winter of

1942–43 a removal of 6,539 was made by hunting. Park removals were intensified in 1956 (2,635 elk, 75% by shooting). Total removals averaged 1,774 from 1956 to 1962 (hunting, 9%; park, 91%), and at these levels park removals appear to have nearly substituted for hunting removals outside the park. Park removals were further intensified in 1962, and from 1963 to 1968 total removals averaged 1,649; hunting, 29%; park, 71%.

Minimum autumn populations from 1935 to 1968 were estimated by adding removals to calculated winter populations (Fig. 3.2). Calculated $\bar{r}$ values for 1935–56, 1956–62, and 1962–68 were −.010, −.041, and −.205, respectively, as human predation increased. A trend in autumn populations for this period was produced by fitting a quadratic regression to these estimates. Occasional huge removals (e.g., during 1943, 1956, and 1962) show that these calculated trends for winter and autumn are far smoother than actual trends. The 1943 and 1956 removals abruptly reduced the population. The possible effects of these two removals were calculated by subtracting an estimated 16% calves from the 1943 and 1956 autumn numbers to produce minimum winter populations for 1942 and 1955 (Fig. 3.2). The abrupt decline in winter numbers between 1961 and 1962 (Fig. 3.2) resulted from the 1962 park reduction.

These fitted lines represent trends in only the broadest sense, especially for 1930–55. The population did decline over this period, but the actual rates of decline and the numbers present in any one year could have differed substantially from those shown by the trend lines.

The 1969–79 Period

A moratorium on elk removals from the park began in 1969 (Cole 1969b). The period from 1969 to 1979 represented an attempt to rely more upon natural regulation of ungulate numbers within Yellowstone and to reconcile different management objectives inside and outside the park (Houston 1979).

Sixty-three aerial total counts (using Piper Supercub aircraft) were made during December–May periods between December 1967 and February 1979 to monitor elk numbers and distribution. Flight procedures are described in detail by Barmore (1980). Recent counts have required 11–12 hours flying time, usually on two consecutive days (5–6 hours/day). The 121 counting units were covered systematically at altitudes of 90–150 m (56 units where the highest elk densities occurred averaged 10.9 km^2 in area). Since 1970, the maximum counts were obtained during mid-December to late January, when elk seemed to be exceptionally visible (Fig. 3.3). Positive aspects of the 1967–79 counts included:

1. Several flights were made annually.
2. Flight procedures were similar, and the same counting units were used.
3. Only three observers were involved over the entire period (pilot–observer D. Stradley made all flights).
4. The range was usually completely snow covered for the winter counts.
5. Elk were comparatively undisturbed by shooting prior to making counts, except during 1968 (maximum counts of 1976, 1978, and 1979 were made before winter hunts were conducted outside the park).
6. Elk occupancy of forests appeared to be very low during early winter.

FIGURE 3.3.

Elk in the Lamar Valley, 21 December 1977. Optimum counting conditions occurred when the range was completely snow covered and groups of elk foraged on grasslands. Conspicuous trails and feeding craters in new-fallen snow provided clues to the presence of elk in an area before they were actually observed.

Negative aspects included:

1. Counting efficiency probably declined by the end of each daily flight because of observer fatigue.
2. Movements of elk could have occurred between halves of each flight.
3. Snow conditions and elk occupancy of forests still varied among early winter flights.

Outlying areas with much lower elk densities were overflown last each day to reduce the effects of point (1), and observations of elk and their trails suggested that aspect (2) was of little consequence, particularly where the precipitous canyon of the Yellowstone River separated halves of each flight.

The maximum counts from 1969 to 1979 were obtained under circumstances quite different from those made earlier. Counts were still below the absolute numbers present, but, with one exception, I have used the actual counts to represent the minimum numbers of elk present in early winter. The exception was 1977, when counting conditions comparable to those of the other years simply did not occur. Snow cover was mostly absent in early winter, and by late winter elk had dispersed into forests. I have omitted the 1977 count from some analyses. For others, an estimate of the minimum numbers present in 1977 of 10,741 was produced by subtracting the proportion of calves of the year from the 1978 autumn population of 12,941 (Fig. 3.2). Elk subsequently killed in winter hunts held outside the park in 1976, 1978, and 1979 were subtracted from the maximum early winter counts of those years. Counts ranged from a low of 4,305 in 1969 to 12,607 in 1975. Close comparison of the 1969–79 counts with earlier aerial counts requires caution, because the 1969–79 counts were obtained earlier in the winter (Fig. 3.2) and usually with much less precount disturbance of the population.

The growth trajectories of winter populations from 1968 to 1975 and of autumn populations from 1969 to 1976 were of particular interest because human predation was low (less than 1 or 2% of autumn populations) and all removals were made by hunting outside the park (Table 3.2, Fig. 3.1). The annual $\bar{r}$ values were .305, .253, .273, .121, .195, .053, and .180 for winter populations from 1968 to 1975. The annual $\bar{r}$ was .232, .288, .124, .201, .058, .172, −.032 for autumn populations from 1969 to 1976. The mean $\bar{r}$ for winter populations from 1968 to 1971 was .279, which also represented a crude estimate of r_p, the potential rate of increase, with human predation nearly eliminated (Caughley 1977:109). [Barmore (1980) estimated $\bar{r}$ at .242 for 1968–70 by using slightly lower spring counts for 1969 and 1970 than used here.] The annual $\bar{r}$ declined significantly for winter populations from 1968 to 1975 (i.e., a regression of $\bar{r}$ on time showed the slope to be significantly less than 0, $P < .05$). Similarly, the $\bar{r}$ for minimum autumn populations declined significantly ($P < .01$) from 1969 to 1976.

The growth trajectories were deflected as large numbers of elk were removed by human predation in the winter of 1976 and again in 1978 (Table 3.2, Fig. 3.2). The $\bar{r}$ for winter populations from 1976 to 1979 (the poor count of 1977 omitted) was .006; for autumn populations, −.027.

Interpretation: History and Numbers

My interpretation of the history of the northern Yellowstone elk differs in several respects from previous accounts. Archaeological data show that elk have been present in the Yellowstone area for millennia. Earliest written observations indicate that the Yellowstone area was historical summer range for large numbers of elk. This interpretation is in agreement with Murie (1940), Murie (1951), Cole (1969a), Lovaas (1970), and Gruell (1973). Interpretations that the area was not a major historical summer range (Skinner 1927, 1928; Rush 1932a) appear to have been based upon incomplete reviews of the literature and the use of select negative information, as pointed out by Murie (1940).

The presettlement distribution and density of the northern Yellowstone elk in winter have been the subject of controversy. Skinner (1928), Grimm (1939), and National Park Service (1957) speculated that (1) the park was not historic winter range, (2) elk in the northern herd formerly wintered farther down the Yellowstone River, and (3) elk were subsequently compressed into the park.

However, my review of the available records indicates that the valleys of the Yellowstone and Lamar Rivers served continuously as winter range for large numbers of elk from the 1870s. Actual densities cannot be determined, but judging from accounts there must have been many thousands. Earlier records do not exist, but it seems likely to me that elk have inhabited these areas in winter for as long as postglacial climates and plant communities would support them. Consider that elk migrate into energy-rich but only seasonally available ecosystems (spring, summer, autumn ranges). Such migrations permit maintenance of a greater biomass than would otherwise be possible (Hall 1972). Complete occupancy of all available winter range, the most limited seasonal energy source, probably evolved early on. The alternative interpretation of Skinner (1928) and others is not supported by the records and also requires postulating an unlikely biological vacuum if elk moved from the area.

Accounts indicate that large numbers of elk, bison, and pronghorn wintered historically in the Paradise Valley (24–64 km north of the park) and farther down the Yellowstone River when large numbers of elk were also reported in the park (Meagher pers. commun.). The evidence concerning the summer distribution of these ungulates is equivocal, i.e., point (2) cannot be evaluated. I have been unable to confirm Cahalane's (1941) comment that the elk from the northern herd formerly wintered "down the valley to the present site of Livingston or farther, a distance of about 70 miles," which unfortunately continues to be cited as fact (Craighead et al. 1972). I suspect that the ungulates wintering in the Paradise Valley largely summered in the mountains north of the park on both sides of the Yellowstone River. If this was so, then elk from the lands that became Yellowstone Park would have encountered a biological barrier in the sense that the area was already occupied. Whatever their summer distribution, bison and pronghorn were extirpated during settlement of the valley, and only about a thousand elk have recolonized the margins (Constan pers. commun.).

The historical accounts also do not support the interpretation that large numbers of elk were compressed into a smaller area in the park—point (3). First, intense hunting inside and outside the park continued into the mid-1880s and greatly reduced elk densities overall. Second, subsequent densities on the northern winter range were not nearly as high as has been previously reported. Finally, increased elk densities resulting from accelerated immigration and restricted emigration would likely have been balanced through reduced natality and survival because the winter environment in the park is quite rigorous.

Historical records suggest that the present distribution and densities of elk are best interpreted as a remnant of a once far greater biomass of ungulates that occurred in the region, rather than as an artifact created by establishment of the park. This interpretation does not preclude the possibility that densities are somewhat different now (either higher or lower) for other reasons, e.g., climatic changes, plant succession, levels of predation.

The need for this reevaluation of the history of the northern elk transcends purely historical accuracy; management through 1968 was predicated largely on the history as we then understood it. For the past half-century nearly every account of the population dynamics of the northern elk, every interpretation of habitat conditions, and many interpretations of the relations of elk with associated herbivores have been based upon one or more of the following premises: (a) the park was not historical winter range, (b) following establishment of the park the population erupted to 35,000 by the early 1900s, and (c) the population crashed to 10,000–12,000 between 1917 and 1920— attendant range deterioration is often suggested. Similarly, the need for management of the elk—which has included winter feeding, predator control, and elk reductions within the park—appears to have been buttressed by one or more of these premises. My review of the historical records suggests that all these premises and interpretations were incorrect. The previously accepted history of the northern Yellowstone elk possibly resulted from accepting selected premises or conclusions of previous authors without always reexamining their supporting evidence. Consecutive reports and publications built upon and reinforced what appears to have been largely an incorrect historical account.

Euro-American man has had a variable and sometimes substantial direct influence on elk numbers from first contact in the early 1800s to the present. Predation by modern man was probably negligible until the mid-1870s. Determining specific effects of unregulated hunting, poaching, and livestock grazing on elk numbers during the late 19th century is difficult, and the following is an educated guess, based upon the available accounts. Intense hunting must have reduced or eliminated accessible herd segments. This may have occurred by the mid-1880s and early 1890s, as suggested by the sporadic reports of elk wintering and being taken by hunters north of the park, or of elk wintering around Mammoth Hot Springs. Large numbers still occurred on some interior portions of the winter range. Elk wintering near Mammoth and outside the park increased during the early 1900s as elk reoccupied these portions of their original range. The extent of this increase has been greatly exaggerated by erroneously interpreting estimates of elk summering within the entire park to apply to the northern herd and by some faulty censuses and calculations. Further confusion led to the interpretation that the population erupted and crashed between 1910 and 1920, which appears to be incorrect. The magnitude of change from the 1870s through the 1920s *may* be that winter herds were reduced to 5,000–8,000 and increased to 12,000–16,000.

From the 1930s through 1968 human predation (hunter removals and park reductions) reduced winter numbers from around 12,000 to around 4,000. Park reductions were intensified in 1956 and appear to have progressively substituted for hunter removals. The greatest short-term fluctuations in numbers over this period seem to have resulted mainly from intense human predation rather than from changes in food supplies, weather conditions, etc.

Following the 1969 moratorium on elk removals from the park, the population increased to around 12,000 by the mid-1970s. Hunting removals outside the park increased greatly from 1976. The period of population growth from 1968 to the autumn of 1976 was of particular interest because human predation was very low. The decline of $\bar{r}$ as elk numbers increased suggests that the population was approaching an equilibrium produced largely by natural processes.

CHAPTER 4

The Elk Population—
Seasonal Distribution

MOST ELK IN THE NORTHERN HERD migrate between summer and winter ranges. The distinction between seasonal range areas is not clear-cut, and a few elk remain on the winter range year long. Highest densities occur on the winter range during November–April.

Winter Distribution

Although the entire northern winter range is about 100,000 ha, elk are progressively excluded from the periphery by increasingly severe environmental conditions. Distribution is very fluid, however, and elk reoccupy some peripheral sites if winter conditions moderate.

Results from 27 ground or aerial counts made during 23 different years from 1916 to 1967 showed elk distribution within broad areas of the winter range during January–15 April periods (Table 4.1). Data were generally from censuses designed to determine numbers and not necessarily distribution down the elevational gradients of the Yellowstone and Lamar Rivers during periods of maximum environmental severity. All data are actual counts and have the same bias errors discussed previously. The proportions counted by area provide some perspective on earlier distribution, but comparisons are difficult because of changes in management activities within the park and in land uses outside. About 1,600 ha of winter range were added to the park in 1932. Artificial regulation of elk wintering in the park occurred sporadically from 1935 to 1968, with greatest effects after 1956. Winter feeding of ungulates occurred from 1904 to 1945 (some bison were fed through 1952), but affected significant numbers of elk only from about 1908 to 1937. Effects were greatest between 1921–37, when the largest quantities of hay were fed. Feeding may have had relatively little influence on

TABLE 4.1
Distribution of Northern Yellowstone Elk During January–15 April Periods, 1916–67[a]

Date	Inside Park			Outside Park	Total Counted
	Upper Range	Lower Range (BLA)	Total (%)	Total (%)	
1916 M[b]	4.4[c]	4.2	8.6 (89)	1.0 (11)	9.6
1927 F	4.2	5.0	9.2 (74)	3.2 (26)	12.4[d]
1928 A				2.6	
1929 A[e]	5.7	3.4	9.1 (99)	0.1 (1)	9.1
1930 F	4.0	2.3	6.3 (87)	1.0 (3)	7.2
M	3.7	3.1	6.8 (83)	1.4 (17)	8.2
1932 J	4.5	2.6 (1.5)	7.1 (82)	1.5 (18)	8.6
A[e]	5.2	3.7 (0.9)	8.9 (84)	1.7 (16)	10.6
1933 A	4.3	4.1 (0.8)	8.4 (73)	3.1 (27)	11.5
1934 M[e]	7.0	2.7 (0.7)	9.7 (97)	0.3 (3)	10.0
1935 M	4.8	3.5 (0.9)	8.3 (82)	1.9 (18)	10.1
1936 M	4.0	4.9 (1.0)	8.9 (86)	1.4 (14)	10.3
1937 A[e]	4.1	4.2 (0.7)	8.3 (95)	0.5 (5)	8.8
1938 M	2.5	4.6 (1.9)	7.1 (64)	3.9 (36)	11.0
1943 FM[f]	1.1	2.2 (0.7)	3.3 (40)	5.0 (60)	8.2
1946 M	3.4	4.8 (0.9)	8.2 (96)	0.4 (4)	8.5
1948 F	2.0	3.4 (1.4)	5.4 (69)	2.4 (31)	7.8
1949 M	4.3	3.7 (1.3)	7.9 (84)	1.6 (16)	9.5
1956 M	3.0	2.9 (1.0)	5.9 (85)	1.1 (15)	7.0
1959 M				4.7	
1961 M[e]	5.8	2.3 (1.1)	8.1 (99)	0.1 (1)	8.2
1962 A[f]	1.0	1.7 (1.0)	2.7 (45)	3.1 (55)	5.8
1964 J				0.1[g]	
1965 F				0.6[g]	
A	2.5	1.9 (0.7)	4.5 (92)	0.4 (8)	4.9
1967 J	1.6	1.6 (0.9)	3.2 (100)	[h]	3.3
M	2.0	1.6 (0.4)	3.6 (94)	0.2 (6)	3.8

[a] Survey technique and sources as in Table 3.2.
[b] Month of count.
[c] Thousands of elk.
[d] Questionable count, but proportions by area may be useful.
[e] Mild winters.
[f] Very severe winters.
[g] Montana Fish and Game Department records.
[h] Less than .1%, but number outside park is underestimated.

overall elk numbers because the volume fed was small relative to the winter forage requirements of the population, but feeding influenced local distribution. This was certainly true in the BLA (see Chap 8, Human Developments and Activities), where feedgrounds concentrated elk that would otherwise have dispersed more widely within and probably outside the park.

Changes in land use and human populations have influenced the availability of elk winter range outside the park. The largest human populations occurred around 1900–10, with another short-lived increase in 1940 when mining increased (Table 4.2). Differences in land use patterns are not wholly reflected by census figures. The greatest conflicts with the forage available to wintering elk occurred in the early 1900s

TABLE 4.2
Human Populations on the Winter Range of the Northern Yellowstone Elk Outside Yellowstone National Park[a]

DATE OF CENSUS	NUMBER OF PERSONS
1880	50[b]
1890	349
1900	1,627
1910	1,104
1920	540
1930	588
1940	1,070
1950	595
1960	650[c]
1970	650[c]

[a]Data from U.S. Department of Commerce census records for areas from Gardiner and Jardine to Dome Mt.
[b]Estimate based upon historic accounts.
[c]Estimate based on the Gardiner–Cooke City census district.

from grazing by livestock. Livestock grazing was reduced in the mid-1920s (Rush 1932a). The net result of continued changes in land use, including reductions in the human population and in livestock, is less conflict with wintering elk on ranges outside the park boundaries now than at any time since the 1880s.

Although bison wintered historically in the Lamar Valley, they were extirpated by poaching (Meagher 1973). Bison were reintroduced into the Lamar Valley in 1907 but were maintained in semidomestication and fed during winter. This herd exceeded 1,000 from 1929 to 1932 but was artificially reduced to 143 by 1952 as management objectives changed from a ranching-oriented approach to one of allowing bison to free range without supplemental feeding. Foraging by the artificially large bison herd and cutting hay for winter feeding of bison and horses reduced winter forage supplies for elk, particularly during 1919–49, when 400 or more bison occupied the area.

Because of this formidable array of variables, few generalizations may be made about elk distribution from these census data. Apparently with winter populations of 10,000 or more elk, about 70–80% were counted in the park most years. This declined to 40% on occasional very severe winters, and over 90% occurred in the park during very mild winters. Late March or April counts probably underestimated the proportion of the population wintering outside during the more severe, early parts of winter. Also, these counts were conducted after elk removals had been made.

Perhaps 3,000–5,000 elk occurred on the upper winter range (Fig. 2.1) most winters; 5,000–6,000 wintered there during especially mild winters; but only 2,000 remained during the occasional very severe winters. (The 1942–43 winter was particularly severe, and 1,123 elk were counted after 691 had been removed.) Records from scout diaries and station log books for 1898–1919 also suggested herds in the 3,000–5,000 range for this general area most years (Houston 1974, 1980).

About 20–30% of the elk were counted outside the park many winters. These consisted of elk that summered in the park and others that never ranged inside the park.

During many years most elk wintering outside the park had summered within it. Intensified efforts to reduce the northern herd since 1935 reduced disproportionately those segments wintering outside the park. Increased reductions within the park and hunting outside reduced numbers until by the mid-1960s, with herds of about 5,000, the numbers wintering outside the park were usually negligible.

Ungulate densities in the BLA of the park have been of particular concern. Winter feeding led to concentrations of 2,500 or more elk in the 1920s. Narrative accounts (Albright 1932, Rush 1932a, Olsen 1938) suggest that public hunting outside the park also contributed to these concentrations of elk. A thousand or more elk were counted in the BLA from 1932 to 1967 (Table 4.1), but numbers concentrated by hunting cannot be determined because counts were made following closure of hunting seasons.

Elk distribution and density were measured in more detail during December–May periods from 1967 to 1979. Distribution was recorded on maps during each of 63 flights made from December 1967 to February 1979. Surveys began during the last year of herd reductions in the park and continued as the winter population increased to over 12,000. A comparison of range occupied during early and late winter shows the reduction of available range caused by progressively more severe weather conditions (Table 4.3). The late winter periods shown in Table 4.3 usually represent the time of maximum range constriction as elk move northwest down the Yellowstone River and its tributaries. The period of minimum range availability has begun any time from mid-December to late April and has lasted for a few weeks to over two months. The exceptional 1976 winter also illustrated the variation in winter conditions on the area. Two snowstorms in late November and early December combined to rapidly reduce range availability. By late February the area occupied increased by 6,000 ha as some

TABLE 4.3
Elk Numbers, Distribution, and Density during Winter, 1968–79

Winter Periods[a]	Elk[b] (10³)	Hectares (10³) Occupied Overall and (ha/elk)		Outside Park	
		Dec.–Jan.	Feb.–15 Apr.	Hectares (10³) Occupied	Elk (10³)
1968	3.2	—	17 (5)	c	d
1969	4.3	31 (7)	28 (7)	c	d
1970	5.5	39 (7)	21 (4)	c	d
1971	7.3	75 (10)	42 (6)	4	0.6
1972	8.2	76 (9)	43 (5)	5	1.3
1973	9.9	59 (6)	48 (5)	3	0.8
1974	10.5	72 (7)	53 (5)	3	0.8
1975	12.6	67 (5)	39 (3)	6	2.7
1976	10.8	43 (4)	49 (5)	12	1.7
1977	10.7[e]	65 (6)	42 (4)	c	d
1978	11.9	52 (4)	51 (4)	13	2.2
1979	10.8	51 (5)	—	11	1.5

[a]1968 = winter 1967–68, etc. Data for 1968–70 from W. J. Barmore (pers. commun. 1978).
[b]Maximum winter counts minus numbers removed in late-season hunts.
[c]Estimated 2,000 ha or less by elk moving from the park plus 200–400 "resident" elk.
[d]Estimated fewer than 500 including residents.
[e]Calculated minimum number present for 1977.

elk moved farther down the Yellowstone River outside the park and others moved back into peripheral ranges throughout the area as weather conditions became more mild.

The area occupied during early winter increased considerably but not significantly between 1967 and 1979 (linear regression of hectares occupied on time, $r^2 = .02$, P $> .10$), mainly because of variation introduced by occasional severe early winter storms. In contrast, the area occupied during late winter, when environmental conditions were more consistently severe, increased significantly over the 12 years ($r^2 = .61$, P $< .005$). Thus, much of the increase in elk numbers was accommodated by occupying a larger area, particularly areas that had very low densities following the reduction activities. A rough expression of overall density (area occupied/maximum early winter count) shows that December–January density averaged about 5.4 ha/elk during 1973–79, when populations were clearly over 10,000. Density increased during late winter from about 5–7 ha/elk in 1968–69 to around 4 by 1977–78, but the trend on time was weak ($r^2 = .31$, P $> .10$). Recognizing the crudeness of these calculations (e.g., the duration of periods of minimum range availability is not considered, and calculated densities are low because not all elk present are counted), apparently 40,000–50,000+ ha of range may be available, and densities of around 4–5 ha/elk may occur during the period of maximum compression many years. The 3 ha/elk density for 1975 was too high, even granting that 12,600 was a minimum population figure, because substantial winter mortality had occurred by the time this mid-April estimate was made. Numbers of elk moving outside the park and range area occupied there increased substantially but irregularly as the overall population increased. The frequency and size of these movements seem broadly density-dependent, with departures from this relationship reflecting the highly variable winter environment. Even though the population was large in 1977, the winter was so mild that no substantial movement from the park occurred. An additional 1,207 and 825 elk that moved outside the park in 1976 and 1978 were subsequently killed during late hunting seasons (Houston 1979).

The changes in distribution over time were, of course, more complex than indicated by these broad comparisons. Maps of winter elk distribution at the lower populations of 1969 and the higher populations of 1976 and 1978 were compared to more clearly show changes in distribution over time and by area (Fig. 4.1). At any population level, late winter distribution becomes more discontinuous than early winter distribution as environmental conditions become more severe. However, the elk reduction program apparently created a much more discontinuous distribution (as opposed to a uniform low density) compared to more recent times. At low populations, higher densities remained farthest from the roads. Either disproportionately high removals occurred from groups that frequented areas near roads or survivors were habituated to avoid these areas or both. Much of the population increase was associated with reoccupation of areas where reductions had been made and by larger movements outside the park. Large increases in density have generally not occurred in areas that retained high densities at low population levels.

Elk distribution and numbers on the upper winter range have been of particular interest. Even during the severe winters of 1975, 1976, and 1978 around 3,500 elk appeared to remain in this area (Fig. 4.1). This estimate was based upon actual late winter counts of about 1,500, 1,200, and 900 elk for the respective years. However, these counts were very low, because most elk were foraging in forests.

Elk numbers in the BLA increased from an average maximum of 1,400 ± 200 during the winters of 1971–73 to about 2,300 in December 1976. Large migrations from the BLA to areas outside the park occurred in late December 1976 and again in

FIGURE 4.1.

Elk distribution and approximate densities for selected early and late winter periods, 1969, 1976, and 1978. Areas not surveyed (NS) were outside the park when there was no evidence of elk movement beyond the boundary. Only about 100–200 "resident" elk occurred on ranges outside the park in 1969. Actual densities for late winter were considerably higher than shown here, because elk foraged in forests and were difficult to observe. Data for 1969 from W. J. Barmore.

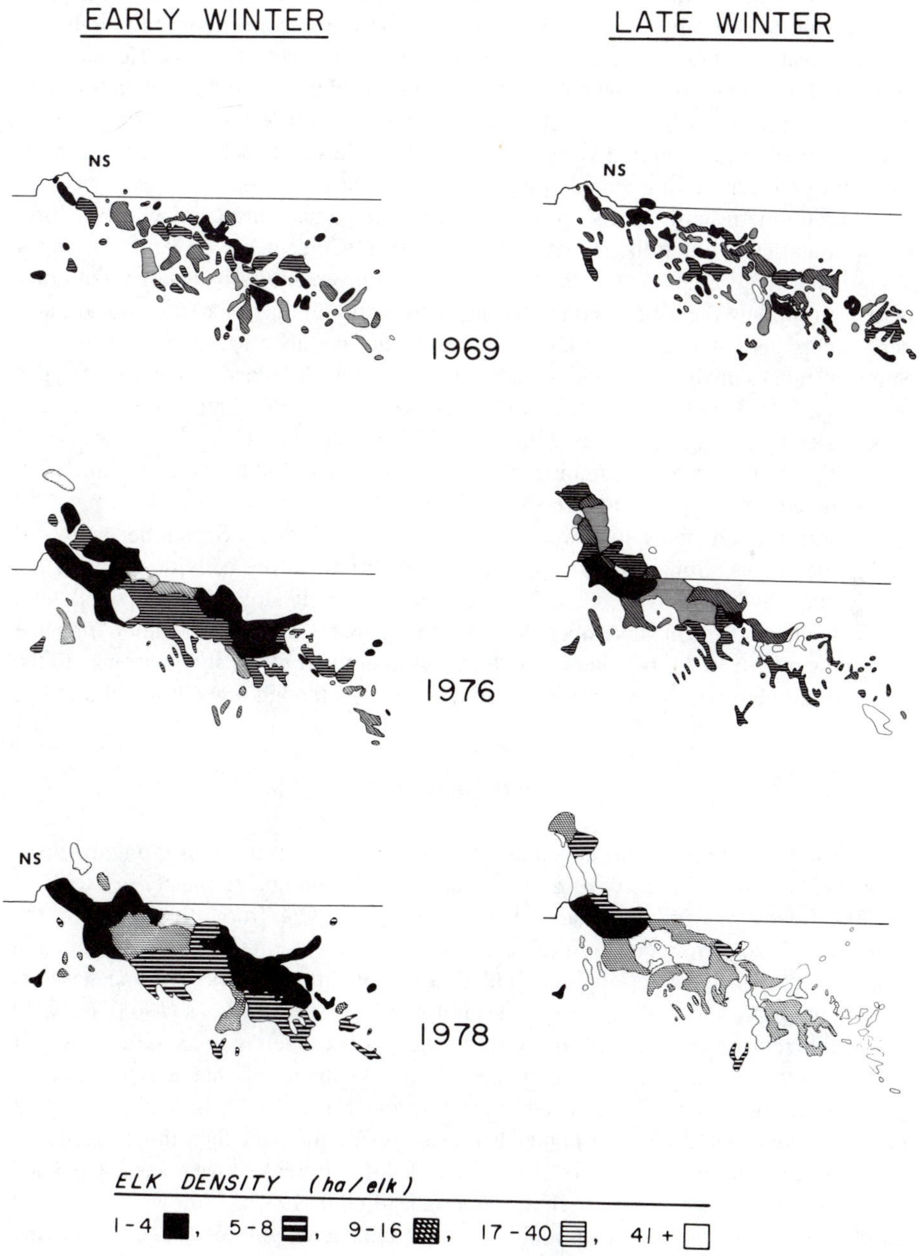

EARLY WINTER   LATE WINTER

1969

1976

1978

ELK DENSITY (ha/elk)

1-4 ■,   5-8 ▤,   9-16 ▦,   17-40 ▤,   41+ □

1978 and 1979 when early winter counts were around 2,000 elk (see Elk Management, Chap. 12).

Spring, Summer, and Autumn Distribution

The time and pace of spring migrations from the winter range vary as environmental conditions moderate. Large-scale movements off the winter range began from early April to mid-May during 1971–78. Elk spread outward from winter concentrations into higher elevations. Observations of the northern herd (Barmore unpubl., Houston unpubl.) and of the Jackson Hole elk (Cole 1969a) showed that elk did not always follow retreating snow lines but sometimes crossed many kilometers of continuous snow cover to reach areas seemingly less hospitable than those left behind. Consequently, the areas used for calving varied considerably in different years.

The northern herd moves up the Yellowstone, Lamar, and Gardner Rivers and their tributaries to intermingle with elk from other winter herds on summer ranges along major hydrographic divides. This pattern of movement is characteristic of other herds surrounding the Yellowstone plateau. During the summer, elk from the northern herd occupy as much as 4,700 km^2 in the park and possibly 1,000 km^2 north of it. Summer ranges include a wide variety of grasslands, herblands, and forest types between 2,300–3,000 m. The approximate summer ranges of different herds within the park, based upon tagging studies (Johnson 1951, Brazda 1953, Cole 1969a, Craighead et al. 1972, Mullen pers. commun. 1973, Shoesmith 1978, Rudd pers. commun. 1979) and some educated guesswork are shown in Fig. 4.2.

Autumn movements to lower elevations begin following September snows at higher elevations. Some males, apparently spent from rutting activities, are on the winter range by late October, to be followed by increasingly larger numbers of elk with the first major storms in November. Migration may span 1,500 m in elevation for some elk, and stretch 130 km between the extreme southern part of the summer range to the extreme northern part of the winter range (Fig. 4.2), although few elk travel that far.

Herd Segments

A total of 1,270 elk was ear-tagged as newborn calves (549) or trapped on the winter range (721) from 1924 to 1958, from winter herds that numbered mostly in excess of 10,000. Recoveries prior to March 1959 totaled 361 (32% from elk trapped on the winter range; 24% from newborn calves). Tag recoveries required having the animal in hand, i.e., subsequent retrapping, field shooting within the park, hunting harvests outside the park, and finding animals dead of natural causes. Kittams (1963) analyzed 357 usable returns and reported strong tendencies for elk to return to areas of the winter range where they had previously wintered, but he believed that the presence of feedgrounds might have influenced some returns. Elk tagged adjacent to the park boundary contributed more to hunter harvests outside the park than those tagged on interior areas. During the winters of 1964–67, 1,448 different elk were ear-tagged and neck-banded for individual recognition (Craighead et al. 1972), from winter herds of 5,000±. "Recoveries" of identifiable animals included sightings as well as having animals in hand (1,448 initial tagging locations, 1,153 locations for trapped elk, 1,722 free ranging, 147 hunter returns). Shoesmith (1978) provided an additional 536 sight-

FIGURE 4.2.

Yellowstone Park region showing winter ranges (dark shading) of nine different elk herds and their overlap on summer range within the park (light shading for northern herd, dashed lines for others). The elk herds are (1) Northern Yellowstone; (2) Sunlight–Crandall Creek; (3) North Fork Shoshone River; (4) South Fork Shoshone River; (5) Greybull River; (6) Jackson Hole (Gros Ventre River and National Elk Refuge segments); (7) Madison–Firehole River; (8) Gallatin River; and (9) Paradise Valley.

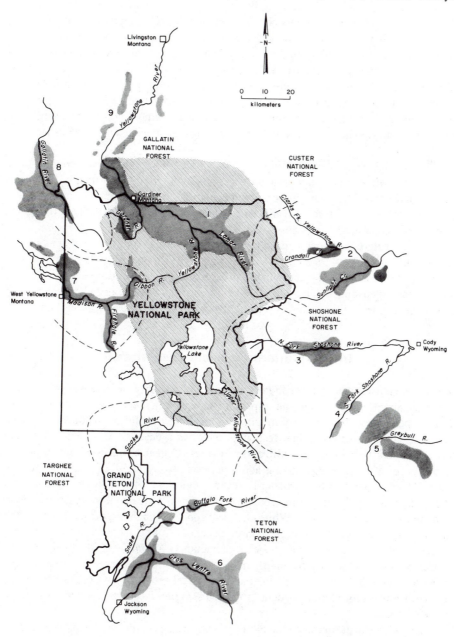

ings of these collared elk for 1968. These combined studies for 1964–68 also showed tendencies for marked elk to return to specific winter and summer range areas. Shoe-smith (1978:57) observed that a minimum 40% of 95 tagged elk returned two or more years to their summer ranges on the Mirror Plateau and that some returned to specific sites. Females apparently showed greater fidelity to summer range areas than males. Interpretations of the movements of tagged elk within the winter range for 1964–68 are difficult, because intense disturbance during these studies may have overridden traditional or environmentally influenced movements. Groups of elk were herded long distances each winter with helicopters to obtain herd reductions. [Greer (1967:3) describes the hazing of elk from the park, including tagged animals, into hunting areas outside the boundary.] Still, over 99% of 915 winter observations of 546 elk initially tagged in the Lamar Valley were subsequently observed in the same general area (Craighead et al. 1972:46). Some few elk from this upper range area were observed outside the park on the Yellowstone River each year from 1964 to 1967 (Shoesmith 1978:65). Unfortunately, the sex and age of animals making such movements were not all reported.

These and other studies (Knight 1970, Fuller 1976) suggest that fidelity to a portion of a winter range among adult elk is relatively high. This affinity for winter home ranges and differences in herd composition for elk on different portions of the northern winter range (see Sex and Age Composition, Chap. 5) support the broad concept of winter herd ''segments'' (elk with similar affinities for specific range areas and similar patterns of movement in response to changing environmental conditions). The occurrence of herd segments also was suggested by detailed studies of elk movements in deep snow during the winters of 1976 and 1978 (Houston 1979). Elk that initially migrated onto winter range along the park boundary tended to comprise a larger proportion of those moving outside the park than did those from interior areas.

Interpretation: Seasonal Distribution

As part of an overall ecological strategy to cope with a highly variable and periodically harsh winter environment, elk can respond to increasingly severe environmental conditions either by moving from an area or by remaining but shifting to different forage sources. The sum of individual responses provides a descriptive model of how elk occupy the northern range and utilize its resources. Evidence suggested that fidelity to a portion of a winter range among adult elk is relatively high but that affinities are modified or overridden by particularly severe environmental conditions. Throughout the winter range in the park some elk remain in a specific area under very severe winter conditions as others move out. While the broad concept of herd segments seems useful, actually there are gradients of response, depending upon the severity of weather, forage availability, and probably social interactions. A *differential sieve* descriptive model of how elk occupy the northern range and utilize its resources seems more consistent with the evidence than the partition model proposed by Cole (1969b) (i.e., divide the area into interior resident groups and migratory groups farther west on the winter range).

The winter distribution of the elk population is especially important to managers because the park is not a complete ecological unit for the population. Experimental elk reductions in the park with hunts outside reduced winter populations to around 4,000 by the late 1960s. Together those removals greatly reduced the numbers of elk that periodically wintered outside the park. The population increase through the 1970s was largely accommodated by reoccupying areas from which reductions were made, rather than by massive increases in local densities. This observation is particularly relevant to various management strategies (see Chap. 12). A review of the information available led Cole (1969b) to propose a descriptive model of elk distribution and management that included the following hypotheses: (1) A portion of the elk herd remains in the park under the most severe winter conditions and is unavailable for hunting. These animals might be "naturally regulated," i.e., reductions were unnecessary. (2) Migratory segments of the population could be restored. Some of these animals would regularly move outside the park and be cropped by public hunting. Subsequent data on winter distribution have permitted an assessment of these hypotheses.

Cole's (1969b) hypothesis that 2,500–3,500 elk may remain on an upper winter range in the park is generally supported by both historical and recent evidence, notwithstanding that other elk move from this area and out of the park. As a broader generalization, the park will contain 8,000–10,000 elk most winters, in excess of 10,000 during mild winters, and as few as 5,000 during very infrequent, extremely severe winters.

The hypothesis that migrations outside the park could be restored is generally supported, even though migrations may occur only one year in two or two years in three. This frequency was also suggested by data from the 1930s to 1950s, prior to extensive park reductions.

The occurrence of herd segments and the nature of the documented changes in elk distribution and density suggest that analysis of the dynamics of the overall population requires caution. Representative sampling of attributes such as natality and the sex and age composition of winter populations is made more difficult by intrapopulation variation. Although large herd reductions seemingly increased available resources per elk, the potential for density-dependent responses in natality and mortality may not have been fully realized, because the smaller winter populations were not distributed uniformly at lower densities.

CHAPTER 5

The Elk Population: Dynamics

THE POPULATION ATTRIBUTES OF NATALITY, MORTALITY, AND DISPERSAL are examined in relation to changes in the size of the elk population. Density-dependent relationships are generally considered to occur when either the percentage of mortality increases or the reproductive rate decreases as the elk population rises (Sinclair 1977). The data are from unpublished files of the National Park Service, Montana Fish and Game Department, and U.S. Forest Service, as well as from personal records of individuals who have worked with the elk, from occasional published accounts, and from my own research. These data include field classifications or other samples of the sex and age composition of winter populations, collections of female reproductive tracts, samples of the age distributions from elk shot or found dead, and observations of the movements of tagged elk.

Natality

A sample of 3,050 uteri obtained from elk during winter herd reductions from 1935 to 1968 was used to determine the incidence of pregnancy. Twins usually represented 1.0% or less of the pregnancies in all samples; multiple births were of little importance in the dynamics of the population. The frequency of twins in the 1963–68 samples from low populations showed no change from the frequency at high populations. Also, *in utero* mortality of fetuses was very low (Greer 1966b, pers. commun. 1973).

In addition to the 2,885 uteri from yearlings and adults tallied in Table 5.1, the uteri of 165 calves 6–11 months old were examined for 1950–67. None was found to be pregnant at any population size.

Some elk reached sexual maturity as yearlings. The uteri of 357 yearlings collected from 1935 to 1968 were of particular interest because of the low and variable

TABLE 5.1
Pregnancy Rates, Northern Yellowstone Elk, 1935–68

AGE CLASS	DATE	N	PREGNANCY RATE	SOURCE
Adults[a]	1935 JF	129	.75[b]	Mills (1935a)
	1937 JF	134	.91[c]	West (1937)
	1943 J	156	.90	Murie (1943)
	1949–50 DJ	375	.79	Kittams (1953)
	1951 JF	259	.94	Kittams (1953)
	1960	118	.82[c]	NPS files
	1961–62 NJn	731	.88	Greer (1966b)
	1963 OJn	163	.95	Greer (1966b, 1967, 1968, pers. comm. 1973)
	1964 OJn	116	.93	Greer (1966b, 1967, 1968, pers. commun. 1973)
	1965 NJn	107	.95	Greer (1966b, 1967, 1968, pers. commun. 1973)
	1966 NJn	104	.95	Greer (1966b, 1967, 1968, pers. commun. 1973)
	1967 NJn	136	.96	Greer (1966b, 1967, 1968, pers. commun. 1973)
Yearlings	1935	5	.20	Mills (1935a)
	1949–50 DJ	14	.00	Kittams (1953)
	1951 JF	25	.04	Kittams (1953)
	1961–62 NJn	70	.09	Greer (1968)
	1963 OJn	13	.00	Greer (1968, pers. commun. 1973)
	1964 OJn	32	.28	Greer (1968, pers. commun. 1973)
	1965 NJn	35	.09	Greer (1968, pers. commun. 1973)
	1966 NJn	27	.04	Greer (1968, pers. commun. 1973)
	1967 NJn	44	.34	Greer (1968, pers. commun. 1973)
	1968 NJn	92	.13	Greer (1968, pers. commun. 1973)

[a] Two years and older.
[b] Some selection for specific individuals and may include some yearlings.
[c] Adults plus yearlings.

pregnancy rates (0.00–0.34). Studies of nutrition and growth (Chap. 6) suggested that both population density and severity of the previous winter (i.e., time $t - 1$, when the sampled yearlings were calves) and those of the next earlier winter ($t - 2$ when yearlings were *in utero*) would be useful independent variables upon which the observed differences in pregnancy could be tested for association. Elk numbers at $t - 1$ and $t - 2$ were used to represent density. The total number of females, young, and yearling males in the population was also tested for association, because many adult males wintered separately from females and young. Indices of winter severity for December–March and December–April periods were calculated from the precipitation and temperature measurements for Mammoth Hot Springs as described by Picton (1979). The indices provided a single numerical estimate of relative severity constructed by algebraic summation of the signs (+ or −) of the monthly deviations from the long-term monthly mean values of temperature and precipitation. The signs of all precipitation values were reversed because snow hinders feeding (Picton 1979:117). Minor modifications of Picton's calculations included adding additional signs for each standard deviation exceeded by a particular monthly value and shifting the scale to provide positive indices when fitting the regression models. The arcsine transformations of pregnancy rates were used as dependent variables to stabilize the variance (Neter and Wasserman 1974).

Exploratory regression models that incorporated numbers and indices at $t - 2$, estimates of population size minus adult males, terms to account for interaction among the variables, and various quadratic terms all failed to explain significant amounts of variation over the simpler model of the form

$$Y_i = b_0 + b_1 N_{t-1} + b_2 I_{t-1}.$$

Yearling pregnancy rate (Y_i) was significantly and negatively associated with population size (N_{t-1}) and the December–March index (I_{t-1}) for the previous winter ($.005 <$ P $< .01$, $R^2 = .75$, Appendix IV), indicating, as expected, that yearling pregnancy declined as numbers and winter severity increased. The coefficient of partial determination for the winter severity index with winter population size already in the model ($r^2_{I \cdot N} = .73$) and for population size with index present ($r^2_{N \cdot I} = .38$) suggest that much of the variation in pregnancy could be associated with winter severity.

The pooled pregnancy rate of .87 for adults (two years and older) from the high winter populations of 1943–62 was significantly (χ^2, P $< .005$) lower than the rate of .96 for lower populations of 1963–67 (Table 5.1). However, these differences could reflect either changes in age-specific rates, changes in age distributions, or both. Greer (1966b) suggested that the significant increase in adult pregnancy rate from .88 in 1962 to .94 in the 1963–66 collections resulted partly from a reduction in the proportion of older, less productive females in the latter sample. More age-specific rates are examined below, but for fewer years.

Most females reached sexual maturity as two-year-olds. The pregnancy rates for this class ranged from .73 to 1.00 in the 1950–67 collections (Table 5.2). Exploratory regressions, similar to those for yearlings suggested that the model

$$Y_i = b_0 + b_1 N_{t-1} + b_2 I_{t-1}$$

best explained the association of pregnancy on numbers and winter severity during December–March periods (Appendix IV). Significant negative associations of pregnancy ($.01 <$ P $< .025$, $R^2 = .78$) occurred with the previous winter's severity and population size. The coefficients of partial determination ($r^2_{I \cdot N} = .56$, $r^2_{N \cdot I} = .44$) suggested that although pregnancy rates were still strongly associated with the severity of the previous winter, population size seemed to influence two-year-olds more than yearlings. Using somewhat different estimates of population size, Fowler and Barmore (1979) also reported a decline of pregnancy rate on population size for two-year-olds.

The effect of two-year-olds removed, a pooled pregnancy rate of .86 for three-year and older elk from high populations of 1950–62 still differed significantly (P $< .005$) from the rate of .96 for the lower populations of 1963–67. Pregnancy rates by age *class* were available for only part of the 1962 collection and for the 1963–67 samples (Table 5.2). Pregnancy for age class three to seven varied from .92 to 1.00 from 1962 to 1967. No significant relationships with population numbers (the 1962 sample is the only one drawn from a high population) or winter severity were detected using regressions. Calculations from Greer (1966) suggested that the pregnancy rate of

TABLE 5.2
Schedules of Pregnancy for Elk Two Years and Older, 1950–67

AGE	1950[a]		1951		1962		1963		1964		1965		1966		1967	
x	f_x	P_x	f_x	P_x	f_x	P_x	f_x	P_x	f_x	P_x	f_x	P_x	f_x	P_x	f_x	P_x
2	11	.73	19	.95	117	.94	19	.89	18	.89	17	.94	25	1.00	21	1.00
3–7	364[b]	.79[b]	240[b]	.94[b]	364	.93	101	.98	62	1.00	47	.98	49	.92	79	.99
8–15					25	.84			————		167	.96[c]	————			
16+					16	.38			————		21	.33[c]	————			

[a] f_x, sampled number; P_x, pregnancy rate.
[b] Values for ages 3 and above combined.
[c] Values for 1963–67 combined.

a small sample of three-year-olds taken in 1962 ($N = 15$) did not differ from a pooled sample of 56 collected from 1963 to 1966. Apparently, pregnancy for three-year-olds was similar over the population sizes and winter conditions experienced.

The pregnancy rate for age class 8–15 was significantly lower in the high population of 1962 (.84) than in the much lower populations of 1963–67 (.96, $.01 < P < .025$). The pregnancy rate of a smaller sample of 8- and 9-year-olds taken in 1962 ($N = 15$) did not differ from a pooled sample of 81 collected from 1963–66 (calculated from Greer 1966b). These results suggest that the rates for 8- and 9-year-olds may not have changed within the 8–15 age class. The overall increase observed within the class was then due to either an increase in age-specific pregnancy rates among 10- to 15-year-olds, changes in the proportion of 10–15-year-olds in this class, or both.

Females in the 16-year and older class showed significantly lower rates of pregnancy than the 8–15-year-olds in both a small sample from the 1962 collection and the pooled 1963–66 sample ($P < .005$).

Some additional limitations of these data are best mentioned here. First, representative sampling of this elk population was very difficult, and the area of winter range where some samples were drawn was unknown to me. Some of the variability in yearling pregnancy, for example, was likely the result of the collection site. Calculations from Greer (1967, 1968) suggested that the pregnancy rate of yearlings taken in 1967 differed significantly ($P < .005$) in the Lamar Valley (.17, $N = 35$) and the Gardiner area (.69, $N = 13$). Similarly, yearling pregnancy in 1968 differed ($.025 < P < .05$) between Lamar Valley (.06, $N = 48$) and the Blacktail Plateau (.20, $N = 44$). Second, age estimates based on tooth replacement and wear have considerable error. The criteria used for distinguishing even yearlings is vague for the early samples and may have been unreliable (Flook 1970). Third, population estimates are crude, and numbers per se may not accurately reflect effective winter density (see Winter Distribution, Chap. 4). Finally, the index of winter severity is similarly crude, and severity can vary greatly over the winter range.

Sex and Age Composition

Fifty-five samples of the sex and age composition of autumn and winter populations were obtained by various methods from 1928 to 1979 (Table 5.3). The primary purpose of field classifications was to obtain a representative sample of population com-

TABLE 5.3
Sex and Age Composition of Northern Yellowstone Elk, Autumn and Winter, 1928–79

PERIOD	PERCENT COMPOSITION[a]						RATIOS/100 F				SOURCE
	N	F	Yg	YrM	AM	TM	Yg	YrM	AM	TM	
Field classifications											
1930	1,158	65	19			17	29			26	NPS files[b]
1930–32	10,446[c]	69	17	2	12	14	25	4	17	21	Rush (1932a)
1932	3,419	73	12	3	12	15	16	5	16	21	NPS files
1949	956[d]	63	23	3	11	14	36	5	17	22	Kittams (pers. commun.)
1950	949	64	22	4	10	14	34	7	16	23	Kittams (pers. commun.)
1951	2,757	64	16	8	12	20	25	12	18	30	Kittams (pers. commun.)
1952	5,300	64	18	5	13	18	27	8	20	28	Kittams (pers. commun.)
1953	2,656	64	23	3	10	13	18	5	16	21	Kittams (pers. commun.)
1954	4,061	62	21	6	11	17	33	10	17	27	Kittams (pers. commun.)
1955	4,089	68	16	6	10	16	23	9	14	23	Kittams (pers. commun.)
1956	4,429	65	18	5	12	17	28	8	18	26	Kittams (pers. commun.)
1957	3,646	68	19	3	10	13	28	4	15	19	Kittams (pers. commun.)
1963	1,408[e]	65	23			12	36			18	Barmore (1980)
1964	1,383	54	27			19	49			18	Ellis (1964)
1965	1,936	58	21	5	17	22	37	19	28	37	Barmore (1980)
1967	621	55	20	6	20	26	34	11	36	47	Barmore (1980)
1968	952	54	20	6	20	26	37	14	36	47	Barmore (pers. commun.)
1969	1,694	49	23	7	21	28	45	12	39	51	Barmore (pers. commun.)
1970	1,654	48	22	8	22	30	47	17	46	52	Barmore (pers. commun.)
1971	2,267[f]	50	21	8	21	29	44	15	42	57	This study
1972	2,795	54	19	7	20	27	35	13	37	50	This study
1973	2,589	57	19	5	20	25	33	8	35	42	This study
1974	4,442	57	17	7	19	26	30	12	33	46	This study
1975	3,449	60	15	6	19	25	25	11	32	42	This study
1976	2,352	63	18	3	16	19	29	5	25	30	This study
1977	3,253	76	13	2	9	11	17	3	12	14	This study
1978	2,664	66	17	5	12	17	26	8	18	26	This study
1979	3,982	66	16	4	14	18	24	6	21	27	This study

Field reductions in park

Year	N									Source
1943	686	80	9				10			13	MFG files
1950	507	71	9			11	11			27	NPS files
1951	476	71	11			20	12			25	NPS files
1956	1,974	66	21			18	15			19	NPS files
1957	717	79	7			12	32			18	NPS files
1958	536	48	22			14	10				NPS files
1960	674	50	18			30	75			62	NPS files
1961	1,284	62	16			32	36			64	NPS files
1962	4,215					23	26			38	NPS files
1967	224	75	5	8	12	20	11	10	22	27	Greer (1967)

Helicopter trapping in park

Year	N									Source
1963	671	65	27			8	42				Barmore (pers. commun.)
1964	1,740	56	33			11	58			34	NPS files
1965	1,668	59	26			15	45			25	Barmore (1980)
1966	1,467	63	20	6	11	17	31	9	17	26	Barmore (1980)
1967	1,609	54	24	9	13	22	45	16	24	40	Barmore (1980)
1968	1,031	55	24	12	10	22	44	23	17	40	Barmore (1980)

Hunter kill outside park

Year	N									Source
1928	1,506	62	10			28	28	16		45	USFS files
1935	1,747	64	13		21	23	20	3		36	MFG files
1936	2,346	64	16	2		20	26		33	32	USFS files
1938	3,586	45	14			42	31			94	NPS files
1939	2,226	45	14			41	31			93	NPS files
1943	6,314	47	15			38	27			81	MFG files
1951	1,070	57	9	10	24	34	16	18	43	61	MFG files
1965	759	34	11	6	49	55	32	19		162	Greer (1965b)
1967	655	50	28	7	15	22	54	14	32	46	Greer (1967)
1976	1,207	30	12	9	49	58	39	32	162	195	MFG files
1978	801	30	24	19	27	46	80	63	90	153	MFG files

[a] Females older than young of the year (F), young (Yg), yearling males (YrM), males older than yearlings (AM), total males older than young (TM).
[b] National Park Service files, U.S. Forest Service files, Montana Fish and Game Department files.
[c] Cumulative classification over winter periods.
[d] Kittams 1949–1950 made from September–December; 1951–1956 made mostly in December.
[e] Number in December–January ground classifications. Classifications adjusted based upon percent males in aerial samples of 3,540–5,226 from 1963 to 1970.
[f] Numbers in January ground classifications. Classifications adjusted based upon percent adult males in aerial samples of 5,945 to 10,318 from 1971 to 1979.

FIGURE 5.1.

Adult male elk wintering on the periphery of the northern range at about 3,000 m. Photos by M. Meagher and D. Stradley.

position; the purpose of other samples, i.e., hunter harvests, field reductions in the park (shooting elk on the open range by teams of men), and helicopter live trapping was to reduce the population. These data differ from those reported previously, as I have omitted cumulative mixtures of samples obtained from early live trapping and from small hunting kills.

The extent to which a sex or age class is underrepresented by sampling obviously results in overrepresentation of remaining classes, and the data contain sampling errors that need to be evaluated. Only calves of the year (six to nine months old), yearling males, adult males, and females older than calves can be distinguished reliably in winter classifications. Adult males (two years and older) were underrepresented in field classifications conducted from the ground because many tend to winter in small groups at remote higher elevations (Fig. 5.1). Only about 52 ± 7% of the adult males were observed in ground classifications as compared with aerial classifications from 1972 to 1975 (thereafter I made no serious attempt to classify males from the ground). The aerial classification covered the entire winter range and provided a much larger sample. The proportion of males observed differed significantly between sampling methods each year (χ^2, P < .005). Even though the procedures used to obtain ground classifications from 1930 to 1957 were unknown to me, I assumed that the true proportion of adult males was underrepresented by one-half. This adjustment could be of the right magnitude, because Kittams (cited by Barmore 1980) reported that total males (yearlings plus adults) represented 34% in an aerial classification of 4,020 elk in 1956 when an early winter ground classification gave 17%.

Field classifications were compared to field reductions, hunting kills, and samples obtained by helicopter trapping to see if these removals (or any portion of them) might be useful to represent the composition of the population for years when no field classifications were made (field classifications were usually completed prior to the winter removals). Adult males were known to be underrepresented in field reductions and helicopter trapping because of their winter haunts and because removals were deliberately aimed at large groups of antlerless elk. The proportion of calves in field reductions of 1950, 1951, and 1956 (but not in 1957) was significantly lower (P < .005) than the field classifications for those years because their comparatively smaller size often results in negative shooting bias (Kittams 1953, Caughley 1970). Comparisons of the sex and age classes in the 1976 and 1978 hunting removals with the respective field classifications showed significant differences (P < .005). This resulted mainly from the disproportionately high numbers of adult and yearling males. (These classes occurred in about the same proportion in the hunted groups as in the overall population.) Hunter selection was especially conspicuous in 1976, when nearly half of the elk killed were adult males. Field observations clearly showed that hunters were selecting the larger antlered males. Yearling males may also be especially vulnerable to hunting removals (Cole 1969a). Comparisons of field classifications with helicopter trapping removals from 1963 to 1968 showed that the proportion of females with young at heel differed significantly (P < .05) and was always higher in trapped samples. Field observations indicated that adult females were comparatively more successful than calves in escaping the helicopter hazing used to move elk into the traps (Barmore pers. commun. 1975, Nuss pers. commun. 1976). Not surprisingly, these comparisons indicated that the proportions of sex and age classes removed often differed from their occurrence in the population. Removals were then of limited value in describing composition, and I have used only the young/female ratios from four very large (1936, 1938, 1943, 1962) removals for some analyses. Elsewhere I have considered the sex ratios of calves obtained from the various removals to be useful. With greater reservations, the sex ratios of yearlings and the proportions of yearling females to adult females were sometimes used.

It may be a practical impossibility to obtain truly representative samples of the sex and age composition of ungulate populations (Caughley 1966), and these data are considered approximations, but they do suggest changes in the composition and dynamics at different population levels. Prior to the intensive park removals begun in 1956, and considering the various sampling biases, the composition of the overall winter populations fluctuated around 57 ± 3.3% females (yearlings and older), 16 ± 3.2% calves, and 27 ± 2.3% males, with yearlings averaging 16 ± 6.2% of males and 5 ± 1.8% of the population. Ratios of calves and yearling males/100 females were 27 ± 6.0 and 7 ± 2.6, respectively. For the much lower winter populations of 1964–70, females averaged 53 ± 3.8%, calves 22 ± 2.6%, males 25 ± 4.0%, with yearlings calculated as 25 ± 3.1% of males and 6 ± 1.1% of the population. Ratios of calves and yearling males/100 females were 42 ± 6.3 and 15 ± 3.4, respectively. The composition of the overall population changed steadily as elk numbers increased during the 1970s. The proportions of adult males, yearling males, and calves decreased; adult females increased. These changes are examined in detail elsewhere. From 1973 to 1979, with winter populations again over 10,000, females averaged 64 ± 6.7%, calves 16 ± 2.0%, males 20 ± 5.5%, with yearlings at 23 ± 5.8% of males and about 5 ± 1.7% of the population. Ratios of calves and yearling males were again about 26 ± 5.2 and 8 ± 3.2.

The composition of samples sometimes differed within the winter range, with the proportion of young being lower on the upper winter range (i.e., generally the Lamar Valley area, Fig. 2.1). Data from Greer (pers. commun. 1973) showed that the proportion of females with young at heel differed significantly (χ^2, P < .005) in a large sample ($N = 1,196$ females and young) taken during the 1962 field reductions; with 11 calves/100 females on the upper range, 26/100 on the lower range. Similarly, field classifications showed that the proportion of females with calves at heel was lower on the upper range each year from 1971 to 1979. For six of these nine years the differences were significant (P < .05), with samples taken on the upper range averaging 7 ± 3 (3–11) calves/100 females lower. One likely interpretation of these differences, given the fidelity to home range areas of some females, is that the dynamics of herd segments on the upper range (i.e., production and survival of young, age distribution of females, etc.) differs from those usually wintering farther down the Yellowstone River. These latter groups may be hunted more frequently at higher population levels and some also winter at lower elevations and contend with less severe snow conditions. These differences again underscore the difficulties of sampling this population.

Recruitment

With such difficulties in mind, the occurrence of calves in 24 winter populations from 1951 to 1979 was taken as an index of recruitment (i.e., addition of young to the population six to nine months after birth) and examined for association with population size and winter severity. The proportion of calves in winter populations and ratios of calves/100 females (analyzed as the proportion of females with calves at heel) were used as dependent variables in regression models. I used samples obtained in early winter; those made prior to 1951 were omitted, because samples were composites obtained over an entire winter, because they were obtained in late winter, or because they included autumn samples obtained prior to the major elk migrations onto the winter range. Following much the same rationale as described for regressions of pregnancy rates, the dependent variables were tested for association with populations at $t - 1$, populations minus the adult male component, and indices of winter severity at $t - 1$.

Models that included numbers and winter severity for December–March at $t - 1$ returned highly significant regressions with negative slopes for both the proportion of calves in winter herds (P < .001, R^2 = .59) and the proportion of females with calves at heel (P < .001, R^2 = .62, Appendix IV). Since the proportion of females with calves at heel is not influenced by the questionable estimates of the proportion of adult males, this represents the better index of recruitment. This regression model showed $r^2_{N \cdot I}$ = .61 and $r^2_{I \cdot N}$ = .04, which indicated that virtually all the variation explained by the regression was associated with population size. The steep decline in recruitment with increasing population size is illustrated in Fig. 5.2.

Similarly, the occurrence of yearling males in 21 winter populations from 1951 to 1979 was tested for association with population size and winter severity. The ratios of yearling males/100 females on population size at $t - 1$ returned a significant negative association (P < .005, r^2 = .39, Appendix IV). The index of winter severity did not improve the model. The low r^2 value indicates that although the recruitment of yearling males declined at higher populations, the regression was not particularly successful in explaining the variation observed (Fig. 5.3). This might be expected because, in addition to the other sampling difficulties, the yearling male ratio was influenced by the variable presence of undetermined numbers of yearling females, and perhaps by the disproportionate removal of calves during the previous winter at the lower population levels.

FIGURE 5.2.

The relationship between calf recruitment and population size.

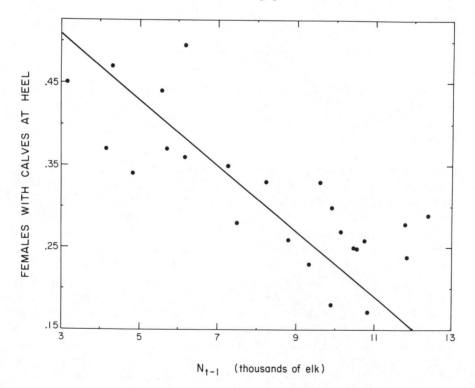

FIGURE 5.3.

The relationship between recruitment of yearling males and population size.

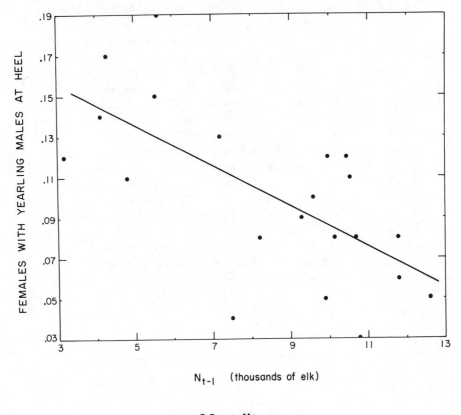

N$_{t-1}$ (thousands of elk)

Mortality

Changes in age-specific mortality are examined here in relation to population size.

Sex Ratios

Changes in the sex ratios at different stages in the life history of elk imply differential mortality or dispersal (Table 5.4). Sex ratios *in utero* were available from seven collections made between 1935 and 1968. Neither the separate nor combined samples from the higher populations of 1935–62 or the lower populations of 1963–68 showed ratios that differed significantly from 100/100 (χ^2, P > .05). However, the 1962 sample with a greater proportion of males differed from the 1963–68 sample with fewer males (P < .005). While proportionately fewer males may have been carried *in utero* at lower populations, too much could be made of this, because males were not consistently favored at high populations, and the 1963–68 sample was pooled over six years. The sex ratio of 507 calves captured and ear-tagged at birth or shortly thereafter between 1947 and 1955 showed no significant difference from parity, implying no differential *in utero* mortality by sex. The sex ratios of six–nine-month-old calves differed significantly from parity in large samples drawn from the high populations of 1936–54 (P < .01) and 1976–79 (P < .025). (Annual samples were combined by

TABLE 5.4
Sex Ratios, Northern Yellowstone Elk

AGE	DATE	N	M/F	SOURCE
in utero	1935	94	88:100	Mills (1935a) direct reduction
	1937	122	88:100	West (1937) direct reduction
	1943	130	110:100	Murie (1943) direct reduction
	1950–51	538	102:100	Kittams (1953) direct reduction
	1935–51	884	100:100	
	1962	637	103:100	Greer (pers. commun. 1973) reductions and biological collections
	1963–68	379	89:100	Greer (pers. commun. 1973) reductions and biological collections
Birth	1947–55	507[a]	95:100	NPS files, calf-tagging records[a]
6–9 mo.	1936	386	56:100[b]	MFG files, hunter kill
	1943	916	84:100[b]	MFG files, hunter kill
	1950–54	516	75:100[b]	MFG files, hunter kill
	1962	95	76:100	Greer (pers. commun. 1973) direct reduction
	1965–68	1060	88:100[b]	NPS files, Greer (1968) helicopter trapping
	1976–78	309	76:100[b]	MFG files, hunter kill
18–22 mo.	1951	39	63:100	Quimby (pers. commun. 1973) direct reduction
	1962	230	92:100	Greer (pers. commun. 1973) direct reduction
	1965	208	100:100	NPS files, helicopter trapping
	1965	—	86:100	Calculated from biol. collection (see text)
	1967	263	114:100	NPS files, helicopter trapping
	1967	—	110:100	Calculated from direct reduction
	1968	256	94:100	NPS files, helicopter trapping
	1976	—	68:100	Calculated
	1978	—	72:100	Calculated

[a]Tagged mostly within a few hours to few days after birth.
[b]Differs significantly from parity; see text.

period in Table 5.4 when χ^2 tests for homogeneity could not be rejected.) These data indicate a differential mortality of males during their first six–nine months of life. The combined samples from low populations of 1965–68 also differed from parity (P < .05) but did not differ from the sex ratios of fetuses *in utero* from 1963–68. The higher mortality of male calves at high populations may be relaxed at lower population levels.

The samples of yearling sex ratios were especially difficult to interpret. The 1951 and 1962 samples from high populations had low proportions of males that did not differ from parity, but these samples also did not differ from the ratios of calves characteristic of the collection periods. The 1965, 1967, and 1968 yearling ratios from helicopter trapping suggested increased proportions of yearling males during two years, but samples did not differ significantly from parity or from the 1965–68 sex ratios of calves. The sex ratios in trapped samples were highly variable, and Greer (1968:11) commented that, "A male and female yearling ratio of 36:64 percent from the Frog Rock trap was apparently significantly below seasonal proportions [in 1968]. Yearling males were notably absent from three groups obtained in this trap in February." Calculations from Greer (1968:12) showed that the yearling ratios were 173, 66, and 40 males/100 females at the three trap sites. Crude yearling sex ratios were calculated from the yearling male/100 female (older than calves) ratios in field classifications of 1965, 1967, 1976, and 1978, when the proportions of yearling females to older females were also available from shot samples (hunter kills in 1976 and 1978). These also suggested lower yearling male:female ratios in three samples, but a higher ratio occurred in 1967. I have little faith in any of these yearling ratios, but the variation recorded by Greer suggested that the trapped samples may not have been representative of the population. The low ratios characteristic of six–nine-month-old calves may have been carried through the yearling age class at higher populations, but differences in yearling sex ratios were perhaps less at lower populations.

Calculations from the winter field classification suggested ratios of 26–44/100 for elk older than yearlings, which reflects continued differentially high mortality (plus perhaps dispersal) of males throughout their adult lives.

Mortality of Young

NEONATES

Calf mortality from birth to six–nine months was estimated from age-specific pregnancy rates, standing age distributions of female elk, and field classifications of calves/100 females in early winter populations (Table 5.5). Mortality was calculated as pregnancy

TABLE 5.5
Elk Mortality from Birth to Six–Nine Months

YEAR[a]	PREGNANCY[b]	FEMALES WITH CALVES AT HEEL	MORTALITY
1935	.73	.26	.64
1937	.91	.31	.66
1943	.84	.27	.68
1950	.76	.25	.67
1951	.86	.27	.69
1960	.82	.26	.68
1962	.81	.26	.68
1963	.88	.49	.44
1964	.79	.31	.62
1965	.74	.41	.47
1966	.81	.34	.58
1967	.88	.37	.58
1968	.84	.45	.46
1969	.85	.47	.45
1970	.84	.44	.48

[a]Year of pregnancy sample (t) compared to $t + 1$ calf/female ratios as $(P_t - \text{Calves}_{t+1})/P_t$. The 1943 pregnancy was compared to 1943 direct reduction, 1960 and 1962 compared to 1962 direct reduction. The 1936 and 1938 calf ratios are from hunting kills. All these are given in Table 5.3.
[b]Weighted mean including proportions and rates for yearlings from Tables 5.1 and 5.6. The 1968–70 adult pregnancy estimated as the 1963–67 mean. The 1968–70 proportion of yearlings estimated from the 1963–67 mean, and the proportion pregnant estimated from regressions of pregnancy rate on population size and winter severity.

rate at time t minus calves/female at $t + 1$/pregnancy rate at t. For example, the 1951 pregnancy of yearling and older females of .86 (from Tables 5.1 and 5.6) and the calf:female ratio in autumn 1952 of .27 (Table 5.3) gives a mortality rate of .69. In several cases, either age-specific pregnancy rates or the calf proportions at $t + 1$ were unavailable, and estimates for the period were used. These calculations, which are actually a sticky blend of data and guesswork, suggest that mortality over the first six–nine months of life was significantly greater (Tukey's quick test, $P < .0005$) at high populations of 1935–62 (.67 ± .017) than at the lower populations of 1963–70 (.51 ± .071). Mortality may have been around .46 when the population was at the lowest levels of 1968–69. Based upon equal sex ratios *in utero* and 75 males:100 females by six–nine months, the calculated mortality rate for male and female calves was .72 and .63, respectively, for the high populations of 1935–62. Pregnancy rates of .74 and .72 for the high populations of 1976 and 1978 were calculated from the proportions of yearlings in hunter kills, the regression equations for yearling pregnancies, and an estimated pregnancy rate for two-year and older females of .79 (this was the lowest rate recorded from 1953–62 and would produce conservative estimates of calf mortality). This information was used to estimate calf mortality at .77 and .67 for 1976 and 1978 by subtraction of the 1977 and 1979 calves at heel of .17 and .24. The shortcomings of these comparisons are discussed elsewhere, but they do suggest that mortality of calves was greater at the higher population levels. Barmore (1980) used somewhat different estimates of pregnancy and calf ratios to arrive at a mortality of .67 for three years from 1935–51, and .53 from 1963–69.

OVER-WINTER MORTALITY

Barmore (1980) also calculated a significantly greater over-winter mortality (Wilcoxon two-sample test, $P < 0.05$) for male calves (40 ± 19%) for eight winters at high populations during 1949–57 than for six winters at the low populations of 1964–70 (21 ± 13%). These rates were calculated from the field classifications of winter populations by comparing the calculated male calf/100 female ratios (male calves estimated at 44% of total calves) with the yearling male/100 female ratio at time $t + 1$. For example, the 1957 yearling male/100 female ratio of 4 was subtracted from the 1956 calculated male calf/100 female ratio of 12 (i.e., 28 × .44). The difference, 8, was divided by the male calf ratio to produce an estimated mortality of 68%. The calculations actually estimate mortality from around 6–9 months to 18–20 months of age, but Barmore considered most to have occurred over winter, i.e., before calves reached one year old. I calculated over-winter mortality of male calves at 29, 32, 47, 20, 15, 55, 78, 5, and 45% for the years 1970 to 1978, using Barmore's procedures and the field classifications (Table 5.3). Mortality of female calves could have been about the same. Mean over-winter calf mortality was 36 ± 28% for populations of 10,000 or more for 1973–78, but annual estimates obviously varied widely. All estimates suggest greater over-winter calf mortality at higher populations and are examined further under Annual Mortality (below).

Mortality Patterns and Adult Mortality

The standing age distributions of male and female elk older than calves were sampled six and seven years, respectively, between 1951 and 1967 (Tables 5.6 and 5.7). No samples were available prior to the first herd reductions, and no collections were made

TABLE 5.6
Age Distributions of Female Elk, 1951–67

Age[a]	1951	1962	1963	1964	1965	1966	1967
1	24 (10)[b]	120 (12)	16 (7)	32 (18)	33 (21)	22 (16)	13 (8)
2	20 (8)	117 (12)	26 (12)	22 (13)	23 (15)	25 (18)	24 (14)
3	12 (5)	146 (15)	20 (9)	14 (8)	11 (7)	16 (11)	28 (17)
4	13 (5)	68 (7)	38 (17)	18 (10)	8 (5)	9 (6)	16 (10)
5	18 (7)	87 (9)	16 (7)	13 (7)	6 (4)	13 (9)	18 (11)
6	22 (9)	87 (9)	13 (6)	14 (8)	11 (7)	8 (6)	11 (7)
7	31 (13)	58 (6)	32 (15)	18 (10)	13 (8)	13 (9)	16 (10)
8	32 (13)	64 (7)	12 (6)	10 (6)	11 (7)	10 (7)	17 (10)
9	26 (11)	35 (4)	15 (7)	14 (8)	14 (9)	8 (6)	7 (4)
10–15	31 (13)	78 (8)	23 (11)	12 (7)	20 (13)	13 (9)	15 (9)
16+	16 (7)	113 (12)	7 (3)	9 (5)	5 (3)	3 (2)	2 (1)
N	245	973	218	176	155	140	167
Source	c	d	d,e	e	e	e	d

[a] Based upon tooth replacement and wear (Quimby and Gaab 1957).
[b] Percent given in parentheses.
[c] Biological collection (Quimby, pers. commun. 1973).
[d] Direct reduction (Greer, pers. commun. 1973).
[e] Biological collections (Greer, pers. commun. 1973).

with the primary purpose of sampling age distributions. Age determinations for all of these shot samples were based upon tooth replacement and wear (Quimby and Gaab 1957). Females sampled during the winter of 1951 from a population of over 10,000 were used to evaluate pregnancy rates (Kittams 1953) and as part of a study to develop criteria for age determination (Quimby and Gaab 1957). Since no attempt was made to select specific animals during the shooting, Kittams (1953) considered the sample to be representative of adults. The 1962 samples were part of a winter reduction in which nearly half of the population of 10,000 was removed, but followed a period beginning in 1956 when human predation within the park was intensified. Portions of the 1962 sample of females were originally placed in broad age classes (i.e., three–seven years,

TABLE 5.7
Age Distributions of Male Elk 1951–67[a]

Age	1951	1962	1963	1964	1965	1967
1	15 (26)	110 (32)	19 (35)	10 (29)	7 (24)	17 (38)
2	6 (10)	77 (23)	6 (11)	9 (26)	2 (7)	5 (11)
3	3 (5)	↑	2 (4)	1 (3)	5 (17)	8 (18)
4	8 (14)		11 (20)	4 (11)	4 (14)	4 (9)
5	3 (5)	108 (32)	5 (9)	6 (17)	3 (10)	2 (4)
6	5 (9)		7 (13)	3 (9)	2 (7)	2 (4)
7	12 (21)	↓	3 (5)	0 (0)	3 (10)	2 (4)
8	4 (7)	↑	1 (2)	1 (3)	3 (10)	5 (11)
9	0 (0)	46 (13)	0 (0)	1 (3)	0 (0)	0 (0)
10–15	2 (3)	↓	1 (2)	0 (0)	0 (0)	0 (0)
N	58	341	55	35	29	45

[a] Age determinations and sources as in Table 5.6, except 1963 is a biological collection only. Percent given in parentheses.

eight years and older), which I further subdivided into year classes based on a smaller subsample ($N = 87$) collected concurrently (Greer 1966a). Attempts were made to obtain random samples of females during the 1962–66 biological collections from populations of 4,000–6,000 (Greer, pers. commun. 1972). These samples were mainly taken from winter populations but did contain females shot during other seasons. The 1963 direct reduction and biological collection of females were combined when no significant differences were detected between the sample distributions (χ^2, P > .05).

The areas of winter range from which these samples were drawn varied. The 1951 and 1962 collections were taken over most of the range but were probably concentrated on elk accessible from roadsides (Kittams 1953, Greer, pers. commun. 1972). The direct reduction and biological collections of 1963–66 were apparently mainly from the Blacktail Plateau–Lamar Valley areas. The 1967 direct reduction was made largely from several peripheral range areas after 1,105 elk had already been removed by helicopter trapping. Some of these elk were hazed long distances over several days to the traps, and field shooting began after all accessible groups had been trapped (Morey 1967). The proportion of yearling females in trapped groups (.15, $N = 861$ females older than calves) differed significantly (P < .025) from the shot sample (.08). This difference suggests either that the direct reduction sampled groups had previously not been cropped so intensively or that yearling females, like calves, were more vulnerable than adults to helicopter hazing (which would make yearlings proportionately less available in the sample shot subsequently) or both. The 1967 age distributions have been omitted from some further analyses because of these biases in the collections.

Comparisons of the six age distributions for females (Fig. 5.4) showed that they differed significantly, one from the next, over time from 1951 to 1964 (χ^2 tests for homogeneity, Appendix IV). The 1964 distribution did not differ from that of 1965, and 1965 did not differ significantly from 1966. The proportion of females (arcsine transformed) in each age class was regressed on time to examine the differences among the distributions. A sample reported by Kittams (1953) to contain 4% yearlings and 3% two-year-olds in 375 females taken in 1950 was also used in this analysis (older females were classed only as 3+). This 1950 distribution also differed significantly from the 1951 distribution collapsed into similar age classes (Appendix IV). The proportion of yearlings increased significantly over the 1950–66 period (i.e., a *t*-test showed that the slope of the regression was significantly greater than slope $b = 0$, P < .025). The proportions of two-year-olds also increased (P < .005; Fig. 5.5). The proportions of 10+ females declined significantly over the 1951–66 period (P < .05). No other class changed significantly over time.

Four smaller samples of the standing age distributions of males from 1951 to 1965 showed that few males survived beyond 9 or 10 years (Table 5.7). The nature of the reduction programs and the biological collections suggested that yearling males could occur in greater proportion relative to older males in shot samples than in the population, but few data were available to correct for this effect (Fig. 5.6). Yearlings represented 26% of the sample shot in 1951 and might have occurred at about 22.6% of total males older than calves, based upon an adjusted field classification. Yearlings represented 24% of total males in the sample shot in 1965 and occurred at about 22.7% of males in the population. With yearlings omitted and ages collapsed into 2, 3, 4–6, and 7+ year classes, the distributions differed significantly one from the next, except that the 1963 distribution did not differ from that for 1964 (Appendix IV). Regressions of age class on time for 1951–65 showed no significant changes. However, these tests were based upon very small samples and upon partial age distributions.

Life tables are frequently constructed from standing age distributions to describe

FIGURE 5.4.

Standing age distributions of female elk, 1951–66.

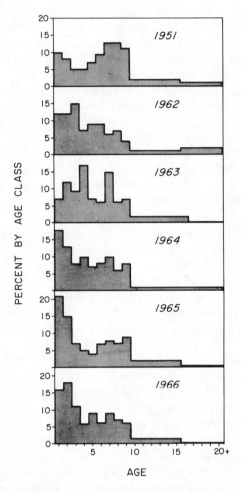

the mortality patterns of populations. Useful life tables can be developed only from stable age distributions, which occur when the rate of increase (*r*) has been constant for two or three generations. Rate of increase should not have fluctuated substantially over this period and should have been measured with accuracy (Caughley 1977). Further, age determinations must be accurate, because errors are not compensatory (Caughley 1967). These criteria are not met by the age distributions in Tables 5.6 and 5.7. As discussed above, the female distributions from 1950 to 1964 were unstable—i.e., the proportions in some age classes changed continually. A consideration of just changes in *r* as shown in the analysis of the census data indicated that distributions were unstable. Even though *r̄* was generally negative during 1950–64, it fluctuated considerably because of sporadic and periodically heavy human predation. The seemingly high proportion of females judged to be six–nine years old in 1951 most likely reflected changes in natality, mortality, and rate of increase following the very large removal of 1943. Since a female cohort might require 15 or more years essentially to pass through this population, the distributions from 1962 to 1966 were also generally unstable. In addition, age determinations based upon patterns of tooth wear were unlikely to be

FIGURE 5.5.

Changes over time in the proportion of standing age distributions of females in the yearling (●), two-year-old (○), and 10+ (▽) age classes. A linear regression was fitted here for purposes of illustration, other procedures were used for analysis.

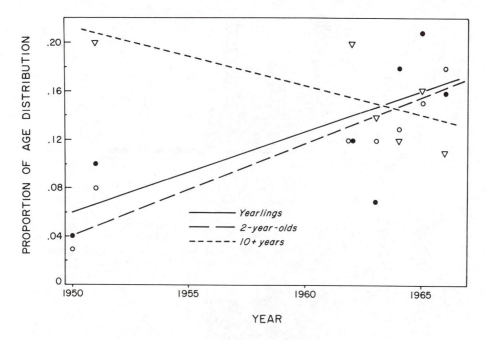

sufficiently accurate for the older classes (Quimby and Gaab 1957, Mitchell et al. 1977:38).

Human predation on elk generally increased over the period of these collections. The instability in the age distributions over time suggests that adult mortality could have been fluctuating in response to this intense predation, which tended to remove adults in proportion to their occurrence in the population (i.e., this force of mortality was largely independent of age). However, shifts in unstable age distributions reflect changes in fecundity, mortality, and rate of increase combined; they do not necessarily imply changes in mortality rate (Caughley 1977:121). For these reasons, and those mentioned above, little can be said about changes in age-specific adult mortality rates.

As an aside, standing age distributions are not generally useful indicators of the sign of *r,* although they are sometimes used erroneously to determine whether a population is increasing, decreasing, or stationary (Caughley 1977:120). This point is well illustrated by the age distributions from the northern herd. All samples were drawn from populations that were probably decreasing, and certainly those from 1964 to 1966, with the highest proportions of yearlings and two-year-olds, were from populations in steady decline from human predation.

The 1950 and 1951 samples for females hint at the characteristics of the stationary age distributions to be expected without intense human exploitation. These would be characterized by proportionately few yearlings and two-year-olds and relatively high proportions of females loaded into the older classes. Another early sample lends support to this speculation; Mills (National Park Service files) reported 6% yearlings in a sample of 89 females older than calves taken in the winter of 1935.

FIGURE 5.6.

Standing age distributions of male elk, 1951 and 1965. Proportion of yearlings adjusted from field classifications.

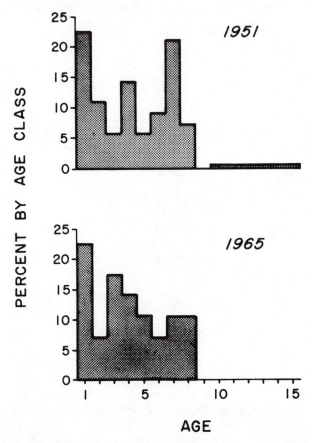

Additional age distributions were available from 727 elk found dead on the winter range in the park during 1975–78. Mortality occurred from November to May, but most died from March to May. Calves of the year represented 319 of the dead elk, and this class probably was found less frequently than its actual occurrence among the dead animals. Also, calves were so completely consumed by carnivores that often the sex could not be determined (Houston 1978b). The remaining 408 elk included 160 females and 248 males aged one year or older (Tables 5.8 and 5.9). Ages were determined from tooth replacement and wear through age two years (Quimby and Gaab 1957) and by counts of growth layers in the dental cement for older animals (Mitchell 1963, 1967). Life tables were constructed following the procedures of Sinclair (1977) to represent the pattern of mortality as the population increased from the lows of the late 1960s. Synthetic cohorts were produced for males and females from the calculated mortality of calves (age class 0) and the age frequency distributions as follows:

1. Calculations suggested that for every 1,000 female calves born at high populations about 625 died by six–nine months of age. Another 135 of the 375 survivors died over winter at the high populations of the 1970s (i.e., 375 × .36 over-winter mortality estimate), for a total first-year mortality of 760 of the

TABLE 5.8
Life Table for Northern Yellowstone Female Elk

Age x	f_x	kd_x	$kd_x e^{rx}$	d_x	l_x	q_x
0	—	760	760	.323	1.000	.323
1	17	26	30	.013	.677	.019
2	2	3	4	.002	.664	.003
3	2	3	4	.002	.662	.003
4	4	6	10	.004	.660	.006
5	3	5	9	.004	.656	.006
6	7	10	21	.009	.652	.014
7	2	3	7	.003	.643	.005
8	2	3	8	.003	.640	.005
9	5	7	22	.009	.637	.014
10	3	5	17	.007	.628	.011
11	5	7	28	.012	.621	.019
12	5	7	31	.013	.609	.021
13	13	19	96	.041	.596	.069
14	9	14	81	.034	.555	.061
15	5	7	46	.020	.521	.038
16	13	19	140	.059	.501	.118
17	14	21	176	.075	.442	.170
18	15	23	218	.093	.367	.253
19	12	18	194	.082	.274	.299
20	7	11	134	.057	.192	.297
21+	15	23	317	.135	.135	1.000
Total	160	1000	2353	1.000		

TABLE 5.9
Life Table for Northern Yellowstone Male Elk

Age x	f_x	kd_x	$kd_x e^{rx}$	d_x	l_x	q_x
0	—	819	819	.639	1.000	.639
1	34	25	28	.022	.361	.061
2	5	4	5	.004	.339	.012
3	5	4	6	.005	.335	.015
4	5	4	7	.005	.330	.015
5	15	11	21	.016	.325	.049
6	40	29	62	.048	.309	.155
7	47	34	82	.064	.261	.245
8	28	20	54	.042	.197	.213
9	23	17	52	.041	.155	.265
10	9	7	24	.020	.114	.175
11	15	10	40	.031	.094	.330
12	11	8	36	.028	.063	.444
13	4	3	15	.012	.035	.343
14	4	3	17	.013	.023	.565
15+	3	2	13	.010	.010	1.000
Total	248	1,000	1,281	1.000		

original 1,000. Similar calculations suggested that 819 male calves died before age one for each 1,000 born.

2. The age frequencies of elk one year and older (f_x) were adjusted proportionately to give cohorts of 1,000 (kd_x) when combined with the mortality estimates for the 0 age class.

3. Each frequency was then multiplied by $e^{\bar{r}x}$ with $\bar{r}$ calculated at .125 from the 1968–78 census data $(kd_x e^{\bar{r}x})$. This was necessary to adjust for the effects of population growth on age distribution.

4. The frequency of mortality (d_x) in the life tables was produced as $kd_x e^{\bar{r}x}/\Sigma kd_x e^{\bar{r}x}$.

5. Survivorship (l_x) was calculated as

$$1 - \sum_{0}^{x-1} d_x$$

and the mortality rate (q_x) as d_x/l_x (Caughley 1977).

The calculated mortality rates, shown in Fig. 5.7, give the most direct projection of the mortality pattern and are least affected by sampling bias (Caughley 1966).

The general U-shaped mortality pattern is probably correct. This indicates high mortality in early life, followed by several years of relatively low mortality, and then steeply rising mortality with advancing age. The differences between the sexes seem broadly reasonable. Male mortality is higher the first year of life, and the steep rise in mortality occurs at younger ages than for females. However, both mortality patterns are distorted. The mortality for age 0 is based largely upon some questionable calculations and assumptions. Since these samples were collected from 1975 to 1978, elk that were 12–16 years and older were from cohorts born prior to the 1962 reduction. Populations were declining before this reduction and for several years thereafter, not increasing as implied by the $e^{\bar{r}x}$ adjustment. The female distribution in particular was distorted by using this adjustment, and the $q x_0$ is quite low. Thus, $\bar{r}$ varied too much to produce reliable mortality curves for females. The male curve may be less distorted because most males died much earlier than females.

Annual Mortality

NATURAL VERSUS HUMAN

The amount of annual mortality and the proportions contributed by human predation and by "natural" mortality were of particular interest.

Barmore (1980) calculated mean annual mortality at 26.1% of the autumn populations ($\bar{X} = 10,491$ elk) from 1949 to 1956. Annual natural mortality averaged 4.6% (excluding mortality of calves from birth to autumn); human predation averaged 21.4%. Mean annual mortality from 1962 to 1970, generally the period of most intense human predation and lowest populations, may have averaged 24.1% of autumn populations ($\bar{X} = 5,797$), with natural mortality and human predation averaging 2.6 and 21.5%, respectively. These relationships were calculated from the census data, the numbers of elk removed by human predation, and the proportions of calves in autumn populations. As emphasized by Barmore, these are crude calculations that underesti-

FIGURE 5.7.

Calculated age-specific mortality rates for male and female elk.

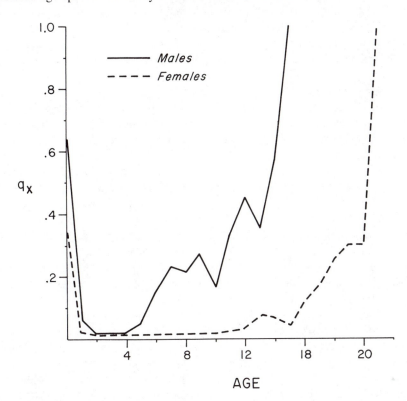

mate natural mortality over winter and at best suggest general relationships at two different levels of human predation. Barmore also calculated mortality of calves from birth to autumn at 34 and 25% of mean autumn populations for 1949–56 and 1962–70, respectively. Using his data, and the assumption that mortality of elk one year and older was negligible over summer periods, mortality then can be calculated from the birth pulse. The relative contributions of human predation and natural mortality to annual mortality changed dramatically when mortality of neonates was included. Total annual mortality was 44.7% of the calculated mean birth pulse populations ($\bar{X}$ = 14,058) for 1949–56, with human predation contributing 16.0% and natural mortality 28.7%. Natural mortality represented 64.2% of total annual mortality. Annual mortality was calculated at 39.3% for birth pulse populations ($\bar{X}$ = 7,246) for 1962–70. Human predation contributed 17.2% of the mortality; natural mortality, 22.1%. Natural mortality represented 56% of the annual mortality. Human predation apparently reduced natural over-winter mortality during these periods (Barmore 1980), even granting that natural mortality was underestimated. When total annual mortality was calculated from the birth pulse, the proportion of elk dying naturally remained large throughout.

DENSITY-DEPENDENT MORTALITY

Some of the relationships between human predation and natural mortality were also examined as the population increased from 1969 to 1975. The numbers of elk in each sex and age class were calculated from the winter counts and the samples of the sex and age composition (Appendix IV). The proportion of calves dying before reaching age one and the proportion of males about 17 months and older dying each year were estimated from these data. (Preliminary attempts showed that these data were too inaccurate either to estimate the proportions of adult females dying annually or to extend the calculations beyond 1975—mainly because the 1977 estimate of elk numbers present in winter was in error.) Human predation on calves was very low throughout this period (Table 3.1). The estimated proportion of naturally dying calves increased significantly ($r^2 = .93$, $P < .001$, Appendix IV) when regressed upon the estimated birth pulse population (Fig. 5.8). The proportion of males dying naturally also increased significantly ($r^2 = .62$, $P < .025$) when regressed upon winter population size (Fig. 5.8).

Such regressions are suspect because the variables are not independent measurements. Therefore, the suggested density-dependent relationships were examined further using the k-factor analysis of Varley and Gradwell (1968), as modified for vertebrates with overlapping generations by Southern (1970) and Sinclair (1977). The k-value is the "killing power" of a particular mortality factor on a log scale. For calves these were calculated as $\log_{10}$ (initial number/final number) at each stage of mortality (Appendix IV). The sum of the k-factors (k_0 = reduction in fertility from the maximum possible, k_1 = neonatal mortality, k_2 = human predation, k_3 = over-winter mortality) represents the total annual reduction in numbers of young (K). Each reduction was considered to act in sequence with negligible overlap in time, and each was calculated as described in Appendix IV. Few of these reductions were measured directly, and they depend upon estimates of the proportions of yearling females in the population and the reduction in fertility. Values for each k factor are considered to be crude estimates ($\hat{k}$) of the actual reductions. A plot of the $\hat{k}$ values on time suggested that $\hat{k}_1$ contributed the greatest change in $\hat{K}$, and by definition, it is considered the "key factor" (Fig. 5.9). The $\hat{k}_0$ was estimated essentially as a constant, and $\hat{k}_2$ was very low throughout.

FIGURE 5.8.
Natural mortality of calves and of males 17 months and older as the proportion of the numbers dying on initial population size, 1969–75. Initial population for calves was the birth pulse population; for males, the post hunt population.

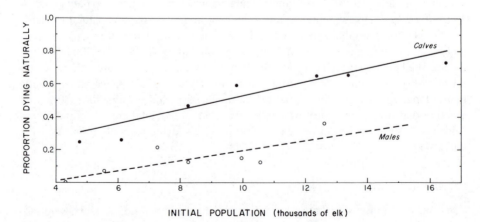

FIGURE 5.9.

The $\hat{k}$-factors for calf mortality, 1969–75. The $\hat{k}_0$ represents reduction in fertility; $\hat{k}_1$, neonatal mortality; $\hat{k}_2$, hunting mortality; $\hat{k}_3$, over-winter mortality summed to give $\hat{K}$, the total annual reduction.

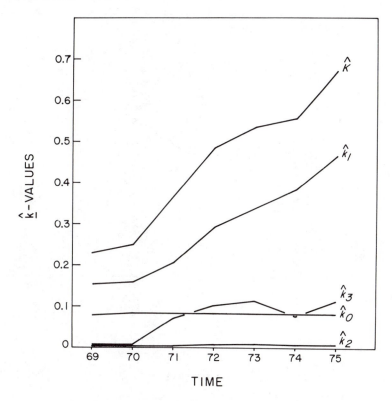

Regressions of $\hat{k}_1$ and $\hat{k}_3$ on $\log_{10}$ initial population sizes (Fig. 5.10) both returned slopes differing significantly from slope $b = 0$ (Appendix IV), which suggested a density-dependent relationship.

However, Varley and Gradwell (1968) emphasized that plots of the k values on $\log N$ ($k = \log N_{\text{initial}} - \log N_{\text{final}}$) also are not independent measurements, and normal regression methods are invalid. (Also for standard regression models N must be measured without error—which most certainly was not true here.) If the initial numbers (I) and final numbers (F) of calves are both determined from separate samples, as were both $\hat{k}_1$ and $\hat{k}_3$ (although I and F for $\hat{k}_1$ both were derived from the estimated autumn numbers, the I was subject to the errors involved in estimating the proportion of adult females and the reduction in fertility), demonstration of density-dependence requires that both the regression $\log I$ on $\log F$ and $\log F$ on $\log I$ produce slopes that differ significantly from $b = 1$ and that these occur on the same side of a slope of unity (Varley and Gradwell 1968:135; see also Luck 1971 and Slade 1977 for discussions of plotting these relationships). The I and F values for $\hat{k}_1$ and $\hat{k}_3$ were tested in this manner (Appendix IV), and both conformed to the above requirements for density-dependence.

The mortality of males older than 17 months was also examined using k-factor analysis, with k_1 representing hunting mortality and k_2 natural over-winter mortality

FIGURE 5.10.

Calf mortality. The $\hat{k}$-factors on log initial total population. For $\hat{k}_1$, the initial population was the birth pulse population; for $\hat{k}_3$, the posthunt population.

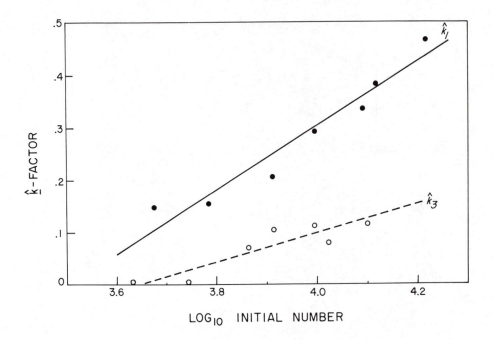

FIGURE 5.11.

The k-factors for males, 1969–75.

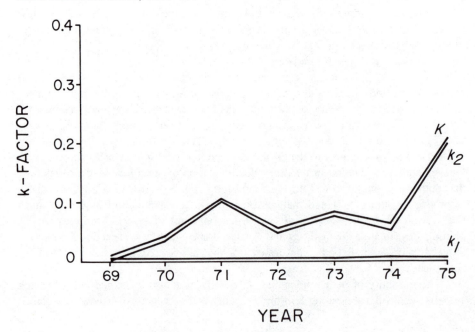

(Appendix IV; Fig. 5.11). Human predation was low, and k_2 was considered to be the key factor. However, the regression of k_2 on initial total population was not significant ($r^2 = .55, .10 > P > .05$; Appendix IV), and density-dependence was not established.

Dispersal

Tagging studies have shown that the northern Yellowstone elk intermingle on summer ranges along major hydrographic divides within the park with other discrete winter herds from Jackson Hole, Gallatin River, Sunlight–Crandall Creeks, Shoshone River, and Madison River (Fig. 4.2). Dispersal (emigration and immigration) occurs among these herds. Elk born into or wintering with the northern herd but that subsequently winter with other herds (or were taken in late fall or early winter hunting seasons on range areas of other herds) are considered emigrants.

Kittams (1963) considered that 3% of 358 returns from elk tagged between 1924 and 1958 had emigrated (5 to Gallatin River; 3, Madison River; 1, Jackson Hole; 3, Yellowstone River but well downstream from the usual winter range of the northern herd). Cole (1969a) reported 1–3 tagged emigrants per year from the northern herd present on the refuge segment of the Jackson Hole herd from 1962 to 1967. Craighead et al. (1972) reported 3 additional northern herd animals killed by hunters in the Jackson Hole area during this same period. One northern herd emigrant was reported in the North Fork of Shoshone River herd for 1963.

Tagged immigrants to the northern herd have originated from all surrounding herds. Peek et al. (1967) reported 6% of 372 returns from 1,082 newborn calves tagged in the Gallatin herd from 1938 to 1960 were made on the northern range. Cole (1969a) reported 1–2 marked elk from the Jackson Hole herd on the winter range of the northern herd in each of the winters from 1962 to 1967. Park records for 1963–66 show 21 tagged immigrants from the Crandall–Sunlight herds and 3 from North Fork Shoshone wintering on the northern range.

Thus, most tagged elk recovered were taken from the area occupied by their respective herds, but a few dispersed. Interchange seemed inversely proportional to the distances between wintering areas—i.e., interchange was greater between the northern herd and the Gallatin and Crandall–Sunlight herds than between the northern herd and the Jackson Hole herd. These tagging studies were designed mainly to define seasonal range and migration routes; none was designed expressly to measure dispersal. Dispersal rates could be underestimated, because sometimes disproportionately large numbers of adult females were tagged. Younger elk, particularly young males, may well be more likely to disperse. The samples were too small, probability of recovery too different between areas, and the time lapse between tagging and recovery too great to determine the age classes that dispersed.

In addition to emigration as defined here, suitable unoccupied range areas within a drainage basin have been recolonized by adjacent established populations within the basin. Apparently this has occurred twice within the past century on the northern winter range. Habitual use of winter ranges outside the park was restored following near elimination of these segments in the late 1800s. Groups wintering outside the park were nearly eliminated again during attempts to reduce the herd between 1935 and 1968, but recolonization occurred as elk numbers increased during the 1970s. Recent observations of these wintering elk suggest that adult males are first to recolonize and are then followed by females and young.

Carrying Capacities

The interaction of ungulates with vegetation typically leads to a stable equilibrium at an *ecological carrying capacity* (Caughley 1976b, 1979). A range of lower sustained yield densities may be imposed upon a population, down to or below *economic carrying capacity* (which produces a maximum sustained yield). As Caughley has pointed out, these concepts and their implications are not widely recognized. This has led to confusion in the management of ungulate populations—particularly those in national parks. Ecological carrying capacity (K_I) characterized by a higher standing crop of animals and a lower standing crop of edible vegetation, is usually the level that is relevant in national parks. Economic carrying capacity (K_c), characterized by much lower standing crops of animals and higher standing crops of vegetation, is of primary interest to range managers, whose objective is to maximize the yield from herds of livestock, and to game managers, whose objective is to maximize the hunting harvest from wild ungulates.

The pattern of population growth from the winter of 1968 to the autumn of 1976, when human predation was very low, was used to estimate K_I and the intrinsic rate of increase (r_m) for the northern herd. The r_m is the maximum rate a population with a stable age distribution can increase when no resource is limiting (Caughley and Birch 1971, Caughley 1977). As reported earlier, the growth trajectory of the population was deflected by heavy human predation in the winter of 1976. In some respects this was unfortunate, because the nature of the growth curve was obliterated as K_I was approached.

Assuming that the population was growing toward a steady K_I, then $(N_{t+1} - N_t)N_t$ has been shown to be linear on N_{t+1} during logistic growth; both K_I and r_m can be calculated by regression (Morisita 1965, cited by Caughley 1977:181). The winter population numbers from 1968 to 1975 returned estimates of K_I and r_m of 17,058 and .36, respectively. The autumn numbers for 1969–76, which extended the growth pattern one more year toward this presumed equilibrium, gave k_I and r_m of 14,910 and .38. Caughley and Birch (1971) and Caughley (1976b) suggest that logistic growth may mimic some populations, even though the biological assumptions behind the use of the curve are inappropriate. When r_m is below about .30 and if artificial reductions in density have not disrupted the social organization of the population, the logistic curve may be useful. These constraints and others (population still was hunted lightly, age distributions were unstable) were not met in this case; thus the estimates represent crude first approximations. Also, the population may have been overshooting K_I because of lags in age distributions and in effects of elk upon their food supplies. If so, the estimates of K_I could be too high. On the other hand, since these calculations used the actual counts to predict K_I, the absolute numbers of elk present would be higher because counts were biased downward.

Interpretation: Population Dynamics

Natality

The winter environment apparently modifies the effects of population density on the pregnancy rates of yearlings. Females two years and older showed the .85 – .95

pregnancy rates characteristic of many exploited elk populations in the Rocky Mountains (Kittams 1953, Cole 1969a, Knight 1970, Flook 1970). The overall pregnancy rate for these elk increased following herd reduction, but separating age-specific responses from changes in age distribution was difficult. Rates of pregnancy of two-year-olds increased at lower populations but were apparently still influenced by winter severity. The three–seven-year-olds and perhaps eight–nine-year-olds had very high pregnancy rates that apparently did not change significantly with density. Also, females 16 years and older showed significantly lower rates than younger animals, and this pattern did not change with density. The increased pregnancy of elk three years and older probably resulted mainly from increased age-specific rates for 10–15-year-olds, the significant reduction in the proportion of females 10 years and older in the population, or both.

The effects of density on pregnancy of the northern herd seemed greatest on certain younger and older age classes. These effects on the overall production of offspring were less than might be expected because of the extended female age distribution and the high pregnancy rates of three–nine-year olds, a group averaging about 60% of females older than calves. The average calculated overall pregnancy rates were the same at high populations for 1935–62 (.82 ± .06) and at lower populations for 1963–68 (.82 ± .05, Table 5.5). Yearlings averaged only about 8 ± 3% of females older than calves at high populations and 13 ± 4% at low populations. Their low and variable rates of pregnancy, which seemed to be strongly influenced by winter conditions, also had less influence on total reproduction than anticipated.

Thus, while density certainly affects natality, the overall influence on young born seems relatively small at the population levels examined. The contribution of changes in natality to any population regulation is apparently less than changes in mortality.

Mortality and Recruitment of Young

The recruitment of calves to six–nine months declined sharply as population size increased. Recruitment, as measured here, is the net result of changes in age-specific natality, in mortality of both young and adults, and in age distributions of females. The same recruitment could be produced by many combinations of these variables. Since the reproductive output of the population did not appear to change greatly, it seems likely that changes in the mortality of calves over their first months of life were a strong influence on the density-dependent effects observed. The recruitment of yearling males also declined as population size increased, although the relationship was more variable. In addition to being influenced by the production and survival of young, the occurrence of yearling males was also an index to the survival of male calves over their first winter.

The comparisons of pregnancy with calves at heel suggested that mortality over the first six–nine months was greater at high populations (~ .68) and considerably less at the lowest populations (~ .46). Changes in sex ratios suggested that greater mortality of male than female calves occurred by six–nine months, but this difference was less at the lower population levels. Causes of mortality of neonates include starvation, disease, and predation (see Chap. 6). Although predation needs further investigation, my own observations and those of Johnson (1951), Robinson (1952), Kittams (1959), Barmore (1980), and Knight (pers. commun. 1980) suggest that predation by coyotes, black bears, and grizzly bears may be more frequent than is generally appreciated. Over-winter mortality of calves was greater at high ($\sim$ 40%) than at low populations ($\sim$ 21%).

The estimates of postnatal and over-winter mortality involve comparisons of ratios—which are treacherous. Caughley (1977:105) has pointed out that ratios cannot be used to track changes in mortality rate from year to year unless "the population has a stable age distribution appropriate to a zero rate of increase." At best, the comparisons made here should be viewed as crude indices of the mortality of young. Slippery as they may be, the data suggest a strong density-dependent relationship between population size and calf survival over the first year of life.

Adult Mortality and Mortality Patterns

The age distributions, for all their limitations, did suggest the mortality patterns to be expected in the absence of intense human predation. These would be characterized by high mortality the first year of life; comparatively low mortality among younger adults; and steeply rising mortality, beginning perhaps at 6 years of age among males and 12 years of age among females. Such U-shaped mortality patterns seem characteristic of mammalian populations (Caughley 1966, Spinage 1972). Males died faster than females; few males survived beyond 10–12 years. Flook (1970) also reported higher mortality among males than females in elk populations from the Rocky Mountain parks of Canada.

A comment on population fluctuations is prompted by examinations of the age distributions. Human predation on the northern herd over the past 50 years or so sometimes occurred as sporadic large removals that abruptly reduced elk numbers (e.g., 1943). Such removals would disrupt trends toward stable or stationary age distributions as schedules of fecundity and mortality changed. In an area with such variable winters, creation of highly unstable age distributions, with consequent time lags as the distributions changed into other forms, could increase the amplitude of the rebound in elk numbers beyond that which would otherwise occur. Such an overshoot might have been anticipated in the 1970s following termination of the park reductions in 1968, but this effect may have been dampened by the resumption of large-scale hunting outside the park in 1976.

Annual Mortality

All aspects of the mortality of elk must be appraised relative to the objectives of the park. Natural mortality was substantial even at the low elk populations of the 1960s when human predation was most intense. Natural mortality during winter is often conspicuous to the human observer and has sometimes caused concern. The historical records show that appreciable natural winter mortality has occurred in the northern herd since Euro-American man was first present as a witness. Early reports and recent studies show that calves and older elk were most affected. Although elk die every winter, mortality was sufficient to attract administrative comment during the winters of 1880, 1892, 1897, 1899, 1910, 1917, 1920, 1927, 1939, 1943, and 1962. Actual counts of dead elk following occasional severe winters (which certainly included those killed by native predators) were 1,888, 558, 514, 533. 872, 476, 581, 300, and 325 in 1917, 1927, 1935, 1939, 1943, 1962, 1975, 1976, and 1978, respectively. (About one-third of those counted in 1917 were on newly enlarged winter feedgrounds, and this count is not strictly comparable to the others.)

Interpretations of this sporadically heavier winter mortality have changed. Early accounts indicate that winter mortality was accepted as inevitable in a variable and periodically harsh environment (Appendix II). In later accounts, all natural mortality on winter ranges seems to have been interpreted as a "loss" to be avoided. This interpretation led to the establishment of feedgrounds and to predator control. More recently yet, this mortality, while still considered to be a loss, has also been interpreted as symptomatic of "overpopulation" and range "deterioration"—attributed in part to the earlier predator control. The role of the natural mortality of elk in ecosystem dynamics is discussed in detail (Chap. 11). Here I suggest only that elk dying within the park are food for native carnivores and that it is misleading to consider such mortality as loss.

Attempts to examine the roles of human predation and natural mortality for density-dependent relationships as the population increased in the 1970s were not particularly successful. The k-factor analysis suggested that mortality of calves from birth to autumn and during winter could have been density-dependent. Human predation on both calves and males 17 months and older was inconsequential from 1969 to 1975. The density-dependence of winter mortality of males could not be demonstrated; however, highly variable mortality might mask density-dependent relationships (Varley and Gradwell 1968). I suspect this was the case for the variable winter mortality, which strongly affects adults only during occasional winters and could then have a density-independent component as well. These k-factor analyses should be viewed with great caution, because a series of sampling errors (elk numbers, sex and age composition, hunting removals) and estimates (reduction in fertility, proportions of yearling and adult females) were compounded to the extent that density-dependence would have to be strong to be detected. Sampling errors were large enough that an analysis of adult female mortality, likely much lower than calves or males, could not be made.

Dispersal

Although dispersal occurs between the various elk herds in the Yellowstone region, the data did not permit examinations of dispersal rates for density-dependence or for the net effects on population size. Howard (1960) suggested that both environmental (density-dependent) and innate (density-independent) components of dispersal might occur among vertebrates. Since nearly all elk populations are now maintained at densities below ecological carrying capacity, our view of the extent and nature of environmental dispersal could be quite distorted. As an intriguing illustration, Rickard et al. (1977) recorded a winter dispersal of a group of elk from an established population more than 155 km into a previously unoccupied area of Washington. The group reproduced successfully and established a separate population (Rickard pers. commun. 1979). Dispersal, though seemingly low in the Yellowstone area, might be frequent enough to influence measurements of other attributes of the population's dynamics; e.g., data on survivorship could reflect both mortality and dispersal.

Carrying Capacities

Historically, various attempts have been made to estimate a carrying capacity of the northern range for elk using methods developed by agriculturists for livestock. Concern over the condition of the vegetation during the drought of the 1930s led to calculations of carrying capacity that ranged from 7,200 to 11,700 elk (Grimm 1939, National Park Service 1938) using the "forage acre factor" system (Stoddart and Smith 1943). This approach has since been abandoned as unworkable by both agriculturalists and wildlife managers. Individuals making these calculations recognized the crudeness of the approach and some of the tacit assumptions (e.g., food habits and use of range by elk were similar to cattle; methods developed for livestock foraging on grasses during the growing season also applied to elk foraging on dormant vegetation during winter; the ecological niches of elk and other native ungulates overlapped completely; and the factors, which were calculated during the depths of a drought, were general), and arrived at an estimated carrying capacity of 7,000 elk until the drought eased. In 1953, a winter population of 5,000 was suggested for a three–six-year trial period to test several research hypotheses involving range conditions (National Park Service 1953). During the subsequent controversial herd reductions, this suggested population level was defended or misinterpreted as an established carrying capacity. In 1963 the Soil Conservation Service suggested a "stocking rate" of 20,000–25,000 animal unit months for the combined ungulate fauna after a brief range survey (Soil Conservation Service 1963). The assumptions and criteria used in arriving at all these estimates were those developed to calculate K_c for livestock and appear to be wholly inappropriate to estimate K_I for native ungulates in a national park.

Human predation on the northern herd has been sufficiently intense during the past 50 years or more to obscure the nature of the equilibrium at K_I. Granting the many sampling errors of the censuses and the confusion surrounding the earlier historical accounts, it seems less likely that the population would be characterized either by stable limit cycles or by unstable "equilibria" (the vegetation–elk system oscillates with increasing amplitude when displaced) than by a stable equilibrium where the system returns to equilibrium when displaced (Caughley 1976b:211). Such stable equilibria seem characteristic of most ungulate populations (Caughley 1976b).

The estimate of K_I at 15,000 or thereabouts provides a useful perspective. The overall elk population is currently held below K_I by cropping animals that move from the park. These elk may be held at densities even below K_c (see Chap. 12, Elk Management). At the same time, because of the size of the winter range in the park and the fidelity of elk to specific areas, some herd segments in the park probably occur at K_I. Several estimates have been made of overall equilibrium numbers with different levels of human predation. Based upon eight censuses made during average to severe winters from 1929 to 1961, Cole (1969b) postulated that winter populations of 5,000 – 8,000 could be maintained in part by cropping groups that moved outside the park. By 1974 additional historical data and the dynamics and distribution of the population showed that this interpretation had to be rejected as an underestimate (Houston 1974). The data suggested that winter herds of around 12,000 (range, 10,000–15,000) were more likely. Changes in land use in and out of the park (reduced bison grazing inside, reduced livestock grazing outside; see Chap. 8, Human Developments and Activities) limited the predictive usefulness of this estimate but did suggest that it could also be too low. Fowler and Barmore (1979) predicted a late winter equilibrium of around 11,000 – 12,000+ from a variable projection matrix model that assumed that hunting removals in the future would be similar to those for 1935–56. Future hunting removals could be lower than those of 1935–56 because many of the early hunting removals were not closely regulated; the equilibrium population could then be somewhat larger than predicted.

The population attributes of density and standing biomass provided further perspective on the calculated equilibrium numbers of elk. Densities in early winter of 7.1–8.3 ha/elk would occur with equilibrium numbers of 12,000–14,000 elk on 100,000 ha of winter range. Densities of around 3.6–4.2 ha/elk may occur during the periods of maximum winter severity if around 50,000 ha are available. Winter weights of elk and the sex and age composition of recent winter populations were used to calculate a standing winter biomass of 2.7×10^6 kg or 27 kg/ha for 12,000 elk and 32 kg/ha for 14,000 in early winter.

Population Regulation

The concept of population regulation through density-dependent factors has been reviewed by Sinclair (1977), who also demonstrated such regulation from field studies of the African buffalo. A brief and oversimplified consideration of how current ideas of population regulation apply to the northern Yellowstone elk seems appropriate here. Borrowing Sinclair's terminology, a population is considered to be regulated when the attributes of natality, mortality, or dispersal show negative feedback from population density. This means that density-dependent responses increase the percentage mortality or reduce natality as a population grows. Populations may be limited by the availability of a resource such as food or by other external agents such as predation. A resource-limited population might be regulated by intraspecific competition that affects natality, mortality, or dispersal in a density-dependent fashion.

Examination of the northern herd for density-dependent effects and for actual or potential population regulation was complicated, in some respects, by the same human predation that also provided insight into the dynamics. Because of the complex setting and the different management objectives applied to this single population, segments of the herd experienced different levels of human predation. The intensity of human predation and the herd segments affected sometimes varied considerably from one year to the next. Rarely in the past half-century has the *overall* population been at K_1 because of human predation, and it has likely never been long enough at this level for stationary age distributions to develop. At the same time there were segments of the population in the park that experienced little direct human predation and probably approached K_l. Consequently, representative sampling of this population was extremely difficult; many of the best samples were drawn from very low populations. Relatively little is known about the occurrence or strength of some potential density-dependent effects at K_l. Extrapolation of the density-dependence shown at low numbers to the population near K_l could be misleading. Fowler (1978) suggests that density-dependent responses may operate sequentially as juvenile mortality, age of sexual maturity, birth rate of adults, and adult mortality as the population approaches K_l. If correct, many density-dependent responses are nonlinear and would be fully expressed only at high population levels.

The natural density-dependent processes of the northern herd were sometimes signaled through the variable human predation and the peculiar difficulties of sampling this population. The growth trajectory of the population in the 1970s following the moratorium on park removals suggested that density-dependent processes were operating to move the population toward an equilibrium at K_I. Analysis suggested that the age of sexual maturity of females was somewhat density-dependent. The density-dependence shown by the population's natality rate was less than might be expected, due in part to the affects of human predation on female age distributions. Survival of young over their first year was strongly density-dependent, especially neonatal survival. The density-dependence of male survival, although suggested, could not be demonstrated. Since some aspects of natality and mortality were density-dependent, the overall population can be considered to show regulation, even though numbers in some herd segments are more or less determined by human predation. Changes in elk nutrition with population size seem to be the ultimate cause of many of these density-dependent responses. These relationships are discussed next.

CHAPTER 6

Physiological Ecology

ELK NUTRITION, GROWTH, AND CONDITION are reviewed briefly as influences on natality and mortality. Following McCullough (1969), Caughley (1971), Geist (1971a), and Mitchell et al. (1977), I consider the European red deer and North American elk to be forms of *C. elaphus*. In addition to being more acceptable from a taxonomic view, the extensive European literature on the physiology of red deer can be used to understand the northern Yellowstone elk. The data reviewed in some detail here are mainly from biological collections of elk from the northern herd. Laboratory studies and field studies conducted elsewhere are cited to establish some relationships.

Nutrition

Seasonal changes in food intake and rumen physiology of elk are related to stages in their reproductive cycle and to the quality and quantity of food consumed. Daily food intake is highest in summer, when demands for growth, lactation, and fat storage are greatest (Mitchell et al. 1977). Lactating females eat more than nonlactating females. Intake is apparently reduced in both wild and captive *C. elaphus* in winter, even though in captive studies food was freely available (Pollack 1974, Mitchell et al. 1976, 1977, Westra and Hudson 1979, Robbins et al. 1981). Mitchell et al. (1977) suggest that since intake is regulated partially by rate of food passage through the gut, the reduced intake in the wild could be due in part to lower digestibility of winter forage and to longer retention in the rumen. Both wild and captive male elk show a marked reduction in food intake during the rut (Pollack 1974, Mitchell et al. 1976, 1977).

The seasonal changes in plane of nutrition (i.e., quality and quantity of food) are reflected in elk rumen contents and fermentation rates. McBee and Worley (1962, 1964) examined the rate at which volatile fatty acids (VFAs) were produced by micro-organisms in the rumens of 58 elk shot on the northern range from 28 February to 11 June 1962 and of 46 shot from 4 October 1962 to 8 September 1963. (VFAs are products of rumen fermentation that provide a major source of energy to ruminants.)

Changes in fermentation rates over seasons are difficult to interpret because of diurnal variations (Short et al. 1969); however, the Yellowstone samples were mostly collected at daybreak. Fermentation rates were uniformly low during late winter, increased markedly with the appearance of green vegetation in April, and were highest in summer. Calculations from McBee and Worley (1962, 1964) suggested that the mean fermentation rate of 1.11 ± 0.54 milliequivalent (mEq) acids/100 g/hour from 34 animals shot during January–March was significantly lower than the rate of $2.41 \pm .71$ SD from 19 elk shot from 15 May to July (Tukey's quick test, $P < .0005$). Samples taken during the April–May periods of transition to higher fermentation rates and the September–December transition to lower rates were omitted. This also excluded the effects of the rut, which caused greater variation in fermentation rates. Elk might require production of at least 1.6 mEq VFA/100 g/hour of rumen contents to maintain body weight, but the majority of elk examined produced less than this from December to mid-April (McBee and Worley 1962).

The average protein content of rumen samples from 13 elk examined in December–March ($9.3 \pm 1.3\%$) was significantly lower than samples from 7 collected between 15 May and 15 August ($23.9 \pm 3.4\%$, $P < .0005$). Protein content increased markedly when green grass became available in spring (McBee and Worley 1962, 1964). Dry weights of rumen contents were significantly greater for elk shot during January–March ($19 \pm 9\%$) than for those collected from 15 May to August ($15 \pm 2.1\%$, $P < .0005$). These comparisons also suggest that greater amounts of poorly digestible materials were consumed in winter (McBee and Worley 1962, 1964).

The dominance of the rumen microbes by relatively few species of bacteria in winter also was interpreted as indicative of low-quality winter diets on the northern range (McBee et al. 1969, McBee, pers. commun. 1979).

Concurrent studies of seasonal changes in body weights (see below) showed that most elk lost considerable weight during the 1962 winter. Declines in body weight and condition continued to occur in winter even at the low population levels of 1963–68. Undernutrition may be considered to occur when any constituent of the diet (e.g., protein, energy) drops below levels necessary for body maintenance. The combined studies of rumen physiology and seasonal changes in body weights show clearly that most classes of the population were undernourished in winter.

Determining the reductions in quantity and quality of nutrients that produce undernutrition in this wild population is not entirely possible from the available data. Since elk were still undernourished at very low populations, low food quality is clearly important. At high populations, both low quality and reduced quantity per elk likely contribute to undernutrition. Given the variation in food habits among individual elk, the spectrum of forage production and availability, and the vagaries of environmental conditions known to occur on the northern range in winter, undernutrition could be produced by combinations of deficiencies that vary among years and between areas of the range. Other studies suggest, however, that deficiencies in available and digestible energy and in usable nitrogen (indexed as crude protein content of forage) are likely (Dietz 1970, Halls 1970). As a first approximation, an adult female elk on the Madison River of Yellowstone Park may require 6,035 kcal/day in winter to meet demands for metabolism and activity (Nelson and Leege 1979). This requirement must be met from daily intake and body reserves. Requirements increase considerably during periods of extreme cold and during the later stages of gestation. About 5.5–6.0% dietary crude protein may be needed for body maintenance during winter (Nelson and Leege 1979). However, specific dietary requirements usually cannot be determined because, among other reasons, the availability of one nutrient often depends upon the digestibility of another. Thus, reduced digestibility of crude protein can inhibit VFA production in the rumen, with consequent reduction in energy supplied to the ruminant, in the presence of otherwise adequate energy sources (Annison and Lewis 1959). Elk, with their symbiotic rumen microbes, have considerable capacities to digest low-quality forage and to recycle nitrogen when it is in short supply (Mould 1980, Westra and Hudson 1979). (Nitrogen, as urea, is recycled to the rumen, where it is synthesized into microbial protein; this is subsequently digested by the ruminant.) These capacities are strained by the forage available on the northern range in winter, nutritional requirements are not met (whatever these may be), and most elk are undernourished, apparently even at low population levels.

Growth

Body weight and skeletal measurements have been used as indices of growth for elk. Rush (1932a:31) reported an average birth weight for elk of "37 pounds [16.8 kg], the smallest weighed 23 pounds and the largest 45 pounds." These data are difficult to interpret, because sample size and sex were not reported, and it is not clear if these weights included elk from just the northern herd (Rush 1932a:27). Calculations from Johnson (1951) gave birth weights for 23 newborn to day-old calves at 14.8 kg (8.6–20.5) for the adjacent Gallatin River herd (standard deviation not reported), and similar variations in birth weights probably occur among the northern Yellowstone elk. Male calves averaged 2 kg more than females. Mean weight of 48 calves considered to be two–four days old was 16.4 kg (9.5–21.8). Weights for two–four-day-old calves must be interpreted with caution, because mortality of small neonates probably has already begun. Interpreting these weights as birth weights gives inflated values. Nevertheless, these wide ranges in weights are of considerable interest.

From a birth weight of 15 kg around 1 June, the surviving female calves on the northern range average about 102 kg live weight by January; surviving males, 115 kg. This represents roughly a seven-fold increase in weight over seven–eight months. These live weights were calculated from dressed carcass weights (Greer and Howe 1964), which are about 67% of whole weight (Quimby and Johnson 1951).

Dressed carcass weights from 83 yearling females collected from the northern herd during December 1961–February 1962 averaged 112 ± 14 kg; 126 two-year-olds, 144 ± 19 kg; 337 three–seven-year-olds, 156 ± 20 kg; 256 eight year and older, 155 ± 20 kg (Greer and Howe 1964). Yearlings and two-year-olds were significantly lighter than the next older age classes (P < .05). Flook (1970) reported that both body weight and hind foot length (a measure of skeletal growth) of 310 females shot from winter populations in Banff National Park increased significantly through three years of age. This continued growth of females through at least three years of age is relevant to interpretations of natality (see below). Age-specific comparisons showed that the dressed weights of 435 pregnant females shot from the northern herd during December 1961–February 1962 were significantly greater than weights from 89 nonpregnant animals (Greer and Howe 1964). These relationships existed even at low population levels. For example, data from Greer (pers. commun. 1979) showed that dressed carcass weights from 8 pregnant yearling females (131 ± 8.0 kg) were significantly higher (Tukey's quick test P < .0005) than weights from 17 nonpregnant animals (120 ± 8.3 kg) shot from the Blacktail Plateau during 18 January–21 February, 1968.

Comparisons by age class showed that male elk are heavier and larger than females and reach maximum body weight at an older age than females (Greer and Howe 1964, Flook 1970). Dressed weights for 26 males eight years and older from the northern range averaged 196 ± 28 kg (Greer and Howe 1964).

The seasonal changes in body weight and skeletal growth are of particular interest. Mitchell et al. (1976) described the annual cycle of body weight for adult *C. elaphus* that involves accumulation of body materials (fats and proteins) in spring and summer, followed by a decline in winter. Males lost about 15% of body weight over the rut; females showed no such loss. Data suggest that this general pattern occurs in the northern herd. Using a sample of 17 males three years and older, Greer (1965a) suggested that losses of 20–25% of dressed carcass weight might occur during the rut. Females did not show significant losses during the breeding season. Greer and Howe (1964) showed that 719 females two years and older lost about 7–9% of dressed carcass weights from 11 December 1961 to 17 February 1962. Males ($N = 155$) of corresponding ages lost a greater proportion of weight than females. Yearling males ($N = 76$) from this collection also showed significant weight losses. Yearling females ($N = 83$) showed a smaller loss that was not significant. The 1962 winter was severe; data were not obtained from late February to April or May, when weight losses probably were accelerated. Dressed weights of females three years and older also declined during December–February periods of 1963, 1964, and 1965 even at lower overall population levels (Greer 1965b). Greer (1965a) reported that weights of females three years and older declined from around 195 to 125 kg in a sample of 84 shot from October to May 1965. However, detailed analyses of these data for age-specific weight loss in relation to population size or environmental conditions have not been made (Greer, pers. commun. 1978).

Mitchell et al. (1976) reported that *C. elaphus* calves from wild populations in Scotland grew in body weight until October. A long ''growth check'' occurred (i.e., body weight remained constant) until April or May. Skeletons of some calves continued to grow slowly over winter. Greer and Howe (1964) showed that male calves declined in body weight from 11 December 1961 to 17 February 1962; female calves may have maintained weight over this part of the winter. These data suggest that calves in the northern herd also undergo a check in growth and, more likely, lose weight over winter. In contrast, captive calves and those on feedgrounds in Wyoming can be made to gain weight over winter periods, if fed supplementary food (Thorne 1970a, Dean et al. 1976). Thus the growth check in wild populations reflects in large part the decline of the plane of nutrition of the calf (and perhaps that of the lactating female).

Condition

Fat reserves are a useful index to the condition of *C. elaphus*. Changes in superficial body fat (e.g., rump fat) reflect changes at the upper end of the spectrum of condition, kidney fat for the middle range, and bone marrow fat for the lower range of condition (Flook 1970, Mitchell et al. 1976). Consequently, an elk showing depletion of marrow fat has largely exhausted other reserves.

Flook (1970) showed that kidney fat indexes of adults were at a low in spring and recovered slowly over summer in populations from the Rocky Mountains of Canada. This was followed by a decline over winter. Adult males lost substantial fat reserves during the rut and entered the winter with smaller reserves than adult females. Males older than 7 years and females older than 10 had substantially lower reserves in early winter than did younger adults. Trainer (1971) reported that lactating 3–10-year-olds had kidney fat reserves significantly smaller than nonlactating females in western Oregon. Mitchell et al. (1976) also showed that lactating females were consistently leaner than nonlactating females in wild populations from Scotland. Further, fat reserves of calves were very low over the year.

These same general relationships of condition to season of the year, sex, and age apply to the northern herd but have not been reported in detail. The cycles of weight changes over time reflect, in part, changes in some fat reserves. When the northern herd was smallest (1967–68), marrow fat reserves were considered to be high (fat content $\geq$ 81%) in most yearling females (N = 92) through January but declined significantly over winter (χ^2, P < .005), until by March none had fat content above 80%, and 5 of 15 were in extremely poor condition ($\leq$ 20% fat) (Greer 1968). The elk population increased after 1968, and during the late winter and spring of 1975 at least 12% died. The femur marrow in 88% of 226 elk that died indicated extreme depletion of fat reserves prior to death (Houston 1978b). Calves of the year and old adults (males 7 years and older, females 12 years and older) comprised most of 716 elk that died during the winters of 1975, 1976, and 1978. Substantial mortality of yearling males and females also apparently occurred in 1978.

Interpretation

Some of the mechanisms whereby nutrition affects natality and mortality through differences in growth and condition can be established for the northern Yellowstone elk. This is necessary to explain some aspects of the population dynamics and also to develop one aspect of the vegetation–elk relationship.

The amount of winter forage is essentially fixed by autumn (Chap. 9) and is reduced over winter as it is consumed. Even at low population levels the winter plane of nutrition was inadequate to maintain body weight and condition. Presumably, the rate and level of decline in condition, and the classes showing extreme decline (i.e., the extent and severity of undernutrition), depend upon the rates at which fixed forage supplies are consumed and body reserves expended. These in turn depend upon population density and winter conditions. Winter forage is emphasized in this oversimplified view, because the level to which elk must recover or grow during spring and summer seems largely determined over winter. I recognize that forage varies both in quantity and quality during late gestation in spring and during summer periods of growth, lactation, and fat storage. However, since the northern elk have dispersed over a very large area at comparatively low densities by summer, they will usually have access to abundant spring forage and will virtually always encounter abundant summer forage of high quality along the gradient in elevation covered by their migration.

Nutrition influences natality through several mechanisms. Sexual maturity in *C. elaphus* apparently depends upon attaining a critical minimum body size or weight rather than any particular age (Mitchell 1973, Mitchell and Brown 1974, Mitchell et al. 1977). Such a relationship appears to be true for most ungulates studied (Sadlier 1969, Sinclair 1977). This means that sexual maturity is strongly influenced by growth rate, with faster-growing animals maturing at an earlier age. Since growth rate is partly a function of nutrition, the increased pregnancies shown by two-year-old elk at lower population densities on the northern range likely resulted from faster growth through better nutrition. Variable winter conditions modified the response of two-year-olds to changes in density and appeared greatly to modify the effects of density on pregnancy rates of yearlings.

Whether or not an elk continues to reproduce annually as an adult apparently depends upon her ability to regain a critical level of condition or size by the rutting season (Trainer 1971, Mitchell 1973). On the northern range, samples showed that pregnant elk were generally heavier than nonpregnant females in early winter. The generally high pregnancy rates among adults suggested that most females attained the required condition annually. The possibly higher pregnancy rates among 10–15-year olds at lower population levels could also reflect improved nutrition. The substantially lower pregnancy rates among old females (16+ years) suggest that, among other reasons, they were unable to regain the size and condition necessary, irrespective of population size.

Nutrition has conspicuous direct effects and more subtle delayed effects upon mortality rates. Experimental manipulations of the diets of captive elk (Thorne et al. 1976) suggest that the great variation in birth weights for wild elk results from the plane of nutrition of pregnant females. Poorly nourished captive females that lost more than 3% of their own body weight (15% loss if weights of fetus, fetal membranes, and fluids were included) between January and parturition gave birth to calves that were significantly smaller than those from females that lost less weight. Small calves survived poorly even under captive conditions. Thorne et al. (1976) also showed that calves born to undernourished females had a significantly lower growth rate (measured as average daily weight gain) their first month than did calves born to better nourished females. This may have been due to reduced reserves of protein and energy in undernourished females, which in turn suppressed milk production. Field studies in Scotland showed that heavier and fatter calves were associated with heavier and fatter females that produced more milk (Mitchell et al. 1976).

The thresholds of weight and physical condition necessary for survival of young could be quite high on the northern range, where spring conditions can be extremely harsh for neonates. Calves must survive spring storms, travel long distances across difficult terrain, cross rivers in flood stage, and escape a variety of predators. Substantial mortality of neonates occurs postpartum. Mammary glands and uteri of 45 recently parturient elk shot in late May–early June of 1965–67 on the northern range suggested that 20% were not nursing (Greer 1965a, 1966a, 1967). Calves born to these females were assumed to be dead. Under experimental conditions, both delayed onset of lactation and desertion led to starvation of neonates born to undernourished white-tailed deer (Verme 1962, Murphy and Coates 1966). On the northern range, elk calves probably die from starvation and disease, in addition to predation. The reduced mortality of calves from birth to six–nine months at lower populations probably resulted, in part, from a higher proportion of larger calves born to a larger proportion of females in better condition.

The relationships between nutrition and winter mortality are complex when the proximate agents of mortality also are considered. As reported above, those classes dying over winter were mostly elk with the lowest energy reserves—calves of the year and aged adults of both sexes (sometimes yearlings of both sexes). Adult males seemed especially vulnerable because of their low fat reserves following the rut. Elk with low reserves may be especially vulnerable to some types of predation (Cole 1972, 1978). Cursory field inspection of moribund elk in 1975–76 suggested that those with low reserves were also heavily parasitized and diseased. Sinclair (1977) proposed that only moderate undernutrition in a host ungulate (African buffalo in his case) could impair its immune response, which requires adequate protein to function properly. The effects of incipient undernutrition thus are amplified through the immune response and may quickly lead to pathogenic infection. A positive feedback relationship may occur where undernutrition leads to disease and in turn accelerates undernutrition, leading to even more rapid declines in condition. Many elk on the northern range appeared to die very quickly in winter—too quickly for death to be attributed simply to inanition. The series of causal relationships proposed by Sinclair (1977) probably occurs generally among resource-limited herbivores; including the northern Yellowstone elk. Even though the proximate causes of winter mortality include diseases and parasites, I consider the ultimate cause to be undernutrition.

Reduced winter mortality of calves at lower populations also can be attributed in part to improved nutrition during their first winter and to larger neonates born to females in better physical condition. Human predation substituted for some other agents of adult mortality at low population levels and obscured some of the relationships between mortality and nutrition. However, as the population increased in the 1970s, much of the conspicuous mortality of aged elk with low body reserves could be attributed to undernutrition.

Thus the evidence suggests that the northern Yellowstone elk could be limited by the quality and quantity of winter forage and that human predation modifies this resource limitation. Some density-dependent aspects of natality and mortality are related to nutrition; the mortality of neonates, the strongest density-dependent mortality identified, seems to be clearly linked to nutrition of maternal females. The quality and quantity of winter food is discussed elsewhere, as are considerations of controls on forage abundance and availability. The nature of intraspecific competition for food and mates is reviewed next.

CHAPTER 7

Elk Behavior

THE SOCIAL BEHAVIOR OF ELK is considered here in relation to intraspecific competition for resources. The occurrence of seasonal migrations and the fidelity shown to range areas were discussed earlier; these aspects of elk behavior also are relevant to the discussions that follow. The data are from studies of the associations among tagged elk and from field observations of the social interactions in groups of untagged elk.

Group Constancy and Associations Among Individuals

Elk society is matrifocal, with groups of females and young generally living apart from adult males, except during the rut. The relationships among adult females in these "cow–calf" groups and the degree of group constancy [i.e., the tendency for a group to remain together (Knight 1970)] have been of interest. The frequency and context of social strife might be strongly influenced by the level of group constancy.

Shoesmith (1978:95) described the changes in group size and composition for the northern Yellowstone elk that occurred during the June–November periods of 1966–68. Groups generally numbered 20 elk or fewer and appeared to be dynamic; size and composition changed considerably over seasonal periods. The largest groups typically occurred from June to mid-August and then declined during the rut. Cole (1969a) reported that elk group size varied considerably among years (1962–66) on summer ranges in southern Yellowstone Park in apparent response to the abundance of biting insects. Elk groups were much larger, several hundred or more, when molesting insects were abundant. Knight (1970) observed that the largest groups of elk in Montana's Sun River herd occurred in winter. Cow–calf groups were largest in January and February and decreased in size over winter. Comparable data are not available for the northern Yellowstone herd in winter, but field observations made from 1970 to 1979 suggest the same general relationships. Cow–calf groups of several hundred or more were observed in early winter when elk foraged on highly productive grasslands and shrublands (see Chap. 9). Group size often declined during severe late winter periods as elk dispersed into forests. Groups of adult males typically contained fewer individuals than cow–calf groups.

Few lasting associations occurred between individually marked elk in the northern herd during the 1963–68 period (Shoesmith 1978:75, 1979). Shoesmith concluded that the basic social group was limited to the family unit (i.e., cow–calf plus perhaps yearling); clans of closely related adult females did not occur. Marked individuals frequently entered and left aggregations of elk. However, Shoesmith (1978:137) rejected the occurrence of clans with considerable reservation, because the intense human predation on females and young affected his results. Any potential social organization to the clan level would likely have been in considerable disarray during the prolonged elk reduction program. Additionally, marked elk caught in subsequent trapping operations were released, whereas untagged members of the same aggregation were transplanted from the park (Meagher, pers. commun.). Such removals were hardly conducive to the study of social relationships, as pointed out by Shoesmith. [Curiously, these same reservations are not expressed in a recently published summary (Shoesmith 1979).]

Social Dominance

Dominance hierarchies (dominant–subordinate relationships) occur in elk groups (Struthsaker 1967, McCullough 1969, Lincoln et al. 1970, Lieb 1973, Franklin et al. 1975, Franklin and Lieb 1979). Hierarchies are established and maintained by social behavior patterns described by the above authors and by Geist (1966, 1979). Social rank among males shows a complex relationship to antler size and development (Lincoln et al. 1970). Dominant males tend to be older, larger elk that possess the largest antlers during seasons when antlers are fully developed. The social hierarchy changes when antlers are growing; formerly dominant males that have cast their antlers or males possessing new velvet-covered antlers may become subordinate. In cow groups the older, larger females are dominant over younger females (Lieb 1973, Franklin et al. 1975, Franklin and Lieb 1979). Calves are subordinate to all older classes. Knight (1970) observed that low group constancy did not preclude the occurrence of dominance hierarchies among aggregations of elk. Such hierarchies must be far more complex when group constancy is low—the apparent situation among the northern Yellowstone elk—than when groups are stable (see below).

I examined aspects of the social hierarchies of feeding ''cow–calf'' groups on the northern winter range from 1973 to 1979 (such groups frequently contained small numbers of yearling males and occasionally very few older males). These groups were of particular interest because of the potential role of social dominance in gaining access to resources. I recorded 462 agonistic (conflict) interactions between individuals in 70 cow–calf groups during late November to early March periods. About 80% of these interactions were observed in their entirety; i.e., I recorded the class and activities of both elk prior to the interaction, the type and sequence of behavior patterns displayed during the interaction, and the behavior of the participants immediately following the encounter. Groups were observed with a 15–60× spotting scope at distances or in situations where my presence appeared to have no influence on their activities. The average distance to the observed groups was around 300 m, but some were observed at distances of 500–700 m. This means that the interactions recorded represent the bare minimum that occurred; subtle interactions were surely underestimated.

About 16 behavior patterns were recordable under the conditions of this study. Terminology generally follows Geist (1966, 1971a, 1979). The aggressive behavior patterns included the "weapon threats": the head high threat (Hh) with variations described by Geist (1966), the front kick (Fk), the rising onto hindlegs and flailing with forefeet (Fig. 7.1) (Rh), the bite (Bi), the "horn" threat (Ht), and the butt (Bu). The "present threats" included the low stretch (Lo) and the broadside display-parallel parade (Bp) shown by males. Horning (Ho) and sparring (S) were also recorded. Additional aggressive patterns included the head-on-rump (Hr) and mount (M). Displacement (D) was also observed (Struthsaker 1967); i.e., one elk simply shouldered a subordinate aside. Submissive patterns included lowering head (sometimes with jawing or headshake), looking away, and walking or running away. The elk displaying the first pattern of the interaction was termed the *initiator;* the other, the *respondent.*

The number and classes of elk in the entire group also were recorded [females, calves, yearling males, adult male I (smaller 4- and 5-point bulls that were mainly two or three years old) and adult male II (all larger, mature bulls)]. Snow depth was recorded as no snow or partial snow cover (class 0) and, thereafter, at depth increments of six inches ($\sim$ 15 cm). Snow density was estimated roughly by the degree of crusting: severe snow crusts were recorded when calves were supported while walking on the surface; moderate crusts occurred when calves broke through but when large angular snow blocks were still being pawed with difficulty from feeding craters; less severe conditions with no visible crusts or only light crusts were combined. The observation period was recorded in minutes.

Trial observations in 1973 and 1974 showed some of the limitations of the field techniques:

1. Social interactions could be frequent and subtle.
2. Observations had to be terminated frequently when members of a group moved from sight or when snow flurries and failing winter daylight obscured my vision.
3. Also, one person simply could not observe and record all the interactions in very large groups of elk, even while using a tape recorder.

The classes of elk involved in 364 agonistic interactions, observed in their entirety, in 70 cow-calf groups are summarized in Fig. 7.2. The first two behavior patterns displayed by a class of initiator toward a class of respondent and the context of the interactions also are shown. Females initiated interactions only toward other females (N = 188, or 63% of all interactions initiated by females), toward calves (35%), or toward yearling males (2%). The Hh and Rh threats represented 90% of the first two patterns displayed by female initiators to female respondents. In contrast, the Hh, Fk, and D patterns were most important in female-to-young interactions. Calves initiated interactions only against other calves, and again, the Hh and Rh patterns were most important. Yearling males initiated interactions with females, calves, and other yearling males; the Ht was displayed most frequently. Adult males initiated interactions against most other classes, but the number of interactions observed was low. In 112 female-to-female interactions the initiator appeared to be larger than the respondent in 56% of the encounters (and often had a dark, well-developed throat mane); the initiator and respondent were of equal size in 40% of these encounters; the initiator appeared to be smaller in 4%. In the 6 female-to-yearling male interactions the females always were larger. In 16 yearling male-to-female interactions the initiating males were larger in only 13% of the cases; they were equal in size to the females in 31%;

FIGURE 7.1.
Dominance hierarchies in elk are established and maintained by aggressive behavior.
Photo by H. Engels.

FIGURE 7.2.

Summary by sex and age class of 364 agonistic interactions observed in 70 elk cow--calf groups. Total number of interactions (IAs) observed between two classes is shown at upper left of each box, along with the (percent) of total IAs launched by class of initiator. The behavior patterns displayed by a class of initiator (I) against a class of respondent (R) are listed. The context and outcome of the interactions are also shown.

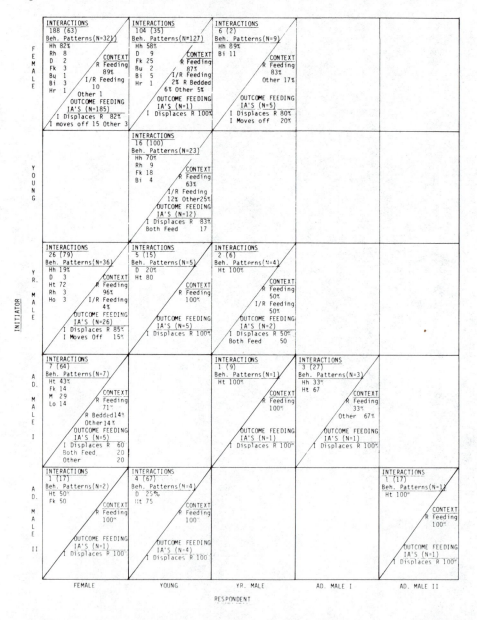

smaller in 56%. In addition to the 5 interactions of adult males with other males in Fig. 7.2, 22 more were obtained from watching 15 male groups. Together, these showed that larger males dominated smaller males and also that the Ht was the most frequent behavior pattern displayed (64%) by initiators in feeding groups during the winter.

This description was a necessary introduction, but none of it represents particularly new information. The social status of the elk interacting in dominance hierarchies has been established with some finesse by several of the authors cited above. In particular, male hierarchies have been studied intensively and manipulated experimentally in the field by Lincoln et al. (1970) and Appleby (1980). Lieb (1973) tested dominance relationships in cow–calf groups. A high percentage of the elk in his study groups were individually marked, and their social rank had been observed for several years. Lieb's findings are especially relevant here: the oldest females with the longest residence on an area were dominant over others; interactions were often most intense between females of the same age class; such "peer-bonded" females tended to split "wins" and "losses" in aggressive encounters, whereas older females usually won encounters with younger animals.

The context and outcome of the interactions observed in the cow–calf groups of the northern Yellowstone herd are of more interest (Fig. 7.2). About 94% of all interactions observed were classed as feeding contexts, i.e., either the respondent was feeding immediately before the interaction (93%) or the initiator and respondent were both feeding in proximity (1%). Over all classes of feeding interactions the initiator displaced the feeding respondent in 87% of the observations. The potential for interactions in contexts other than feeding seemed to me to be far greater than observed. Elk often moved about in feeding groups; they passed by one another and passed by other standing or occasionally bedded animals. Dominants apparently sought out and displaced feeding subordinates. The initiator displaced the respondent in 82% of 186 female-to-female feeding interactions. In another 15% of these encounters, the initiator's behavior patterns were met in kind by the respondent until the initiator showed a submissive pattern (this outcome is described as "I moves off" in Fig. 7.2). These outcomes are considered here to be unsuccessful attempts to gain access to the feeding site, although other interpretations are possible (i.e., reinforcement or establishment of the hierarchy). Females always displaced young in 93 female-to-young feeding interactions. Yearling males usually displaced feeding females in 26 interactions and always displaced feeding calves in 5 interactions. About 70% of 25 adult male-to-adult male interactions occurred in feeding contexts. Larger males always displaced smaller males. The only injury I observed in all these agonistic encounters occurred when a class I male approached an exceptionally large class II bull that was feeding and displayed the horn threat. The large bull lunged from his feeding site and horned the smaller animal in the hindquarters as it turned to flee. The thrust drew blood from at least one point.

The significance of these feeding interactions is best appreciated by observing a group of elk foraging in deep or crusted snow. Pawing a feeding crater through deep snow can be a laborious, energetically expensive task. To be displaced frequently from established sites during severe winter conditions is of no small consequence. I interpret the data on the feeding interactions to show that interference competition (Miller 1967) for food was a common occurrence among wintering elk.

Forty-nine of the wintering cow–calf groups were observed for periods of 10 minutes or longer from 1975 to 1979 (mean observation period was 26 ± 14 minutes). Group sizes ranged from 7 to 120 ($\bar{X} = 36$), but only two groups contained more than 100 elk. A total of 319 agonistic interactions was observed among all classes in 29 groups; 20 other groups showed no interactions during the period of observation. About 75% of these encounters were observed in their entirety. Males older than yearlings were involved in less than 3% of these; i.e., most involved the interaction of the female, young, and yearling male classes.

An index to the rate of interaction for each group was computed as interactions/

elk/minute of observation × 1,000. This was plotted against the relative ease of foraging as determined from observations of snow depth and crust. All conditions with less than about 15 cm of snow were classed as essentially *unrestrictive*. Snow depths of about 46 cm (18 inches) or greater, with or without crusts, were classed as *restrictive*. The only observation of a group feeding with a moderate snow crust in 30–46 cm of snow was also classed as restrictive. All other snow conditions were grouped as *moderately restrictive*. The rate of interaction increased as snow conditions became more restrictive; i.e., interference competition increased when foraging was more difficult (Fig. 7.3). Many variables were unaccounted for in these observations, and objections could be raised to this interpretation. First, the rate of interaction is a function of group composition as well as group size. Even though most of the interactions involved the female, young, and yearling male classes, the opportunity for interaction varied among groups. Second, nothing whatever was known about the constancy of the groups observed; groups could have included temporary aggregations

FIGURE 7.3.
The relationship between the frequency of agonistic interaction and the relative ease of foraging for 49 cow–calf groups. The means, ranges and standard deviations of the index of interactions/elk minute × 1,000 are shown for each class of snow condition.

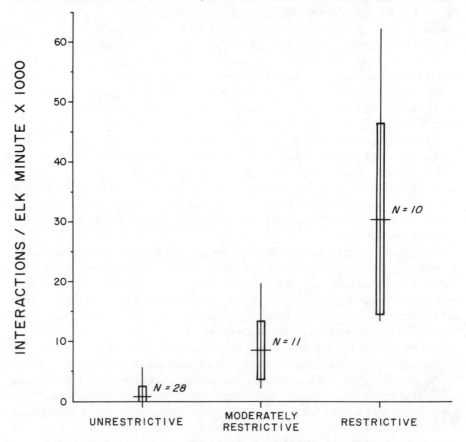

brought together by particular winter conditions, as well as groups with well-established social hierarchies. Finally, there was no direct measure of food supply, only estimates of snow conditions. Still, when examined at this crude level, there seemed to be a broad tendency for the rate of interaction to increase as snow conditions became more restrictive. Similar relationships have been reported for other species; intraspecific aggressive behavior for winter feeding sites increased with snow depth for both Rocky Mountain goats and male bighorn sheep (Petocz 1973).

Interpretation

Group constancy and lasting associations between adult elk apparently were quite low in the northern herd during the period of elk reductions in the 1960s. Knight (1970) also reported low association between individually marked elk on the Sun River. The Sun River population also is seasonally migratory, and some herd segments are heavily hunted. In striking contrast to these findings, very stable associations (i.e., high group constancy) occurred among nonmigratory cow groups at Prairie Creek Redwoods State Park, California (Lieb 1973, Franklin et al. 1975, Franklin and Lieb 1979). These "cow herds" occurred as subgroups usually only for short periods during the rut and when individual females left to calve. Group stability resulted from lasting social bonds between adult females and their female offspring, and also because of bonds between females in peer groups. Jenkins (1980) reported that nonmigratory cow groups in the Hoh River drainage of Olympic National Park, Washington, showed high group constancy.

Clearly, the level of group constancy varies among elk populations within quite broad limits; the level expressed depends upon the environment of the particular population. Franklin et al. (1975) suggest that group stability in an elk population may pass through phases of development from early, less stable conditions to quite stable groups. The occurrence of seasonal migrations and the level of human predation are two important influences on the degree of stability that can be achieved. The nature of the group constancy expected to develop in the northern Yellowstone herd with greatly reduced human predation is unknown, but I would expect constancy to increase from the conditions reported by Shoesmith (1978). The occurrence of seasonal migrations, a highly variable winter environment, and continued hunting of herd segments outside the park all seemingly preclude the development of group constancy to the level reported for populations that are nonmigratory and unhunted.

The same environmental conditions that influenced group constancy most likely resulted in complex and labile dominance hierarchies in the northern Yellowstone herd. Interference competition for food occurred along these hierarchies in winter, and competitive interactions appeared to increase as foraging became difficult. Age-specific rates of mortality and natality are probably mediated partly through these dominance hierarchies because interference competition affected the food intake and energy expenditure of all sex and age classes; the effects on some social subordinates seemed clearly to be negative. Particularly graphic examples of these relationships occurred during the severe winters of 1975 and 1976 when large cow–calf groups foraged in deep snow along the Lamar River. Calves frequently were displaced from feeding sites by older elk. Calves declined rapidly in condition, and a high percentage died during both winters. Both the pregnancy rates of subordinate females and the mortality of neonates born to subordinates are probably affected adversely through dominance hierarchies. The mortality rates of adult males were affected by the intense competition for mates that occurred during rut, plus competition for winter food. The older dominant male elk are most successful in gaining access to females (Geist 1979); these same animals expend their fat reserves during the rut and are particularly vulnerable to winter mortality. Additionally, Craighead et al. (1973) observed that some of the large males dying on the northern range in the winter of 1962 carried injuries apparently inflicted by competitors during the rut. I observed males with similar injuries among those dying during the November–January periods of the 1970s.

The interpretations made here are supported by a recent study showing well-defined agonistic hierarchies among free-ranging male *C. elaphus* groups in Scotland (Appleby 1980). Many of the disputes between males involved access to food. Dominance rank was apparently associated with differential access to food during periods of winter food shortage. Appleby (1980:306) suggests that, "Acquisition of high social rank might therefore be selectively advantageous through reduction of winter mortality and improvement in body condition."

Thus, intraspecific competition along dominance hierarchies affected access to scarce resources—winter food for all classes and, for males, mates. This brief examination of social behavior was necessary to provide another causal link between the dynamics of the northern Yellowstone elk and their food supply. The nature of this food supply, its changes over time, and the foraging strategy of elk are examined next.

CHAPTER 8

The Vegetation: Statics and Dynamics

THE PRESENT AND PAST VEGETATION OF THE STUDY AREA and documented changes in vegetation are described here. The effects on the vegetation of ungulate grazing, climatic change, fire, and human activities are discussed in detail. The data are drawn from a wide variety of sources; methods of study are presented separately in each section. Scientific names of plant species are listed in Appendix X.

The Present Vegetation

About 79% of the terrestrial area of Yellowstone Park is forested. About 81% of the forest is dominated by lodgepole pine, which occurs from 2,300 to 2,600 m. Subalpine fir and Engelmann spruce represent about 9% of the forest and occur mostly above 2,600 m. Whitebark pine is a major component (5%) of this forest zone near the timberline. A small zone of Douglas-fir (4%) is recognized below 2,300 m (Despain 1973, Despain, pers. commun. 1975, Cooper 1975). Nonforested areas include lower-elevation grasslands and sagebrush steppes of the northern range (discussed below), various forest parks, wet meadows, herblands, and alpine tundra. Cole (1969a), Meagher (1973), and Barmore (1980) provide descriptions of various nonforested plant communities.

The vegetation types and the characteristic vegetation of the northern winter range in the park were mapped from 1:15,840 color aerial photos (Table 8.1). Maps were checked by field observations and, for grasslands and shrub steppes, by extensive descriptive sampling of the vegetation. The categories are arbitrary; much of this vegetation would more properly be described as continua along environmental gradients (Whittaker 1967). Type is a collective term denoting major units of vegetation. Combinations of characteristic plants that occurred in presumably "climax" situations

TABLE 8.1
Vegetation on the Northern Winter Range Within Yellowstone National Park

Vegetation Type	Characteristic Vegetation	General Distribution	Approximate Hectares (%)
Upland forest	*Douglas-fir assns.*	Small stands throughout the area: mostly 1,500–2,100 m.	16,100 (20)
	Lodgepole pine associes	North slopes throughout the area: mostly 2,100–2,500 m.	10,600 (13)
	Engelmann spruce/subalpine fir assns.	Streams and north slopes throughout the area: mostly above 2,300 m.	6,600 (8)
	Whitebark pine assns.	North slopes: mostly above 2,700 m.	400 [a]
	Aspen associes	Small groves along forest grassland ecotones, flood plains, and stream banks	1,400 (2)
Upland steppe	*Idaho fescue/bearded wheatgrass assn.* and others (mesic steppe)	North slopes (NE–NW): 2,000–2,400 m throughout the area, some south slopes over 2,100 m	16,300 (20)
	Bluebunch wheatgrass/Idaho fescue assn.–xeric phase, bluebunch wheatgrass/Sandberg bluegrass assn. (xeric steppe)	Ridgetops and steep south slopes throughout the area: mostly over 1,800 m.	4,100 (5)
	Other native steppes		1,500 (2)
	Exotic grasslands (old fields)		500 [a]
Shrub steppe	*Big sage/bluebunch wheatgrass assn.*	Most abundant shrub steppe. Alluvial soils on valley floors and west, south, and east slopes: mostly 1,800–2,500 m.	18,300 (22)
	Big sage/Idaho fescue assn.	Mostly south slopes below about 1,800 m.	
Wet meadows	*Hair grass/sedge associes*	Deep alluvial soils along rivers and streams and wet sites throughout the area.	3,200 (4)
Riparian shrub	Willow species	Along rivers, streams, and springs throughout the area.	300 [a]
	Other	As above.	
Misc. vegetation			600 [a]
"Unvegetated"	Rock outcrops, etc.		2,500 (3)
Human developments	Roads, buildings, etc.		200 [a]
Total			82,600

[a]Less than 1%.

were called *associations* (assn), those in seral stages were called *associes* (Daubenmire 1952). Characteristic plants comprised a conspicuous portion of the vegetation.

Some of the characteristic vegetation requires explanation. About 41% of the area is coniferous forest occurring in small stands at lower elevations and as larger contiguous stands around the periphery of the winter range. Much of the area mapped as coniferous forest at low elevations (especially Douglas-fir) has a very open canopy with a bunchgrass understory. Special effort was made to determine that the aspen associes occurs on about 2% of the area. (Many aspen stands were too small to map. The area of unmapped stands was determined in the field and included in the final estimate of aspen abundance.) Barmore (1980) reported 2.8% aspen on the same area. Because of the limits of accuracy of the techniques used, the true value probably lies between 2 and 3%. In addition to the forest types shown, a few hectares each of limber pine and Rocky Mountain juniper are present. The *Idaho fescue/bearded wheatgrass assn* is highly variable and on some slopes grades into an *Idaho fescue/Richardson's needlegrass assn*. These associations also grade into the wet meadow type in many swales. The amounts of the xeric phase of the *bluebunch wheatgrass/Idaho fescue assn* and of the *bluebunch wheatgrass/Sandberg bluegrass assn* are underestimated because they occur on small ridgetops throughout other extensive grasslands. The other native steppes are mostly in the BLA: a *needle-and-thread/blue grama assn* (650 ha) and a *bluebunch wheatgrass/Junegrass assn* (800 ha), the latter on peculiar edaphic mudflows. Grasslands and shrub steppes are described in greater detail in Appendix VI. Old fields are dominated by smooth brome, timothy, crested wheatgrass, or cheatgrass. The hairgrass/sedge meadows also include small marshes dominated by rushes or bulrush. The riparian shrub type was mapped by ground and aerial work and contains vegetation of special interest. Over 295 ha of marsh willows occur on the area (this includes estimates for stands of just a few square meters around springs, etc.). Species such as Geyer's willow, Bebb's willow, mountain willow, blueberry willow, and Wolf's willow dominate these sites but occur with mountain alder, red osier dogwood, and red birch. Perhaps 16 ha of linear-leaved willows (subfamily Longifoliae) occur on sand and gravel bars throughout the area. About 12 ha of various cottonwoods grow along streams and rivers. The combined total of all riparian shrubs is about 0.4% of the northern range in the park; species of willow may account for 0.3%.

The winter range outside the park is dominated by shrub steppe and upland grasslands. Small amounts of Douglas-fir and lodgepole pine occur on upper slopes. Nearly all of the arable bottomland is under cultivation, and part of the upland steppe is grazed by livestock.

The appearance of low-density vegetation, composed of native plant species, on ridgetops and upper slopes of the winter range has been of particular concern (see Past Vegetation, Narrative Reports of Range Conditions, this chapter). In 1970, I mapped (10 cm/1.6 km) the distribution and abundance of vegetation showing 40% or less canopy cover on ridgetops and slopes. About 2,420 ha, mostly upland steppe, are in this category (Table 8.2). The vegetation on these sites grows under extremely harsh topoedaphic conditions and is subject also to periodically heavy ungulate grazing and trampling. The condition of about 640 ha results mainly from peculiar topoedaphic influences. This is especially true on mudflows in the BLA and on the mudstones of Mt. Everts. The remaining 1,780 ha were tentatively classed as "zootic climax" sites (Daubenmire 1968). Given that the area of these sites might be underestimated by 20% because of failure to locate them all, 2,140 ha or 3% of the park winter range may be in

TABLE 8.2
Distribution and Abundance of Ridgetop and Upper-Slope Vegetation with 40% or Less Canopy Cover for Vegetation

VEGETATION TYPE	AREA IN HECTARES	
	BLA	Other Range Areas
Upland steppes[a]	569 (352)[b]	1,758 (288)
Shrub steppe (*big sage/bluebunch wheatgrass assn.*)	10	82
Total	579	1,840

[a] Mostly xeric phase of *bluebunch wheatgrass/Idaho fescue assn.* or *bluebunch wheatgrass/Sandberg bluegrass assn.*, but including other xeric grasslands in the BLA (see Appendix VI).
[b] Hectares due primarily to topoedaphic conditions.

a zootic climax. The ecological significance of these sites is discussed throughout this chapter. The composition and standing crop of the vegetation and the harsh physical environments characteristic of these sites are described in Appendix VI. Sites are dominated by low densities of a comparatively small number of native plant species.

Past Vegetation

Holocene Trends

Pollen profiles show that forests similar to those now present over much of the park have persisted for over 10,000 years—with fluctuations in the relative abundance of major species paralleling fluctuations in climate (Baker 1970, Waddington and Wright 1974). Tundra, which developed at 2,000 m on the northern range following retreat of the main Pinedale glaciers (see Climatic Trends, below), was replaced by a whitebark pine forest about 11,800 years BP (Gennett 1977). This forest was next replaced by lodgepole pine, which was in turn replaced by an open Douglas-fir steppe about 6,600 years BP. Cooler and wetter climates about 1,600 years BP next led to a more dense Douglas-fir forest and to an increase in lodgepole pine, conditions which persist to the present.

Vegetation of the Historical Past

Three hundred nineteen early photos of the park and adjacent areas were collected; vegetative changes were assessed by rephotographing earlier scenes as close to the same season and time of day as possible. Two hundred forty-four of these photos were taken on the seasonal ranges of the northern Yellowstone elk. Additionally, I was able to examine G. Gruell's collection of more than 100 comparative photos of the Bridger-Teton National Forest immediately south of Yellowstone, most of which have been published recently (Gruell 1980a). We (M. Meagher photographed nearly half of the scenes) have used many outstanding early photos by W. H. Jackson and J. P. Iddings. Iddings worked as a geologist in Yellowstone from 1883 to the early 1890s; most of his photos were not captioned. We believe his photos were taken about 1885 except where otherwise indicated.

Discussions of vegetation are based upon the entire collection of comparative photos. Fifty-one pairs are reproduced here (Appendix V). Photos of grasslands, aspen, and willows are greatly overrepresented because of our interest in these communities. Photos of extensive coniferous forests are underrepresented. Most of the original photos were not taken to illustrate conditions of vegetation. The entire collection is on file at Yellowstone National Park.

Photos were especially valuable for showing changes in the extent, composition, and relative density of tree and shrub communities. They often showed the pattern and relative density of herbaceous vegetation and occasionally suggested species composition. Sometimes, we inferred the probable composition of herbaceous vegetation in the original photos by comparisons to present vegetation, from early narrative descriptions, and from the history of human and ungulate use. These interpretations were tempered with the knowledge that the appearance of grasslands can show great annual variations (see Vegetation Measurements, below).

The photos were particularly useful in assessing the appearance of pristine vegetation and evaluating the amount and rate of successional change because of the land-use objectives of the park (to maintain a natural area). They provided a perspective, obtainable in no other way, from which to assess the influence of Euro-American man. The earliest photos from 1871–90 gave the best approximation of pristine conditions. Euro-American man's influence on the vegetation was probably insignificant when the earliest photos were taken (see Chapter 3 and Haines 1977). This was followed by a period of market hunting in and around Yellowstone that reduced native ungulates; photos taken then could show vegetation with less biotic influence than occurred under pristine conditions. Settlement increased around the park by the end of this period; small areas within the park were being grazed by livestock, and attempts at fire suppression began. Still in all, man's direct influence on the vegetation was probably very minor. Photos from 1891 to 1920 record a period that began with minimal potential for influence on vegetation. However, fire suppression increased, several exotic grasses and forbs were introduced (some through cultivation), winter feeding of some native ungulates began, and locally heavy livestock grazing occurred by the end of this period. Photos from 1921–43 were included primarily because they spanned the decade of drought of the 1930s. These also were used to suggest rates of plant succession when compared to the earliest photos.

Although the earliest comparative photos provide a glimpse of a time when the effects of Euro-American man were minimal, they should not be viewed as fixed standards. If available, photos for the period 1771–1871 would doubtless show natural changes, just as have those from 1871–1971.

SPRING, SUMMER, AND AUTUMN RANGES

Spring, summer, and autumn ranges include the Yellowstone River and tributaries from about 2,300 m to over 3,000 m (Fig. 4.2). A total of 21 early photos of these range areas is shown as Plates 1–21 in Appendix V. Boundaries of seasonal ranges of the northern elk are not sharply defined, and some areas shown here as spring and autumn range also support small wintering groups.

Photos (Pls. 12, 19) showed that the vast tracts of coniferous forest between about 2,300 and 2,800 m in the central, southern, and eastern portions of the park generally have changed little in appearance or extent during the last century. Exceptions are discussed below. These forests are dominated by lodgepole pine, with subalpine fir and

Engelmann spruce occurring in more mesic areas such as lakeshores, along streams, and on north slopes (Despain 1973). Douglas-fir occurs in scattered stands in Gardner's Hole and along the east shore of Yellowstone Lake. The effects of past fires and forest insects on stand age, density, and composition are clearly visible in some early photos. Early travelers commented on the difficulty of crossing these extensive stands because of the density of fallen trees and logs (Russell, in Haines 1965a)—a situation that exists today.

Coniferous trees have extended into grasslands in many areas (Pls. 6, 7). These changes, though locally striking, have affected relatively small areas, and the same small meadows visible a century ago in tracts of lodgepole pine can usually be distinguished today (Pl. 19). (Subjective assessments of whether a change was "small" or "large" generally were avoided. In several places such judgments seemed warranted—but represent only my impression of the extent of change in relation to the area under study.) No major changes in forest species composition were suggested. Tree densities increased in some areas (Pl. 7), particularly along ecotones. Changes in age distribution were most conspicuous in stands that were burned prior to the time the original photos were taken (Pls. 4, 10).

Above about 2,700 m, forests were dominated by subalpine fir, lodgepole pine, and whitebark pine. These showed either no change (especially on harsh sites, e.g., Pl. 5) or advances into grasslands (Pl. 1). Characteristically shaped meadows were clearly recognizable a century later (Pl. 17). An increase in tree density has occurred in some stands at higher elevations. Changes in size distributions again were associated with recolonization of previously burned forests. Changes in species composition were not apparent.

From 2,100 to 2,300 m (sometimes the periphery of the winter range) coniferous forests have advanced into sagebrush grassland or open bunchgrass steppe (Pls. 3, 2). Stand density and species composition also have changed. Lodgepole pine and Douglas-fir have increased; aspen has declined (Pls. 2, 3). Although the overall changes were confined to relatively small areas, they were striking (a proportionately large change in one species, e.g., aspen) and probably reflected suppression of natural fires.

These changes described in forests have occurred both on a wide variety of soils derived from diverse parent materials and on many different slopes and exposures.

Grasslands above 2,300 m are conveniently divided into forest parks (characterized by sedge and tufted hairgrass, or mountain brome and bearded wheatgrass, or Idaho fescue and oatgrass), herblands (characterized by mountain brome, bearded wheatgrass, stickseed, and many associated forbs), and alpine tundra. Generally very little change was shown in the distribution and extent of these grasslands or in the pattern and density of herbaceous vegetation. Exceptions included reductions due to forest advancement throughout the area and increases in big sagebrush. Forest parks and herblands have also increased in some areas because of decreases in big sagebrush and willow (see below). Herblands [of special interest because of their importance as elk summer range (Cole 1969b, Gruell 1973, 1980a,b)] showed little change in appearance (Pls. 5, 8) except for a minor decrease of big sagebrush (Pl. 7). Harsh, poorly vegetated areas covered with late-melting snowbanks (Pls. 16, 20, 21) remained unchanged. The sparse vegetation on highly erodable Absaroka volcanic substrates showed little change (Pl. 17). The appearance of vegetation on elk bedding areas (Pls. 9, 16) and on small wintering areas (Pl. 1) also was unchanged.

Early photos suggested substantial pocket gopher burrowing in some herblands and meadows (Pls. 5, 6, 9)—which continues at present. Meagher (1973) and Gruell

(1973) have summarized historic narrative accounts of extensive gopher burrowings in high-elevation grasslands.

Although some obvious changes in composition of forbs and grasses were notable on localized sites (e.g., Pl. 4), the evidence does not suggest that these changes have been extensive. Tweedy's (1886) account of species and their relative abundance in higher-elevation grasslands was based upon his 1884–85 collection and others as early as 1871. After allowing for taxonomic changes, this description is still accurate with the exception that exotic species have been introduced inadvertently along established trails and in livestock grazing areas. Fire suppression and climatic fluctuations probably shifted composition of herbaceous species. This effect of fire suppression is probably insignificant at higher elevations, where fires occurred at minimum intervals of 300–400 years (Romme 1979) and where suppression has been effective for only a short period.

Various types of sagebrush grasslands are shown in early photos at elevations of 2,300–2,800 m. These have shown a complex pattern of change. A minor decrease in the distribution of big sagebrush occurred in some forest parks and herblands from about 2,300 to 2,600 m (Pl. 2). Sagebrush has increased on other open grasslands around 2,300 m (Pl. 3), probably influenced by fire suppression. In most areas no change can be detected. The overall change in distribution of sagebrush grassland involved a small total area.

Willow communities have shown a net decrease throughout the area, even at the highest elevations. This has occurred along flood plains (Pls. 7, 14) as well as in forest parks and subalpine meadows (Pl. 18). This same type of change has occurred in other areas of the park (Meagher, unpubl.), outside the park (Pl. 15), and in other mountain areas of Wyoming (Gruell 1980a). In the Gardner's Hole area, evidence suggests that decreases in willow accelerated during the 1930s drought. Other sites showed no change in the distribution of willow (Pl. 10). Primary successional changes from willow to forest parks and subalpine meadows, though locally spectacular and occurring throughout the area, have involved a very small total area. (In selecting photos to show the widespread nature of these changes we may give an exaggerated impression of their extent.) It seemed unlikely that herbivores (elk, moose, beaver, etc.) were a driving force in changes at these elevations.

Hydrosere succession has resulted in local changes as sedge meadows replaced open-water ponds (Pl. 11). This has occurred in other areas of the park (Meagher, unpubl.).

WINTER RANGE

The winter range (shown in Pls. 22–51) was divided into the main park range (Pls. 22–44), the BLA within the park (Pls. 45–48), and the range outside park boundaries (Pls. 49–51), because of very different histories of human use.

The most conspicuous changes shown on the main winter range occurred in the amount, density, composition, and size (age) of forest communities (Pls. 25, 28, 29, 35, 42). These changes took place on a wide variety of soils derived from very different types of parent materials. The amount of coniferous forest cover increased, mostly on north slopes (ENE to WNW) and recolonized burns (evidence for fire exists in the original photos Pls. 24, 29, 34). Forest invaded bunchgrass communities (mainly Idaho fescue), big sagebrush/Idaho fescue steppes, and aspen stands. The increase was much less on south slopes (ESE to WSW) and on valley bottoms. Increases in forest occurred throughout the area along previous forest–grassland ecotones. Based on all photos, especially those showing extensive panoramas, and examinations of the ages of trees in various stands, I estimate that this increase occurred over about 5% of the area.

Changes in composition and density occurred within the forests. Douglas-fir and lodgepole pine have increased on upland sites (e.g., Pl. 34). Engelmann spruce and subalpine fir have increased to a much lesser extent along streams. Minor increases in Rocky Mountain juniper have occurred below 2,000 m (Pl. 32). Aspen has decreased in relative abundance and density throughout the area (e.g., Pls. 33, 34, 42)—mostly on north slopes (ENE to WNW) and in swales, but to a lesser extent along streams and around small springs or seeps on south slopes. Compared to 2–3% of the winter range now in aspen, I estimate that 4–6% was aspen in the original photos. A vegetation map of the winter range made in the early 1930s supported this estimate. Calculations from Barmore (1975:294) suggest that perhaps 3.5–4.0% of 69,025 ha may have been aspen. The decrease since the 1930s has affected 0.5–2% of the winter range. Most aspen was seral to conifers—primarily Douglas-fir but also to lodgepole pine, Engelmann spruce, and subalpine fir. Small amounts were replaced by sagebrush grassland on dry sites or by the exotic timothy grass in wetter swale areas.

The size and, by inference, age distribution of forest stands has changed from variable aged with scattered young stands to older trees in more mature stands. This is especially noticeable in aspen—almost always shown as low, very dense, vigorous-appearing stands in early photos (through perhaps 1900–1920). These stands are now mature with little or no aspen reproduction in the understories.

Other sets of comparative photos suggested that the advancement of conifers has been a slow but continuous process. The decrease of aspen also has been slow but continuous, except that some stands showed vegetative reproduction on at least their margins into the 1920s (Pl. 36). The decrease may have been accelerated by the drought of the 1930s plus more effective suppression of fires (see below).

Three narratives refer to aspen during the 1880s to the early 1930s. Hague (1886) observed that fires had occurred frequently in the northern part of Yellowstone park during the 19th century and that aspen was "the first tree to spring up upon recently burned areas. By so doing it helps conceal unsightly charred trunks, and adds bright color to the landscape." Warren (1926) commented on the beaver cutting of aspen on portions of the winter range from 1921 to 1923. This was extensive enough that Warren recommended a beaver control program. He also commented on a "good many very young aspens about Camp Roosevelt." This represented profuse sprouting on the periphery of some stands cut by beaver (Pl. 34). Skinner (no date, written ~ 1935) also commented on the aspen in the 1920s and 1930s. He was clearly in error on successional relationships of aspen to conifers and overestimated the amount of aspen in the park, but he did provide observations of periodic heavy browsing of aspen by elk and the ability of stands to recover. Skinner also observed sprouting of some stands and commented that this new growth "amply replaces all aspens destroyed by all causes operating *a hundred yards or more from ponds and streams.*" Those closer to water were heavily cut by beaver. Decreases in aspen have occurred outside the winter range during this same period (Pls. 2, 3).

Early photos showed clearly that big sagebrush was present as a dominant overstory shrub (along with rabbitbrush, horsebrush, etc.) among bunchgrasses (probably Idaho fescue, bluebunch wheatgrass, and needlegrasses) on older flood plain terraces, swales, and on lower slopes of all exposures. Sagebrush has increased in extent on a wide variety of slopes and exposures (e.g., Pls. 34, 35). This increase has occurred in swales and on the periphery of the winter range (Pl. 3) where ungulate density was comparatively low. Sagebrush also has declined on some sites (Pl. 32) and has been eliminated by cultivation from other small areas. Sagebrush declined along the Gardner River from Mammoth to Gardiner in areas that once were heavily grazed by livestock. My interpretations of changes at sites formerly grazed by livestock are similar to those made below for the BLA. Historically, the distribution and abundance of big sagebrush showed great variation depending upon fire frequency—just as it would now if fire were allowed to burn unchecked. Based upon the distribution suggested by the original photos, and interpretations of fire history and frequency (Houston 1973), an educated guess would be that 5% more of the winter range is now a sagebrush steppe.

The appearance of bunchgrass communities changed very little for most of the area. Some bunchgrass sites became sagebrush steppe or forest. In many cases bunchgrasses persisted as understory in recently forested areas. Grasslands may show large annual changes in appearance because of precipitation (see Vegetation Measurements, below), but we have little evidence to suggest that substantial changes have occurred in composition. Tweedy's 1886 description of the relative abundance and distribution of grasses still would apply to the winter range. Seeming exceptions are the result of changing taxonomy—Tweedy's *Festuca ovina* is clearly *F. idahoensis, Poa tenuifolia* is part of the *P. sandbergii* complex, and *Stipa viridula* is *S. occidentalis*. These latter two species were often confused in early taxonomic literature (Maze pers. commun. 1974, Rominger pers. commun. 1974). Other exceptions would include the effects of fire suppression on species abundance and where exotic grasses or forbs have become established.

The low-density herbaceous vegetation on certain ridge tops and steep slopes (Pls. 23, 25, 32, 37, 38, 43) was of special interest. These sites, representing very harsh topoedaphic conditions, received consistently heavy foraging and trampling by elk and other ungulates during winter and spring. Early photos (17 photos, 1871–90; 12 photos, 1891–1921) showed the presence of such sites a century ago; retakes suggested no change in size or density of vegetation. Such sites represent about 3% of the winter range in the park. Based upon these photos and studies of habitat use and forage utilization (Chap. 9), most of these were considered to represent naturally occurring zootic climax vegetation as influenced by the extremely harsh physical environment. Similar sites are found in early photos of winter ranges in the Jackson Hole area (Gruell 1980a).

Photos also showed that sedge meadows (often containing rush and hairgrass) increased slightly as hydrosere succession occurred—frequently associated with the activities of beaver (Pl. 29). The sedge and hairgrass component decreased in some meadows where the exotic timothy grass invaded or was formerly cultivated (Pl. 31).

Willows and associated riparian vegetation (mountain alder, cottonwood, red birch) have shown a net decrease. Although locally spectacular (Pl. 44), this change has affected relatively small areas overall. Some sites showed little or no change; on others, riparian vegetation apparently increased. Both narratives and photos (see Spring, Summer, and Autumn Ranges, above) suggest that the decreases in willows occurred mostly during the 1930s drought, on upper flood plain terraces. Photographic evidence together with field reconnaissance of flood plains suggested that not much more than twice the present amount of willow and associated shrubs (300 ha) occurred on the area 100 years ago with the decrease affecting less than 0.5% of the area. In particular, there was no evidence for vast reductions in willow on the winter range. Photos show that willows decreased outside the ungulate winter ranges as well during this period.

Photos show other things of interest. Clumps of native wildrye grass apparently persisted for very long periods (Pl. 41). Early roadbeds were quickly revegetated with native species when abandoned (Pl. 40). Some conifers showed a browse line as a result of ungulate foraging on lower branches (Pls. 34, 38). These were present in both early photos and retakes but are more conspicuous in the latter because of increased tree density. Browse lines also are conspicuous in historic photos of elk winter ranges in the Jackson Hole area (Gruell 1980a).

The Boundary Line Area.   The history of human use, the semiarid climate, and the very different geology and soils (Frazer et al. 1969) made the interpretation of vegetative changes in the BLA (mostly 1,500–1,800 m in elevation) very difficult. We lack photos taken before 1893 for the area, so the character of the pristine vegetation must be inferred from photos of immediately adjacent sites. Early travelers commented on the area in unflattering terms. Gillette (1870) observed in August 1870 that the BLA was "very rough and barren, has a little the appearance of the Badlands of the Missouri River." Doane (in Bonney 1970) commented on the area from the Devil's Slide to the Gardner River (traversing most of the present BLA) in August 1870 as "passing from a dead level alkali plain to a succession of plateaus covered with a sterile soil" (almost certainly a series of mudflows). He also commented that the area at the mouth of the Gardner River was their first poor campsite, with "grass being very scarce." Elements of these descriptions apply today. At present the 4,900-ha BLA is composed of mud or earth flows with bentonite clay soils (820 ha), abandoned agricultural fields in bottomlands (230 ha), and other geologic substrates including alluvial deposits, various glacial deposits, and a series of Cretaceous deposits of sandstones, mudstones, etc. (3,850 ha).

Photos suggested that historically the upland alluvial and glacial deposits were mostly bunchgrass steppe—probably dominated by needle-and-thread and bluebunch wheatgrass, with winterfat, fringed sagebrush, and prickly pear on xeric sites (see Winter Range Outside the Park, below). Big sagebrush occurred in more mesic swales. Open Douglas-fir forests occurred on north slopes, with Idaho fescue as the dominant grass. Scattered Rocky Mountain juniper occurred at lower elevations. The area doubtless was swept periodically by fires. Photos taken during later periods show few changes on the more mesic north slopes (Pl. 48), except that Douglas-fir forests have increased in extent and density and aspen has decreased. Other photos showed changes in the density and extent of big sagebrush. Some showed high densities of sagebrush in areas that were grazed by livestock up to 1932, followed by its decrease and a marked *increase* in native perennial grasses (Pl. 45). The abundance of big sagebrush on some of these upland sites probably represents a grazing disclimax (see Daubenmire 1968:237) induced by livestock and reduced fire frequency. Sagebrush decreased in this semiarid area and perennial grasses increased following the removal of livestock— even during the drought of the 1930s. This interpretation was also supported by Pl. 45, which shows sagebrush persisting *inside* the park where heavy livestock grazing still occurred in 1972 and by measurements of vegetation at this site (see Grasslands in BLA, Appendix VI). This return to more pristine conditions occurred *despite* winter and spring grazing by native ungulates. The decrease in sagebrush was accelerated during the drought (see Bauer's 1938 report, Appendix VII).

The pristine vegetation of abandoned hayfields may have been bunchgrass steppe (needle-and-thread and bluebunch wheatgrass), with sagebrush in more mesic sites. Exotic grasses (smooth brome, timothy, quackgrass, crested wheatgrass, and cheatgrass) are now the dominant vegetation in old fields, although native species are invading the peripheries of some stands.

The character of pristine vegetation of mudflows and earthslides remains an enigma. Our earliest photo, taken about 1893 (Pl. 46), suggested that ridgetops and upper slopes were such extremely harsh sites that only low-density herbaceous vegetation could exist. Swales supported a variety of grasses and shrubs—dominated by big sagebrush. Photos of some mudflows suggested no change. Others taken during intervening periods of livestock grazing showed little change in the appearance of upper slopes (Pl. 47); some showed scattered big sagebrush. Big sagebrush has subsequently decreased on slope and swale sites (Pls. 46, 47) following removal of livestock and concurrent with increased grazing on sagebrush by native ungulates. The decrease accelerated during the drought.

This decrease of sagebrush in swales could be interpreted as unnatural retrogressive succession (i.e., succession from an established climax to a more pioneer sere) caused by native ungulates artificially concentrated along the boundary. This interpretation is supported by the persistence of sagebrush in swales where native ungulates generally were excluded (e.g., cemetery, exclosures) but is confounded by at least three other formidable variables. First, the decrease in sagebrush has been associated with a concurrent change in shrub composition, with greasewood, saltbush, winterfat, spiny hopsage, and rabbitbrushes either increasing or becoming more conspicuous (Pl. 47)—some of these are quite palatable to native ungulates. Also, sagebrush has persisted as a dominant in swales adjacent to sites from which it has disappeared (Pl. 48); seemingly if native ungulates could eliminate it from one site they should have been capable of causing more widespread decreases. (This observation could also mean that sagebrush plants on mudflows were simply less capable of withstanding intense browsing.) Finally, the character of the entire swale plant community has been changed with the introduction and dominance of cheatgrass and quackgrass (Pl. 47). If swales capable of supporting sagebrush occupied 50% of the mudflows, then the conspicuous net decrease covered 410 ha—a relatively small area.

Winter Range Outside the Park. My main interest was to establish the character of the pristine vegetation on the winter range outside the park, rather than to document the effects of increased livestock grazing and settlement during intervening years. W. H. Jackson's 1871 photos (Pls. 49–51) did this nicely. Much of the range appears originally to have been a bunchgrass steppe, probably dominated by needle-and-thread and bluebunch wheatgrass, with sagebrush steppes occurring in swales and on lower slopes. Rabbitbrushes, winterfat, and prickly pear occurred in the steppes. Small stands of Douglas-fir grew at higher elevations, scattered Rocky Mountain juniper at lower elevations. Suggested changes included a minor increase in extent and density of forests and increased distribution of sagebrush steppe with a corresponding decrease in bunchgrass steppe. Virtually all arable bottomlands now are under cultivation. I attribute most of these changes to some combination of increased fire suppression and a long history of settlement, with attendant grazing by livestock.

Vegetation Measurements

Measurements of the vegetation on the winter range have been made for the period from 1930 to 1978 (Table 8.3). The purpose of these repeated measurements has been

TABLE 8.3

Summary of the Types of Vegetation Measurements Repeated over Time on the Northern Winter Range, 1930–78

VEGETATION AND MEASUREMENTS[a]	SAMPLE UNITS (No.)		YEARS MEASURED 1930	1940	1950	1960	1970	1980
Herbaceous vegetation								
Herbage production quads	A[b]	4–15 (4)[c]		×××××××			×	××
Excl. m² quads	B	10–20 (4–8)	× ××	××××	×			
ft² density tr.	C	11 (4)		×× ×				
Photo tr.	D	10 (6)			×××××××××			
Photo points	D	10 (9)			×××××××××			
Parker tr. 1957, 1962 excl.	E	20–38 (8–12)				×	×	×
Chart quads 1957, 1962 excl.	B	24–37 (8–12)				×	×	×
Parker tr.	E	14 (6)			×[d]		×	×
Herbaceous vegetation—harsh physiographic sites								
ft²-density tr.	C	9 (3)		×				
yd² quads	B,D19	(6)			×××××××××××		×××××××	×××
Line intercept tr.	B	19 (13)			× ×			
Agronomy cage-yd² quads	D	10 (4)			× ×			
Trees and shrubs								
Excl.—aspen	F	4		×××××××××			×	
Aspen reproduction	F	20 ?			×××××			
Aspen reproduction	F	4–20 ?					×××××× ×	
Excl.—willow	F	1		?				
Photo points—sage	D	21–24 (21–24)				×××××××××××		
Belt tr.—aspen 1957, 1962 excl.	F	4–5				×	×	×
Belt tr.—willow 1957, 1962 excl.	F	9				×	×	×
Belt tr.—shrubs 1957, 1962 excl.	F	2–3				×	×	×
Belt tr.—sage 1957, 1962 excl.	F	6–10 (2–3)				×	×	×

[a] Quadrats (quads), transects (tr.), exclosures (excl.).

[b] Types of measurements include: A, clipping and weighing herbage; B, measuring basal area or basal intercept—sometimes with crown cover of shrubs; C, estimating foliage area; D, visual examination of density, composition, or herbage production; E, plant frequency and photos (grass vigor measured in exclosure studies in 1962, 1965, 1967, 1977); F, density, canopy area, and height.

[c] Number of units in BLA given in parentheses.

[d] Mostly in 1955, some in 1954 and 1956.

to evaluate attributes of plant communities or plant species—density, succession, and composition—in relation to climate and ungulate foraging.

Sample units on *Herbaceous vegetation* were located on bunchgrass steppe, wet meadow, and sagebrush steppe, and measured a wide variety of species, including some shrubs. Units on *Herbaceous vegetation–harsh physiographic sites* usually sampled xeric bunchgrass steppe on ridgetops or steep slopes characteristic of about 3% of the winter range. Units on *Trees and shrubs* usually sampled single woody species. All exclosure studies were designed to compare the treatment of grazing with the treatment of no grazing by native ungulates.

About 69% of the 308 sample units were on steppe; 27% of the steppe units were on harsh physiographic sites. Measurements of trees and shrubs were nearly all on either aspen, willows, or big sagebrush. About 27% of all measurements were in the BLA (and many were located on mudflow substrates). Some units were remeasured for 17–30 years. In addition to repeated measurements, several descriptive measurements and surveys of the vegetation have been made.

Few areas have a backlog of vegetation measurements that seemingly could be used to measure attributes of plant communities and the effects of foraging by native ungulates. Furthermore, the opportunity to evaluate these effects by using large-scale experimental manipulations of native ungulate populations is rare, especially in national parks. Elk herd reductions gave a perspective on ungulate–habitat relationships that could have been obtained in no other way. Pronghorn and bison populations also were reduced (Chap. 10). Measurements from the early 1950s to 1978, including those associated with exclosures established in 1957 and 1962, therefore, were of particular interest, because they spanned the period of ungulate reductions and subsequent increases.

An analysis of each set of measurements in relation to climate and ungulate foraging is given in Appendix VI and is summarized here.

Herbaceous Vegetation

Three herbage production studies spanned a 29-year period from 1935 to 1963 and showed that annual variation in the autumn standing crop of herbaceous vegetation on certain upland sites was four to five times greater during periods of abundant precipitation than during droughts. Production also varied annually on wet meadows and mesic upland steppes. The samples were not a true measure of annual above-ground biomass production by plants, because plants were sometimes grazed in spring prior to being clipped in the autumn. They exaggerated the annual variations in the absolute abundance of forage on the winter range, because other sites (lower slopes, forest, shrubs, bottomlands) were not representatively sampled. Nevertheless, there were substantial annual fluctuations in the absolute abundance of forage on the winter range as a result of variation in growing conditions.

Only limited interpretations were possible, but the square-meter quadrats and square-foot density transects measured from 1930 to 1943 suggested that the decrease and subsequent increase in basal area and plant cover paralleled changes in growing conditions and showed little relationship to elk numbers. Narrative accounts from this period supported these observations. Vegetation (as recorded on transects) in the BLA also may have been recovering from the effects of past livestock grazing. Exclosure fences affected microclimates and precluded an assessment of the effects of grazing on plant area.

Photo transects and photo points measured from 1949 to 1958 showed annual fluctuations in autumn standing crop (most pronounced in BLA) but no consistent change in composition or density. Abundance of annual species varied greatly. Individual perennial plants persisted throughout the study period. Variations in standing crop appeared to be related to growing conditions, although these effects were not easily separated from effects of reduced elk densities in the BLA.

The square yard quadrats measured from 1948 to 1978 on harsh physiographic sites were heavily utilized and trampled by ungulates but did not show progressive changes in density, composition, or basal area over the study period. Some perennials appeared to persist over the entire period. A temporary increase in standing crop of perennial grasses (also influenced by accumulations of herbage) reflected a combination of grazing and climatic influences. Elk may have maintained a reduced autumn standing crop of vegetation but may not have greatly influenced annual productivity, since these plants also were grazed in the spring. Increased crown size on certain shrubs probably reflected less browsing. Litter did not accumulate on most sites, even with reduced grazing.

The square-foot density transects, measured in 1943 and 1947, and the line intercept transects, measured in 1948 and 1952, were located on harsh physiographic sites and apparently measured fluctuations in plant cover and basal area associated with growing conditions. Changes measured on the line intercept transects showed little correlation with adjacent square-yard quadrats. Agronomy cages measured in 1949 and 1954 showed little evident change in species composition. Cages probably altered microclimates.

Parker transects and chart quadrat exclosure studies measured from 1958 to 1974 showed little or no consistent difference between the treatments of nongrazing and grazing by native ungulates on species abundance, basal cover, and composition. Differences over time appeared to have been related more to fluctuations in growing conditions. Some perennial grasses decreased with protection from grazing, although at these lower plant densities the maximum inflorescence height or leaf length was somewhat greater, especially on ridgetop and upper-slope sites. Ungulate browsing did influence crown size and possibly density of certain shrubs, especially on ridgetop and upper-slope sites. Accumulations of litter sometimes were greater on protected plots, but litter did not accumulate on some ridgetop sites, even with protection. Parker transects and chart quadrats on mudflows in the BLA showed an increase in canopy size and density of big sagebrush inside exclosures; no change occurred outside, even at greatly reduced densities of elk and pronghorn.

Parker transects located on the open range and measured from 1954 to 1974 suggested that fluctuations in composition and abundance of perennial grasses and forbs were related more to growing conditions and occasionally to pocket gophers than to ungulate densities (BLA excepted). Increased crown size of some shrubs on ridgetop sites was probably related to lower ungulate densities. The increase in perennial grasses and forbs for 1955–67 on BLA transects clearly occurred with both reduced ungulate grazing and more favorable climatic conditions. Other measurements or photos in this same area prior to ungulate reductions also showed great annual variation that seemed more closely associated with climate. Separation of biotic from climatic effects was especially difficult in the BLA. Changes in perennial grasses and forbs may have been related more to climatic fluctuations than ungulate effects. Increased crown size on shrubs such as rabbitbrushes may reflect reduced browsing.

Trees and Shrubs

The combined aspen studies (exclosure studies 1935–65, aspen reproduction 1948–52 and 1963–69, aspen survey, 1970, aspen belt transects 1958–74) showed that successful aspen regeneration generally failed to occur either before or after elk reductions (exceptions included scattered stands in some roadside areas and in some peripheral range areas). Fences on two small exclosures altered microclimates. Some stands in exclosures showed successful low-density vegetative reproduction; others showed none. Most stands on the winter range showed some vegetative reproduction that was heavily browsed even at low elk densities; i.e., there was little measureable relationship between ungulate levels and utilization.

The combined willow exclosure studies (one exclosure, 1930s; willow belt transects, 1958–74) showed that ungulate browsing suppressed cover and height of willows when compared to a treatment of no browsing. Photos suggested that willows were hedged less from 1962 to 1965 when compared to 1958 and 1974. Utilization of willows was high in 1970–78 and increased along roadsides. Observations for 1960–75 showed heavy utilization of willows on the Blacktail Plateau throughout the period of elk reductions (Meagher pers. commun. 1975). Willow density apparently did not increase in exclosures even with the absence of browsing for 12–17 years. Density did not decrease with continued heavy browsing outside exclosures.

The combined studies on big sagebrush (sagebrush photo points BLA, belt transects 1958–74) suggested that the increased crown size and plant density on ecotones between sagebrush steppe and bunchgrass communities reflected either the reduction in browsing both inside and outside exclosures or the general increase in sagebrush characteristic of the winter range during the past century, related primarily to fire suppression. Browsing of sagebrush in the BLA was substantial (Chap. 10), even at low elk and pronghorn densities (mule deer numbers were not reduced), and no response in sagebrush cover or density occurred on the sample units outside the exclosures. These transects were located on mudflows, where the reduction in sagebrush could reflect, in part, the decreasing density of sagebrush in a grazing disclimax established by livestock. Interpreting rates of change on transects inside exclosures relative to those outside was difficult, because in some cases those inside had both higher initial densities and cover.

Three–six shrub species measured inside and outside one exclosure from 1958 to 1974 showed little consistent relationship to ungulate densities. Browsing suppressed crown cover of serviceberry and rabbitbrush on some slope sites even at low elk densities.

Descriptive measurements of vegetation (Appendix VI) suggested that the decrease in big sagebrush on upland sites in the semiarid environment of the BLA largely represented a return to more pristine conditions following removal of livestock. Differences in vegetation between mudflows and alluvial soils in the BLA were largely inherent, although some departures from natural conditions of vegetation in the BLA from abusive past livestock grazing or from artificially high densities of native ungulates almost certainly occurred in local areas.

Narrative Reports of Range Conditions

Narrative reports by personnel engaged in field studies of the vegetation on the northern range over the period 1930–58 were extracted mostly from unpublished range reports (Appendix VII). These illustrated the conditions of vegetation that were of concern and the changes in interpretations of range conditions over time. Also, many of these findings subsequently have been misinterpreted.

Rush based his assessment of range conditions in the early 1930s primarily upon comparison with his observations during a 1914 horseback trip through part of the winter range (at a time when there were certainly as many elk as in the 1930s). He considered that carrying capacity decreased from his earlier trip because of drought and grazing. The basis for the assessment of a large-scale decrease in carrying capacity is not clear. He may have made a subjective assessment of the appearance of the range or believed that more than twice as many elk inhabited the area about the time of his 1914 trip and that the area was not historical elk winter range. (Both beliefs were incorrect.) Specific mention of overgrazed and eroded conditions referred to three areas within the park where livestock grazing occurred and where a semidomesticated, unnaturally large bison herd ranged for part of the year. He considered ranges outside the park to be in poor condition because of heavy livestock grazing. Rush recognized the cursory and subjective nature of his range assessments, a fact which seems to have been overlooked in subsequent references to his findings.

Observations made by Grimm and Gammill from 1935 to 1947 were especially valuable because they spanned the most severe part of the drought as well as the subsequent recovery. As the drought broke and both the density and composition of herbaceous vegetation showed marked improvement in spite of thousands of wintering elk, they recognized drought as being of overwhelming importance. Little correlation occurred between the reported condition of wintering elk or elk numbers and assessments of range conditions. Grimm also appreciated the difficulty of making short-term interpretations of range conditions in the BLA because of past human use. Low densities of herbaceous vegetation on certain ridgetop sites—"spot damage" (i.e., zootic climax vegetation)—were recognized as probably a natural or at least inevitable situation. The status of aspen and willow was of concern, but Grimm recognized the limitations and possible sources of error in the use of exclosures to assess conditions.

Kittams considered that the northern winter range was overgrazed and in less than desirable condition during 1947–58. Reports show that his primary concerns were the condition of the vegetation in the BLA (especially the herbaceous vegetation on mudflow substrates and the decrease in big sagebrush) and the appearance and utilization of herbaceous vegetation on ridgetop and steep slope sites throughout the winter range. Specific comments on erosion and illustrative photos both refer to such sites. Kittams equated such sites to "critical winter range" and viewed them as having retrogressed from pristine conditions. The utilization of aspen and willow stands was also of major concern.

Certain concerns were common to these narratives. The condition of herbaceous vegetation over much of the range was considered to have retrogressed during the drought, but assessments of general retrogressive plant succession ceased at the break of drought conditions. The condition of herbaceous vegetation on small ridgetop and steep slope areas was sometimes viewed as retrogressive succession and sometimes as natural. The interpretation that these sites had retrogressed was apparently always based upon the *assumption* of what such sites "should" look like; i.e., no data supported this interpretation. Herbaceous vegetation in the BLA was considered to illustrate retrogressive succession resulting from past human activities and livestock grazing, although past human use was often omitted from the later writings. Both the presence of big sagebrush in the BLA and its subsequent decrease were interpreted as plant retrogression due to grazing. Much of this decrease occurred during the drought (Bauer 1938). All range assessments of this period expressed concern over the condition and utilization of willow and aspen. Grimm and others recognized that drought contributed to the decrease of these species, but the effects of fire suppression were not fully appreciated. Bauer (1939) documented the mortality of aspen during the drought with associated browsing. Studies in eastern Montana also documented extensive mortality of sagebrush and "damage" to flood plain species such as cottonwood during this drought (Ellison and Woolfolk 1937). References to erosion in the park apparently refer to areas grazed by livestock, to small ridgetop and steep slope sites, to mudflows, and probably to the Cretaceous mudstones of Mt. Everts (see Erosion). Most processes of erosion were temporarily accelerated during the drought of the 1930s.

These writings also illustrated frustration with concepts of range management designed primarily for livestock and with the limitations of conventional range measurements that used "rules of thumb" for "proper utilization," etc. Techniques that initially seemed promising were repeatedly abandoned, followed sometimes by greater reliance on range reconnaissance. The futility of attempting to separate cause from effect and to interpret short-term changes in vegetation appearance was also apparent from these writings. These authors recognized the great variability in weather conditions and the contingencies for elk to obtain forage during adverse conditions. Elk numbers showed no relationship to the range manager's assessments of changes in carrying capacity. The carrying capacity of concern was economic carrying capacity; the distinction between this capacity and ecological carrying capacity usually was not recognized.

Windswept ridgetops and steep south slopes were classed as "critical winter range" for elk during the latter part of this period. This designation apparently was based on observations that these sites provided the most available forage source and were heavily utilized and trampled. The assumption also was made that the vegetation had retrogressed from a climax condition. The term "overgrazed" was loosely used throughout this period to refer to everything from heavy *utilization* of cured grass leaves and of individual plants to presumed *retrogressive* succession. The term, as used, was really a subjective assessment that had little clear biological meaning.

In addition to these observations by park personnel, several reports of range conditions originated from short-term inspection trips during this period (Wright 1934, Wright and Thompson 1935, Cahalane 1943). These writers were unfamiliar with the history of human and livestock use on certain sites and sometimes used photos of the BLA, old horse pastures, elk feedgrounds, etc., to illustrate overall conditions. They also underestimated the effects of drought, fire suppression, and edaphic influences.

Abiotic Influences on the Vegetation

Climatic Trends

The climate of the past century or two was of particular interest because of the documented changes in vegetation of the park. Weather records, available for Mammoth Hot Springs since 1887 and for other stations for shorter periods, were examined for climatic trends. I have drawn from recent tabulations and analyses by Dirks (1974, 1975) and Dirks and Martner (1978).

The Pinedale glaciation of approximately 25,000–10,800 or perhaps 8,500 years BP (Richmond 1965, 1972, Keefer 1972, Bryson and Hare 1974) provides a useful perspective for assessing recent climatic trends in Yellowstone. About 15,000 years BP nearly all of the area that became Yellowstone Park was covered with an ice sheet that may have exceeded 900 m in depth. Mean annual surface temperature differences from full glacial to the present interglacial may have been only 4–6°C on a global basis (Bryson 1974). Baker (1970) calculated that the moist cold late-glacial climate of the Yellowstone plateau had a mean annual temperature about 4°C colder than at present.

The warming that terminated the Pinedale glaciation on the Yellowstone plateau increased rapidly about 11,500 years BP (Waddington and Wright 1974). This trend culminated in the warmer, drier "Altithermal," variously dated from about 9,000 or 7,500 years to 4,500 years BP (Baker 1970, Richmond 1965, Waddington and Wright 1974, Gennett 1977). Mean millenial temperatures for 40–90°N latitude might have been 1.6–1.9°C warmer during the Altithermal when compared to the previous millenium (Bray 1971). Richmond (1972) calculated a mean July free-air temperature at orographic snowline for the Yellowstone area as 2.6°C higher during the warmest part of the Altithermal than at present.

In Yellowstone, the Altithermal was terminated by a return to colder climates, which generally have continued to the present. This interpretation was suggested by changes in pollen profiles (Baker 1970, Waddington and Wright 1974, Gennett 1977) and by the occurrence of at least two neoglacial stades (Richmond 1965, 1972, Porter and Denton 1967). A colder, moister climate (the Temple Lake neoglacial stade) occurred in Yellowstone about 2,800 years BP (Richmond 1965, 1972, Baker 1970). Milder climates returned but again reverted to colder conditions during the Little Ice Age (LIA) from about 1550 to 1900 AD (the Gannett Peak neoglacial stade). The LIA marks the most significant climatic aberration to have occurred during the past 2,000 years; a wealth of documentary materials exists to support its occurrence and effects (Bray 1971, Porter and Denton 1967). Evidence for the occurrence of cirque glaciers during Gannett Peak times occurs throughout Yellowstone (Richmond 1965, pers. commun. 1971). Although the precise dates of the stade have not been determined for Yellowstone, Benedict (1968) dated the occurrence of the Gannett Peak advance in the Colorado Front Range from 1650 to 1850 AD. On a global basis, the coldest part of the LIA may have occurred from about 1650 to 1700 AD. An upward trend in temperatures began after the early 18th century and was especially pronounced in the 1930s. Periodic reversions to colder climates also occurred during this period (Bray 1971). Richmond (pers. commun. 1971) suggested that changes in mean temperatures for the Yellowstone area during Gannett Peak advances would have been small, but that a decrease of a few degrees in mean July temperatures may have occurred. The climate during advances may have been characterized by later springs, earlier autumns, more cloudy weather, more water in streams, larger springs, and more swampy ground. South-facing slopes would still have been very dry in summer.

Annual and seasonal trends in temperature and precipitation for Mammoth Hot Springs are shown as moving averages in Figs. 8.1 and 8.2. Moving averages are an artificial time series that smooth short-term fluctuations to give long-term trends (Barry and Chorley 1968), but they have the disadvantage of losing some of the data at each end of the series and of obscuring extremes that may be of biological importance.

FIGURE 8.1.

Annual and seasonal temperature trends at Mammoth Hot Springs, Yellowstone National Park, as 15-year moving averages.

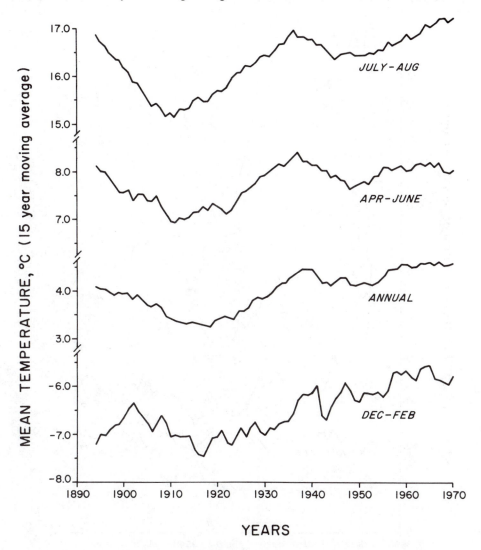

YEARS

An increase in mean annual temperature of 0.5–1.0°C occurred from the late 1890s to 1972. A period of especially low temperatures occurred during 1910–20; especially high temperatures, 1930s and late 1950s into the 1960s. Seasonal temperatures generally showed similar trends. Those for December–February suggested a short period of relatively warmer temperatures in the late 1890s to early 1900s, followed by colder temperatures, which were then followed by a rise of nearly 2°C from about 1915 to the present. This increase in annual winter temperature was significant (Cox-Stewart test, P < .05) over the 1887–1977 period, but changes in the methods of making climatic readings meant that it was necessary to evaluate these records to determine whether or not indicated trends were real. Wahl (1968) tested early measurements that were collected in a manner similar to Yellowstone's and concluded that changes in

FIGURE 8.2.
Annual and seasonal precipitation trends at Mammoth Hot Springs, Yellowstone National Park, as 15-year moving averages.

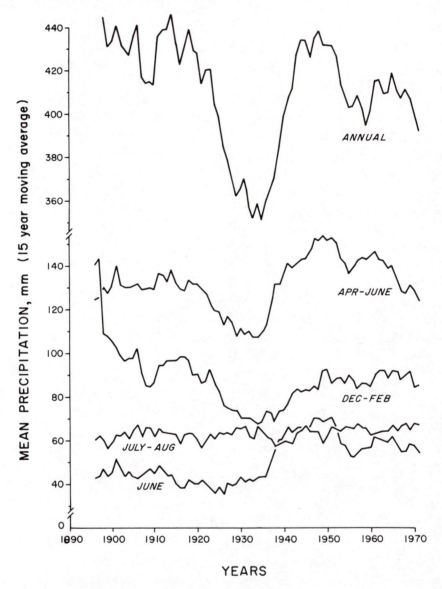

methods could not explain the differences observed; the records could be used to show trends. The Mammoth data were tested to determine if inhomogeneities existed in the record that could be attributed to instrumentation, station location, etc. (Stockton 1973, Bradley 1974). None was found. Shorter January–February records for the Lamar Ranger Station (1923–72) and Tower Falls Ranger Station (1933–72) generally paralleled those for Mammoth, except that fluctuations were slightly less pronounced, probably because of cold air drainage along valley floors at these locations. Comparisons of these records with those of other areas were limited because few other stations were located in high-elevation mountainous areas. Mitchell (1961), in a detailed analysis, suggested that a mean increase in annual temperatures of about 0.9°C occurred from 40° to 70°N latitude from 1880 to the 1940s. Mean winter temperatures increased about 1.3°C during the same period. The trends for Mammoth generally paralleled those shown by Dightman and Beatty (1952), Mitchell (1961), and Bray (1971). The Mammoth records did not suggest the return to cooler conditions reported for some areas in the 1950s and 1960s (Mitchell 1970). Bradley (1974) found that other areas in the Rocky Mountains also did not show this return to cooler conditions. These comparisons suggested that the direction and magnitude of temperature trends were real.

Some additional data exist for Yellowstone during the late 1800s. Douglas and Stockton (1975) attempted to reconstruct past seasonal climates of the Yellowstone area for the period 1751–1910 from tree-ring records. Tree rings were calibrated using the historical climatic records for the 1912–71 period. Their calculations showed that winters of the 1860s and those from 1885 to 1900 were unusually cold (perhaps by 5 or 6°C) when compared to the long-term winter mean.·

Measurements of precipitation are subject to a variety of errors due mostly to winds, which affect the catch of the gauge and must be interpreted with caution (Dirks 1974). Annual precipitation trends for Mammoth suggested highs in the late 1890s, during 1910–20, and again in the 1940s to early 1950s. Low precipitation occurred from about 1900 to 1910, during the 1930s, and periodically in the 1950s. December––February precipitation showed a marked decrease from the late 1890s through the 1930s, followed by an increasing trend. April–June precipitation declined in the late 1920s and 1930s, and also showed a longer-term shift in June precipitation. July–August precipitation, which usually occurred as local thunderstorms, showed no consistent trends over time. Annual precipitation at Lamar 1925–72 generally paralleled Mammoth. Mean annual precipitation at Lake 1930–36 was 34.54 cm compared to 51.54 cm for 1950–67. The Lake records showed that the drought of the 1930s also affected higher elevations.

Dirks (1975) used a seven-year weighted binomial running mean to detect a decrease in annual precipitation at Mammoth from the early 1900s into the drought of the 1930s. This trend was even more pronounced at Lake Station. Dirks also analyzed the frequency of precipitation—another important but often overlooked aspect of climate. The frequencies of precipitation ≥ 1.27 cm/day and of no precipitation for 15 or more days in September and October–April periods also showed the summer droughts and decreases in winter precipitation of the 1930s. Interestingly, a conspicuous decrease in frequency of precipitation ≥ 1.27 cm/day occurred from 1946 through 1954 for both seasonal periods.

Wahl and Lawson (1970) calculated (from widely scattered observations) that annual precipitation for the Yellowstone region of the Rocky Mountains may have been up to 20% greater for the 1850–70 period when compared to 1931–60 "normals," and that winter precipitation was perhaps 10–30% greater. Bradley (1974) suggested that winter and spring precipitation from 1865 to 1900 were above the comparable 1951–61 averages over much of the Western United States. The climatic reconstruction from tree rings suggested that the highest winter precipitation for the entire 161-year (1750–1910) period occurred from about 1877 to 1890 (Douglas and Stockton 1975).

Additional data from independent sources were compared with measurements from weather stations. Trends in annual runoff from the Yellowstone River at Corwin Springs (5 km north of the park boundary) from 1910 to 1974 generally paralleled trends in annual precipitation at Mammoth (Fig. 8.3) (Farnes, unpubl.). Note that minimum runoffs below 1,850,000 dkm³ occurred during the drought of the 1930s and that the 1934 minimum of 1,700,000 dkm³ was only 44% of the maximum of 3,890,000 dkm³ recorded in 1913. The combination of reduced precipitation and increased temperatures of the 1930s clearly reduced runoff and confirms narrative reports (Appendix VII) of the severity of the drought. Additionally, runoff values were compared to April 1 snow water equivalents from 10 snow courses in Yellowstone for the period 1937–74 (Farnes, unpubl.). These values paralleled those shown for annual runoff. These comparisons suggested that trends in climate shown in the Mammoth weather records were real and reduced the hazards of relying heavily upon one station to indicate climatic trends.

The available evidence shows that the climate of Yellowstone has indeed gone through several changes in the past few hundred years. The most pertinent trends are those of the periodically cooler and perhaps wetter LIA—especially the colder, wetter winters of the late 19th century—followed by the more recent rise in temperatures. These increasing mean temperatures coincided with substantial reductions and shifts in seasonal precipitation, especially during the 1930s.

FIGURE 8.3.

Annual runoff for the Yellowstone River at Corwin Springs, 1910–74. Data are for water years (Oct. 1–Sept. 30) plotted as five-year moving averages. Years with runoff below 1,850,000 dkm³ and above 3,700,000 dkm³ are also shown, ⊙. Mean April 1 snow water equivalents from 10 snow-course surveys from 1937 to 1974 are shown as five-year moving averages. All data from Farnes (unpubl.).

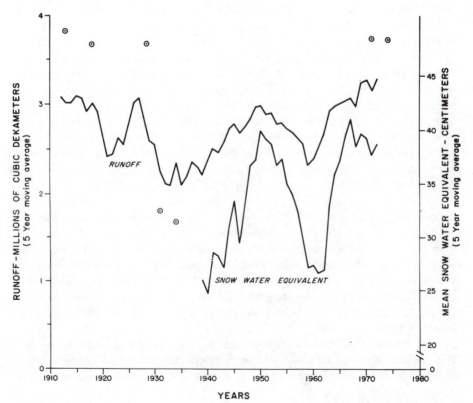

Climatic changes of the LIA have affected human migrations and agriculture and the distribution of vegetation (Hastings and Turner 1965, Bray 1971). Some of the changes in the vegetation of Yellowstone seemed related to the documented climatic changes (see Interpretation: Vegetation, below).

Fire

Natural fires have significantly influenced plant succession on the winter range (Houston 1973). Best estimates of frequency from a relatively small sample of fire-scarred trees ($N = 40$) suggested mean intervals of 20–25 years between fires during the past 300–400 years, with perhaps 8 or 10 extensive fires in that same period. Euro-American man reduced fire occurrence for about 80 years and virtually eliminated fire from the system for perhaps the last 30 years. Much of the area probably would have burned at least one–four times since establishment of the park were it not for suppression.

A comparison of the vegetation on four burned and adjacent unburned shrub steppes at 9–13 years since burning is shown in Table 8.4. The Blacktail and Junction Butte fires occurred in *big sagebrush/Idaho fescue assn;* the airport and Gardiner fires in *big sagebrush/bluebunch wheatgrass assn.* All four fires were intense; big sagebrush was eliminated. Sagebrush was slowly reinvading the Junction Butte and Blacktail burns. Examinations of sites where fires burned during the 1930s and 1940s showed that sagebrush had reinvaded fescue grasslands by the early 1970s. These observations showed the fire-sensitive nature of big sagebrush (inability to resprout from a root crown) and indicated that reestablishment of sagebrush might take 10–30 years. Perennial grasses sometimes showed increased coverage on burned areas. Measurements and photos (Fig. 8.4 and 8.5) suggested that standing above-ground biomass of vegetation was greater on unburned sites. Nine years after the fire, the burned Blacktail site showed 79 g/m^2 air-dried weight (nearly all perennial grasses); unburned, 138 g/m^2 (56 g/m^2 grasses, 82 g/m^2 shrubs). Corresponding values for Junction Butte were 84 g/m^2 on the burn, 130 g/m^2 (69 grasses, 61 shrubs) on the unburned. Values for shrubs included only estimated annual production. If the entire shrub biomass had been weighed, that of unburned sites would have been much greater than that of burned sites. Despain (pers. commun. 1975) found that the weight of all big sagebrush leaves, twigs, and inflorescences at 10 sagebrush steppe sites averaged 122 g/m^2; the entire above-ground sagebrush plants averaged 684 g/m^2. Limited observations of recently burned sites suggested that sprouting of perennial species occurs immediately following the fire but that standing biomass is much lower by late autumn or winter following the burn than on unburned sites (Fig. 8.6). Samples were too small to assess the effects of fire on individual species of perennial grasses.

The probable historic role of fire in maintaining dense reproducing stands of aspen on the northern range in the presence of large numbers of ungulates has been discussed elsewhere (Houston 1973). In 1974, three small aspen stands (total area < .10 ha) known to have burned in September 1939 were relocated on the periphery of the northern range (Houston unpubl. memo to Supt., YNP 1974). The largest of these (Fig. 8.7) contained stems 3–5 m tall and had a tree density of 2.5 stem/m^2. By contrast, the closest unburned stand showed trees 8–12 m tall, had a tree density of 0.3 stems/m^2, and showed no successful reproduction. The unburned stand was typical of most other aspen stands on the northern range, as shown in the comparative photos.

In 1976, I examined a site about 5 km north of the park boundary in Cinnabar

TABLE 8.4
Comparisons of Canopy Coverage and Frequency (CC/F) of Plant Taxa on Burned and Unburned Sage Steppe[a]

TAXA	LOCATION[b,c] (YEARS SINCE BURN)							
	Blacktail (9)		Junction Butte (6)		Airport (11)		Gardiner (13)	
	B	U	B	U	B	U	B	U
Bluebunch wheatgrass	45/100	10/60	15/92	3/52	25/88	18/80	17/68	23/84
Idaho fescue	17/52	21/80	21/96	41/96				
Needle-and-thread	6/76	*/12	*/8	*/4	6/20	*/12		
Sedges		3/16	*/12	*/24				
Junegrass	*/32	4/56	5/60					
Thickspike wheatgrass	*/20	*/8	5/60					
Sandberg bluegrass		*/20			*/4	*/8	*/4	
Indian ricegrass					2/12	1/8	14/72	4/32
Other grasses			*				*	*
Total grass	69	38	47	45	31	19	32	28
Phlox	*/4	*/8				*/12		
Milkvetch	*/16	*/20	3/16	12/76			*/4	1/12

	Moderate/south Loam 1980	Moderate/east Loam 2100	Gentle/south Sandy loam 1580	Steep/south Sandy loam 1580
Pussytoes	*/8			
Prickly phlox	1/28	*/4		
Lupine	1/56	5/40	1	*
Other forbs	*/4	4	1	1
Total forbs	6	14	18	1
Big sagebrush	30/92	40/80	23/76	18/44
Horsebrush	2/20			
Green rabbitbrush	1/20	7/44	3/24	
Fringed sage		5/36	1/8	2/28
Other shrubs		5	1	*
Total shrubs	34	43	25	20
Bareground and rock	1	12	5	43
Litter	3	4	46	44

[a] Measured (August and September 1972) and calculated using method of Daubenmire (1959) with 25 plots/transect.
[b] B = burned, U = unburned.
[c] Asterisk indicates less than 1% canopy coverage.

FIGURE 8.4.
The Gardiner Airport burn of June 1961 showing the effects of fire in the *big sage-brush/bluebunch wheatgrass assn.* 14 years postburn (UTM Coordinates 520 E, 4987 N; elev. 1,600 m; 8/27/75). Upper photo within the burn shows a vigorous stand of bluebunch wheatgrass with needle-and-thread and fringed sagebrush. Lower photo shows big sagebrush with the same grass species in the adjacent unburned area.

FIGURE 8.5.
The Blacktail Creek burn of 1963 showing the effects of fire on a *big sagebrush/Idaho fescue assn.* 12 years postburn (UTM 533 E, 4977 N; elev. 2,100 m; 8/25/75). A dense big sagebrush canopy remains on the unburned area at left. Grasses in the burn at retake were Idaho fescue and Richardson's needlegrass. Big sagebrush was initially eliminated by the fire but was reinvading by 1975.

Basin on the northern range known to have burned 23 August 1963 (Houston unpubl. memo to Supt., YNP 1976). The fire mostly burned lodgepole pine forest but did burn 1–2 ha of aspen. A 1956 aerial photo showed that the preburn aspen stands were composed of tall "over mature" stems with open canopies. Thirteen years after the fire the burned stands showed dense vigorous reproduction (Fig. 8.8); adjacent unburned stands were still characterized by open canopies and no successful reproduction.

On 22 April 1977 a small prescribed burn (~10 ha) was conducted by the U.S. Forest Service in Yankee Jim Canyon on the northern range. About 1.5 ha of aspen with associated shrubs (chokecherry, rose, dogwood) was burned. By July 1977 dense sprouting had occurred (Fig. 8.9), and by September 1977 sprout densities for the four species of shrubs averaged 359,300/ha at five sites; aspen sprouts averaged 234,900/ha. Over 95% of the aspen and chokecherry sprouts were browsed during the winter of 1977–78 and again in 1979. Despite intense browsing, many aspen stems over 2 m tall and chokecherry 1–2 m tall occurred in dense stands when examined 18 September 1980.

By contrast, a 0.9-ha prescribed burn at Bunsen Peak on the northern range in September 1966 resulted in some initial increases in aspen sprouting, but the burn failed to kill the majority of overstory trees, and sprouts did not grow vigorously (Barmore 1968).

FIGURE 8.6.

A sagebrush steppe burn occurred near Gardiner, Montana on 29 July 1974 (524 E, 4986 N; elev. 1,800 m). Upper photo was taken 29 August 1974, and only scattered resprouting of grasses had occurred. The middle and lower photos show grasses (blue-bunch wheatgrass, Junegrass, needle-and-thread) at the same site one and four years post burn. Big sagebrush was virtually eliminated. Dense vigorous bunchgrass occurred by 1978. Historically, wildfires in late summer and autumn reduced the available forage for ungulates on burned areas for the upcoming winter.

1974

1975

1978

FIGURE 8.7.
A dense aspen stand (2.5 stems/m) on Bunsen Peak known to have regenerated follow-ing a September 1939 fire (upper photo; 523 E, 4974 N; elev. 2,300 m; 8/26/75). Lower photo shows large, low-density (0.3 stems/m²) trees in the nearest unburned stand (about 100 m from burned stand). Periodic burning appears to be necessary to maintain vigorous aspen on the area with the present climate and native ungulates.

FIGURE 8.8.

Aspen regeneration in the Cinnabar Basin 13 years after the 1963 fire (photographed 24 August 1976; 508 E, 4993 N; elev. 2,100 m). Densities were around 1.7 stems/m^2 and stems were up to 4 m in height.

These observations suggested that periodic burning (by hot fires) was required to maintain aspen reproduction on the area. Gruell and Loope (1974) and Gruell (1980a,b) arrived at similar conclusions for ungulate winter ranges in the Jackson Hole area. It might be more difficult now to kill the large scattered trees in the remaining aspen stands with fire and get successful regeneration, because clones have deteriorated (Schier 1975). These studies and observations supported the interpretation that many of the changes in vegetation on the winter range shown in comparative photos were the direct result of fire suppression.

Erosion

Examples of geologic erosion occur throughout the range of the northern Yellowstone elk. Erosion from friable Absaroka volcanics (Pl. 17) on local summer range areas at high elevations add significantly to the sediment load of the Lamar River. Cretaceous mudstones and sandstones of Mt. Everts on the winter range (Pls. 23 and 25) erode into the Gardner River during spring and following hard summer rains. The role of elk in erosional processes required careful evaluation because of past reports of accelerated erosion due to grazing on the area.

FIGURE 8.9.

Aspen regeneration on 22 July 1977 at the Yankee Jim Canyon prescribed burn of 22 April 1977 (509 E, 5002 N; elev. 1,600 m). Sprout densities exceeded 500,000/ha at this site. Despite heavy browsing each winter, aspen exceeded 2 m in height by 9 September 1980 (lower photo).

FIGURE 8.10.
A steep south slope (78%) showing erosion rills following late winter rains at Oxbow Creek (537 E, 4978 N; elev. 2,100 m). Upper photo by D. Beal, 4/9/56; lower by D. B. Houston, 9/23/75. The slope is heavily grazed by elk during winter and spring. Thirteen of 43 photos taken to illustrate erosion on the northern range were taken here. The site is largely a colluvial deposit from cliffs above. Douglas-firs, which show exposure of lateral roots, were over 300 years old (upper left and right). Trees less than 150 years old showed no significant root exposure. A robust stand of bluebunch wheatgrass occurred at meter stake (arrow and inset). Note: we were unable to match lens used in original.

FIGURE 8.11.

Gardiner area view west along old park boundary (522 E, 4986 N; elev. 1,600 m).
Upper photo by J. A. Griswald, 6/9/32; lower photo by D. B. Houston, 6/17/71.
Interval between photos is 39 years. Wright and Thompson (1935) interpreted the
upper photo as follows: "Erosion is under way. As evidenced by remaining stubs, this
gulch was once well protected by grass and shrubby growth. It is now stripped naked,
and the fertile topsoil is washing away. Erosion is hard to stop once it starts." My
interpretation is that an isolated sandstone outcrop, essentially unchanged, projects
through surrounding mudflows. The site represents a topoedaphic condition very atypical of the winter range. The area is on the original park boundary and was subjected to
livestock grazing and artificial concentrations of native ungulates (the area behind the
fence was added to Yellowstone in 1932). Little change is apparent in earth movements
or vegetation on this site, which is characterized by an extremely harsh microclimate.
Certainly this is not convincing evidence for accelerated gully erosion. Wet but drying
soils in original account for differences in appearance at retake.

Earlier reports (Appendix VII), when specific, usually referred to erosion on areas grazed by livestock or by a semidomesticated bison herd. Other areas, especially mudflows in the BLA, geologic formations such as Mt. Everts, and small ridgetop and steep-slope sites were sometimes mentioned. References to general erosion were common during the drought of the 1930s. Forty-three photos taken to illustrate this erosion since the 1930s (41 in Yellowstone Park files, 2 as Fig. 8.10 and 8.11) have included 2 or 3 on mudflows; 25 on small, very steep, south slopes (Fig. 8.10) at four different sites; 3 on ridge tops (including 2 at the top of a cliff in the BLA); 1 in a gully of Mt. Everts; and 1 along a contact between two dissimilar geologic formations that was interpreted as gully erosion (Fig. 8.11). Ten other photos, though clearly showing accelerated erosion, were taken of sites resulting from road construction and had nothing to do with ungulate grazing.

The bases of 10 steep slopes (60–78%) on the winter range, including the site shown in Fig. 8.10, were examined for buried soil profiles, which could represent recent accelerated erosion (a suggestion made by D. T. Patten). Presumably such erosion also should have exposed the roots of trees on the shallow soils at these sites. Ten–twelve Douglas-fir on each of three slopes (including Fig. 8.10 and Pl. 37) were cored to determine age and examined for root exposure. To date, no buried soil profiles have been found. Although the proximal ends of some lateral roots on several fir trees over 300 years old were exposed at each site, no substantial exposure occurred on roots of trees less than 100–150 years old. Whatever the erosion rate and influence of elk at these sites, neither has been sufficient to provide evidence of recent acceleration. In contrast, ungulates clearly were accelerating the movements of materials at mineral licks located on steep slopes (60–75%) along lower Blacktail Creek (Pl. 26).

Many processes of erosion probably increased temporarily during the drought; artificial concentrations of livestock or bison also might have caused unnatural acceleration. An assumption implicit in past interpretations of erosion at other sites, such as Mt. Everts, various ridgetops and mudflows, and the sandstone outcrop of Fig. 8.11, was that these sites once looked very different. If such were true, great differences should have been visible in the comparative photo series (Appendix V), and extensive field evidence of head-cutting gullies, sheet erosion, etc., should have occurred on the area.

The evidence generally does not support these interpretations. Mudflows in the BLA sometimes resembled sites that suffered massive accelerated sheet erosion. The photographic evidence suggests that these areas have changed little (but does not preclude accelerated erosion during periods of livestock grazing or at elk feedgrounds). Ephemeral erosion rills occur following thaws and spring rains on some small, very steep slopes (Fig. 8.10); elk could contribute to these conditions. Some investigators considered that elk foraging and trampling on such sites unnaturally accelerated erosion (see Packer 1963). All these interpretations were based on the assumption that such sites once looked very different and were the major forage source for wintering elk. Studies of habitat use and forage relationships showed that some of these sites were utilized heavily at low elk densities (Chap. 9). Comparative photos showed these sites to be unchanged. The available evidence does not support interpretations of widespread or accelerated erosion on the area.

Human Developments and Activities

Human developments, including roads, buildings, campgrounds, etc., occupied less than 1% of Yellowstone Park (Swan pers. commun. 1975). About 200 ha or 0.3% of the northern winter range in the park were developed (about 120 ha of roads, 80 ha of buildings, etc.). Developments have decreased on the ~1,600 ha of winter range added to the BLA of the park in 1932 (Fig. 2.1). Homesteads, with associated live-stock grazing, occupied this area from the mid-1870s until 1932. Other developments included a livestock slaughterhouse and the Cinnabar railhead with several hundred people between about 1883 and 1903. Abandoned building sites, roads, and railbeds can be located on the ground but now are largely revegetated.

The ecological effects of some existing developments on native ungulates were complex. All developments removed areas from forage production, but during winters the plowed roads provided snow-free travel routes that could be energy saving for ungulates.

Generally, the native vegetation of the park has not been grazed by livestock. Exceptions on a parkwide basis included locally heavy summer horse grazing in the past along roadsides and in meadows around developments, local summer pastures for milk and beef cattle, and small areas subsequently added to the park. Considering the numbers of park visitors and later use of autos, grazing, except in the BLA, would have been greatest from about 1900 to 1915. The location and size of livestock grazing, haycutting, and feeding of native ungulates on the winter range are summa-rized in Table 8.5 (from materials filed in the Yellowstone Park archives). In addition to livestock grazing shown in Table 8.5, transient summer horse grazing must have occurred by aboriginal people during summer periods on the Bannock Indian Trail from about 1838 to 1878 (Haines 1962). I suspect horse grazing during these periods was ecologically insignificant. As with the rest of the park, heavy summer horse grazing from park visitors and others must have occurred along roadsides and meadows of the winter range. The U.S. Army kept meticulous records of grazing activities; we were unable to confirm Rush's (1932a) statement of 3,000 horses on the Blacktail Plateau up to 1916.

Meagher (1973) provided details of the management of the semidomestic bison herd in the Lamar Valley. Native ungulates were fed during some winters from about 1904 to 1945 (some bison fed through 1952) at certain sites on the winter range. These animals were fed mostly native hay cut from wet meadows at the feedground site; some hay was also cut from cultivated fields of exotic grasses on site. (Small-scale irrigation was used to increase yields on some native and cultivated grasslands as early as 1908.) Records showed that feeding of ungulates other than bison was greatest from about 1920 to 1937. This feeding caused artificial winter concentrations with resultant heavy use of vegetation on and adjacent to feedgrounds. In addition to feeding, the construc-tion of 7 km of woven wire fence 2 m high along the north boundary in 1913 probably restricted winter distributions of some ungulates, especially pronghorn. This fence was removed about 1932. Unnaturally high elk concentrations in the BLA resulted from prolonged hunting seasons outside the park. Sporadic use of salt grounds in the early 1930s also caused local ungulate concentrations.

These assessments of the ecological effects of livestock grazing and winter ungu-late feeding are made after extensive field observations. Excluding the BLA, in no case was there evidence of extensive physical damage to the environment (massive soil erosion). Indications of these past activities now exist as close, parallel, grazing terraces or trails along Rose Creek, at Soda Butte, north of Mammoth Hot Springs, and in portions of the Gardner River Canyon. Terraces have revegetated with native peren-nial grasses. A minor increase in big sagebrush occurred on upper slopes north of Mammoth. Sagebrush has since decreased following removal of livestock, whereas perennial grasses increased. Livestock grazing, haycutting, and cultivation altered the

TABLE 8.5
Livestock Grazing, Haycutting, Winter Feedgrounds, and Other Developments on the Northern Winter Range

General Area	Period and Type of Use	Size of Operation
Lamar Valley	Late 1870s: summer cattle	Small[a]
	1880s–1890s: year-round cattle and horses	Small and short-term
	1880s–1890s: native hay cut at Slough, Rose, and Soda Butte creeks	Small and short-term
	1907–52: bison held in semidomestication—fed in winter on native hay and from cultivated haylands	Over 1,000 bison during 1929–32, 100–900 tons of hay fed
	1920–37: elk sometimes fed with bison and horses on Slough Creek	25 up to maximum of 500 tons fed one winter
	1940–51: horses raised at Rose Creek	Small
Blacktail Plateau	Late 1870s: summer cattle	Few hundred animals
	1890s–1915: June–Oct. periods—horses YP Transportation Co. Also Army and NPS horses into 1950s(?)	500–800[b]
	1882–1903: year-round livestock grazing with haycutting—Yancey's Hole	100–300[b]; Less than 20 ha
	1920s(?) to 1930s: NPS horses and probably some elk fed in winter—Yancey's Hole	50–70 tons
	1935–42: bison pasture—Antelope Cr., ~220 ha	25–30 bison in summer
Mammoth Hot Springs–Gardner River to BLA	1879–1920(?): periodic year-round horse grazing with very heavy spring–fall grazing around developments and roads—mostly affected 730 ha	Small

Boundary line area		
1. Inside original park boundaries (3,300 ha)	1904 to ~ 1920: periodic winter feedgrounds for elk, deer, bighorn	Small—less than 50 tons
	1902–20s(?): bison "show" pasture, perhaps 2 km²	Less than 20 animals
	Early 1880s–1905: year-round livestock grazing was terminated with construction of 7 km of fencing in 1905. A military rifle range and golf course also occurred in the area.	Locally heavy
	1905(?)–1937: periodic winter feedgrounds for pronghorn, deer, and elk	Sometimes large, with 100 tons up to 400 in 1920, then declined, several thousand elk occasionally fed 1915–25
2. 1932 boundary addition (1,600 ha)	1870s–1932: heavy year-round livestock grazing included Van Dyck slaughterhouse operation. Formerly cultivated fields occur throughout the area.	
	1932–37: winter feedground elk	
Gardner's Hole	1885 to 1915–18(?): summer horse, cattle, sheep	Small, ~25–100 tons
	1. Wylie Camping Co.	50–100 milk cows[b]
		275–400 horses[b]
	2. Van Dyck Livestock Co.	50–100 cattle[c]
		100–250 sheep[c]

[a] "Small" = mostly less than 100 livestock.

[b] Animals brought on in June with most dispersed throughout the park from mid-June to mid-September, then reassembled in September or October and driven from the area.

[c] Numbers estimated to be present at any one time—summer operation usually processed 200–300 beef cattle and 700–1,000 sheep from 1909 to 1915.

composition of some plant communities. Various shrubs, including willows, were cleared from wet meadows at Soda Butte, Rose Creek, Slough Creek, and Yanceys Hole (Albright 1920b:60). About 180 ha of formerly cultivated fields still dominated by smooth brome or timothy have persisted on the winter range (excluding the BLA). Colonization of these fields by native species has been slow, and timothy has spread to other local grasslands on the winter range. Species composition and successional relationships were altered at these sites, but productivity was not. Timothy, for example, formed dense productive stands (Pl. 31) and was highly palatable to native ungulates. Other exotic plants occurred locally in areas formerly grazed, but native species usually predominated.

Activities in the BLA had the greatest potential for causing lasting departures from natural conditions. There are about 230 ha of formerly cultivated fields. Most are dominated by smooth brome or crested wheatgrass. Native species reinvaded former fields in some areas, but exotics remain dominant. Cheatgrass invaded some abandoned fields and swale areas of adjacent grasslands. Cheatgrass also occurred at scattered sites along roadsides and heavily used trails, around talus fields on steep south slopes, and on pocket gopher mounds below about 2,000 m (mostly below 1,770 m) in other areas of the winter range. Cheatgrass may have reduced winter forage supplies, but it is highly palatable in early spring. Its distribution did not appear to be changed greatly from that reported in the 1930s and 1940s (Rush 1932a, Grimm 1943). Native grasslands in the BLA, excluding mudflows, are generally dominated by vigorous native species such as bluebunch wheatgrass, needle-and-thread, Junegrass, etc. This represents a recovery following heavy use by livestock. Big sagebrush has decreased on certain sites, representing a return to more pristine conditions following removal of livestock. Mudflows in the BLA (820 ha) show terraces from heavy livestock grazing and a major elk feedground. These activities may have contributed to the impoverished appearance of vegetation on these sites, but they appeared to have inherently poor soils.

Early photos suggested that shrubs and trees of all kinds were utilized heavily during winter periods on and adjacent to feedgrounds. A consideration of frequency of use and size of feedground suggested that this effect was most pronounced in the BLA around Gardiner and extended 3–5 km south up the Gardner River drainage. These effects were mostly short-lived.

Major human activities on the winter range such as market hunting and fire suppression have been discussed earlier.

Rush (1932a) described heavy livestock grazing on the winter range outside the park. Much of this either has been eliminated or closely regulated. The winter range outside the park is still dominated by native perennial grasses and shrubs. Vigorous fire suppression is practiced, although several small prescribed burns in sage steppes have been conducted recently. Arable bottomlands are used for agriculture.

Interpretation: Vegetation

Interpretations of vegetation conditions are based upon the accumulated data from historical photos and narratives, measurements of vegetation, climatic records, fire history, the documented influences of modern man, and studies of elk–habitat relationships (from Chap. 9).

Spring, Summer, and Autumn Ranges

PHOTO COMPARISONS AND EARLY NARRATIVES

The following interpretations are suggested for changes in vegetation on the spring, summer, and autumn ranges of the northern Yellowstone elk. The combination and timing of minor increases in area and density of forest at higher elevations (2,300± m to timberline), suggestions of subtle changes in composition of some meadows (Pl. 4), decreases in riparian shrubs (especially willow), seral ponds, and increased establishment of conifers on formerly braided flood plains all seemed consistent with the hypothesis of a climatic change to warmer, drier conditions. Note that any single change in vegetation described here would be difficult to interpret, but collectively, observed changes suggest causal relationships. Considering the known climatic events surrounding the termination of the LIA, it would be surprising if effects on plant communities were not visible. Hastings and Turner (1965) and Bray (1971) have documented the sensitivity of vegetation to seemingly small changes in climate. Franklin et al. (1971) attributed increased forest invasion of subalpine meadows in the Pacific Northwest to a warmer, drier climate since the late 1800s. Gruell (1980b) suggests that an increased density of herbaceous plants in some subalpine and alpine communities of northwest Wyoming during the past century (conspicuous in some of his comparative photos) could be attributed, in part, to warmer climates.

The effects of fire on succession were apparent in many photos and involved changes in density, age distribution, and sometimes composition of forest communities. These effects were less visible at high elevations, where fires were infrequent, but became more visible at lower elevations (~2,300–2,600 m). Generally, grasslands and herblands showed little change. Sparsely vegetated snowbank sites, erodable volcanic substrates, and elk bedding areas showed little change. Herbivores, including elk, probably had only a small role in the changes observed.

The data from this study and those of Cole (1969a), Gruell (1973, 1980a,b), and Meagher (1973 and unpubl.) support the interpretation that vegetation on spring, summer, and autumn ranges did not show departures from natural conditions that could be attributed to native ungulates. [The biotic effects of elk on the vegetation of some summer ranges in and adjacent to southern Yellowstone have been controversial. Earlier concerns about these effects (Beetle 1952, 1962, Anderson 1958, Croft and Ellison 1960) have not been supported, in my view, by more detailed studies (Cole 1969a, Gruell 1973, 1980a,b) and by continued monitoring of conditions (Wood pers. commun. 1980).] Human developments, the local effects of past livestock husbandry, and recent fire suppression resulted in departures from natural conditions. The former two effects were small-scale or ephemeral; the latter seems reversible with the ongoing fire management program.

Winter Range

PHOTO COMPARISONS AND NARRATIVES

Changes in vegetation on the lower-elevation northern winter range of the park (excluding the BLA) generally were limited in area but did result in striking changes in the distribution and appearance of some plant communities. The increased distribution of fire-sensitive big sagebrush, increased density and distribution of coniferous forests, decrease in aspen, and changed age distribution of forests were consistent with the hypothesis of a reduced natural fire frequency because of active suppression (Houston 1973). These changes occurred within the framework of a warmer, drier climate and were influenced by grazing. Studies of vegetation on recent burns strengthened the interpretation that fire suppression played a major role.

The changed distribution of riparian vegetation would be consistent with the climatic changes but was influenced by fire suppression, herbivores, and modern man. [Fire suppression could have altered the hydrologic characteristics of the smaller streams on the area and reduced stream cutting (Houston 1973, Romme 1979). Consequently, the amount of gravel bars and other pioneer habitat suitable for colonization by willows and alder has declined.]

The vegetation of the BLA has been most affected by modern man—especially the land added to the park in 1932. The area set aside as elk winter range outside the park retained its character as a native grassland, despite a period of heavy livestock grazing. Arable bottomlands now are used for agriculture.

The role of herbivores, especially elk, in influencing specific changes in vegetation and the effects of such changes on ecological carrying capacity for ungulates are discussed below. None of the photos supports a clear interpretation of progressive retrogressive plant succession or a decline in carrying capacity that could be attributed to free-ranging native ungulates (BLA excepted). Small sites with low densities of vegetation that received periodic heavy grazing in winter and spring were present in the earliest photos; they apparently remained unchanged. Photos and other work did not support interpretations of widespread erosion resulting from the foraging activities of free-ranging elk. The distribution of aspen and willow has changed on the northern winter range where ungulate densities were comparatively high, on other seasonal ranges within the park where ungulate densities were low, and, for willow, on certain areas outside the park where ungulate densities were very low.

Photos, supported by early narratives, showed that conspicuous effects of modern man on the vegetation appeared to have been local (cultivation, construction, clearing shrubs), temporary (haycutting, winter feeding of ungulates, livestock grazing), negligible in changing productivity (introduction of exotic plants), or probably reversible (fire suppression). Exceptions to these interpretations have occurred in the BLA.

VEGETATION MEASUREMENTS

Consideration of both the array of vegetation measurements made on the winter range and the manipulations of ungulate populations suggested that the sample units in grasslands have, to date, mostly measured fluctuations in plant communities rather than long-term directional changes. Fluctuations seemed related more to short-term climatic conditions, or occasionally to the localized biotic effects of pocket gophers and grasshoppers, than to the effects of ungulates. On some sample units the effects of ungulate foraging could not be clearly separated from climatic effects, especially in the BLA. The most striking aspect of the grassland measurements was the fluctuation in standing crop, plant area, and density. This made for substantial annual fluctuations in absolute abundance of forage available to wintering ungulates as a result of variations in growing conditions.

Plant species encountered on grassland transects and their relative abundance were generally those expected in climax grass communities of the region (Barmore 1975; see also Appendix VI). Exceptions included species growing on some harsh physiographic sites and exotic grasses. Measurements spanning the drought of the 1930s suggested classic retrogressive succession in grasslands. However, the shift of succession toward climax vegetation in spite of extensive grazing by native ungulates suggested that the drought was of overriding importance. Native ungulates did not have the capacity to maintain retrogressed conditions on most grasslands. Seemingly, if they ever had the ability to do so, it should have been during this drought.

None of the measurements repeated over several to many years could be interpreted as showing continued retrogressive succession. Measurements also showed that persistent heavy winter and variable spring grazing, with associated trampling on harsh physiographic sites characteristic of 3% of the area, did not cause extensive plant mortality or progressive changes in density or basal area. Individual plants persisted for decades under the most severe environmental and grazing treatments; i.e., these plant communities appeared to be quite stable over time, even though seasonal grazing was intense. Litter did not accumulate on ridgetops when grazing was reduced or absent (in exclosures). The topographic and edaphic influence may well be as important as the grazing influence in determining composition and density on such sites.

Studies of grasslands spanning the period of major elk herd reductions showed little or no consistent difference between treatments of nongrazing and grazing by native ungulates on species abundance, basal area, or composition. Fluctuations of the magnitude shown were common in other grazed and ungrazed steppes of the western United States. The overall species composition and the remarkable fluctuations measured from year to year, or from one period to the next, showed the dynamic nature of grasslands but argued against the following interpretations: (1) that grasslands had retrogressed beyond recovery, (2) that elapsed time was insufficient to measure a response from lowered ungulate densities, or (3) that techniques were insensitive to changes due to reduced grazing. Rather, the measurements tended to indicate that winter grazing on cured grasses and dormant shrubs had little lasting effect.

Measurements suggested that big sagebrush increased on all but the BLA portions of the winter range. This mostly reflected continued fire suppression, with possibly reduced browsing on upper slope sites. Measurements of big sagebrush on mudflows in the semiarid BLA showed heavy browsing and continued mortality at low ungulate levels. These observations and measurements of the influence of livestock grazing suggested that these changes reflected, in part, a return to more pristine vegetation and, in part, the unnatural effects of artificially high densities of some ungulates in the BLA.

In general, the ungulate effects on aspen (heavy browsing of low-density reproduction) and willow (reduced crown size and height) showed few measurable relationships to population densities; i.e., utilization remained high even at the lower ungulate levels. While ungulate foraging contributed to the present condition of these vegetation types, the ultimate cause of their changing status seemed related more to continued fire suppression and climatic changes (see below).

The effects of ungulate foraging as measured on different vegetation types in proportion to their occurrence on the winter range are summarized in Fig. 8.12. This summary should not be interpreted to mean that ungulates were having no other effects—only that other possible influences went unmeasured. Ungulate effects have

FIGURE 8.12.

Percent occurrence of major vegetation types on the northern winter range in the park and the influences of ungulate foraging as measured by vegetation sample units.

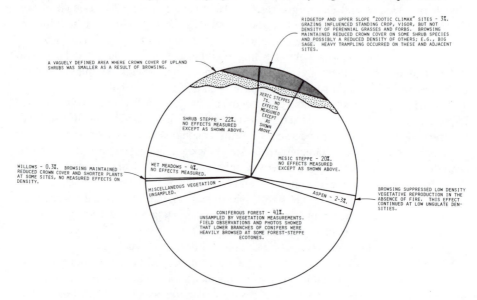

not been measured on about 90% of the area, partly because most forest types were unsampled and partly because sample units were often deliberately located on the most heavily utilized sites. The ecological implications of these effects are discussed below.

Vegetation measurements also illustrated the formidable difficulty of sampling vegetation on an area as diverse as the northern range. Statistical analysis and interpretation were even more difficult. The ungulate exclosures, for example, provided a measure of grazing effects, but it was inappropriate to consider them as controls for grazed plots. Exclosures provided an artificial treatment of no grazing for comparison with grazed sites on an historical ungulate winter range. Continued protection inevitably will result in vegetation inside exclosures that will differ from that outside due to litter accumulations, etc. Vegetation so derived should not be considered a management goal or natural.

"Deterioration" of the Winter Range

Range sample units and narrative accounts showed that earlier interpretations of deterioration of vegetation on the northern range were based primarily upon the decrease of aspen, the appearance and utilization of herbaceous vegetation on ridgetops and steep slopes characteristic of about 3% of the area, and the decrease of big sagebrush in the 1932 addition to the BLA. The effects of browsing on coniferous trees and on the distribution of willows have been of secondary concern. It is necessary, recognizing the redundancy, to summarize the data and to give my interpretations of the role of native ungulates in these conditions.

ASPEN

Almost without exception the earliest photos of the northern range showed low, very dense aspen stands that were apparently of fire origin. Historically, the winter range had a comparatively high frequency of natural fires, but suppression attempts began in the late 1880s. Narratives and photos indicated that vegetative reproduction occurred in some stands through the 1920s. This occurred in the presence of thousands of elk and other ungulates. Accounts and photos showed that while stands were periodically browsed, browsing did not prevent their maturation into stands showing a low density of large trees. Exotic grasses invaded the understories of some stands. Suppression became efficient to the point of eliminating fire. The combination of the drought of the 1930s and browsing apparently killed some stands. Most remaining mature stands showed a low-density vegetative reproduction that was heavily browsed.

Most aspen was clearly seral to coniferous forest, with fire suppression and the climate of the past century. (These aspen appear to occur at the lower elevational limits of the species distribution on the Yellowstone River, particularly as a component of transition zones between coniferous forest and grasslands. Thus, they could be especially vulnerable to extreme droughts.) Aspen decreased from about 4–6% to 2–3% of the area. These same changes occurred outside the winter range and outside the park where native ungulates occurred at remnants of historic densities (e.g., Clarks Fork of the Yellowstone, at sites where livestock grazing appeared to be minimal) and apparently throughout the northern and middle Rocky Mountains (Schier 1975, Gruell 1980a,b, 1982). Some stands on the winter range showed successful reproduction if given complete protection from browsing, but densities and growth rates often did not approach those suggested in early photos. The large reduction in the elk population generally failed to reduce utilization or permit escapement of the low-density vegetative reproduction; i.e., there was no measurable feedback with elk densities.

Data from the northern range and adjacent areas showed that aspen often reproduced successfully when burned in the presence of ungulate populations. These data seemed consistent with the hypothesis that the decrease in aspen was largely the result of fire suppression carried out by Euro-American man in a changing climate (the number of stands that would have been inevitably seral to conifers or that would have died during the drought even with burning is unknown). Herbivores doubtless affected the rate of postfire succession but were not the force that determined the direction and timing of events. The role of fire in these relationships needs to be tested further. The role of ungulates in the decline of aspen elsewhere in the Rocky Mountains has been controversial [see Boyce and Hayden-Wing (1979) for a compendium of views]. The evidence, in my view, favors the interpretation of Gruell and Loope (1974) and Gruell (1980b, 1982) that widespread fire suppression was the primary cause of the decline.

VEGETATION OF RIDGETOPS AND UPPER SLOPES

Interpretations that the low density of vegetation on ridgetops and upper slopes, characteristic of 3% of the area, represented range deterioration were based upon the assumptions that these sites formerly supported higher densities or a different composition of vegetation, that their present appearance was due to recently intensified grazing and trampling by native ungulates, and that these sites determined carrying capacity. These sites appeared in the earliest historical photos of the area (and of adjacent winter ranges) and in all cases appeared to be unchanged. Studies did not support the inter-

pretation of massive recent accelerated erosion from these sites. Protection from grazing generally did not result in substantial changes in composition, density, or, in some
cases, accumulation of litter. Some sites remained heavily grazed and trampled at very
low ungulate densities (exceptions included some roadside areas where elk were greatly reduced) and remained heavily grazed from 1970 to 1978 as the elk population more
than doubled. These data seemed consistent with the hypothesis that such sites represented stable zootic climax vegetation strongly influenced by abiotic forces. Such sites
appeared to be the inevitable consequence of having even very low densities of native
ungulates on the area. Data did not support the interpretation that these sites determined ecological carrying capacity (Chap. 9).

The term zootic climax, as used here, designated a naturally occurring influence
on herbaceous vegetation by native ungulates; the concept is not unique to this study.
That herbivores might maintain a biotic climax or a zootic climax was recognized by
Tansley (1935) and Daubenmire (1968), although both used domestic herbivores to
illustrate the concept. Cole (1969a) interpreted ridgetop and upper-slope sites on elk
winter ranges in Jackson Hole, Wyoming, as zootic climaxes and considered the term
synonymous with natural biotic disclimaxes. Bergerud (1967:640) reported the occurrence of what appeared to be ecologically equivalent sites on caribou winter range.

Historic accounts suggested that large herds of bison and elk along the Yellowstone River, northeast of the area that became the park, must have maintained extensive areas as zootic climax vegetation—conditions that some range managers would
now class as fair to poor range [see Bureau of Land Management (1969) for summary].
Unfortunately, all of these "grazing systems" were destroyed before they could be
studied; the intensity of the biotic effects on vegetation from native ungulates at K_I is
outside the experience of most North American biologists. In fact, the disciplines of
plant ecology and range and wildlife management evolved here in systems that were
largely faunally impoverished.

BIG SAGEBRUSH IN BLA

Early photos suggested that big sagebrush occurred historically in swale areas with the
semiarid climate and natural fire frequency of the BLA. The combination of intense
year-round livestock grazing with fire suppression resulted in increased densities of
sagebrush on many upland sites. Sagebrush decreased on upland sites when the area
was added to the park in 1932, as livestock were removed, and as aggregations of
native ungulates occurred (feedgrounds and conditioned avoidance behavior). The
decrease accelerated during the drought. Sagebrush was replaced on many upland sites
by native perennial grasses. Sagebrush persisted in swales throughout the BLA with
heavy winter grazing by native ungulates. It has persisted on upland sites in the park
with a treatment of heavy summer livestock grazing and winter browsing by native
ungulates.

The decrease of sagebrush in swales of mudflows has been of particular interest.
Exclosures showed that sagebrush persisted and increased in mudflow swales when
given complete protection from browsing. Elk and pronghorn reductions failed to
reduce utilization of sagebrush outside exclosures on mudflows. These data seemed
consistent with the hypothesis that the decrease in big sagebrush over most of the area
represented a return to more pristine conditions following a grazing disclimax established and maintained by livestock (also influenced by fire suppression). Barmore
(1975) made a similar interpretation. The decrease in swales, especially on mudflows,
can be fairly, but not clearly, interpreted as an exaggerated unnatural biotic effect.

The vegetation established over the entire area by cattle grazing may have resulted in higher densities of some native ungulates (pronghorn, mule deer) than would otherwise have occurred (see Barmore 1975:259), which in turn permitted effects not otherwise possible. This interpretation cannot be separated from the effects of unnaturally high ungulate densities in the BLA through conditioned avoidance and artificial feeding or of drought and the introduction of exotic grasses. If the decrease in sagebrush in swales is interpreted as a departure from natural conditions, it was most conspicuous on about 1% of the winter range in the park and resulted from a boundary line situation, atypical of the rest of the area. Vegetation composition changes (exotic plants) and boundary area status may preclude reversing that change.

CONIFERS

High-lining of conifers (heavy browsing of lower branches) has been interpreted as evidence of range deterioration. Early photos showed high-lined trees on the northern range and in adjacent areas. These are more conspicuous presently along some forest–steppe ecotones, probably because of increased distribution and density of forests. Browsing of conifers occurs during severe winter conditions but also throughout the year. Male elk were commonly observed sweeping lower branches from Douglas-fir, Rocky Mountain juniper, and limber pine with their antlers as soon as they came onto the winter range. The browsing, rubbing, and horning of lower branches and mortality of trees caused by elk and bison affected the rate of forest advancement into steppe along some ecotones. Photos showed that with fire suppression, browsing was incapable of preventing trees from invading grasslands. These data showed that ungulates had a minor influence on rates of forest succession, but this effect cannot be appropriately interpreted as range deterioration.

The failure of scattered Rocky Mountain juniper stands between Mammoth and Gardiner to reproduce has been mentioned as evidence of deterioration. This is inconsistent with observations showing increased densities of juniper at slightly higher elevations and throughout the lower elevation Yellowstone River canyon from Hellroaring to Crevice Creeks. The canyon has the highest ungulate densities on the area. Failure of junipers to reproduce at some sites with abundant reproduction elsewhere suggests a failure of seedling establishment at certain microsites, possibly a result of present climatic conditions. Increased distribution of juniper at other sites is related to fire suppression; field observations show that the species is easily killed by fire.

WILLOWS

Early photos showed riparian shrubs, mainly various willow species, on some flood plains. The distribution of willows and other riparian vegetation may have declined to about 0.4% of the area from roughly twice that amount during the past century. Heavy winter browsing was observed on many stands (Chap. 9). Some willows were physically removed to cut hay. Mortality was most conspicuous on upper flood plain terraces and occurred mainly during the drought of the 1930s. Elimination of ungulate browsing by exclosures produced increased height and canopy but usually no significant increase in numbers of plants. Willows persisted with heavy browsing outside exclosures but at reduced canopy size and height.

The following observations are crucial to an interpretation of willow changes. Many species of willows still grow throughout the winter range (Fig. 8.13) and colo-

FIGURE 8.13.

Robust stands of many species of willows occur on the northern winter range. Upper photo shows a stand of Geyer's willow with scattered blueberry and Wolf's willow on Blacktail Creek (532 E, 4977 N; 8/25/75); lower, a stand of interior willow on the Yellowstone River (537 E, 4984 N; 8/23/78). Willows at both sites were heavily browsed each winter from 1970 to 1978 by ungulates and were also cropped sporadically by beaver in late summer and autumn.

nize pioneer substrates (Fig. 8.14). These stands are often on active flood plains, are usually heavily browsed, and in some areas are adjacent to sites where ungulates were thought to have caused other stands to decrease. Willows were also seral to grassland and forest on areas *outside* the winter range and *outside* the park (at high elevations) during this same period. Willows still occurred on summer ranges throughout the park where they received consistent summer browsing (Fig. 8.15). These decreases in willow occurred at sites where it seemed most unlikely that the biotic effects of ungulates (and beaver) could have been the driving force behind succession.

Although moose occurred in parts of Yellowstone by the late 1860s (but apparently not in the 1830s), a detailed historical review showed no observations of moose on the northern range until about 1913 (Meagher pers. commun. 1975; see also Chap. 10). They are now commonly observed year-round. Willows were so limited on the winter range that it seemed unlikely that moose could have materially increased winter utilization except that they are capable of consistently foraging in deeper snow than elk. Increased utilization of willows (perhaps aspen?) by moose may now occur during spring to autumn periods.

Studies and photos in the Jackson Hole area suggested that consistently heavy winter browsing did not cause changes in willow density or composition on sites where soil moisture content was optimum (Houston 1968, 1978 unpubl. memo, Gruell 1980a,b). Patten (1968) showed that the ability of willows to survive heavy browsing along the Gallatin River in and adjacent to Yellowstone Park varied by species along a soil moisture gradient. Plants on sites with optimum soil moisture near the river were most able to withstand browsing by elk and moose. In contrast with the Jackson Hole observations mentioned above, photos taken in the Gallatin area prior to the mid-1920s clearly showed that by the 1940s willows had decreased. This was attributed to increased browsing by elk (Patten 1968, Lovaas 1970, and others). An alternative interpretation is that browsing may not have increased but that soil moisture decreased on flood plains with the drought of the 1930s, thereby reducing the plants' ability to survive browsing. This is suggested by a study of the hydrology of the river (Farnes and Shafer 1972), which showed greatly reduced runoff in the 1930s (the 1934 runoff was about 37% of the 1890–1971 mean). Interpretations of changes on the Gallatin River were additionally complicated because of periodic concentrations of elk produced artificially by winter feeding and by hunting outside the park boundary.

Observations of the *timing, location,* and *direction* of changes seemed consistent with the hypothesis that while ungulates and other herbivores affected the rate of primary succession, changes in distribution of willow were mostly climatically determined. (As mentioned earlier, fire suppression may also have adversely affected soil moisture relationships for willows at lower elevations.) Additionally, some changes in plant species distribution were to be expected as an area was colonized by a formerly absent species of ungulate (Caughley 1970, 1976a). It seems appropriate to interpret such changes as predictable habitat modification rather than as deterioration or retrogression.

One final observation of willows is worthy of note, because it illustrates the difficulties of trying to interpret vegetative change in terms of just one or two ungulate species. I witnessed two consecutive years (1971, 1972) of complete defoliation and subsequent mortality of a stand of interior willow along the Gardner River by *Disonycha pluriligata,* a small native beetle. The stand was on an upper flood plain terrace and may have been under environmental stress so that it became especially susceptible to defoliation—possibly soil moisture availability, because adjacent stands at the edge of the river were defoliated and yet survived. The result was a dead stand that now,

FIGURE 8.14.
Willows colonized pioneer substrates along streams. By 1978, stands of interior willow had colonized this gravel bar, which was deposited in the Gardiner River during spring floods of 1974 (524 E, 4982 N; elev. 1,700 m). Inset shows stem densities by 1978. Plants were heavily browsed each winter. Sweet-yellow-clover, rather than willow, dominates the left of the foreground bar.

1974

1978

FIGURE 8.15.

Robust stands of willows occur on spring, summer, and autumn ranges of the northern Yellowstone elk. These receive summer browsing by elk and moose. A net decline of willows occurred at even the highest elevations of the park during the past century. Upper photo shows a stand of Geyer's willow with scattered blueberry and Wolf's willow on Obsidian Creek (521 E, 4967 N; 8/25/75); lower, somewhat similar stand on Beaverdam Creek (565 E, 4907 N; 8/24/75; photo by M. Meagher).

because of breakage, is indistinguishable from some stands earlier thought to have been killed by ungulate browsing. So far as I am aware, no one has been studying the ecology of *D. pluriligata;* indeed, we were unaware of its presence until 1971.

In general, departures of vegetation from pristine conditions on the winter range appeared to have been due mostly to the direct or indirect effects of modern man. This resulted in an increased expression of climatic climax vegetation through fire suppression. Cultivation and local livestock grazing changed species composition and introduced exotic plant species in small areas. This is unfortunate and may be largely irreversible. The combination of events occurring in the BLA gave departures from natural conditions of vegetation that would otherwise not have occurred. These events were cultivation, livestock grazing, and artificial concentrations of native ungulates on feedgrounds and as a result of hunting outside park boundaries. These changes also may be irreversible.

Ungulate Effects on the Vegetation

Further consideration of the effects of elk and other ungulates on the vegetation of the northern winter range is necessary because of the controversy surrounding their management. I have used the concepts and terminology of North American plant ecology and range management throughout this chapter (i.e., climatic climax vegetation, zootic climax, grazing disclimax, retrogressive succession), but these perspectives on vegetation and on the effects of ungulates on vegetation can sometimes become a trap. This may be especially true when dealing with native ungulates in national parks, as emphasized by Caughley (1976b, 1979), Sinclair (1977, 1979), and McNaughton (1979a). Vegetation–ungulate systems are often interactive; the grazed vegetation may differ substantially in structure, composition, and biomass from the ungrazed state (Caughley 1976b; see also Chap. 9). Furthermore, range and wildlife managers usually strive to obtain the vegetation–ungulate equilibrium at economic carrying capacity (K_c), which, as mentioned earlier, is characterized by a comparatively large standing biomass of vegetation and a small biomass of ungulates. A very different equilibrium occurs at ecological carrying capacity (K_I); this is characterized by a much larger biomass of ungulates and a smaller biomass of edible vegetation. It follows that the biotic effects on the vegetation are much more intense at K_I. These concepts have not been widely appreciated; consequently, whenever the vegetation characteristics used to measure K_c are applied to national parks, where K_I is the appropriate objective, the vegetation is invariably reported to be overgrazed and deteriorated (Caughley 1976b, 1979). Ecological carrying capacity is the perspective from which the ungulate–vegetation system of the northern range needs to be evaluated.

The presence of high densities of long-lived ungulates in a variable and periodically harsh environment means that ungulates must leave some measure or expression of their presence on the landscape. The exceptionally difficult question to be addressed is how great a biotic effect should be expected from populations near K_I and how should these conditions be distinguished from more intense effects heralding the destabilization of a grazing system through some influence of modern man?

The hypothetical extirpation of ungulates from the northern range provides a useful perspective from which this question may be addressed. This hypothetical extripation was simulated by exclosures, by herd reductions in the park, and by reduction or elimination of some resident native ungulate species outside the park. The data from this study suggest that the initial observable or measureable effects would be small. This is because negative feedback on the ungulate populations in this grazing system mainly occurs in winter from dormant or cured vegetation (see Chap. 9). Nutrients in these dormant plants have been translocated and stored in roots of grasses and in roots and older stems of shrubs (Garrison 1972); these plant resources are largely unavailable to wintering ungulates.

Vigor and standing crop of grasses would increase on ridgetop and upper-slope sites. Crown size and density of some shrubs on these and adjacent upper slopes would increase. Without fire, some aspen stands would reproduce, but in many cases densities would be insufficient to replace parent clones. Conifers would continue to replace aspen. Height and crown size of willows, and possibly density, would increase at some sites. Coniferous forests might advance more quickly into some grasslands. Conspicuous trail systems, bedding areas, wallows, etc., would become vegetated. Trampling of xeric grasslands would be eliminated.

With time, subtle but profound changes would occur. Species composition, dynamics, and genetic makeup of some plant populations could shift as the selective force of grazing was eliminated. Grasslands would become more homogeneous as the vegetation mosaics produced from both the grazing and nongrazing (walking, bedding, wallowing, dung and urine deposition, etc.) activities of ungulates disappeared. [This effect has not been well measured on the northern range, but my impression from comparing grasslands inside and outside exclosures is that this would occur. Also, this effect is characteristic of any grazed vegetation (Harper 1977:449)]. In short, although the vegetation would become different, many differences would be subtle.

Data from this study showed that even at very low ungulate densities on the northern range, and in the continued absence of fire, most aspen would fail to reproduce; willows would be heavily utilized; and ridgetop and upper slopes would be maintained as stable but heavily grazed vegetation. These effects occurred because of the quantitative relationships of these plant communities to the major forage supplies of the ungulate populations; i.e., these forages were consumed incidentally to those that in the aggregate determined ungulate densities (Chap. 9). As a consequence, ungulates on the northern range had the capacity to influence the rate of some primary seres (willow) and postfire secondary seres (aspen) when the timing and direction of change were determined by other agents. It is worth noting that the vegetation on ridgetops and upper slopes remains in stable condition because early spring grazing of growing plants is followed by an absence of late spring and summer grazing—ungulates move to other sites or off the area. Early spring grazing on native grasses and forbs has less effect on production and survival than was once supposed—provided that no further use occurs during the growing season (Stoddart 1946, McCarty and Price 1942, Blaisdell and Pechanec 1949, Mueggler 1967).

There is no definitive answer to the question of how great the biotic effects should be from free-ranging ungulate populations near K_l. There are *a priori* reasons to think that these could be substantial; i.e., extensive areas could be maintained as a zootic climax (when compared to a theoretical climatic climax or to vegetation within an exclosure) or rates of plant succession could be greatly affected, particularly when set in motion by other agents and when these have little quantitative feedback as food sources. In general, the studies to date show surprisingly light biotic effects overall and suggest a relatively stable ungulate–vegetation system. Certainly the evidence does not support the interpretation of progressive pathological range deterioration.

In sum, the limited departures of vegetation from pristine conditions that occurred on spring, summer, and autumn ranges of the northern Yellowstone elk resulted from fire suppression and the local introduction of exotic plants. Greater departures occurred on the winter range in the park from fire suppression and to a lesser extent from cultivation and introduction of exotic plants. The effects of fire suppression may be largely reversible as fires are again permitted to burn. The role of elk and other herbivores in these departures appeared to be much less than originally supposed. Artificially high densities of elk and other ungulates contributed to conditions of vegetation in the BLA that otherwise would not have occurred, but even in this area, cultivation and livestock grazing appeared most important.

In general, elk did not appear to be having effects on vegetation exceeding those expected from a population approaching a K_l in a stable vegetation–ungulate system. Portions of the BLA are excepted. The hypothesis that a vegetation–ungulate equilibrium appropriate to the park can be maintained without cropping in the park is generally supported by these data. That the existing vegetation–ungulate equilibrium may still differ from the pristine—and what, if anything, need be done to compensate—is considered elsewhere (Chap. 12).

These interpretations are different from those made in the past and will require monitoring further to refine, reformulate, or reject the hypothesis now held. They differ mostly by considering abiotic influences on vegetation, distinguishing a BLA on the winter range, and recognizing that native ungulates have some natural effects on their environment and that populations near K_l will have greater effects than those at K_c.

CHAPTER 9

Elk–Habitat Relationships

THE SEASONAL USE OF DIFFERENT HABITATS, food habits, forage quality, and measurements of forage utilization by vegetation type are presented in this chapter. The data are mainly from extensive field studies; methods are discussed separately by section.

Habitat Utilization

The combination of vegetation type and slope/exposure was considered a habitat (Barmore 1975). Vegetation types used in studies of elk foraging activity generally were similar to those in Table 8.1, except that a swale physiographic type was added.

Elk foraged seasonally in virtually every vegetation type in the park. Even during winter, when most elk occupied lower-elevation grasslands and forests, some foraged on the highest windswept alpine areas. Their versatility in obtaining forage under variable and periodically harsh winter conditions proved especially difficult to sample or describe. My objectives were to examine the strategy elk used to exploit this environment, to determine the locations of food supplies that maintained the population, and to evaluate foraging contingencies under variable environmental conditions.

Barmore (1975) recorded elk feeding activity by location, vegetation type, slope/aspect classes, behavior, and snow depth while regularly traveling vehicular routes through the northern winter range from October to May 1967–70. Routes covered 76 km; the area observed was about 8% of the winter range (Barmore 1975). Results from these studies have been described in great detail. I continued this sampling from October 1970 to May 1974. My sampling began about 10–15 days later on the average than Barmore's, and only the Lamar Valley route was sampled from October 1973 to May 1974. Our methods were similar. Slope/aspect categories used were not quantified (e.g., "gentle," "moderate," etc.), and interpretations may have been more variable. Winter–spring fixed-wing plane flights also were used to sample elk distribution, numbers, and habitat use patterns (see Chap. 3, The 1969–79 Period).

Observations by vegetation type of 59,784 feeding elk during three seasonal periods from 1967 to 1974 are shown in Fig. 9.1. Foraging patterns, as measured by this method, varied considerably among years within seasonal periods, and percentage use of some types showed progressive changes over the seven years. From 80 to 90% of the observations of foraging elk during October to December occurred on the combination of four highly productive types (mesic upland steppe, shrub steppe, swale grasslands, and wet meadows). The percentage of observations increased annually on wet meadows during this seasonal period; use of xeric steppe and other types combined often was low. January–March use was highly variable, with 30–85% of foraging elk observed on the combined high-producing grasslands. From 11 to 65% of the observations occurred on xeric steppe. There was also a marked change in the percentages of feeding elk observed on some types over the seven years; a decrease occurred on xeric steppe, an increase occurred on wet meadows (the extent of this increase is exaggerated because only the Lamar route was sampled in 1973–74). From 30 to about 90% of April–May observations occurred on high-producing grasslands, especially mesic upland steppe and shrub steppe. Foraging in these types sometimes continued to be on cured grasses during severe late winter conditions on the upper portions of the winter range—but foraging more often reflected use of new spring growth of vegetation. A decrease in percentage of observations on xeric steppe occurred over this period; observations increased on sagebrush steppe. Minor increases in observations on mesic upland steppe and wet meadows also were suggested.

Observations of 45,541 feeding elk by slope and exposure classes for three seasonal periods from 1970 to 1974 are summarized in Fig. 9.2. Seasonal sample sizes are the same as Fig. 9.1. Slope/exposure classes reflected the locations of the vegetation types discussed above. Level to gentle slopes of all exposures accounted for about

FIGURE 9.1.

Observations of 59,784 feeding elk by vegetation type and seasonal periods, 1967–74. Data for 1967 to May 1970 from Barmore (1975). Observations for 1973–74 are from the Lamar route only. See text.

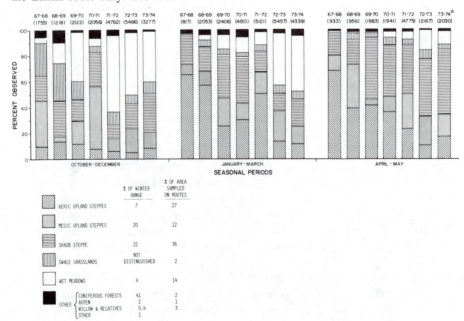

FIGURE 9.2.

Observations of 45,541 feeding elk by slope and exposure classes, 1970–74. Lamar route only in 1973–74.

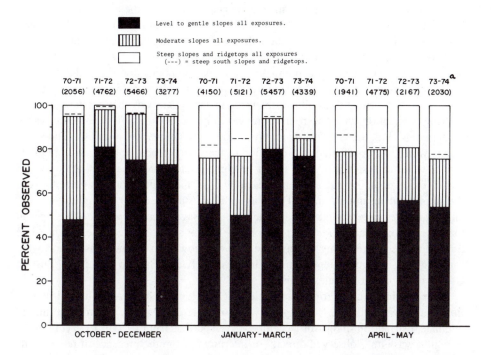

50–80% of the observations of feeding elk during October–December periods over the seven years; moderate slopes, 15–45%. About 50–80% of the observations for January–March occurred on level to gentle slopes; moderate slopes showed 8–27%. Feeding on steep slopes of all exposures and ridgetops increased to 6–25%; steep, south slopes and ridgetops accounted for 5–18%. Foraging on level and gentle slopes decreased to 45–55% during April–May periods; use of moderate slopes increased to about 20–35%; steep slopes and ridgetops, 20–25%. Elk sometimes shifted to ridgetops and upper slopes in preference for spring growth. Because of sampling biases (see below), use on moderate slopes probably was underestimated; use of gentle and steep slopes, ridgetops, and level areas was overestimated.

Snow depths in which elk foraged were recorded during route coverage. About 94% of 19,067 feeding elk observed during January–March periods for 1971–74 foraged in about 30 cm of snow or less; 6% fed in 30–75 cm of snow. These observations were particularly difficult to interpret because there was no measure of depths where elk were not feeding and no measure of snow crusting or density, which probably was more important in limiting feeding activities. During the severe late winter and spring of 1975, I recorded female–young elk groups regularly feeding in 45–60 cm of snow; groups of adult males fed in 60–75 cm of snow in the Gardner's Hole area. Barmore (1975:419) analyzed snow depths in which elk foraged during 1967–70 and reported that "snow density and hardness appeared to be more constraining than depth up to about 24 inches [60 cm], but depth alone was constraining in deeper snow."

Elk utilization of different habitats was influenced by many variables. These included the depth, density, duration, and distribution of snow cover and the rate and extent of spring greenup of grasses. The elk population also increased from around 4,000 to over 10,000 during the study period. Further, the behavior of the elk changed following termination of herd reductions in 1968. Reductions appear to have either greatly reduced groups that frequented areas near roads (i.e., the area sampled during habitat utilization studies) or conditioned survivors to avoid the open, highly productive grasslands and wet meadows where they were more vulnerable to human predation (at least during daylight hours). I attribute some of the progressive change in habitat use over the seven years to a combination of increasing population size and a lessening of this conditioned avoidance behavior, as well as highly variable snow conditions.

The most serious difficulty in interpreting these data was that habitats, as indicated by vegetation types, were not sampled in proportion to their occurrence on the winter range (Fig. 9.1). Of the major types, the xeric steppe, wet meadows, and shrub steppe were overrepresented in proportion to their occurrence on the area; coniferous forests were undersampled. This might be compensated for by calculating correction factors based upon the true amount of each type—if the assumption was made that use was similar on unsampled areas. This was not always the case. For example, it was not unusual in late winter for elk to leave the extensive sagebrush steppe on south slopes in the upper Lamar Valley; recorded use on this habitat showed a decrease. At the same time, however, fixed-wing flights (see below) showed that thousands of elk were foraging on sagebrush steppe on south slopes between Buffalo and Little Buffalo Creeks at slightly lower elevations.

Fixed-wing flights provided a somewhat different perspective on habitat utilization. Numbers of elk and foraging activities of large groups were recorded during 20 ungulate distribution flights for December–April periods from 1970 to 1975 (Fig. 9.3). Foraging was either observed directly or interpreted from the presence of recent trails and feeding craters during periods of snow cover. Snow cover usually was complete for December–March flights. Maximum counts were obtained in December and January. This was coincident with extensive foraging on high-producing grasslands, especially wet meadows, swales, sagebrush steppe, and mesic steppe on lower slopes. In some years, elk were able to utilize these productive grasslands throughout the winter and aerial observations were similar to those made from the ground. Little foraging was observed in and around coniferous forests during early winter.

Numbers counted decreased to 55–85% of maximum counts in late January, February, usually in March, and sometimes into April—in a direct relationship with the severity of environmental conditions. I attributed this decrease primarily to increased foraging in forests, although it was sometimes influenced by differences in counting conditions (partial snow cover) and mortality. The decreases always corresponded with observations of elk and signs of their foraging in forest areas. Flights were made on those rare days between prolonged stormy periods and as a result still underestimated the importance of forest areas. This forest habitat use pattern was not detected from ground studies.

Extensive foraging in sagebrush steppe on south slopes also was commonly observed during severe environmental conditions. Foraging also increased on all other slope sites and on ridgetops during these periods. During conditions of deep crusted snows, elk foraged in mesic steppe on slopes where the snow was deeper but uncrusted. Elk counts sometimes increased again in April when spring growth of vegetation began (May counts were omitted from Fig. 9.3, because many animals had moved off the area). This was coincident with observations of foraging on xeric and mesic upland steppes and shrub steppes. The relative use of these various types depended

FIGURE 9.3

Elk counted during fixed-wing flights as percent of maximum annual count, and generalized foraging activities. Maximum winter counts given in Table 3.2.

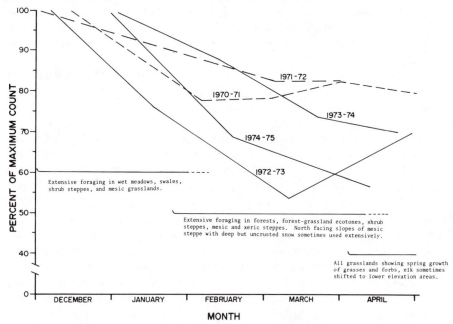

upon spring conditions. Rapid widespread onset of growth led to dispersed foraging activities throughout the area; retarded spring conditions with prolonged cold and snow cover led to increased short-term foraging in the xeric steppes on ridgetops and upper slopes. Elk sometimes shifted to lower elevations during spring greenup.

This is a very generalized description of foraging activities; the timing of the changes in foraging varied considerably. For example, the most severe environmental conditions I observed occurred during a mid-April 1975 flight when deep, crusted snows occurred throughout the area. Other years the elk were foraging on green grass by mid-April. Furthermore, foraging conditions often varied considerably in different areas at the same time: elk at Gardiner and Mammoth foraged on green grass in mid-May 1975, while those in the Lamar Valley foraged in forests and on ridgetops in deep, crusted snow; elk in the Lamar remained on valley bottom grasslands in February 1978, while deeper snow forced others on the Blacktail Plateau to forage in forests.

Sampling difficulties, areal and temporal variations in environmental conditions, and changes in behavior of elk limit interpretations of these observations. A generalized winter foraging strategy for elk seems to be as follows: after arriving on the northern winter range, extensive foraging occurs on the highest-producing grassland vegetation types; on bottomlands, swales, and lower slopes. Elk continue to forage on these types throughout some winters; other winters they return to them with any easing of conditions. This strategy seems to be one of obtaining a maximum amount of the highest-quality food (see below) in the least time with the least expenditure of energy. All vegetation types on all slopes and exposures become more important as environmental conditions increase in severity, with crusted or deep snows excluding elk from lower slopes and bottomlands. Under these conditions forests, ecotones between forests and upland steppes, sagebrush steppes, and xeric steppes become especially important foraging areas. The combination of forests with adjacent slope steppes is an especially crucial forage source during severe winters. Wind-swept upper slopes are important late winter forage sources at higher elevations. Spring foraging on growing grasses is highly variable; some years, ridgetops and upper slopes are heavily used for short periods; other years, elk disperse throughout all grasslands, from bottomlands to ridgetops.

Barmore (1975) analyzed data for 1967–70 and came to somewhat similar conclusions. Differences between our interpretations seemed related largely to the winter conditions observed and to greater use of roadside habitats as the population increased and avoidance behavior lessened.

Habitat use patterns on summer ranges were not sampled during this study. Cole (1969a) sampled elk use of vegetation types on summer areas in southern Yellowstone from 1962 to 1966 on ranges shared by the northern and southern Yellowstone elk herds. Elk foraged extensively in forest parks, old burns (upland forest types burned since 1930), and subalpine herblands from mid-June through July. Elk often made extensive use of forest types from mid-August through September. The time, duration, and intensity of use of each type was *highly variable* among years; use apparently depended upon snow conditions (extensive snow banks may persist into July), plant phenology, and the presence of molesting insects. Cole (1969a:58) suggested that the conspicuous August dispersal from high-elevation ranges into forests might be caused by female avoidance of early sexual behavior of adult male elk. An additional influence on these movements may be related to food quality. Plant development in forest understories lags behind that at other sites, and understory plants may also be less susceptible to early killing frosts; thus, food quality could remain relatively high in forests during late summer and autumn as it declines elsewhere. Gruell (1973) provided additional observations of the highly variable nature of elk summer use of vegetation types on ranges adjacent to southern Yellowstone Park from 1967 to 1971. Summer use varied so greatly between years that Gruell (1973:40) likened summer elk grazing to a complex deferred rotation grazing system—plants grazed one year may go unused the following year, and a substantial quantity of forage is left untouched. This pattern of use contributed to the survival of individual plants. Observations made by me during 1970–78 in conjunction with other field work suggested that similar, highly variable use of vegetation types occurred on spring, summer, and autumn ranges. Spring distribution and use of vegetation types was particularly variable (Houston: unpubl. flight reports 1970–78).

Food Habits

Quantitative data on seasonal food habits of the northern Yellowstone elk were provided by two studies. Greer et al. (1970) analyzed 793 rumen samples collected mostly (97%) from January 1962 to June 1967. Rumens were from elk killed in herd reductions or during periodic special collections. Because food habits were not the primary study objective (Greer et al. 1970:1), the vegetation types from which animals were collected were not recorded, nor were elk collected in relation to their occurrence on vegetation types. Cole (1969a) studied food habits of the Jackson Hole elk from 1962 to 1967 by recording instances of plant use at elk feeding sites on different vegetation types. Most of the 20,714 instances of plant use recorded at 118 feeding sites, during

July–September 15, on five mountain vegetation types was done in southern Yellowstone on ranges shared by both elk herds.

Rumen samples showed great individual variation at all seasons, even when collected from the same groups of elk at the same time. For this reason, and for others discussed below, only the broadest generalizations seem possible. Grasses (including sedges and rushes as grasslike plants) averaged 80 ± 14.2% (56–92%) by volume in 247 rumens collected during January–March periods. (The winter sample of 1966 consisted of only 9 rumens collected during March and is omitted here.) Browse averaged 17 ± 14.9% (6–43%) and increased in volume during severe winters. Forbs averaged only 3 ± 2.1%. Rumens collected from April to June (323) contained predominantly grasses (80–90%) but showed increased consumption of forbs (2–18%). Nearly all rumens contained small amounts of shrubs (1–9%) during this period. July–August rumens (22 collected for 1963 only) suggested that grasses continued to be most important (58%), but the use of forbs increased over April–June values (to 26%). In marked contrast, studies of 118 feeding sites for July–September 15 showed forbs to be the most frequently eaten forage class (47–85%) on forest park, herblands, burns, and coniferous forest vegetation types (Cole 1969a). Grasses and forbs were consumed equally on subalpine meadows. Grasses were usually the most abundant items in rumens (192) from September to December (37–75%). During the same period, forb consumption decreased and shrub consumption sometimes increased.

Certain forages are discussed here because of interpretations of habitat conditions and plant succession made in other sections of this report. Late spring and summer diets of forbs (which were much less available at other seasons), supplemented with leaves of actively growing grasses and shrubs, represented an extremely high plane of nutrition (see Geist 1974). This was also the period of growth, lactation, and accumulation of large energy reserves as fat deposits. Grasses and grasslike plants predominated in diets from autumn to spring, although shrubs increased during winter periods. It is important to note that this grass forage consisted largely of cured, dried (i.e., dead) leaves and culms of dormant plants for October to mid-April periods when highest elk densities occurred on the winter range. The remainder of the winter diet consisted mainly of twigs from dormant deciduous shrubs. Exceptions included big sagebrush which retained leaves and conifers which retained needles year-round. Both were eaten in small amounts by elk throughout the year, with increased consumption shown during severe winter conditions. While these forages were less palatable than many others, their year-round occurrence in the diet suggests that they were not just emergency food. Willows usually occurred only in trace amounts and in low frequency during January–March periods (true for other seasons as well). Aspen usually occurred in trace amounts or low percentages during October–March periods. Exceptions occurred in the January–March 1962 (14%) and the October–December 1965 collections (38%). The 1965 sample was taken from elk shot in aspen stands (Greer et al. 1970:24), and a grouping of the 1962 collections by forage categories (Greer et al. 1970:47) suggested similar collection sites. The small amounts of both aspen and willow on the area made them quantitatively insignificant in the winter forage requirements of the elk herd.

Clearly, it was extremely difficult to sample the food habits of an animal as versatile as elk. All methods, even analysis of rumen contents, may return surprisingly biased results (Nelson and Leege 1979). In addition to selection for plant species, the seasonal selection for plant parts, not reported in these studies, may represent a very important aspect of dietary change (see Sinclair 1975, 1977). Observations made during summer and autumn of 1970–78 showed that feeding elk often selected: (1) only the youngest leaves from some species of shrubs (leaving older leaves and stems), (2) the youngest, actively growing parts of forbs, and (3) the inflorescences and seed pods from a wide variety of forbs, grasses, and shrubs. This represented selection for extremely high-quality diets. Thus, the studies reported here should be considered approximations. The same herd reductions that so influenced interpretations of habitat use patterns also affected rumen collections. Collections probably undersampled animals that foraged in wet meadows and forests (the former were greatly reduced, the latter would have been comparatively more difficult to collect). Individual rumen samples, collection sites, and times varied considerably during the study (Greer et al. 1970:48–49). Changes in seasonal diets from one year to another were interpreted as reflecting different environmental conditions and elk population levels (Greer et al. 1970). This was doubtless true to some extent, but differences also may have reflected changes in collecting sites and in elk behavior that occurred during reductions.

Forage Quality

The seasonal changes in nutritional quality of forage available to elk and other ungulates in the Rocky Mountains are too well known to require lengthy comment (Cook 1972, Geist 1974, 1979, Hobbs et al. 1979, Nelson and Leege 1979). In general, quality is highest during late spring and early summer periods of rapid plant growth; quality declines over summer and autumn as vegetation matures; quality is lowest during winter when plants are dormant (Hobbs et al. 1980). Definitions of food quality vary; quality depends upon the complex interplay between the chemical composition of the plants and their digestibility in relation to the seasonal changes in physiological demands on the ungulate (Dietz 1970, Nelson and Leege 1979, Hobbs et al. 1979). I do not intend to venture far into these relationships, but a broad view of the quality of forage available to elk wintering on the northern range seems useful to interpret the information on food habits and habitat use.

The amount of nitrogen, as crude protein, in forage is very important to wintering elk (see Chap. 6; see also Hobbs et al. 1979, Nelson and Leege 1979). Following Crampton and Harris (1969), Cowan et al. (1970), and Sinclair (1977:230), I used crude protein (CP) content as a rough index to forage quality. CP levels were very low for grasses collected from four different vegetation types on the northern range during the winter of 1978 (Fig. 9.4). (Large samples for each type were clipped at three different sites and pooled for analysis. CP was determined by the Chemistry Station Lab, Montana State University.) The cured leaves and culms of bluebunch wheatgrass in xeric grasslands from ridgetop sites had the lowest values throughout the winter. Idaho fescue in mesic grasslands on lower slopes had the highest values in November and January, but these declined by March (small amounts of green leaves remained at the bases of these snow-covered plants during the first two collections). Samples from wet meadows and forest understories had CP levels that were intermediate to the other types; these remained at less than 5% throughout the winter (forage density was sometimes quite low in forest understories; see Appendix VIII). CP increased rapidly with the spring greenup of grasses on ridgetops and upper slope sites (Fig. 9.4).

Data on late autumn and winter CP levels of shrubs and trees on the northern range were even more limited: aspen twigs, 5.2%; rabbitbrush, 9.2% (Rush 1932a); "willows," 6.6%; Douglas-fir, 6.1% (Craighead et al. 1973); big sagebrush leaves

FIGURE 9.4.

Percent crude protein of grass and sedge species for four vegetation types during winter 1978.

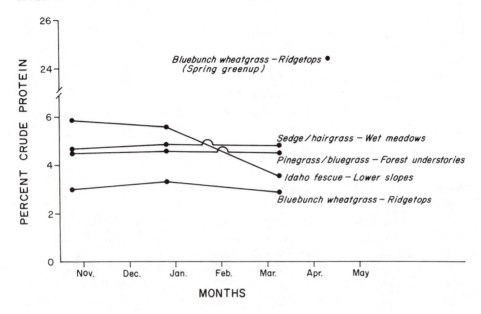

and twigs, 13.3–14.1% (Rush 1932a, this study); big sagebrush seed stalks, 9.1%; and green rabbitbrush, 7.0% (this study). A broader picture can be drawn of CP in woody plants if these data are combined with other studies from adjacent areas (Craighead et al. 1973, Houston 1968, Morton 1976, Stewart 1975). Fourteen samples from nine species of deciduous shrubs (aspen, cottonwood, chokecherry, smooth sumac, rose, four willow species) had mean CP for twigs of 6.9 ± 1.6 (5.0–9.8)%. Seven samples from four conifers (Rocky Mountain juniper, Douglas-fir, lodgepole pine, subalpine fir) had 6.7 ± .89 (5.6–7.9)% CP. Eight samples from evergreen shrubs (big sagebrush, fringed sage, rabbitbrushes) had 10.2 ± 2.37 (8.6–14.1)% CP. These data showed that while shrubs usually contained somewhat greater amounts of CP than grasses, the overall values were still quite low. Some of the highest values, e.g., big sagebrush, were in the less palatable species.

CP values by species vary somewhat between winters and collection sites (Morton 1976), but these values probably represent general conditions on the northern range. The values for shrubs and grasses are quite similar to those from an elk winter range in Colorado (Hobbs et al., 1980). Although less than satisfactory, these measurements did indicate the low overall quality of the winter forage available for elk. These values underestimate the CP levels in the diet because of food selection. This could be particularly true of wet meadows, where the bases of sedges and grasses sometimes remained green during most of the winter; elk often appeared to be selecting these. When residual green leaves were separated from cured leaves in a separate January 1978 sample from wet meadows, the CP was 7.2%.

The high density and comparatively high quality of forage available in wet meadows, swales, and lower slopes likely explains elk use of these sites in winter for as long as they are available. The shift to increased late winter consumption of shrubs may reflect reduced availability of herbaceous species as snow accumulates or a food selection tactic to compensate for decreased winter protein levels of grasses (Hobbs et al. 1979) or both. Winter consumption of shrubs, with somewhat greater protein levels, carries a penalty for elk; digestibility of shrubs is lower than for grasses (Hobbs et al. 1979). Increased use of upland sites during spring periods is surely a response to the high-quality food available from new growth. Increased consumption of forbs in late spring and summer could reflect selection for CP levels that are, on average, higher than for grasses (Cook 1972). This crude survey, showing the low quality of winter forage, generally supported the earlier interpretation that winter nutrition was quite poor, and, as a result, elk could be undernourished even at low population levels (Chap. 6). This in turn affected the dynamics of the population (Chap. 5).

Forage Utilization

Winter and spring forage utilization was monitored during May and June 1971–78 on different vegetation types and physiographic sites. A few measurements were also made in 1970. Transects were established throughout the major wintering areas. The winter elk population increased from about 6,000 to over 12,000 during this period. Measurements also included foraging by bison (their population increased from 85 to 230), moose, mule deer, bighorn sheep, and pronghorn. Percent weight utilization of cured bunchgrasses was measured by the ungrazed plant method using 100 plant samples (Cole 1963); percent utilization of grasses and grasslike plants that lacked a bunch form was estimated (USDA Forest Service 1969). An index to utilization of shrubs was based upon estimates of the percent of browsed twigs (Cole 1963). Additionally, supplemental field notes were taken on range use.

Utilization of grasses and grasslike plants at 75 sites on the main winter range is shown in Table 9.1. Twenty-seven ridgetop and upper-slope sites usually showed consistently heavy utilization ($\geq$ 70%) of cured grasses during 1971–78. Mean use during the exceptionally mild winter of 1977 was significantly lower (Tukeys W-procedure, $P < .05$); no significant association was detected between utilization and winter elk numbers ($r^2 = .14$, $P > .10$). Estimates from June 1970 also showed 75–80% utilization on nine ridgetop sites from Hellroaring Creek to Soda Butte Creek. Forty-four sample units on mid- to lower slopes, swales, bunchgrass bottoms, and wet meadows (several abandoned hayfields included) showed highly variable, light to moderate utilization from 1971 to 1978. Use of wet meadows was low in 1976 and 1978 because severe winter conditions restricted access to these sites; use was low in 1977 because animals remained dispersed over a wide area. However, mean use did not vary significantly among years for any type or site ($P > .05$). Utilization at two–four sites in forest understories was light to moderate but highly variable. Use seemed greater during the severe winters of 1975, 1976, and 1978, but differences were not significant. Measurements at some wet meadow and swale sites included utilization by bison in addition to elk; measurements on some upper slope sites included use by bighorn sheep.

Eleven sites in the BLA showed patterns of utilization similar to that of other range areas, except that use was somewhat greater on lower slopes and swale sites. Ridgetop sites showed heavy use with no significant changes over time. Slopes and bottomlands showed highly variable, increasing moderate to heavy use, but again annual differences were not significant. Field notes showed that large amounts of cured grass remained unconsumed in the BLA following the winters of 1970–73 and again

TABLE 9.1
Winter Utilization of Grasses and Grasslike Plants on Northern Winter Range, 1971–78

Sites	Sample Units (No.)	Percent Utilization (Mean ± SD)							
		1971	1972	1973	1974	1975	1976	1977	1978
Main winter range[a]									
Ridgetops and upper slopes	27	76 ± 5.8	76 ± 6.9	74 ± 9.0	74 ± 10.1	74 ± 10.1	66 ± 16.2	61 ± 19.9	71 ± 13.3
Mid- to lower slopes	11	41 ± 18.9	39 ± 22.3	41 ± 22.0	48 ± 18.4	45 ± 19.0	36 ± 22.5	26 ± 19.6	33 ± 22.0
Swales and bunchgrass bottoms	19	33 ± 16.9	37 ± 19.5	40 ± 20.9	42 ± 19.7	45 ± 19.3	37 ± 23.3	33 ± 21.0	30 ± 17.2
Wet meadows	14	23 ± 14.5	28 ± 17.5	31 ± 13.2	32 ± 17.0	34 ± 16.7	18 ± 16.0	20 ± 14.8	19 ± 10.8
Forest understory	4	30 ± 28.3	30 ± 17.3	33 ± 12.6	38 ± 20.6	55 ± 10.0	40 ± 25.8	33 ± 26.3	48 ± 12.6
BLA[b]									
Ridgetops and upper slopes	4	64 ± 7.5	75 ± 5.8	73 ± 9.6	78 ± 5.0	80 ± 0	80 ± 0	65 ± 10.0	78 ± 5.0
Mid- to lower slopes	4	46 ± 31.5	68 ± 15.0	58 ± 25.0	60 ± 24.5	73 ± 5.0	75 ± 10.0	48 ± 28.7	75 ± 5.8
Swales and bunchgrass bottoms	3	50 ± 28.3	53 ± 31.8	75 ± 7.1	80 ± 0	75 ± 7.1	75 ± 7.1	50 ± 0	65 ± 21.2

[a]Ridgetop units sampled bluebunch wheatgrass (14) and Idaho fescue (13); only 25 units in 1972. Midslope units sampled Idaho fescue (9) and bluebunch wheatgrass (2). Swales sampled Idaho fescue (15), bluebunch wheatgrass (3), timothy (1); only 16 units in 1971, 14 in 1972. Wet meadows sampled sedges (11), tufted hairgrass (1), timothy (1), smooth brome (1); only 12 units in 1971, 11 in 1972. Forest understory sampled Idaho fescue under Douglas fir; only 2 units in 1971, 3 in 1972.
[b]Ridgetop sites sampled bluebunch wheatgrass (2) and needle-and-thread (2). Midslopes sampled bluebunch wheatgrass (3) and Idaho fescue (1). Swales sampled bluebunch wheatgrass (1), needle-and-thread (1), and crested wheatgrass (1).

147

after the mild winter of 1977; little or none remained following the other winters. Utilization of these food supplies in the BLA was influenced by increasing elk densities (see Chap. 4), winters that permitted access to bottomlands, and probably by a relaxation of conditioned avoidance behavior following the elk reductions as animals foraged progressively farther from escape cover. (Use at some roadside units on the main range in 1970–74 was also lower than in adjacent areas, probably for this same reason.)

The percentage of browsed leaders on willows and big sagebrush at 26 sites is shown in Table 9.2. Use of big sagebrush was primarily by elk in upper range areas but included foraging by mule deer in the Mammoth area and by mule deer and pronghorn in the BLA. Elk and moose were the primary users of willow. Utilization of willow on the main range was consistently high for 1970–78. Use on one BLA transect from 1973 to 1978 was usually high, but more variable. Field notes suggested that utilization of roadside willow stands increased from 1970 to 1974. Again this was attributed to some combination of increasing elk numbers and to changes in animal behavior following the reductions. The percentage of browsed leaders of big sagebrush on the main range was low to moderate and showed a weak positive association with winter elk numbers ($r^2 = .55$, $P < .025$). As described below, elk made substantial use of the abundant seed stalks of big sage, in addition to the browsing of twigs and leaves recorded here. Sagebrush use in the BLA, as measured on one sample unit and as recorded in field notes, generally was quite heavy, 1977 excepted. Notes also showed that vegetative reproduction of aspen was heavily browsed throughout this period, several roadside stands excepted. Browsing of the abundant green rabbitbrush on upper slope sites usually was heavy, as was use of winter fat and fringed sage in the BLA (1977 again excepted).

Utilization of grasses on xeric steppe located mainly on south or west slopes and ridgetops was highly variable and averaged 30% from 1963 to 1969 (Barmore 1975). Measured utilization was highest in the winter of 1967, when overall elk densities were near their lowest. Utilization was reduced on some ridgetop and slope sites in roadside areas and in the BLA (see Appendix VI, yd^2 quadrats on harsh physiographic sites). However, utilization remained high in areas less affected by herd reductions (Barmore 1975:244), and on ridgetop bighorn wintering areas. Utilization of big sagebrush remained low on much of the range, but high in the BLA. Utilization of aspen generally remained high even at low elk densities. These overall measurements and observations of utilization were quite similar to my own.

Measurements have shown only a rough pattern of plant utilization on the winter range. They do not show the quantitative importance of different sites as a food source. For example, 30–40% utilization of wet meadows, which occupy 4% of the area and produce perhaps 4,500 kg/ha, is a much more important source of forage (when available) than an equivalent area of ridgetop producing maybe 200 kg/ha. Utilization of vegetation in forest areas, though variable and often locally very light, is nonetheless important during extremely severe winter periods.

The combination of range measurements and photographs suggested that the effect of winter grazing on composition, productivity, and vigor of cured grasses was minimal. By contrast, the irregular spring grazing on the new growth of perennial grasses and forbs on ridgetop and upper-slope sites has more influence on the plants (see Chap. 8). The percentage of plants (not percent utilization) showing spring grazing on 12–21 ridgetop sites from 1971 to 1978 was quite variable but often 50–80% on individual transects. The combination of spring grazing and associated trampling of thawing soils contributed to maintenance of those limited sites termed zootic climaxes.

TABLE 9.2
Winter Utilization of Willows and Big Sage on Northern Winter Range, 1970–78

Species and Site	Sample Units (No.)	Percent of Browsed Leaders (Mean ± SD)								
		1970	1971	1972	1973	1974	1975	1976	1977	1978
Main winter range[a]										
Willow	9	91 ± 6.5	92 ± 7.0	93 ± 5.7	92 ± 5.1	90 ± 7.5	93 ± 3.5	94 ± 2.2	83 ± 15.8	93 ± 2.5
Big sage	15		11 ± 9.8	15 ± 25.8	18 ± 14.9	17 ± 11.1	18 ± 8.2	12 ± 11.3	10 ± 12.7	15 ± 17.1
BLA										
Willow	1				60	50	50	70	10	95
Big sage	1		70	50	80	50	25	70	30	50

[a]Only 8 willow units in 1971, 7 in 1972; units sampled mostly blueberry willow and Geyer's willow. Only 14 sage units in 1971, 13 in 1972.

Heavy winter grazing of the dormant vegetation on ridgetops and upper slopes occurred from 1970 to 1978 as the elk population doubled in size. The forage available on these sites was consumed at even low densities of animals, and monitoring of forage consumption on such sites cannot be used to determine ecological carrying capacity. Other forage sources, in the aggregate, seemed more important in determining carrying capacity. Willow, a very limited forage source, was consumed even at low ungulate densities (aspen showed this same relationship).

Some added notes of caution are necessary in interpreting these data. These sample units were located on perhaps a dozen of the hundreds of plant species that occurred on the area. It was difficult, nearly impossible, to monitor satisfactorily use on even the sampled species, because variable winter conditions and elk distributions resulted in a complex and changing pattern of forage consumption. The units were biased by location in the sense that often they were deliberately placed in areas with high winter and spring elk densities. Supplemental field notes showed that over much of the remaining northern range it was difficult even to measure forage removal because it was so light.

Interpretation: Elk–Habitat Relationships

Studies of habitat use and food habits showed that the northern Yellowstone elk were successful generalists able to utilize many different resources. Elk foraged in all vegetation types in the park and ate a wide spectrum of different grasses, forbs, and shrubs. Their ecological strategy included migrations into energy- and nutrient-rich but only seasonally available areas for periods of growth and accumulation of energy reserves. This strategy also included full occupancy of all suitable winter range. While on winter ranges their foraging strategy seemed to be one of obtaining the most high-quality food in the shortest time with the least expenditure of energy. The ability of mature, socially dominant elk to obtain winter maintenance diets during severe environmental conditions was awesome (Fig. 9.5). Combinations of vegetation types and slope/exposures formed a complex mosaic of alternative foraging sites. No single type or slope/exposure determined ecological carrying capacity. Data on forage utilization would not support the interpretation that the limited forage produced on windswept ridgetops and steep slopes (sites sometimes arbitrarily considered as critical winter range) determined this carrying capacity. Calculations suggested that these zootic climax sites supplied only 1–6% of the winter forage requirements of the elk population (Appendix VIII). The combination of seasonal movements and the versatile foraging strategy permitted the maintenance of a much greater biomass of elk than would otherwise be possible.

The Food Supply and the Grazing System

The absolute abundance of winter forage for elk was influenced by climate and, historically, by natural fires. The relative availability of winter forage was influenced greatly by snow conditions; declines in availability could be gradual or abrupt, depending upon the rate of snow accumulation. These abiotic influences interacted to produce a highly variable environment. Some of the largest elk migrations to lower elevations, and highest winter mortality, occurred with the greatest absolute abundance of forage

FIGURE 9.5.
Adult female elk consumed a great variety of comparatively low-quality foods during winter. Photo by M. Sample.

but with a relative shortage due to snow conditions that reduced availability. Biotic influences also affected both absolute abundance and relative availability of winter forage: abundance was reduced by consumption; availability was often reduced when the foraging activities of elk themselves accelerated the maturation of snow cover to form hard crusts that restricted further foraging. Other herbivores, particularly invertebrates, affected forage supplies for elk (see below).

Winter food supplies for elk were essentially fixed by autumn, in marked contrast to the nature of the food supplies available on spring and summer ranges. As emphasized earlier (Food Habits), this food supply, of low quality, was composed mainly of cured leaves and culms of dormant grasses and the twigs of dormant deciduous shrubs (some leaves from evergreens). Calculated forage requirements suggested that populations of 12,000–14,000 wintering elk might consume 9–10% of the fixed supply of herbage on the winter range during 15 November–1 May periods (Appendix VIII). Elk represent about 89% of the winter biomass of ungulates (see Chap. 10), so the combined ungulate fauna probably consumes less than 12% of the standing herbage. These are *not* estimates of the net annual primary production consumed by ungulates. Perhaps 70% or more of the net annual production of plants on the winter range was unavailable to wintering ungulates—either physically unavailable (underground or out of reach) or physiologically unavailable (wood, etc.) (see Chap. 8; see also Walter 1973). Ungulates consume much less than 10% of the net primary production on the winter range, even with allowance for an additional 30 days consumption of growing vegetation in the spring and for year-round use by some of each species of ungulate. Consumption was not, of course, distributed evenly. Elk and other ungulates ate a high percentage of the production on xeric steppes, much less on other types.

Estimates of forage consumption give a perspective on the role of elk in the transfer of energy and cycling of nutrients through park ecosystems that could be somewhat misleading. The influence of elk on ecosystem dynamics and structure is surely more subtle than suggested either by the calculated forage removal or by the documented effects on composition and succession of plant communities. This elk population, which seems to be largely resource limited, influences the rate and timing of nutrient cycling on the winter range—just as other ungulate species affect this process in different grazing systems (Bliss 1975, McNaughton 1976). This effect on ecosystem dynamics could be larger, and the outcome much different in nature, than anticipated from the small proportion of net production consumed, particularly when the various nongrazing effects of elk are included (Chap. 8). Grazing may increase net primary production in long-evolved grassland–ungulate systems by altering plant physiology (McNaughton 1979a,b). Increased efficiency of light utilization through removal of accumulated herbage and nutrient recycling by dung and urine are among the many facets of grazing that increase plant production. These influences occur with winter grazing on the northern range, although plant responses would be deferred until the growing season. Increased production also may result from compensatory or enhanced regrowth of grasses grazed during the growing season. Regrowth involves many different mechanisms: increased photosynthetic rates from residual tissues, reduction in the rate of leaf senescence, etc.—influences that could occur on spring and summer elk ranges. Additionally, browsing increases above-ground production on some species of shrubs (Jameson 1963, Mackie 1973, Wolff 1978, Willard and McKell 1978). Conceivably, elk influence ecosystem dynamics by increasing net primary productivity on all seasonal ranges. The possibility of such relationships would be a fruitful area for research.

Plant–herbivore systems may be classed as noninteractive (herbivores do not influence the rate at which their resources are renewed) or as interactive (Caughley 1976a). The year-round grazing system of the northern Yellowstone elk is interactive, but seasonal systems differ considerably. The winter system might be classed as largely noninteractive because of the dormant nature of the food supply and the small demonstrable effects of grazing. However, after considering the probable role of elk in ecosystem dynamics, this classification would be a mistake. A limited-interactive classification seems preferable—recognizing that the interaction is dampened and deferred because of the dormant vegetation. The winter grazing system might be further classed as a limited-interferential-interactive system (Caughley 1976a), because elk do actively interfere with each other's ability to obtain food.

Changes in Ecological Carrying Capacity Over Time

A consideration of the foraging strategy of elk and of the changes in vegetation documented on the winter range suggested the interpretation that *if* ecological carrying capacity for elk has changed in the park over the past century, it increased and became less variable. Consider just the historic effects of fire. The *immediate short-term* effects of fires in late summer or autumn were to greatly reduce forage on the burned area for the upcoming winter. Fire suppression removed this variation from the system. Next, consider the foraging strategy and environmental conditions that occurred during severe winter periods: the increased density and distribution of forest and of sagebrush steppe may have increased both the relative availability and absolute abundance of winter forage by providing additional foraging contingencies. (There probably is an optimum ratio of forest to grassland necessary to produce high elk densities. A massive invasion of grassland by forest would reduce ecological carrying capacity.) Observations suggested that although snow sometimes accumulated in big sagebrush on upper slopes, snow in sagebrush stands often was more granular and less crusted than on adjacent grasslands. Snow shadows formed under big sagebrush, just as under conifers, and these were important foraging areas (Fig. 9.6). The physical characteristics of snow under conifers were much different than in open areas (see Peterson and Allen, 1974, for a summary of these influences elsewhere). Snows were less crusted, less deep, and the maturation of the snow cover was retarded under forest canopies. Big sagebrush and various conifers provided winter rations that are available now to a greater extent. Wintering elk were often observed eating the matured seed stalks from big sage (also Murie 1951:223). Stalks were relatively high in crude protein (9.1%) and often represented a substantial food supply (226 kg/ha average at three lower slope sites clipped in 1977). Previous interpretations of a decreasing carrying capacity for elk during the past century did not consider these relationships, or the net changes in vegetation. Only the absolute change in one plant species or community was considered; e.g., willows decreased; elk eat willows; therefore carrying capacity decreased.

FIGURE 9.6.

Elk sometimes foraged on grasses in the snow shadows that formed at the bases of big sagebrush plants, Lamar Valley, March 1973. Big sagebrush was also lightly browsed. Snow on adjacent upper slopes was heavily crusted.

Fire suppression contributed greatly to the decline of some palatable plant species (aspen), but suppression may also have increased the density of other palatable but fire-sensitive species, e.g. rabbitbrushes, fringed sagebrush (Robertson and Cords 1957, Coupland et al. 1973).

Just how recent climatic changes might have affected ecological carrying capacity for elk on the northern range is much less clear; carrying capacity has fluctuated with climate and will continue to do so. Warmer winter temperatures coupled with the decrease in winter snowfall and snow accumulation could have increased carrying capacity during the past century. This is not the far-fetched possibility it might seem: large changes have occurred in the distribution and abundance of arctic animals in response to seemingly small climatic fluctuations on the scale of a few decades (May 1979). Similar changes could be expected to affect ungulate populations in harsh, high-elevation areas like Yellowstone Park.

A vigorous defense of these interpretations is unwarranted; I discuss the foregoing possibilities because there is a chance that they are correct and to illustrate the complexity of relationships. Gruell (1980b), for example, takes the alternative view that frequent fires enhanced the historic K_l for elk on the Jackson Hole winter ranges. The influence of Euro-American man in suppressing natural fires, and changing these relationships, whatever they may be, is inappropriate within the park.

Herbivory in Perspective

The effects of herbivores upon the vegetation of the park require another look, because preoccupation with ungulates gives a distorted view of their herbivory in ecosystem dynamics.

Pocket gophers occur throughout the grasslands, herblands, and shrub steppes of the park. Populations of this fossorial rodent fluctuate considerably, and judging from the extent of soil disturbance, gophers reach phenomenal densities in deep soils (Gruell 1973). Gophers have a profound effect (albeit wholly natural, Chap. 8) on plant succession and species composition in these communities (Laycock 1958, Cole 1969a, Gruell 1973). Indeed, the effects of gophers were far more conspicuous on some vegetation transects on the northern range than ungulate grazing.

Next to nothing is known about the roles of invertebrates in the dynamics of park ecosystems. However, grasshoppers sometimes reach densities of $36–42/m^2$ during late July on the grasslands of the northern range (Bergstrom 1964). Conservatively, vegetation capable of supporting such densities makes up one-half of the winter range. The overall grasshopper biomass could reach $9 \times 10^6–10.5 \times 10^6$ kg (grasshoppers weighed about 0.5 g each in July 1973), or over 3 times the ungulate biomass (3×10^6 kg, see Chap. 10). Periodically high grasshopper populations characterized the region historically and profoundly affected the vegetation (Bureau of Land Management 1969:10). Forest insects, particularly pine bark beetles and western budworms, periodically reach outbreak levels and kill vulnerable conifers over vast areas of the park. These insects have conspicuous long- and short-term effects on forest composition, succession, and nutrient cycling that also occurred historically (Despain 1972, 1976, Gruell 1980a; see also Chap. 8) and are regarded as natural biotic forces in the park.

Finally, the minute soil fauna, particularly nematode worms, consume far greater amounts of the net primary production in grasslands than all the above-ground fauna (Scott et al. 1979). We know nothing of these relationships for the grasslands of the northern range.

Any of the species or taxa mentioned probably have far greater roles in the flow of energy and cycling of nutrients through park ecosystems than the large, conspicuous ungulates. The mortality of Douglas-fir caused by western budworms on the northern range during the late 1970s was extensive; by comparison fir mortality from ungulate browsing (Chap. 8) paled to insignificance.

CHAPTER 10

Relationships Among Species of Herbivores

Six species of native ungulates currently occupy the northern winter range. Elk are by far the most numerous, followed by mule deer, bighorn sheep, bison, moose, and pronghorn (Table 10.1). The history, distribution, population trends, and dynamics of the five less abundant species are reviewed briefly to introduce the principal topic: resource division and relationships among species, with emphasis on the effects of elk upon the others. Fortunately, much of the information available on these species has been synthesized recently: Meagher (1973) studied life history, ecology, and management of the bison. Barmore (1980) examined interspecific relationships among the ungulates with field studies conducted in 1962–70. These works include reviews of earlier studies and of historical information. Meagher also has in preparation an ecological history of Yellowstone that involved the extraction and interpretation of thousands of early, first-person observations of species abundance and distribution. I can add little to these accounts; this chapter mainly updates the information from 1970–79 field studies and includes my interpretation of interspecific relationships. As with studies of vegetation, the period from about 1955 to 1979 is of particular interest because of the potential effects on the less abundant ungulates from the large reduction and subsequent increase in elk numbers. Reductions of bison and pronghorn populations also were made during this period.

Methods of studying habitat use, distribution, abundance, and herd composition during 1970–79 were generally as described for elk. Methods also had the same shortcomings described, plus some peculiar to each of the other species.

The Less Abundant Ungulates: History, Distribution, Numbers, and Dynamics

A synopsis of historic populations is presented, followed by species accounts for more recent years. Archaeological studies show that bighorn sheep, bison, pronghorn, and

TABLE 10.1
Approximate Winter Numbers, Biomass, and Density of Native Ungulates on the Northern Range, 1978[a]

SPECIES	WINTER NUMBERS	WINTER RANGE	STANDING BIOMASS		DENSITY	APPROXIMATE FEMALE LIVE WT.[b]
		(km²)	*kg × 10³*	*(% total)*	*(No./km²)*	*(kg)*
Elk	12,000	1,000	2,703	(89)	12.0	240
Mule deer	2,000	150	106	(3)	13.3	60
Bighorn sheep	500	50	32	(1)	10.0	60
Bison	260	60	134	(4)	0.2	450
Moose	200	1,000	56	(2)	0.2	300
Pronghorn	150	30	8	(c)	5.0	50

[a] See text for basis of estimates.
[b] Live weights for respective species from Houston (1978b), Mackie (1964), Thorne (1976), Meagher (1973), Schladweiler and Stevens (1973), and O'Gara (1968).
[c] Less than 1% of standing biomass.

deer (probably both mule deer and white-tailed deer) have coexisted with elk for millenia in the Yellowstone River Valley (Lahren 1976). Populations of mule deer, bighorn sheep, and pronghorn were greatly reduced by human predation from the mid-1870s to late 1880s; bison were extirpated from the northern range (Barmore 1980, Meagher 1973, in prep.; see also Appendix I).

Mule deer apparently recovered quickly, and Barmore (1980) suggests that numbers wintering in the park have been "grossly similar from the early 1900s and, perhaps, since primeval times to the present." Numbers wintering outside the park have been variously influenced by human settlement, livestock grazing, and recreational hunting. Bighorn sheep probably were more abundant historically than currently in the Yellowstone region, particularly during summer in the Absaroka Mountains along the present east boundary of Yellowstone Park (Barmore 1980, Meagher, in prep.). The winter distribution of these sheep is unknown, but snow conditions in these mountains suggest to me that many wintered outside the park along the eastern flanks of the Absaroka Range; most would have been eliminated early on. Barmore (1980) notes that bighorns may have been more abundant historically on the northern range and that seemingly excellent sheep habitat outside the park remains unoccupied. Meagher (in prep.) suggests that although bighorns were reduced on some major terrain features on the northern range, remnants persisted and populations increased from about 1890. Accounts suggest that 1,000 or more pronghorn summered in the park during the 1860s and 1870s (Barmore 1980, Meagher, in prep.). Most pronghorn that wintered along the Yellowstone River outside the park were progressively eliminated, until, by the turn of the century, remnant populations of 500–800 wintered in the park and immediately adjacent areas (Barmore 1980, Meagher, in prep). Bison were reintroduced into the Lamar Valley in 1907, following extirpation of early populations estimated at 200–300 (Meagher 1973). However, these bison were maintained to some degree in semidomestication until about 1952 (Meagher 1973; see also Chap. 4).

Moose have not turned up in archaeological sites or other Holocene faunal assemblages from northwest Wyoming and south central Montana (Lahren 1976, pers. commun. 1978, Anderson 1974, Martin and Gilbert 1977, 1978). [One report from a late Pleistocene site in southeast Wyoming is questionable (Anderson 1974).] Moose apparently had not occupied northwest Wyoming during the 1830s but had colonized the Yellowstone area by the 1870s (Houston 1968), perhaps immigrating through southwest Montana (see Walcheck 1976). This situation was not unique. Moose seem to have been uncommonly slow in colonizing many areas of western North America following glacial recession (Kelsall and Telfer 1974). Moose apparently did not occur on the northern winter range until around 1913 (Chap. 8).

Mule Deer

Mule deer are currently the second most abundant ungulate on the northern range, but are, in many respects, the least known. Deer are seasonally migratory and occupy about 15,000 ha of winter range ($\sim$ 35% in the park, 65% outside) as a strip along the lower Gardner and Yellowstone Rivers, mostly below 1,900 m (Figs. 10.1 and 10.2). Winter distribution is dynamic, and during most years the majority of the population winters outside the park. During the severe winter of 1976 virtually all mule deer briefly moved outside the park. Human predation on the population was comparatively light during the 1970s. Population segments that resided year round outside the park were hunted each autumn, but harvests were reduced after 1976, because only males were hunted. Herd segments moving from the park were essentially unhunted. Some deer remain on the northern range year round; others migrate to high-elevation summer

FIGURE 10.1.
Mule deer often wintered on sagebrush steppes below 1,900 m. Yellowstone National Park photo.

FIGURE 10.2.
Map of the northern range showing winter distribution of mule deer and bison. Maps give a very general view of winter distribution. During severe winters the area occupied by deer, for example, would be considerably smaller than indicated.

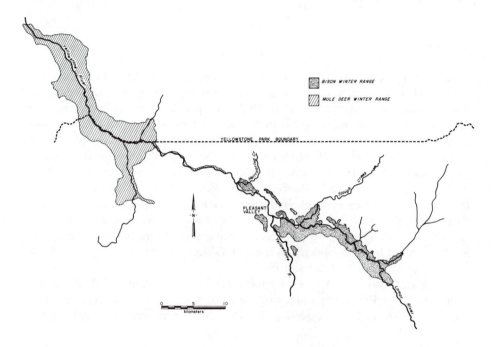

ranges in the park, where they probably intermingle with deer from other discrete winter populations.

About 700–1,100 mule deer were counted during five ground total counts of the northern range during 1930–48 (Barmore 1980). Additionally, 500–800 deer were counted on just the park portion of the winter range during three counts from 1936 to 1946. Deer distribution was monitored periodically during winter and spring fixed-wing flights during 1973–78, but no counts were made. Montana Fish and Game Department personnel counted 1,080 deer by helicopter on 3 April 1979; however, counting conditions were poor on part of the range (Erickson pers. commun. 1979). Tests elsewhere in Montana suggest that 50–65% of the deer present may be observed under such conditions (Mackie et al. 1978, Mackie pers. commun. 1980), thus 1,660–2,160 deer could have been present during the 1979 count. On this basis, I estimated that the winter population was 2,000 during the late 1970s (Table 10.1). Given the limited information available, numbers could have fluctuated around this level for the past 50 years or so.

Early winter deer populations for 1971–79 averaged 45 ± 3.2% females, 40 ± 1.1% young, 4 ± 2.0% yearling males, and 12 ± 3.3% adult males (Appendix IX). These values are broadly similar to those for 1938–39 and 1968–70 (Barmore 1980); differences could easily reflect the time and areas sampled. Comparisons of winter and spring fawn/doe ratios during the late 1930s and late 1960s suggested that, "Variable and sometimes very high over winter fawn mortality [to 76%] . . is apparently characteristic of the population" (Barmore 1980). Predation may be an important proximate cause of winter fawn mortality in the park. I examined 52 dead fawns from 1971 to

1978; coyotes clearly killed 44%. Since most fawns were rapidly and entirely consumed (only rumen contents, hooves, and hair remained), many others could have been predator kills. Deer recruitment is examined below for association with elk numbers and winter severity.

Bighorn Sheep

Bighorn sheep occupy about 5,000 ha during winter (88% in the park) as a narrow, interrupted, strip of cliffs, rock outcrops, and steep slopes along the Yellowstone and lower Lamar and Gardner Rivers (Fig. 10.3). Sheep also winter on similar terrain on mountain peaks around the periphery of the northern range (Fig. 10.4). Most sheep are migratory. Recent seasonal distribution has been discussed by Oldemeyer (1966), Oldemeyer et al. (1971), Woolf (1968), and Barmore (1980). Groups wintering on some major terrain features have been considered to be more or less discrete (Oldemeyer et al. 1971:261, Barmore 1980). Recent studies of the movements of recognizable ewes (Sindt unpubl.) and observations of sheep crossing the Yellowstone River at Mt. Everts (Houston unpubl.) suggest that distribution along the Yellowstone River from lower Specimen Ridge to Bear Creek and Mt. Everts may be quite dynamic; this complex is best considered as one unit. Groups wintering on outlying peaks do seem to be discrete units (Barmore 1980).

Parkwide estimates of sheep numbers were 200–300 from the 1890s to early 1920s (Barmore 1980). Forty-two winter ground counts were conducted during 28 years from 1923 to 1954 (Appendix IX). The counts, areas censused, and counting

FIGURE 10.3.
Bighorn sheep wintered on steep slopes and ridgetops where food density was often low. Photo by M. Sample.

FIGURE 10.4.

Map of the northern range showing winter distribution of bighorn sheep and pronghorn.

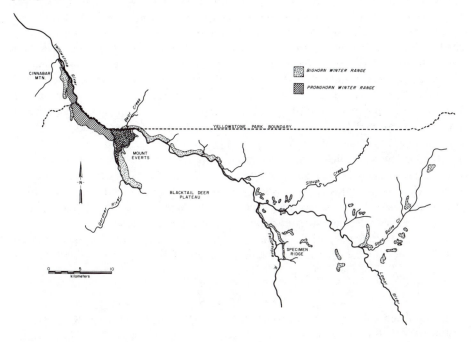

methods varied considerably within and between years. Ground total counts of the entire northern range apparently were made only five years (March 1927, 1940, 1943, 1945, 1948) and probably in 1941 and 1949. Additionally, ground total counts of the northern range in the park were made in 1939, 1946, and possibly 1924. Twenty-three other counts included just the major, more accessible part of the sheep range. The areas censused were not reported for five counts, and in four others only one or two areas were counted. Maximum counts by decade were 346 in 1927, 228 in 1939, and 272 in 1940. The 1927 count was an intense effort launched following reports of sheep mortality from scabies. Accounts suggest that considerable winter mortality occurred during the late 1920s (Barmore 1980). However, the increase in numbers counted from the mid-1930s to 1940 seems to reflect increased coverage (Appendix IX).

My interpretations of sheep counts and population trends differ somewhat from those of Buechner (1960), Oldemeyer (1966), and Woolf (1968), mostly because of additional information available from the Superintendent's monthly reports (Appendix IX). My reported counts and interpretations of areas censused are generally similar to Barmore's (1980).

Seven single aerial total counts were made 1955–67; five by helicopter, one by a combination helicopter–ground count, and one by fixed-wing aircraft (Appendix IX). Counts ranged from 118 to 231. Twenty-five counts were made in 1968–70 by W. J. Barmore and D. Stradley (Appendix IX), including perhaps the most intense effort ever made, in March 1970. Maximum numbers for any single annual flight varied from 178 to 324. Barmore calculated maximum winter populations of 257, 295, and 384 for 1968–70 by combining the maximum counts on major terrain features.

Stradley and I made 33 aerial counts during winter and spring periods of 1971–78.

(Seven other late May to early June flights are omitted here because most sheep had moved off the winter range.) Counts were made in conjunction with elk distribution and census flights (Chap. 3), but a special effort was made to cover bighorn areas. Counts varied greatly (Fig. 10.5), but the interpretation of the results is not quite so discouraging as it first appears. By chance, the March 1972 count was conducted on the first relatively warm days following weeks of wretched weather (windy, cold, with intermittent rain and snow). Snow melt had progressed, however, until the sheep range had recently become snow free. Three hundred fifty-seven sheep were counted, over 100 more than during the late January flight. An early April count at slightly warmer temperatures and with some spring greenup of grasses on the sheep range produced 373 bighorns. From that year forward at least one flight annually was timed to coincide with similar conditions of snow cover, temperature, and greenup. We were more successful some years than others; the desired conditions had to occur simultaneously over the range and before the spring migration. Also, two days without strong winds or fast-moving spring storms were necessary to fly. This happy combination was rare in the mountains of Yellowstone. Late April or May counts were usually much higher than earlier ones, despite mortality during the intervening period.

Several explanations of the higher spring counts are possible: (1) sheep moved onto the area, (2) habitat use and foraging patterns changed in response to warmer

FIGURE 10.5.

Bighorn sheep counted during 33 aerial censuses of the northern range in winter–spring, 1971–78.

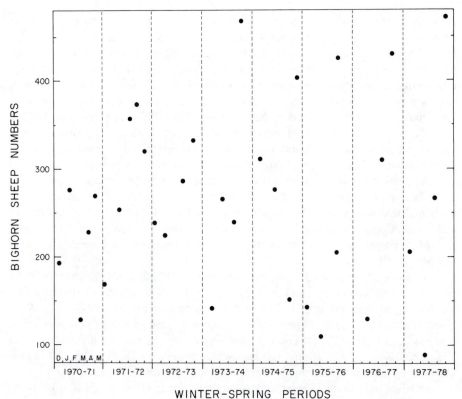

WINTER–SPRING PERIODS

temperatures and vegetation growth, and (3) observability improved with time as the faded, white, spring pelage made sheep more conspicuous against brown and green backgrounds. The failure to locate other large groups of sheep in high-elevation areas surrounding the northern range (Appendix IX) and limited winter movements of marked sheep in adjacent areas (Stewart 1975) suggest that explanations (2) and (3) were far more important than (1).

Sheep numbers were significantly and positively associated with average daily ground temperature at Mammoth Hot Springs during the counts ($r^2 = .52$, $P < .001$; Fig. 10.6). The regression model was improved somewhat by adding the estimated percent of the range with greenup ($R^2 = .62$, Appendix IX). Interpretations are complicated, because greenup is partly a function of temperature. Also, the areas of sheep range showing greenup were crude estimates produced from flight reports. Greenup was retained in the model, with reservations, on the rationale that it may have reflected some cumulative effect of temperature on sheep observability, whereas temperature during a count represented a more instantaneous effect. Time of counts and various interaction terms did not significantly improve the model.

Interpreting trends in sheep numbers from 1955 to 1978, the period of aerial counts, was extremely difficult because of the differences in seasonal observability, counting techniques, areas covered, and observers. The mean observed rate of increase ($\bar{r}$) of sheep for 25 winter counts did not differ significantly from zero [regression of ln

FIGURE 10.6.
Relationship of the number of bighorn sheep observed during 33 aerial counts to mean daily temperature at Mammoth Hot Springs, 1971–78 (years designated 1–8, respectively). Counts made with spring greenup of vegetation on 60% or more of the northern range are indicated ($\bigcirc$).

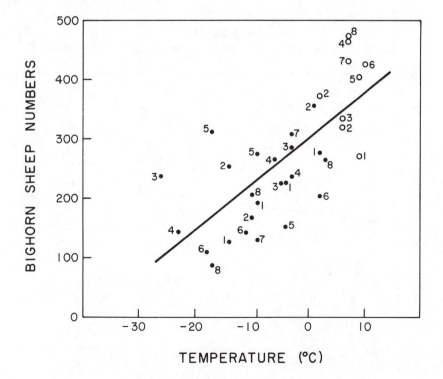

sheep numbers on time, $\bar{r} = b = .011$, P $> .10$; see Fig. 10.7 and Appendix IX (Caughley 1977:51)], suggesting that the sheep population did not change over the 1955–78 period. The data and assumptions used in these calculations require explanation: only single aerial counts made during late January–early April before greenup and without warm temperatures were compared. Winter counts were assumed to be an index of population size, even though they were likely far below absolute numbers. This comparison required the least manipulation of earlier winter counts. Several counts were omitted: the 1966 estimate because it was a combination ground–aerial count; all December–early January 1971–79 counts because previous censuses were made later in the winter. The counts of 247 sheep completed on 21 March 1969 and of 324 on 19 March 1970 seemed most comparable to the others and were used instead of Barmore's (1980) estimates of 295 and 384 sheep from the series of 1969 and 1970 counts.

The $\bar{r}$ for 1955–78 also did not differ significantly from zero when the 32 late January to mid-May counts were adjusted upward as though the 23 winter counts were made at 7°C and 83% greenup ($\bar{r} = b = .0099$, P $= .10$; see Figure 10.8 and Appendix IX). Adjustments were based upon the regression relationships for the 1971–78 counts. The 1961 and 1967 winter counts could not be adjusted from the available data and were omitted. These admittedly precarious manipulations seemed necessary to compensate for differences in observability before comparisons could be made to the recent high spring counts. Some early counts were conducted at very low temperatures, e.g., the temperature during the 1955 census averaged $-17°C$. [Note: Regression of ln maximum spring counts on time for 1971–78 was significant ($\bar{r} = b = .067$, P $< .01$; Appendix IX). This could easily reflect the choice of increasingly better census conditions over time, rather than an upward trend in sheep numbers.]

Additional variables affected interpretations of sheep population trends. Helicop-

FIGURE 10.7.
Relationship of ln sheep numbers on time for 25 winter aerial counts, 1955–78.

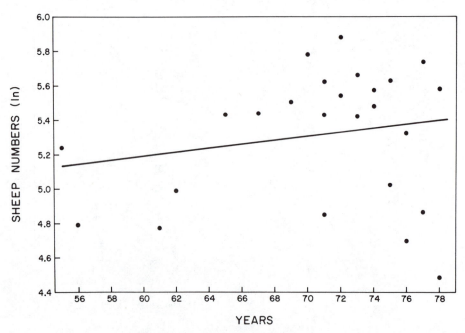

FIGURE 10.8.

Relationship of ln sheep numbers on time for 32 adjusted winter–spring aerial counts, 1955–78. Winter counts adjusted upward as though made at 7°C and with greenup on 83% of the range (see text).

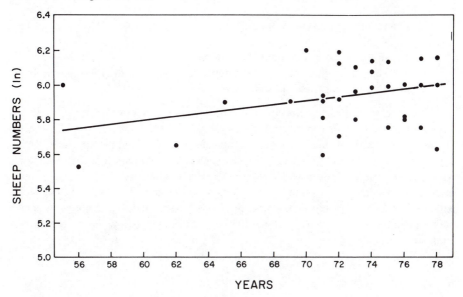

ter counts are difficult to compare to fixed-wing counts: some helicopter counts followed extensive disturbance from elk reduction programs. Also, surprisingly, helicopters may be less efficient than fixed-wing aircraft in counting bighorns (Morgan 1970), particularly in canyons, where the added noise causes sheep to seek cover before they can be observed (D. Stradley pers. commun. 1980, Erickson pers. commun. 1980). There were also some differences in areas searched for sheep during the 1955–78 period. I counted the Beattie Gulch–Devil's Slide area up to 4 km outside the park; other counters apparently did not. Studies of radio-collared sheep show that at least some bighorns wintering at these sites move from the park (Keating 1982). I usually did not cover Abiathar Peak, about 8 km from the northern range; others often did.

This preoccupation with relatively small changes in sheep numbers is necessary because of concern about the extent of interspecific competition between elk and bighorn. Oldemeyer et al. (1971) and Barmore (1980) suggest that the bighorn population increased following the elk reduction, and that this could have been due in part to reduced interspecific competition for resources. They also make a strong case from studies of forage use that potential competition with elk was greatly reduced on some of the sheep winter range during the late 1960s. My interpretation that the overall sheep population did not change significantly is based upon the variation encountered in subsequent counts. Some increase in sheep numbers may indeed have occurred along the Black Canyon of the Yellowstone and on Mt. Everts following the elk reduction (Barmore 1980). The continued high sheep counts during the 1970s, as elk numbers increased, make it less clear that this possible increase in sheep was associated with reduced elk densities (see Effects of Elk Upon the Less Abundant Ungulates, below).

An additional comment on sheep population trends seems appropriate. My interpretation of the ground counts from 1923 to 1950 has been strongly influenced by my attempts to monitor the numbers of this elusive beast from 1971 to 1978. The variability in all counts, the differences in areas covered, and the probability that winter counts are far below actual numbers suggest to me that:

1. There may have been many more sheep on the area since the 1920s than suggested by censuses.
2. Fluctuations in absolute numbers could have been far less pronounced than reported.
3. Variations in counts could reflect entirely the bias errors in the censuses.
4. The status of bighorn sheep on the northern range since the 1920s has probably not been as precarious as sometimes suggested.

Mean early winter composition of the sheep populations in the Mt. Everts area from 1971 to 1979 was $54 \pm 4.4\%$ ewes, $16 \pm 5.1\%$ lambs, $6 \pm 2.9\%$ yearling males, and $24 \pm 6.4\%$ adult males (see Appendix IX). Sheep in the Specimen Ridge, Hellroaring Creek, Reese Creek, and Cinnabar Mountain areas were classified some years; these were combined with sheep on Mt. Everts to represent the overall population, whose mean composition during 1972–79 was $54 \pm 3.7\%$ ewes, $17 \pm 4.7\%$ lambs, $7 \pm 2.8\%$ yearling males, and $23 \pm 4.2\%$ adult males. Variations in annual recruitment of lambs from 1938 to 1979 are examined below in relation to elk numbers.

Bison

Bison herd groups wintered on about 5,800 ha of range, mainly on valley bottoms along the Lamar River and Slough Creek (Figs. 10.2 and 10.9). In addition, many bulls wintered apart from herd groups, some at higher elevations. Changes in the winter distribution of the mixed herd groups (cows, calves, some bulls) during the

FIGURE 10.9.
Bison group foraging on a sedge meadow. Yellowstone National Park photo.

1970s included increased use of Tower Junction–Pleasant Valley and more frequent movement down the Yellowstone River from Hellroaring Creek. Mixed herd groups were seasonally migratory and summered on the headwaters of the Lamar River in the Absaroka Range and on the Mirror Plateau (Meagher 1973:82).

The Lamar bison population was reduced sporadically from 1954 to 1965, following the progressive reductions from 1,000 in 1930 to 143 in 1952 (Meagher 1973). About 85 bison remained after the last reduction in 1965. Only 19 were females (9 yearlings and older, 10 calves) (Meagher 1973). The population increased slowly from 1966 to 1973 (with mean $\bar{r} = .067$) and more rapidly from 1973 to 1980 ($\bar{r} = .117$) (Fig. 10.10). This growth pattern could have resulted from the time lag required for females to reach sexual maturity; most first breed as four-year-olds (Meagher 1973:51). Human predation on bison was low during the 1970s and limited to winter removals made near the boundary as part of a brucellosis control program (8 removed in 1976, 2 in 1978) and to occasional poaching (perhaps 1–2/year). [The control program was designed to prevent contact between bison and cattle. The disease organism, *Brucella abortus,* occurs in bison and elk in the park and is quite possibly native to bison (Meagher 1974, 1976).]

Pronghorn

Pronghorn occupy about 2,900 ha of range (75% in the park) during winter, mostly below 1,700 m and within the narrow 30-cm zone of annual precipitation along the Yellowstone River downstream from Gardiner (Fig. 10.4). Most pronghorn migrate to higher-elevation grasslands on the northern range during summer (Blacktail Plateau, Specimen Ridge, Lamar Valley); others remain on their winter range. Early management of the pronghorn included winter feeding ($\sim$ 1905–35); attempts also were made

FIGURE 10.10.
Bison numbers on the northern range, February aerial counts, 1966–80. All data from Meagher (pers. commun. 1980).

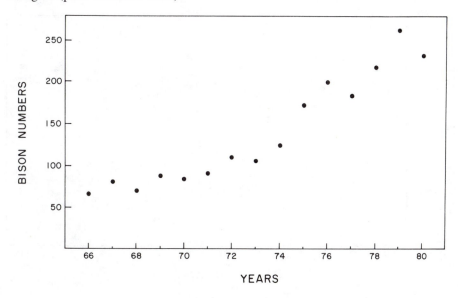

to restrict them to the park during winter by fencing and herding (Barmore 1980; see also Chap. 8).

Ground total counts suggest stable winter populations of 500–700 pronghorns from 1930 to 1937. The pronghorn population increased to 600–800 from 1938 to 1947 after addition of private land to the park and removal of a boundary fence increased their winter range (Barmore 1980). (Barmore also notes that because of their restricted winter distribution, pronghorn counts were comparatively more accurate than counts for other species.) Concern about the decline of big sage in the BLA (Chap. 8) led to periodic pronghorn reductions during 1947–67. Human predation was a major cause of the reduction of winter herds from around 800 in 1947 to about 188 by 1967 (Barmore 1980). The last large reduction (1966) was followed by the severe winter of 1967–68; most pronghorn migrated from the park, and the late winter population declined further to an estimated 122 (Barmore 1980). Pronghorn numbers remained at around 140 during 1969–80 (Fig. 10.11).

Reductions provided insight into the population's dynamics. Pronghorn numbers rebounded to 400–600 following two early removals (1947, 1951); mean annual $\bar{r}$ during the rebounds was .227 (.167 for 1949–51, .287 for 1951–53). The pronghorns failed to rebound 1969–79 from populations of about 140 ($\bar{r} = .008$, regression ln numbers on time, $P > .10$). The 94 pronghorn removed in 1966 (77 were females) represented 34–39% of the population (Barmore 1980). The continued downward trend during the winter of 1968 involved mainly dispersal or mortality of males (Barmore 1980). These combined losses placed the population into a very different state that requires examination. High fetus/doe ratios of about 200:100 for 1965–67 (O'Gara 1968:62) indicate that reduced fertility resulting from changes in vegetation was not responsible for the failure of the population to rebound; mortality and dispersal were responsible. Mortality of fawns from birth to autumn averaged .76 ± .10 from 1963 to 1979. Mortality from birth to winter was .83 ± .01 during 1969–70 (Barmore 1980)

FIGURE 10.11.

Pronghorn numbers on the northern range, 1969–80. Data are aerial counts; those for 1969–70 from Barmore (1980).

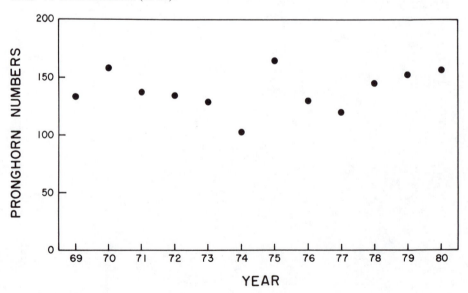

and .80 ± .10 during 1971–79 (Appendix IX). Mortality of neonates resulting from poor condition of the females may not be significant because studies "indicated a better year round level of physical condition for adult females in Yellowstone Park [from supposed poor condition range] than for those on the National Bison Range [supposed good condition range]" (O'Gara 1968:110). Coyote predation has been suggested as the agent of fawn mortality (O'Gara 1968, Barmore 1980). This seems likely to me also, but field evidence of predation is poor. I observed coyotes harassing female pronghorn with neonates at heel on several occasions, and I saw coyotes with a fawn they had apparently killed. Additional known losses to the low population during the 1970s included some poaching and dispersal of males during the severe winters of 1975 and 1976.

Human predation apparently reduced the population from one resource-limited stable state (suggested by the increase in pronghorn following addition of winter range to the park) to a lower state maintained by natural predation, incidental human predation, and dispersal. Coyote densities may be strongly influenced by elk numbers (Chap. 11); consequently, the level of coyote predation on pronghorns has little feedback on coyote numbers. This entire interpretation is, however, largely speculative. Other forces, for example, interspecific competition with mule deer for winter food, could affect pronghorn.

Pronghorn populations averaged 53 ± 4.8% females, 21 ± 8.8% young, and 26 ± 7.1% males during seven December classifications from 1971 to 1979 (Appendix IX). Composition was roughly similar during 1969–70 (Barmore 1980).

Moose

Moose wintered mostly above 1,800 m on the northern range. They were usually solitary or occurred as females with young. Barmore (1980) calculated that up to 200 moose could have occurred on the northern range 1967–70, but considered that 100 was a liberal estimate. No census of moose was made in 1971–78, but numbers were recorded during elk distribution flights. Moose sometimes were quite visible during December (6 flights, average moose/hour of flying = 1.66 ± .92). They often vanished into the coniferous forests during January–March (15 flights, $\bar{X}$ = .33 ± .29) and then reappeared from mid-May–early June (8 flights, 3.05 ± 1.16). Maximum numbers of 48, 49, and 58 were observed during May 1971–73, respectively. Moose winter in many higher-elevation areas of the park, and some of these could have moved down onto the northern range in spring. Moose in forests are notoriously difficult to census (Peterson 1977:25). My estimates of 200 moose on the northern range (Table 10.1) is conservative.

The wintering moose populations averaged 44 ± 4.9% females, 26 ± 4.6% young, and 30 ± 6.9% males during six winters from 1972 to 1978 (Appendix IX). Young/female ratios averaged .54 ± .19, were quite variable (.24–.73), but these were often based upon very small samples.

Resource Division

The nature of resource division that enables the six species of ungulates to coexist is explored here. Since, to some extent, the species are all seasonally migratory, the partitioning of the low-quality, potentially exhaustible winter food (Chap. 9) is of main interest. Interspecific competition, current or past, could be the process whereby food resources are partitioned.

Resource division among the few, often distantly related, species on the northern range (1 antilocaprid, 2 bovids, 3 cervids) seemingly would be straightforward, particularly compared to the complex grazing systems of East Africa, where many closely related species occupy the same area (Bell 1971, Jarman 1974, Jarman and Sinclair 1979). A necessary perspective, however, is that the extant megafauna of North America represent the few survivors of large-scale extinctions during the not-too-distant Pleistocene. The ecology and behavior of these survivors evolved largely under very different selection pressures. Consequently, unraveling existing ecological relationships is difficult, and as pointed out by Geist (1974), pseudoexplanations are easily made. Furthermore, the mechanisms of resource division among ungulates may be quite subtle (Bell 1971, McNaughton 1978, Jarman and Sinclair 1979); the data for the species on the northern range generally permit only a cursory view of resource partitioning.

Differences in body size of the three large (bison, moose, elk) and three comparatively small species (mule deer, bighorn sheep, pronghorn) (Table 10.1) on the northern range place different constraints on winter distribution and food resources. Generally, smaller species require better-quality food (higher protein, less fiber) than larger species because of higher metabolic requirements per unit body weight, even though the absolute quantities of food required by large species are greater (Bell 1971, Jarman 1974, Geist 1974, Jarman and Sinclair 1979). Thus, large quantities of low-quality food, typical of the grasslands of the northern range in winter, are utilized more efficiently by relatively large grazers. Additionally, snow strongly influences winter distribution, and the varying ability of ungulates to contend with snow depth and density seems related to several morphological characteristics (Telfer and Kelsall 1979). Any partitioning of resources among the species through interspecific competition must occur within these broad constraints imposed by metabolic requirements and morphology.

Studies on the northern range, elsewhere in the Rocky Mountains, and in East Africa show that spatial segregation and food preferences contribute to resource division among ungulates (Barmore 1980, Cole 1969a, Mackie 1970, Stelfox and Taber 1969, Telfer and Kelsall 1971, 1979, Hudson 1976, Singer 1979, Jarman and Sinclair 1979). Segregation may occur by broad geographic area or by habitat selection; food preference may occur at the level of forage class (e.g., browse), plant species, or plant parts. Each of these aspects of resource division is examined in turn.

Separation in Space

GEOGRAPHIC AREAS

Segregation of some species into broad geographic areas on the northern range is influenced strongly by the different snow conditions encountered down the elevational gradient of the Yellowstone River (Barmore 1980). Chest heights and foot loads (live weight ÷ area of all hooves to dewclaws) are considered indices of the ability to cope with snow depth and density, respectively (Telfer and Kelsall 1979). Differences in chest height suggest that the ability to cope with deep snow declines in the order:

moose, elk, bison, mule deer, bighorn sheep, and pronghorn (Fig. 10.12). Only small samples were available for some species, but chest heights for moose, elk, bison, and bighorn are broadly similar to those measured elsewhere (Telfer and Kelsall 1971, 1979). Estimated foot loads for adult females predict that the ability to contend with

FIGURE 10.12.

Chest heights for six species of native ungulates on the northern range during winter–spring. Sample sizes with means, ranges, and standard deviations of measurements are shown.

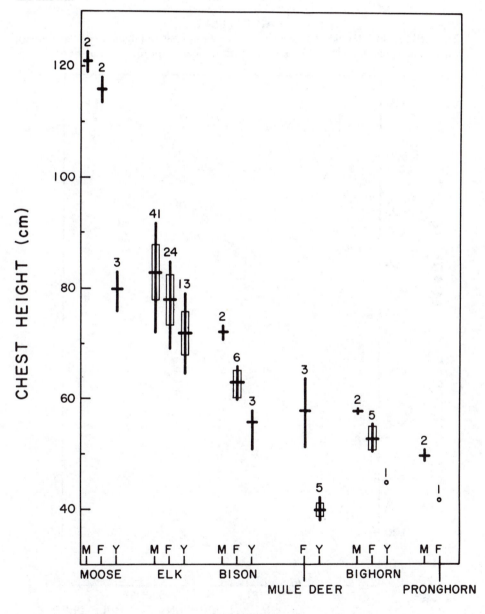

dense snow increases (i.e., foot loads decline) as: bison, pronghorn, elk, bighorn, moose, and mule deer (Fig. 10.13). Foot loads were estimated indirectly from measurements of foot area and mean live weights from other studies (Table 10.1). Relationships among moose, elk, bison, and bighorns generally are similar to those reported by Telfer and Kelsall (1971, 1979), except that foot loads for female bison from the park seem high.

These relationships, especially chest height, make some sense when compared with the upper limits of winter distribution of most of the species. I do not mean to

FIGURE 10.13.

Estimated foot loads of adult females for six species of native ungulates on the northern winter range. Sample sizes for foot area measurements are the same as Fig. 10.12.

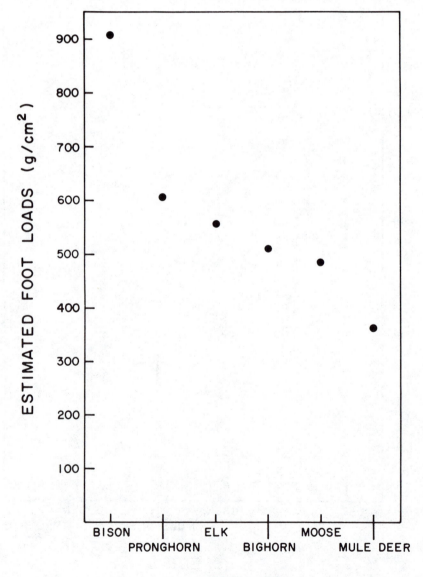

imply that other forces—e.g., predators, interspecific competition, tradition—are not important, just that the general pattern of distribution is strongly influenced by snow conditions. Thus, the three smaller species winter either at the lowest elevations where snow conditions are least severe (pronghorn, mule deer) or where snow is redistributed by wind and gravity or melts quickly (bighorns). Pronghorn seem least able to cope with deep or dense snow and occupy the snow shadow along the Yellowstone River (Figs. 2.3 and 10.4). All feeding pronghorn observed during January–March 1971–74 ($N = 191$) were in about 8 cm of snow or less. Some mule deer winter at higher elevations (Fig. 10.2); 95% of 1,248 deer observed during January–March fed in 8 cm of snow or less, but 5% fed in snow up to 30 cm. The bighorn sheep's ability to occupy windswept cliffs at high elevations gives them a wider but more interrupted winter distribution than pronghorn or mule deer (Fig. 10.4). About 99% of 148 feeding bighorns were in 15 cm of snow or less. However, these observations underestimate the bighorn's ability to cope with deep snow. Sheep wintering at high elevations on the northern range feed in 30–45 cm of snow (Barmore 1980). Among the three large species, moose should be most able to handle deep and crusted snow. Observations of moose feeding on the northern range were too few to be useful, but I observed moose feeding in about 80 cm of snow along the upper Yellowstone River in the southeast corner of the park. Feeding elk can cope with a wide variety of deep and crusted snow conditions (Chap. 9). Chest height and foot load measurements underestimate the bison's ability to forage in deep, moderately crusted, snow. Only 5% of 873 feeding bison were in 30–60 cm of snow, but herd groups in the Pelican Valley of Yellowstone regularly feed in snow to 60 cm; bulls, to 90 cm (Meagher pers. commun. 1980). The massive musculature of their neck and shoulders permits bison to push deep snow from feeding sites (Meagher 1973:73).

Habitat Utilization

Observations of feeding activity by vegetation type for the five less abundant ungulates are summarized for three seasonal periods in Fig. 10.14. Data were obtained at the same time and manner as described for elk (Chap. 9).

The combination of xeric steppe, sage steppe, and mesic steppe (mostly old fields) accounted for over 80% of the observations of feeding mule deer in the park during all periods. Subsequent observations outside the park, where most deer winter, suggest that sage steppe is far more important to the overall population than shown by the segment inside the park. Food habits studies (Barmore 1969) indicate that use of Douglas-fir forests is underestimated throughout the area.

Xeric grasslands accounted for 60–80% or more of the observations of feeding bighorn sheep. My observations of sheep foraging in forests along the base of Specimen Ridge and those of Oldemeyer (1966) and Barmore (1980) indicate that winter use of coniferous forests adjacent to cliffs and slope grasslands may be underestimated. Steep slopes and ridgetops accounted for 42, 51, and 78% of the feeding sheep during October–December, January–March, and April–May, respectively. The importance of steep slopes was underestimated overall, because sheep on the moderate north slopes of Mt. Everts often were more easily observed than those elsewhere. Ewe–lamb groups and most rams rarely fed more than 100 m from cliffs or steep slopes (also Barmore 1980, Oldemeyer 1966, Woolf 1968). However, groups of 10–20 or more rams often fed far from cliffs on the grasslands at the confluence of the Yellowstone and Gardner Rivers.

The combination of wet meadows, swales, and mesic grasslands accounted for

FIGURE 10.14.
Observations of feeding mule deer, bighorn sheep, bison, pronghorn, and moose by
vegetation type during three seasonal periods, 1970–74. Numbers observed by period
shown above each column.

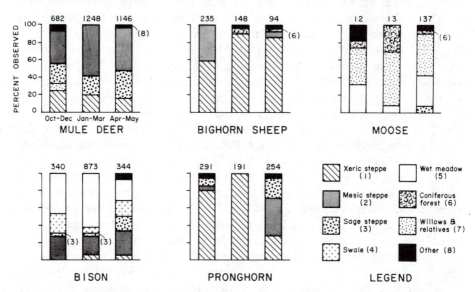

about 70–90% of the feeding bison; wet meadows were particularly important during
January–March.

Xeric steppe, mesic steppe, and sage steppe accounted for 90% or more of the
feeding pronghorns. All feeding during January–March was on xeric steppe. Food
habits studies (Barmore 1969, O'Gara and Greer 1970) and observations of pronghorn
wintering outside the park in 1976 and 1979 suggest that use of sage steppe was
underestimated. About 95% of all feeding pronghorn were on level to moderate slopes.

Willow, sedge meadow, and coniferous forest accounted for 80% or more of the
feeding moose, but October–March observations were too small to be meaningful. Use
of coniferous forests (particularly Douglas-fir, subalpine fir) was underestimated during winter (Barmore 1980).

The use of vegetation types changed substantially for bison, pronghorn, and
perhaps moose during April–May (Fig. 10.14) as all species shifted their diets to green
grass and forbs (Barmore 1980).

These observations of seasonal habitat use were a necessary introduction, but they
add little new information to Barmore's (1980) 1967–70 studies. In a more detailed
analysis of winter habitat preference, Barmore reported that mule deer selected sagebrush and mesic steppes (old fields) over other types; sheep preferred xeric and mesic
grasslands; bison preferred wet meadows and mesic grasslands; pronghorn preferred
xeric steppe. Although interpretations are subject to the same difficulties and limitations described for elk (Chap. 9), these combined studies suggest that differences in
habitat use contribute to resource partitioning among the species.

Food Preference

The feeding strategies that seem to have evolved among ungulates that utilize similar
vegetation are that smaller species *select* high-quality, highly digestible food, whereas

large species are less selective and ingest large quantities of low-quality food (Bell 1971, Jarman 1974, Geist 1974, Jarman and Sinclair 1979). These strategies reflect the higher metabolic rates of small species. Since high-quality food items (e.g., twig tips, scattered green leaves, seeds during winter, and flowers, seeds, new growth in summer) are dispersed and relatively rare in a sea of abundant, low-quality food, small ungulate species are often less abundant (Jarman and Sinclair 1979).

If feeding strategies evolved similarly on the northern range, then the small species should have mouths adapted for selecting discrete food items. The larger species should have adaptations for consuming large quantities of undifferentiated food. Further, the proportion of low-quality winter food that can be cropped rather unselectively (i.e., cured grasses) might be expected to decline with body size, since there would be a minimum body size that could be supported on a diet of cured grass.

Ungulates can be classed as grazers (grasses and forbs), browsers (shrubs and trees), and mixed feeders (Bell 1969). Based upon winter food habits, the moose was classed as a browser; the bison, a grazer; the elk, bighorn sheep, mule deer, and pronghorn as mixed feeders (the latter somewhat arbitrarily) (Table 10.2).

Among mixed feeders and grazers elsewhere the selective species have more pointed faces than nonselective feeders, and this is reflected in skull characteristics (Bell 1969). An index to the relative narrowing of the face is derived by dividing the maximum width across the upper rear molars by the maximum width of the body of the premaxillae (Bell 1969). Also, the incisors of selective feeders are inserted in the lower mandible to meet the palate at nearly a right angle. The angle of insertion is more obtuse in nonselective feeders (Bell 1969).

The relationship between body weight and these indices of the potential ability of grazers and mixed feeders of the northern range to select food suggest that bison, the largest, would be least selective (broadest face, greatest angle of insertion), elk would be intermediate, and the three small species should be most selective (Figs. 10.15 and 10.16). Further, the proportion of grass in winter diets does decline with body size (Fig. 10.17). (The data on diets are presented with reservations discussed in Forage Classes, below).

Body size–metabolic rate relationships suggest that large browsers would be relatively less selective than small browsers, but strict winter browsers are too few to test these relationships. Based upon morphology, moose (narrowness index 2.74, I_1

TABLE 10.2
Ungulate Winter Foods by Forage Class

Species	Percent of Diet[a,b]			Source
	Browse	*Grasses*	*Forbs*	
Elk	17	80	3	Greer et al. 1970
Mule deer	51	32	17	Barmore 1969
Bighorn sheep	22	61	17	Oldemeyer et al. 1971
Bison	*	99	*	Meagher 1973
Pronghorn	82	4	14	Barmore 1969, O'Gara & Greer 1970
Moose	90+?			Estimated from Houston 1968, Stevens 1970

[a] Percent by volume from rumen analyses, except bighorn and moose, which were from examinations of feeding sites.
[b] Asterisk indicates less than 1% of diet.

FIGURE 10.15.

The relationship of relative narrowing of the face to female live weight for five species of grazers and mixed feeders. Points represent the mean index from 10 or more female skulls for each species.

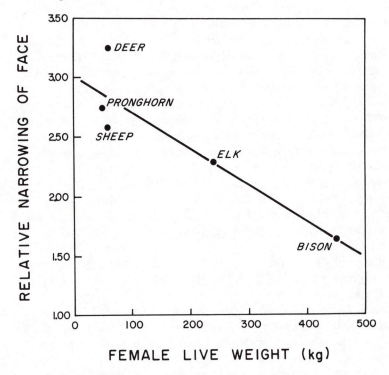

insertion 110°) could be as selective as pronghorn but less so than mule deer if the latter two are considered to be mainly browsers. The diet of moose may contain high proportions of low-quality browse from relatively large-stemmed deciduous shrubs (Houston 1968, Stevens 1970). Pronghorn and mule deer, in contrast, seem to eat greater proportions of higher-quality browse from evergreen shrubs, e.g., big sagebrush, fringed sage, winterfat (Barmore 1969).

FORAGE CLASSES

Although the morphological studies suggest that food selection could be inverse to body size, direct evidence for selection is limited. At a first level of comparison, the proportions of three forage classes in winter diets differ among the species (Table 10.2). These data are rough approximations, and comparisons are necessarily limited (Chap. 9, Elk Food Habits). Bighorn diets are from examinations of feeding sites and are tenuously compared to diets of elk, deer, bison, and pronghorn, based upon rumen analysis. No data are available on winter foods of moose; the browse diet is an assumption based upon studies in adjacent areas. Several ''forbs'' in the winter diets of sheep, deer, and pronghorn share some important characteristics with ''browse'' species. Thus, phlox and pussytoes are small, quite woody perennials that are comparatively high in crude protein [phlox ~ 8% (Stewart 1975)] and would seemingly require considerable selection to consume in quantity.

FIGURE 10.16.

The relationship of the angle of insertion of I_1 to female live weights for five species of grazers and mixed feeders.

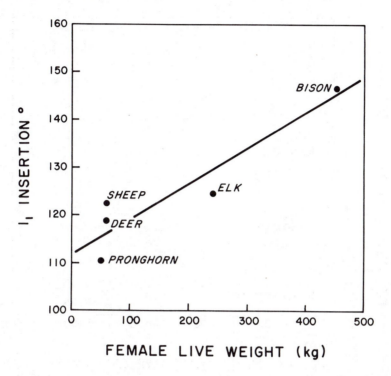

PLANT SPECIES AND PLANT PARTS

Data on the extent of selection within forage classes for plant species and plant parts is practically nonexistent. Examinations of winter feeding sites suggest that bison are quite unselective and leave swaths of grazed grasses and sedges. Although elk select for species and plant parts during spring and summer (Chap. 9), winter grazing of grasses appears to be indiscriminant. In contrast, bighorns in Yellowstone apparently select species of grasses, forbs, and shrubs during winter (Oldemeyer et al. 1971), i.e., plants are eaten with greater frequency than they occur in the community. Sheep wintering adjacent to Yellowstone also select for species (Stewart 1975). They may also select plant parts: sheep ate mainly twig tips, leaves, and seed heads from some shrubs (e.g., winterfat) and the leaves from cured grasses (needle-and-thread, blue-bunch wheatgrass) on Mt. Everts in January 1976 and 1977 (Houston, unpubl.). Elsewhere wintering sheep selected terminal buds from shrubs (Stewart 1975:85). Nothing is known about selection of plant species or parts by wintering moose, mule deer, or pronghorn on the northern range. Pronghorn may be quite selective for plant parts: waste grains form an appreciable part of winter diets in some agricultural areas of Montana (Cole and Wilkins 1958).

All ungulates likely select plant species and parts more during late spring and summer when food is abundant than during winter. During summer moose select leaves from many shrubs, and bighorn sheep select a wide variety of plant parts (Houston 1968, Woolf 1968:75).

FIGURE 10.17.

The relationship of the percent of grasses and grasslike plants in winter diets to female live weights for five species of grazers and mixed feeders.

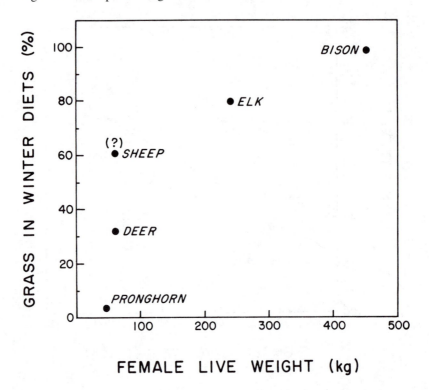

In sum, differences in food preference by forage class are pronounced and represent an important aspect of resource partitioning. Small species of ungulates may be more selective of plant species and parts. Food selection at these levels could represent an important dimension of resource partitioning, but much more information is needed.

Effects of Elk Upon the Less Abundant Ungulates

Even though resource partitioning occurs among the ungulates, the numerical superiority of elk still could influence the abundance of the others because of overlapping distribution and food habits. Perturbation experiments are used commonly to measure the nature and extent of interspecific competition (Schoener 1974, Connell 1975). The large reduction and subsequent increase in the elk population seemingly provided an unparalleled opportunity to test the extent of interspecific competition between elk and the other species, but this proved to be more difficult than anticipated.

If intense interspecific competition occurs between elk and the other species for winter food, then numbers and possibly recruitment of the less abundant ungulates should be negatively associated with elk numbers. The proportion of females with young at heel in early winter was used as an index of recruitment for mule deer, moose, and pronghorn. For bighorn sheep the recruitment index was based on the proportion of females plus yearling males, becasue of difficulties in field classifications (Appendix

IX). The proportion of young in mixed herd groups of bison was used to index recruitment. The proportion of yearling male mule deer also was used as an index of recruitment. Indices of abundance included winter counts of sheep, bison, and pronghorn, and the maximum moose per hour observations from spring flights. The data were mostly for 1968–79, but for bighorn and mule deer some earlier data were available (Appendix IX). Only data obtained after the bison and pronghorn reductions ceased were used for these species.

Since recruitment into populations of some species might be negatively associated with winter severity, the index of severity during the previous December–March ($t - 1$) as well as elk numbers then were used as independent variables in regression models (see Elk Natality, Chap. 5, for a discussion of the winter severity index and elk numbers). Population numbers at $t - 1$ were included in models of recruitment for bison, pronghorn, and bighorn sheep to test whether or not density-dependent intraspecific competition might also explain variation in recruitment. Results are summarized in Table 10.3; regression models are given in Appendix IX.

Interpreting these associations in terms of interspecific relationships immediately places one on dangerous ground, both statistically and ecologically. The more obvious pitfalls include the following points. (1) The indices of recruitment are difficult to interpret (Chap. 5), especially when associated measures of the species abundance are unavailable (e.g., recruitment into the mule deer population is probably influenced by deer density, but no data are available on deer numbers to test this obvious relationship). (2) Indices of abundance are based upon counts that are sometimes questionable

TABLE 10.3
Association of Recruitment and Numbers of the Less Abundant Ungulates with Elk and Winter Severity[a]

SPECIES	DEPENDENT VARIABLE (N)	ASSOCIATION WITH ELK NUMBERS (E) AND WINTER SEVERITY (I)		
		R^2	P	Sign and Degree of Significant Association with Elk
Mule deer	Yg/F (14)	.12	> .10	
	YrM/F (9)	.10	> .10	
Bighorn sheep	Yg/F + YrM			
	Mt. Everts (17)	.16	> .10	
	Overall (8)	.14	> .10	
	Numbers (14) (1955–78)	.17	> .10	
Bison	Yg/Ad (10)	.85	< .001	$-$ $R^2_{\bar{E}|I} = .81$ (P < .001)
	Numbers (11) (1969–79)	.83	< .001	$+$ $R^2_{\bar{E}|I} = .74$ (P < .001)
Moose	Yg/F (8)	.04	> .10	
	Number/hour (11) (1968–78)	.07	> .10	
Pronghorn	Yg/F (9)	.14	> .10	
	Numbers (11) (1969–79)	.01	> .10	

[a] See Appendix IX for variables and regression models. *Abbreviations:* Yg, young; F, female; YrM, yearling male; Ad, adult.

(e.g., bighorn sheep). (3) Threshold effects are common in biological systems; responses of associated ungulate populations to changes in elk numbers could be nonlinear and show complex time lags (e.g., the winter distribution of elk and mule deer overlap on only part of the range. Very large changes in overall elk numbers could occur with no effect on deer.) (4) Regressions do not establish either causation or the nature of interspecific relationships. Recruitment into the deer population might show an inverse relationship with elk numbers that has nothing whatever to do with competition for resources; predation from coyotes, whose abundance may have been linked with the availability of elk carrion, could negatively affect deer recruitment. The two ungulate populations would be linked ecologically, but through an entirely different route. Thus, interspecific competition would have to be pronounced and straightforward to be detected by regression analysis; even then the presence or absence of statistical association must be interpreted with caution.

For all species, scattergrams of dependent variables and their residuals were examined for nonlinear patterns (Neter and Wasserman 1974). Interaction terms and transformations of dependent variables failed to improve models.

Indices of recruitment for mule deer showed no significant association with elk numbers or winter severity (Table 10.3). Similarly, recruitment and indices of abundance for pronghorn and moose showed no significant association with elk numbers or severity. Models of pronghorn recruitment that included pronghorn numbers at $t - 1$ were not significant; neither was a simple regression of pronghorn young on pronghorn numbers. These relationships for pronghorn are not surprising; the status of the pronghorn population seems to be determined largely by other forces.

Regressions of bison numbers and recruitment proved to be more interesting but also underscored the limitations of the regression approach. Bison numbers were significantly associated with winter severity and elk numbers but more strongly with elk numbers (Table 10.3). However, the regression reveals nothing about interspecific relationships. The association was positive, because both populations were increasing following periods of intense human predation (Figs. 5.1 and 10.10) rather than because of interspecific facilitation [one species has a beneficial effect upon another (Sinclair 1979)]. Bison recruitment, however, was associated significantly and negatively with elk numbers (Table 10.3). Bison recruitment also was negatively associated with bison numbers ($r^2 = .41$, $P < .05$, Appendix IX), thus the decline in bison recruitment could reflect both inter and intraspecific competition for resources (Fig. 10.18). The overlap in winter distribution and food habits makes this a plausible interpretation, which was predicted early on (Meagher 1974). An alternative interpretation is possible, however, because the index of bison recruitment was influenced by males older than calves in herd groups. Thus, changing proportions of males as well as young could affect apparent recruitment. Detailed comparative studies of the dynamics of Yellowstone's three bison populations are in progress (Meagher pers. commun. 1980); these will provide more information on density dependence and interspecific relationships.

Regressions of bighorn sheep numbers for 1955–78 showed no significant association with winter severity or elk numbers (Table 10.3). Similarly, regressions of recruitment into the overall sheep population and for those on Mt. Everts were not significant. Regression of overall recruitment on sheep numbers at $t - 1$ also was not significant. These results are viewed with special skepticism, because sheep population trends are uncertain, the index of recruitment includes yearling males, and the samples of recruitment for the overall population are limited in number. Keating (1982) suggests that interspecific competition occurs between sheep and elk in the BLA. The $\bar{r}$ of

FIGURE 10.18.

The relationship between bison recruitment and elk and bison numbers on the northern winter range, 1970–79.

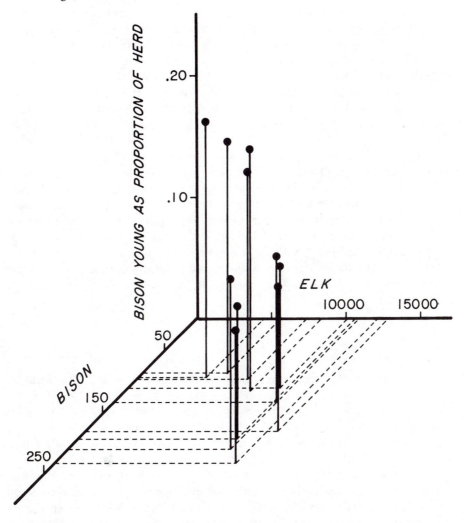

the Mt. Everts bighorns from 1963 to 1981 was negatively associated with winter elk numbers four years earlier (Keating 1982:36). The biological relationships behind the four-year lag are, however, unclear to me.

Given the limitations of the regression approach, the indices of abundance and recruitment for the less abundant ungulates generally showed no significant negative associations with elk numbers. Only bison recruitment declined with increasing elk and bison numbers, and this relationship is questionable.

Other Herbivores

Two other herbivore species require comment because of historical concern about the effects of elk upon their abundance.

White-tailed Deer

White-tails were apparently uncommon on the northern range when the park was established but increased around 1900 (Meagher, in prep.). Small numbers of white-tails (< 100; Meagher, in prep.) wintered in thickets along the lower Gardner River and along the Yellowstone River in and adjacent to the park. The population declined in the early 1920s and was essentially extinct by 1930 (Skinner 1929, Murie 1940, Barmore 1980, Meagher, in prep.).

I observed several white-tails on the northern range in 1974, but resident populations did not occur during the 1970s. Viable populations do, however, occur in dense contiguous thickets along the Yellowstone River beginning about 30 km north of the park.

Apparently, the park and adjacent areas represented the extreme upper limit of marginal winter range (Murie 1940, Barmore 1980). The evidence suggests that a combination of land clearing, livestock grazing, and human predation outside the park was primarily responsible for the decline of the very vulnerable population (Skinner 1929, Murie 1940, Barmore 1980). Fire suppression and artificial concentrations of elk in the boundary area of the park (Chap. 3) also probably aggravated their already precarious state (Barmore 1980). Given that white-tails increased in the presence of very high elk numbers and that man greatly altered their habitat, it seems unlikely that interspecific competition with elk for food was the primary cause of the decline in the deer population.

Beaver

Beaver increased on the northern range and throughout the park around 1900 (Meagher in prep.). Colonies were abundant in aspen stands on the northern range during the early 1920s (Warren 1926). Beaver numbers declined during the 1920s and remained comparatively low into the 1950s (Jonas 1955). Beaver colonies seemed to be quite transitory along small streams on the northern range and in other areas of the park during the 1920s and 1950s (Warren 1926, Jonas 1955).

Beaver occurred throughout the northern range during the 1970s. As earlier, many colonies appeared to be emphemeral; this was also true for colonies on other small streams throughout the park (Meagher pers. commun. 1980). Notable exceptions include populations on the delta of the upper Yellowstone River and colonies along 4 km of Obsidian Creek, both of which feed on extensive stands of willow.

The decrease in beaver on the northern range that began in the 1920s has been attributed to interspecific competition with elk (National Park Service 1961). However, severe competition cannot be established from the available evidence. First, the increase in beaver occurred in the presence of large elk populations. Second, beaver subsequently declined both where elk did and did not winter in the park. An interpretation that seems more consistent with the timing and magnitude of the fluctuations in beaver numbers on the northern range involves the effects of fire suppression on food supplies. Suppression initially permitted aspen to develop uniformly into stands of moderate-sized trees, instead of the variable state maintained formerly by frequent fires (Chap. 8). The beaver population increased in response to this increase in aspen, their main food supply (Warren 1926). Continued suppression, coupled with browsing and drought, progressively reduced the abundance of aspen; thus beavers declined and have remained at lower densities.

Surveys of the distribution, abundance, and turnover of beaver colonies being conducted in Yellowstone (Meagher pers. commun. 1980) should clarify some of the relationships between food supplies and colony stability. Ephemeral colonies may be characteristic of most of the park. The available evidence does not support earlier interpretations of competitive exclusion of beaver by elk.

Interpretation: Interspecific Relationships

Ecological Separation and Refugia

Since elk are versatile generalists (Chap. 9), to persist the less abundant ungulates must be relatively more efficient than elk in exploiting some part of the resource base available on the northern range. These ecological refugia result, in part, from interspecific differences in distribution and food preferences. Some boundaries of the refugia that permit the other species to coexist with far greater numbers of elk are examined here. Resource partitioning between other pairs of species is discussed by Barmore (1980).

The ecological separation between elk, moose, and bison is pronounced. The ability of solitary moose to utilize widely scattered pockets of browse in very deep snow provides a refugium from elk. Bison are able to forage on wet meadows when snow conditions have long since forced elk into other habitats. Bison seem more restricted than elk to this highly productive type; only there can they obtain the large amount of food required by their unselective grazing.

The relationships of the three smaller species to elk are particularly interesting, but aspects of ecological separation are poorly understood. Separation in space is important: sheep occupy cliffs and very steep slopes more efficiently than elk. Mule deer seem to be bound far less by tradition to winter range sites than sheep. To some extent, increased mobility allows deer to move on down the Yellowstone River when either severe snow conditions or potential competition with elk threaten. Such movements, however, bring them into contact with large numbers of other deer.

Differences in food preference at the level of forage class occur among the species, especially between mule deer and elk and pronghorn and elk. These contribute to separation, but there are likely more important ecological consequences of the food selection–body size relationships. I propose the following hypotheses, which need to be tested, to account for the separation between elk and the smaller species. Since the absolute amount of food required daily by deer, pronghorn, and bighorn is small compared to elk, selection for high-quality diets of plant parts and species may permit them to persist on the ''crumbs'' left over from the winter grazing of elk (see Jarman and Sinclair 1979). Further, species may coexist by eating identical foods, provided the food is dispersed differently (Sinclair 1977:272, McNaughton 1978). The small absolute food requirements of bighorn sheep compared to elk (perhaps 2 kg for a ewe versus 6 kg for a female elk) may permit sheep to persist on cliffs and steep slopes where food density is too low to support elk. I recognize that elk sometimes feed on these sites but suggest that sheep feed there more efficiently.

Clearly, the ecological refugia of the smaller species requires deeper examination.

Many of the differences in distribution and food habits that I consider to be important elements separating elk and the other species ecologically are also considered to be of major consequence by Barmore (1980).

Interspecific Competition

Interspecific competition is often difficult to demonstrate from field studies (Schoener 1974, Connell 1975, Abrams 1980, Barmore 1980). Barmore (1980) considered that interspecific competition between elk and the other ungulate species was minimal or lacking during the late 1960s, except with segments of the bighorn sheep population. Even though changes in elk numbers were large, the regression analyses suggest that the elk population and populations of the less abundant ungulates were not closely linked by interspecific competition during the 1970s; i.e., large changes in elk numbers seemingly had little effect upon the other species. Only bison recruitment was negatively associated with elk numbers. While the elk population may not be closely coupled to the others, the data on population trends and recruitment for sheep, deer, and moose were poor enough that this interpretation remains questionable. However, mule deer and moose have high reproductive potentials and could increase quickly if intense competition with elk for resources was greatly reduced. Population responses for these species that were at all commensurate with the reduction and subsequent increase in elk would have been noted, even granting the crudeness of population monitoring. The effects of past human predation on pronghorn and bison continue to obscure their relationships with elk. Possible effects on bison recruitment should become clearer as both bison and elk populations approach ecological carrying capacity (K_I). Additional studies of bighorn sheep numbers, dynamics, and distribution will be required to document competition with elk. Such competition might be pronounced on parts of the sheep winter range (Barmore 1980, Keating 1982). The possibility remains, however, that resources are neatly partitioned, and interspecific competition between elk and other species on the northern range may be low.

Interspecific relationships are not static; competition may act only intermittently, and competitive relationships could change with climate, fire, plant succession, and by chance events on the northern range. Since the interpretations made here cover a relatively short time, when several populations were recovering from human predation, continued monitoring is necessary. Demonstration of interspecific competition for resources between elk and other species, or between pairs of the less abundant ungulates, would add to the understanding of important ecological processes on the northern range. Such relationships *may* have important management implications. However, even the existence of intense interspecific competition is *not necessarily* either cause for alarm or evidence that "corrective" management is required (Chap. 12), as sometimes suggested in the past.

Relationships among sympatric species of ungulates are not limited to competition; facilitation may also be important (Vesey-Fitzgerald 1960, Bell 1971, Jarman and Sinclair 1979). Historically, the modifications of plant communities wrought by huge herds of bison in the Yellowstone region may have been of considerable benefit to the smaller pronghorn (Barmore 1980). Unfortunately, these grazing systems were destroyed, and bison and pronghorn are largely separated in the park. Few examples of facilitation on the northern range occur to me: movements of the small species of ungulates through deep snow may be facilitated by use of trails established and maintained by elk. Elk, over time, may retard forest invasion by periodic heavy browsing of conifers on some slopes important to bighorn sheep. These examples are trivial, but the concept warrants a closer look on the northern range and throughout North America.

Changes in K_l Over Time: The Less Abundant Ungulates

The resource requirements of the less abundant ungulates and changes in vegetation (Chap. 8) suggest that ecological carrying capacities set by resource levels changed for some of these species during the past century, just as for elk (Chap. 9). Changes in the *potential* upper limits of the bison, pronghorn, and mule deer populations are considered because their populations are currently below K_l.

The role of natural fires and fire suppression in the ecology of bighorn sheep has not been fully appreciated until recently. Forests have advanced dramatically over grasslands on low-elevation sheep ranges adjacent to Yellowstone Park (Gruell 1980a,b). This has occurred on the northern range as well (see Pls. 25, 42) and may be more extensive than suggested by the few available photos. Scarred trees show that fires were frequent historically on steep slopes along the Yellowstone River from Quartz Creek to Deep Creek (about 6 km) and on the Gardner River from Lava Creek to Osprey Falls (5 km) (Despain pers. commun. 1980). These sites are adjacent to major sheep wintering areas. Fire was also quite frequent in the Black Canyon of the Yellowstone River from about Bear Creek to Hellroaring Creek (18 km), judging from the abundance of scarred trees (no early photos are available for these sites). Forest cover appears to have increased in all three areas. Bighorn sheep do sometimes forage in forests, but on balance the increase in forests probably reduced K_l for sheep by allowing snow to accumulate on formerly windswept sites and perhaps by reducing the abundance of preferred forage. Similar interpretations of the effects of fire suppression on sheep have been made elsewhere (Stelfox 1976, Gruell 1980a,b, Riggs and Peek 1980).

In contrast, the combined effects of livestock grazing outside the park and fire suppression in and out of the park could have increased the abundance of available shrubs for wintering mule deer and pronghorn (Barmore 1980). Similarly, fire suppression has increased K_l for deer in the adjacent Jackson Hole area of Wyoming (Gruell 1980a,b).

Changes in K_l for moose and bison are less clear. Increases in wet meadows (Pls. 29, 44) may have increased K_l for bison.

The interaction of plant succession with winter climates (Chap. 8) makes these interpretations of changing carrying capacities as speculative as those made for elk (Chap. 9). However, the effects of fire suppression on deer and bighorn sheep could be tested in the park by again allowing natural fires to burn (Chap. 12).

CHAPTER 11

Elk–Carnivore Relationships

THE HISTORY AND STATUS OF THE CARNIVORES associated with elk on the northern range are reviewed. Field studies show that elk are important winter–spring food for predators and scavengers. The incidence of parasitism and disease in the elk herd is established from other studies. The effects of predation, parasites, and diseases on elk numbers are explored.

The Carnivores

As with ungulates, the large carnivores were hunted heavily from the mid-1870s to mid-1880s, with the presumed exception of aboriginal man (Skinner 1927, Murie 1940, Weaver 1978, Barmore 1980, Meagher, unpubl.). In addition, various "control" programs for wolves, coyotes, and cougars were conducted sporadically in the park from the mid-1890s into the 1930s.

The Gray Wolf

The gray wolf occurred historically in Yellowstone. Early numbers are unknown, but reports suggest that wolf densities were low during the periods of exploration and establishment of the park (Weaver 1978, Meagher, in prep.). Wolf numbers increased on the northern range shortly before 1912. Four occupied dens occurred in 1916 and 1920, suggesting the existence of at least four packs. This upsurge in wolves was met with a control program from 1914 to 1926 that apparently devastated the population (Weaver 1978). Large wolflike canids have, however, been reported periodically to the present, but their identity has not been established (Cole 1971b, Weaver 1978). One possibility is that these animals are wolf-coyote hybrids (Weaver 1978). A viable wolf population, with established pack units, does not occur presently on the northern range or elsewhere in the park.

The Coyote

Coyotes also were hunted during the late 19th century and were subjected to sporadic control in the park until 1935 (Murie 1940). In contrast to wolves, the control programs had no lasting effect, and coyotes were abundant on the northern range in the park throughout this study. Coyotes were, however, hunted and trapped heavily outside the park during the 1970s. Attempts to monitor coyote population trends during winter by recording visits to scent stations and by counting elicited howling responses (Linhart and Knowlton 1975, Pimlott and Joslin 1968) were unsuccessful. (Ungulates showed an uncommon interest in scent stations—so much so that the stations would have served better to measure the relative abundance of male bison!) Winter coyote densities on the National Elk Refuge in Wyoming averaged $.72 \pm .18/km^2$ over four years (Camenzind 1978). No comparable data exist for the northern range. However, I am quite familiar with the refuge, and densities on the northern range in the park were roughly similar; 1 coyote/3 km^2 in early winter would be conservative many years. Earlier studies showed that elk were important winter food for coyotes (Murie 1940).

The Cougar

Cougars were present on the northern range historically and seem to have been abundant until perhaps 1930, judging from sightings (Meagher, in prep.) and the numbers removed during the sporadic control programs (Skinner 1927). Mountain lions apparently were uncommon throughout the park from the 1930s through the 1960s (Murie 1940, Barmore pers. commun. 1980), although sporadic sightings were recorded (Houston 1978a). Limited evidence suggests that numbers increased during the 1970s. Barmore (pers. commun. 1980) observed only one or two sets of cougar tracks while spending a great deal of time in the field from 1962 to 1970. By contrast, I regularly observed lion tracks and the "scrapes"or scent stations made by resident males (Seidensticker et al. 1973:45) in the Black Canyon of the Yellowstone River during winter–spring from 1972 to 1978. Lions and their kills (mostly elk) also were observed occasionally. Sightings and tracks showed that females with young occurred on the area in 1972, 1974, 1975, and 1978, indicating that a resident population was present, rather than just transient lions (Houston 1978a).

The Wolverine

Wolverines were known historically (Meagher, in prep.), but may have been reduced to low levels by trapping and poisoning (Murie 1940). Poisoning campaigns aimed at coyotes continued on some federal lands surrounding the park until about 1971. These may have inadvertently maintained this wide-ranging scavenger at very low densities throughout the Yellowstone region. Reliable sightings of wolverines were made in and adjacent to the park throughout the 1970s, but the existence of resident populations has not been established (Houston 1978a).

The Grizzly Bear

Grizzly bears were abundant historically on the northern range (Meagher, in prep.). Up to 350 grizzlies may occur now in the park and the surrounding area (Blanchard and Knight 1980); numbers and population trends have, however, been in dispute (see Craighead 1974, Cole 1976, McCullough 1978, Schullery 1980). Grizzlies were common on the northern range during the 1970s. Elk, as prey and carrion, may be important items in spring and autumn bear diets (Cole 1972, Mealey 1975, Kendall 1980) (Fig. 11.1). The availability of carrion in the park may be important to the reproductive success of grizzly bears (Picton 1978).

The Black Bear

Black bears were also common historically throughout the forests of the park (Meagher and Phillips 1980, Meagher, in prep.). They are common at present; up to 650 may

FIGURE 11.1.
Remains of an adult male elk killed and eaten by a grizzly bear on the northern winter range, October 1970. Photo by M. Sample.

occur in the park (Cole 1976). Black bears were observed frequently on the northern range during spring. Elk carrion was important to these bears, particularly following severe winters with the subsequent delayed spring growth of vegetation (Houston 1978b; see also below). Black bears prey upon newborn elk and occasionally upon adult elk (Barmore and Stradley 1971; see also Chap. 5 and below).

Man

Man occupied the Yellowstone region for over 9,000 years as a hunter–gatherer (Wedel et al. 1968, Lahren 1971, 1976). Archaeological evidence and historical accounts suggest that densities of man were comparatively low in the upper Yellowstone River Valley and the area that became the park (Lahren 1976). Small bands of the Tukudika (Sheepeaters), a subdivision of the Northern Shoshoni, occupied the upper Yellowstone, Wind, and Snake Rivers until the 1870s (Lahren 1976). Additionally, tribal societies developed on the surrounding plains with acquisition of the horse in the 18th century. Several tribes of these very mobile peoples passed through the northern range annually on extended hunting trips. Such long-distance movements apparently were most common from about 1838 to 1868 (Haines 1962).

Accounts of Euro-American man in the Yellowstone area, including early and recent influences on the elk, occupy much of Chapters 3 and 5. Presently, segments of the northern elk herd wintering outside the park boundaries are hunted heavily (Houston 1979; see also Chap. 12). Human predation in the park is limited to illegal hunting. The extent of this poaching is difficult to gauge but probably amounts to fewer than 50 elk per year. Modern man's predation differs in at least two important respects from that of aboriginal man and the native carnivores: (1) there is no feedback from the intensity of predation upon the abundance and dynamics of the predator, and (2) the nutrients in the prey are removed from the ecosystem.

Elk as Food for Carnivores

The importance of elk as food for carnivores on the northern range was determined by monitoring the consumption of 1,084 carcasses of elk that died in the park during three winter–spring periods (Table 11.1). Carcass location and stage of consumption were determined from aerial and ground observations made during November–June. Samples of the dead elk by sex and age classes were used to estimate the amount of food available from the carcasses. Calculations have been described in detail elsewhere (Houston 1978b). In addition to the mammalian carnivores, large numbers of birds— mostly ravens, black-billed magpies, golden eagles and bald eagles—ate the carcasses. Most carcasses were eaten, with 19,000–35,000 kg of elk (about 75–80% of that available) observed to be consumed annually (Table 11.1). Actual consumption may have approached 50,000–85,000 kg, since only about 30–40% of the carcasses present were found (Houston 1978b). Elk were clearly a very important food for carnivores.

These observations also permitted some inferences about the abundance of predators and scavengers. The observed feeding rate for the combined carnivore fauna in 1975 averaged about 194 kg/day of elk over the entire period but was much greater from March to mid-June. The actual feeding rate may have been twice the observed rate. The amounts of elk consumed were underestimated, because figures for elk

TABLE 11.1
Consumption of 1,084 Elk Carcasses by Carnivores on the Northern Range in Yellowstone Park During 1975, 1976, and 1978

WINTER-SPRING PERIOD	ELK CARCASSES MONITORED	CARCASS CONSUMPTION (%)			ELK CONSUMED[b] (KG × 10³)	
		Eaten	Partially Eaten[a]	Uneaten	Observed	Estimated
1975	503	70	22	8	35 (80)[c]	85
1976	256	67	16	17	19 (75)	53
1978	325	76	9	15	21 (80)	65

[a] Estimated 50% consumed on average.
[b] Calculations follow Houston (1978b). About 1,200, 700, and 1,000 carcasses estimated to occur in the park during the three winters.
[c] Observed percentage of kilograms available that was consumed.

mortality were conservative and because completely consumed carcasses were comparatively more difficult to find. Additionally, other ungulate species and other foods were eaten by carnivores during the study periods (Houston 1978b). An impressive predator–scavenger fauna occurs in the park on the northern range, even though little is known about the abundance of any particular species or their relative contribution to the consumption of the carcasses.

Attempts were made to monitor directly the abundance of several carnivore groups by recording their numbers during each flight made to determine elk distribution (Chap. 3). Coyotes and eagles often were conspicuous during February–April periods (two–three flights annually). Coyote observations averaged around 16 per flight many years and ranged upward to 20–25 (Fig. 11.2). Interpreting these sightings in relation to the increasing abundance of elk during the 1970s is difficult. Both aerial and ground observations suggested that coyotes were particularly abundant in 1976, following the prolonged severe winter of 1975 when elk carrion was readily available. However, the 1976 winter also was severe but the 1977 coyote observations were the lowest recorded. Unfortunately, the 1977 winter was so mild that attempts to count elk were unsuccessful (Chap. 3), and attempts at monitoring the abundance of smaller carnivores fared no better. Similarly, the numbers of eagles observed showed little change over time, except that they seemed most numerous during the winter of 1975, when many fed on the carcasses. (These were mostly bald eagles in 1975, but bald and golden eagle sightings are combined in Fig. 11.2 because subadults were not readily identified from the air.)

Bears were observed mainly during the last flight of every winter–spring series, usually made between 25 May and 4 June. The number of grizzly and black bears observed averaged 17 ± 7 during these flights (N = 8), but ranged from 5 to 27. Observations were too few to draw any conclusions about trends in bear numbers on the northern range.

None of these observations could be interpreted convincingly to show changes over time in carnivores that might have been associated with the availability of elk or elk carrion. At best, the observations may serve as a base for future comparisons, because though abundant, some carnivore populations still could be depressed (see Interpretation, Carnivore Populations, below).

The above estimates of elk consumption did not include those killed and eaten

FIGURE 11.2.

Coyotes and eagles counted (mean, range) on the northern winter range during 17 aerial surveys, 1971–78.

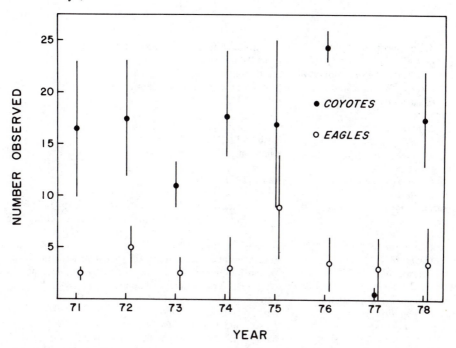

during other seasons. The spring flights sometimes hinted at the predation occurring upon newborn elk (Chap. 5). For example, 27 bears and 9 coyotes were observed during the flight of 28–29 May 1972. My observations, summarized in the flight report, were that, "Bears and coyotes showed marked preferences for major elk calving areas. Eight of the 19 grizzly bears observed were either feeding on newborn elk calves..., chasing groups of elk with calves..., or traveling through high density calving areas... Two of the 8 black bears observed were traveling through high density calving areas, and another medium sized bear was observed to catch and kill a calf in the Mt. Norris area. Five of the nine coyotes observed were either harassing female elk with newborn calves, feeding on a freshly killed elk calf, or traveling through a calving area." Concurrent field studies of bears also suggested that predation on elk calves was frequent some springs (Knight pers. commun. 1980). Studies elsewhere, which have included experimental removals of bears, suggest that black bear predation on elk calves can be quite intense (Schlegel 1976, 1977). Additionally, grizzly bear predation on adult elk is common in Yellowstone during spring and autumn (Knight pers. commun. 1980).

Parasites and Diseases of Elk

In addition to providing food for vertebrate carnivores, elk in the Yellowstone region serve as hosts for at least 25 different parasites and pathogens, 17 of which are known to occur in the northern herd (Table 11.2). These organisms play important roles in the relationship between carnivores and elk and in the dynamics of the elk population.

TABLE 11.2
Parasites and Diseases of Elk in the Yellowstone National Park Area

Organism[a]	Comments and Source
Bacteria	
*Actinomyces sp.	"Necrotic stomatitus," Allred et al. 1944
*Brucella sp.	Brucellosis, Rush 1932b
Fusobacterium necrophorum	From Honess and Winter 1956
Pasteurella sp.	Hemorrhagic septicemia, Thorne 1970b
Clostridium sp.	Howe 1970
Protozoa	
*Eimeria wapiti	Worley and Barrett 1964
*Sarcocystis sp.	Rush 1932a, Mills 1936
Trypanosoma cervi	Kingston and Morton 1975
Cestodes	
Cysticercus tenuicollis	Murie 1951
*Moniezia expansa	Worley and Barrett 1964
*Thysanosoma actinioides	Fringed tapeworm, Worley and Barrett 1964; 41% of 181 northern Yellowstone elk infected, Jacobsen et al. 1969
Nematodes	
*Capillaria sp.	Worley and Barrett 1964
Cooperia sp.	Bergstrom pers. commun. 1977 (tentative identification)
*Dictyocaulus sp.	Thread lungworm, Worley and Barrett 1964; 43% of 348 northern Yellowstone elk infected
Marshallagia marshalli	Bergstrom 1968
*Nematodirus sp.	Worley and Barrett 1964
*Ostertagia sp.	Worley and Barrett 1964
*Protostrongylus macrotis	Worley and Barrett 1964, Bergstrom pers. commun. 1977
Trichostrongylus sp.	Bergstrom pers. commun. 1977 (tentative identification)
*Trichuris sp.	Worley and Barrett 1964
Arthropods	
*Cephenemyia sp.	Bot fly larvae, Worley and Barrett 1964
*Dermacenter albipictus	Winter tick, Worley and Barrett 1964
*Bovicola sp.	Lice, from Mills 1936
*Otobius sp.	Greer 1968
*Psoroptes cervinus	Scabies mite, Worley and Barrett 1964

[a] Asterisk denotes organisms known to occur in the northern Yellowstone elk.

Over 500 post-mortem examinations of elk for parasites were made during the herd reductions of the 1960s (Worley and Barrett 1964, Greer 1968). The winter tick was the most abundant external parasite, and heavily infested elk were observed occasionally. The fringed tapeworm and thread lungworm appeared to be the most common internal helminth parasites (Worley and Barrett 1964, Greer 1968). Lungworms were particularly important, because the incidence of infection was high in all sex and age classes during the 1962–63 collections (calves, 35%; 1–9 years, 36–38%; 10 years and older, 54–62%). The incidence and the average worm burden increased markedly during March–May, when elk were stressed. Individual elk sometimes showed very high worm burdens, accompanied by pneumonias (Worley and Barrett 1964, Worley 1979). About 26% of 90 elk examined from December 1967 to March 1968, when the elk population was at its lowest level, also were infected with lungworms, although the burdens appeared to be lower than those observed earlier (Greer 1968:20).

Less is known about the incidence and pathogenic effects of either the bacterial diseases or protozoan infections. Brucellosis occurs in the northern herd, but the incidence appears to be rather low (Rush 1932b, Meagher 1974, Thorne et al. 1979).

The immediate cause of death for most elk dying naturally on the northern range during winters of the 1970s (Chaps. 5, 6) was not determined, but diseases and parasites played important roles. (The ultimate cause of death of these predominantly young and old elk was undernutrition from intraspecific competition for food.) Heavy tick infestations were observed on some dead calves. Other dead elk, particularly adult males, showed scabby areas on the skin that appeared to be scab mite infestations (Worley and Barrett 1964). Many moribund elk showed symptoms of the pneumonia associated with heavy lungworm burdens (Worley and Barrett 1964).

Parasites and pathogens served as sensitive links between the northern Yellowstone elk and their winter food supplies. As mentioned earlier (Chap. 6), incipient undernutrition leads quickly to pathogenic infection through impairment of the host's immune response. The timing and extent of the lungworm burdens, with the associated pneumonias, indicate that these organisms were particularly important links because they increased the vulnerability of young and old elk to mortality from undernutrition. Moreover, parasitized and diseased elk were more likely to be vulnerable to predation (Anderson 1978).

Interpretation: Carnivores and Elk

Carnivore Populations

Evidence from measuring the consumption of elk carcasses indicates that carnivores are abundant on the northern range. Some of the changes in species composition that occurred during the past century can be attributed directly or indirectly to Euro-American man. The elimination of viable wolf populations almost certainly was due directly to overhunting in and around the park. Indirect effects of man upon the abundance of certain carnivores may persist from the earlier elk reductions. These reductions decreased the natural winter mortality of elk, as well as the occurrence of weakened animals vulnerable to predation, and consequently may have decreased the associated carnivores. The time lags for restoration could be long for carnivores, which must now "learn" about the increased availability of vulnerable or dead elk (e.g., migratory eagles, bears denning in other areas of the park).

The Effects of Predation

The overall northern elk herd is currently held below $\hat{K}_I$ by human predation outside the park, a situation that is expected to continue (Chaps. 5, 12; see also Houston 1979). Predation by native carnivores on elk inside the park may be more frequent than generally appreciated, but its effects on elk population dynamics are not easily documented—except that predation is insufficient to prevent herd segments from being resource limited. At most, current levels of predation in the park might dampen fluctuations in the elk population or extend the intervals between them. [This would certainly be true if predation is used in the widest sense of including parasitism and disease in addition to killing by carnivores (MacArthur 1972:21).]

How the present effects of predation on the elk population differ from historic effects is an important issue. The early accounts of carnivore abundance are generally too limited to determine whether or not elk were more intensely or frequently predator limited. Based upon archaeological evidence and historic accounts, Lahren (1976) speculates as follows: "It seems improbable, during any time of the year, that the hunter–gatherer populations ever operated at a level which significantly affected the evidently large biomass [of their main prey in the upper Yellowstone Valley]." As mentioned above, early wolf densities appear to have been quite low in the presence of abundant ungulate populations. Early accounts also show that substantial mortality of elk occurred on the northern range during severe winters regardless of the levels of predation (Chap. 3). These observations would suggest that even historically, predation did not prevent elk, as the most abundant, large migratory ungulate, from being resource limited.

Still, this early information spans only a half century or so—an instant in the postglacial history of elk and their predators in the Yellowstone area. The historic effects of a large carnivore like the wolf may be discounted too easily when absent (see Pimlott 1967). The effects upon elk of adding wolves to the present system were modeled by Fowler and Barmore (1979). This model suggested that wolves could, in theory, reduce the size of the elk population if the estimated numbers of elk killed by wolves were added to all existing sources of mortality, including the human predation characteristic of the 1935–56 period. These authors were forced to assume a great deal about interspecific relationships. The effects of wolf predation on elk numbers would be less than predicted to the extent that their predation substituted for that of other species, including man. Wolves could reduce or displace other carnivores, including the coyote (Mech 1966, 1970). Wolf predation in the park could substitute for much human predation outside the park, since elk movements to wintering areas outside seem to be density-dependent (Chap. 4). The numbers of elk presumed killed by wolves in the model seem reasonable, but these are difficult guesses in a multispecies system where alternate, more vulnerable prey may be important to wolves (e.g., deer, beaver). Further, large numbers of elk from other herds summer in the park (Chap. 4); these might further dilute the effects of wolf predation on the northern herd. The possibility remains, however, that wolves could reduce the numbers of elk if added to the present system.

Generalizing about the effects of predation by large carnivores on the abundance of large ungulates (i.e., elk or larger) from other studies is difficult; the number of such studies is limited, they are inherently difficult to conduct, and they show that the effects of predation vary. A number of recent studies suggest, however, that predators are unable to prevent large ungulates from being resource limited in several natural ecosystems, particularly if the large ungulates are migratory and also are the most abundant of several alternate prey (Hornocker 1970, Schaller 1972, Kruuk 1972, Carbyn 1974, Sinclair 1977, 1979, Bertram 1979). The series of excellent studies of moose–wolf relationships on Isle Royale now indicate that moose are resource limited (Peterson 1977) instead of being held below this level by predation, as suggested earlier (Mech 1966). Large predators have additional influences in these systems, however, which may include selecting substandard prey (Mech 1970, Schaller 1972), altering prey distribution (Hornocker 1970), and changing the dynamics of prey populations (Kruuk 1972).

Systems where the large dominant ungulates are trapped at lower population levels by predators seem to occur when predation by native carnivores and modern man are combined or when food for the prey is reduced by plant succession or by particularly severe environmental conditions (see Kelsall 1968, Smuts 1978, Peterson 1979, Hilborn and Sinclair 1979).

In contrast to the effects of native predators on large dominant ungulates, the smaller, less abundant ungulates with restricted distributions more often may be limited by predation (Kruuk and Turner 1967, Schaller 1972). This may be true presently for pronghorn on the northern range, although intense human predation was initially responsible for the lower numbers of pronghorn.

In the particular case of the northern Yellowstone elk, the absence of a wolf population does not justify resumption of human predation in the park. Although the proximate agents of elk mortality have changed somewhat during the past century, the existing array of predators, parasites, and diseases would seem to be sufficient to modulate the fluctuations of the elk population. These remarks should not be misinterpreted—it is unfortunate that a viable wolf population does not occur in Yellowstone, but their absence may not be as serious as sometimes suggested insofar as their effects upon elk numbers are concerned. Fortunately, these interpretations, speculations, and models of predation can be put to rigorous field tests, as they should (Chap. 12).

CHAPTER 12

Management

Management Considerations and Strategies

Yellowstone is the world's first National Park. The park was established to conserve unique geothermal features in a sublime setting of mountains and lakes. The preservation of large mammals in the park soon was considered equally important, as these species were being extirpated throughout the Rocky Mountains. The primary purpose of Yellowstone as a natural area still is to maintain these representative and unique ecosystems in as near pristine conditions as possible. In addition to preserving ecosystems for their cultural and scientific values, the park, as a Biosphere Reserve, is now seen as a reservoir of genetic diversity (Franklin 1977) and as an environmental base line to which other, exploited, systems may be compared (see Jenkins and Bedford 1973, Sinclair 1977, Martinka 1978).

These unique land use objectives mean that management of the park is restricted to compensating or correcting for the influence of modern man on ecosystem processes. Criteria used to manage vegetation and wildlife to produce sustained yields are inappropriate in national parks (Cole 1971a, Houston 1971, Caughley 1976b, 1979, Sinclair 1977). (This observation applies to the management of most park resources, but the necessary differences in criteria still are not fully appreciated. Until recently the management of forests and fishes in many U.S. National Parks was nearly indistinguishable from the programs of other land management agencies.) Appropriate management criteria for natural areas are often the most difficult to develop, because these require considerable ecological and historical information. Ecosystems are dynamic, and some component populations may shift from one natural stable state to another (Holling 1973, 1978, May 1977, Peterman et al. 1978). Thus, "one must resist the temptation to manage [natural ecosystems] with a view toward maintaining some arbitrary status quo" (Sinclair 1979:25).

The course of corrective management in parks may be signaled clearly once the changes in ecosystem processes brought about by man have been documented, but sometimes this is not the case. Management must be tempered by considerations of biological feasibility and of biological "side effects." Situations are encountered where the best strategy may be to recognize and accept a somewhat altered state, perhaps temporarily, as less traumatic to the overall system than any attempted "cure." This observation is not an invitation to circumvent the stewardship responsibilities for managing natural areas, but it is intended as a caution that recognizes our ignorance of ecosystem dynamics.

Reconciling situations where a single resource is to be managed differently by two or more agencies, each charged with different objectives, is the most difficult of all. Management of the northern Yellowstone elk falls into this class, as nonconsumptive uses within the park are to be meshed with consumptive uses outside.

Management: Conflicts and Recommendations

Conditions that conflict with the park's objectives of managing the vegetation and animals on the northern range are reviewed, and recommendations are offered. With some reservations, I have included several very specific recommendations. These may be quickly outdated as conditions and information change. On the other hand, a record seems necessary because recommendations are sometimes lost or misinterpreted as personnel and priorities change.

At the outset, I assume that all manipulative management of park biota will be regarded as essentially experimental (see Sinclair 1979:27). This means that hypotheses to be tested, procedures to be used, and criteria to reject or to reformulate hypotheses should be stated clearly in advance. The information obtained from management programs should be reviewed frequently for consistency with the hypothesis being tested.

The Vegetation

FIRE

Many of the changes in distribution and composition of the vegetation documented during this study resulted from the suppression of natural fires. Since 1972, park managers have moved to restore fire to park ecosystems by allowing lightning fires to burn unchecked (National Park Service 1975a). Presently, managers have the option of allowing fires to burn on about 70% of the park, including portions of the northern winter range. Fire behavior and weather are studied to improve predictions of the rate and direction of fire spread and the ultimate size of the burn. The effects of fires on the vegetation, aquatic life, stream flow, and terrestrial vertebrates are either studied intensively or monitored routinely (Sellers and Despain 1976, Despain and Sellers 1977).

The fire management program should be expanded to include the rest of the northern range in the park (except the BLA, see below). This will require a cooperative agreement with the Gallatin National Forest, because some fires originating in the park would spread to the adjacent Forest lands. Such agreements already are in effect between the park and the Bridger–Teton and Shoshone National Forests.

Historically, the northern range burned more frequently than any other part of the park. Thus, the area should be given priority in the fire management program. If several fires start, and manpower or other considerations dictate that some must be suppressed, then those on the winter range should be allowed to burn. Additionally, a limited program of experimental prescribed burns should be implemented in aspen vegetation types. Burns should be conducted on dissimilar sites to test the relative importance of browsing, climate, fire intensity, and fuel loads on stand regeneration.

By contrast, it seems best, at present, to suppress fires in the BLA until an overall plan has been worked out to restore native vegetation (see below). Fires at this low elevation may simply facilitate spread of the exotic cheatgrass at the expense of native plants.

Exotic Plants

A number of exotic grasses and forbs have displaced native species, especially in the BLA. A long-term management goal should be to reestablish native species (e.g., replace crested wheatgrass and cheatgrass with needle-and-thread and bluebunch wheatgrass). Restoration might be facilitated by using biological control agents or highly selective herbicides. The technology available to accomplish these ends is now quite primitive; here the risk is high that a "cure" could turn out to be worse than the affliction.

The Herbivores

Ungulate–Vegetation Equilibria

The major purpose of this study has been to examine the nature of existing ungulate–vegetation relationships. As of September 1980, the data available do not indicate that reductions of elk or of any other ungulate are necessary in the park to alter the present equilibria. This recommendation is made recognizing that aspects of the ungulate–vegetation equilibria have changed during the past century, mainly as a result of fire suppression. Also, the biotic effects of native ungulates on the vegetation of the BLA have been exaggerated (Chap. 8), but even here the relationships seem stable.

This interpretation and recommendation seem consistent with findings from a wide range of other studies. Ecosystems that have evolved in harsh environments where natural "disasters" are relatively frequent (e.g., floods, fires, drought, severe winters) likely will be quite resilient (Holling 1973). This means that systems like the northern range should have a considerable "ability to absorb change and disturbance and still maintain the same relationships between populations and state variables" (Holling 1973:14). Furthermore, studies elsewhere suggest that resource-limited ungulates reach acceptable equilibria with the vegetation in many large national parks without cropping (Houston 1968, Meagher 1973, Sinclair 1977, 1979, Cole 1978, Martinka 1978). Obviously, this possibility can apply only to segments of the northern herd that remain in the park. Although strongly resource limited, the overall herd is not a clean example of a "naturally regulated" population (i.e., one occurring at K_1 and subject entirely to natural regulatory forces), as some segments are hunted.

Certainly additional data on vegetation–ungulate dynamics could cause this interpretation to be modified or rejected. Evidence to reject the interpretation of an acceptable equilibrium should include measurements of vegetation that document progressive declines in the absolute abundance of food for elk. This would involve retrogressive succession on major grasslands; climatic fluctuations and plant successional processes controlled by other agents would have to be separated from ungulate effects. Such effects upon the vegetation should also measureably reduce elk densities. Information from continued studies of the relationships among herbivores or from the elk management programs outside the park also could lead to limited elk reductions in the park (see below).

ELK MANAGEMENT

The objective of maintaining representative natural ecosystems must be modified for the northern Yellowstone elk, because the park is not a complete ecological unit for one segment of the population. I assume that elk hunting will continue on the 17% of the winter range outside the park. The biological rationale for such hunting is to maintain low elk densities that are reasonably compatible with agriculture (i.e., partition forage resources between elk and cattle, and limit damage to private property) and to substitute human predation for some natural mortality. To accomplish the former, elk migrating from the park probably will be maintained at densities far below maximum sustained yields.

Hunting alters the dynamics of this herd segment and otherwise conflicts with park objectives. However, it may be possible, through sensitive management, to minimize these effects. Each agency involved in the cooperative management of the elk (National Park Service, Montana Fish and Game Department, U.S. Forest Service) must respect the very different, equally valid land use objectives of the others. Management of elk moving from the park has been covered by a signed "Memorandum of Understanding" among the agencies, where each agreed to provide part of the necessary biological data for management. Annually, the field personnel of each agency prepared recommendations, based upon their studies, for administrators. Recommendations were forwarded for consideration to the Montana Fish and Game Commission, which had the responsibility for establishing hunting seasons, quotas, etc.

The winter hunting of elk outside the park has been controversial. Over 3,000 elk moved outside the park prior to the hunting seasons of 1976 and 1978. A high percentage of these elk had moved from the BLA (Houston 1979). About 1,283 hunters took 1,121 elk in 1976; 937 hunters took 767 elk in 1978. Numbers and distribution of hunters were controlled by permits. Maximum hunter density was around 1.4 hunters/km^2 in 1976; 1.1, in 1978. The high densities of hunters and elk during these winter seasons means these hunts are a game cropping operation, as opposed to traditional recreational hunting, carried out under difficult biological and social constraints.

A research hypothesis that such hunting could be conducted without causing artificial concentrations of elk in the park through conditioned avoidance behavior was rejected on the basis of the 1976 and 1978 hunts (Houston 1979). Elk moved back and forth across the boundary during hunts, and temporary concentrations occurred in the BLA. However, nearly 500 elk were taken by hunters during a 1980 winter season, apparently without significant movement back into the park (Erickson pers. commun. 1980). This means that it may be possible to conduct such seasons without concentrating elk in the BLA. However, this will require an innovative, experimental approach to management.

Management alternatives that need to be tested outside the park to reduce conflicts with agriculture and to minimize elk concentrations in the BLA include:

1. Provide landowners with reasonable compensation for elk using private lands through a program of "wildlife easements," as opposed to damage claims.
2. Continue to obtain private lands on the winter range, when available, through a program of land exchanges and purchases.
3. Seek more liberal hunting opportunities on the large blocks of private land.
4. Permit only infrequent, very conservative, hunting of some areas to encourage elk use, and conversely, permit periodic near elimination of particular elk groups by hunting in other areas, rather than attempting to provide uniform yields throughout.

These various management strategies could fail if:

1. Elk numbers moving outside the park become too large to be cropped effectively by public hunting.
2. Sociopolitical constraints prevent cropping or trying other management alternatives.
3. Large numbers of elk regularly move back onto the winter range in the park (Houston 1979).

An alternative would be to maintain very low elk densities in the BLA of the park by periodic selective removals of entire herd groups by the National Park Service. This would be a comparatively small-scale program that could have limited influence upon the dynamics and behavior of other elk in the park. Park reductions should be a last resort. These probably would be necessary only to the extent that a flexible program cannot be maintained outside the park because of sociopolitical pressures on the management agencies.

OTHER UNGULATES

With one exception, the available data do not indicate that management of the less abundant ungulates is necessary in the park to maintain equilibria with the vegetation, to alter interspecific relationships among herbivores, or for other reasons. Bison are the exception. A program to prevent contact between bison and cattle will require the sporadic removal of limited numbers of bison at the park boundary. As mentioned earlier, this seems necessary to further reduce the unlikely possibility of brucellosis transmission to local cattle (Meagher 1974, 1976).

A management philosophy of maintaining arbitrary "balances" among the ungulate species by reductions of one to favor another is generally inappropriate in the park. Studies of interspecific relationships do not suggest either that this is necessary to prevent competitive exclusion or, indeed, that such manipulation would even work. A possible exception to this suggested guideline could occur because of winter elk hunting outside the park. Forced concentrations of elk in the BLA could exaggerate their effects upon other species, particularly bighorn sheep. Severe effects *might* be sufficient justification to resume the elk reductions in the BLA as mentioned above, but very reliable data on sheep population trends and dynamics would be required to support such a program.

On a related subject, the present, precariously low, numbers of pronghorn on the northern range resulted primarily from human predation. Consideration should be given to reestablishing pronghorn on the range outside the park. Not only would this expanded distribution more closely resemble historic conditions, but chances for perpetuating the pronghorn would be greatly enhanced.

OTHER HERBIVORES

Occasionally in the past, park managers either have initiated or have been pressured into attempts to "control" outbreaks of native insects in the forests of the park, including forests on the northern range, by using insecticides. Such programs are wholly inappropriate and can only detract from attempts to maintain natural ecosystem processes in the park.

The Carnivores

Maintaining populations of the large native carnivores is an especially important and challenging management objective on the northern range. Large numbers of elk, undergoing periodic extensive winter mortality, may be prerequisite to having vigorous populations of some carnivore species. The welfare of carnivores would have to be considered in any future elk reduction programs in the park.

THE GRAY WOLF

The gray wolf should be restored to the park. The absence of a viable wolf population represents perhaps the single greatest departure from the objective of maintaining natural ecosystems. The biological and social problems of introducing wolves into parts of their former range in the northern Rocky Mountains have been reviewed at length (U.S. Fish and Wildlife Service 1980). Aspects of the specific problem of an introduction into Yellowstone also have been examined (National Park Service 1975b, Weaver 1978, Meagher pers. commun. 1980). No insuperable biological reasons preclude an introduction of wolves into the park. The major difficulty, other than choosing genetically suitable stock and deciding upon the mechanics of the actual introduction, involves wolf dispersal from established park populations into livestock producing areas. Strategies for mitigation have been explored (U.S. Fish and Wildlife Service 1980). The land use objectives and the ungulate prey-base make Yellowstone an ideal site for a wolf introduction. The presence of wolves would provide a needed empirical test of the effects of this large carnivore on a multispecies prey-base.

OTHER CARNIVORES

Viable populations of the remaining carnivores occur in the park, and no introductions seem necessary at present. The wolverine represents a potential exception; continued monitoring of sightings is warranted to determine its status.

EURO-AMERICAN MAN

The difficulties of meshing the consumptive use of elk by man-the-predator with nonconsumptive use by man-the-observer occupy much of this chapter and need no further comment. Conflicts with the management of elk and other large mammals outside the park will accelerate as land is further subdivided and developed. Opportunities should not be missed for government agencies to purchase these private lands on the winter range. Purchased land would be added to the public domain and managed solely as wildlife range. Within the park, it will be necessary continually to review the need to retain certain facilities on the northern range. A long-term goal should be to reduce the size and number of park developments.

The management conflicts facing park managers are, in essence, best defined as problems of managing man. This view, while essentially correct, is also a bit trite and risks missing the other side of the coin. The unique assemblage of species on the northern range is a source of immeasurable interest and pleasure to park visitors. Perhaps the greatest revelation to me was that maintenance of reasonably intact natural ecosystems was, in fact, possible in the presence of large numbers of visitors—the mere presence of man had to be distinguished from his significant ecological effects. The northern range, indeed the entire park, is tangible proof that this can be done.

Monitoring and Research

Monitoring

Monitoring the status of the plants and animals that comprise the complex and dynamic northern range system must be done routinely to guide management and to test the interpretations from research. Such recommendations are far more easily made than carried out, particularly when operating budgets are strained to the limits. However, a program to monitor the presumed key elements of the northern range is essential, and can be done relatively inexpensively.

A monitoring program has been detailed elsewhere (Houston, unpubl. 1978) and is briefed here. Trends in vegetation can be determined by measuring various established transects at intervals as infrequent as five–seven years. Population trends and winter distribution of elk, bison, and pronghorn must be monitored annually from fixed-wing aerial counts. Bighorn sheep could also be counted annually, but since this is so difficult and funds are so limited, a better alternative is to make two–three spring counts once every two or three years when counting conditions seem to be optimum (Chap. 10). The effects on elk distribution inside the park from winter hunting outside always should be monitored. Sometimes small changes in hunter access points, in hunt unit boundaries, and in the timing of the hunts can minimize elk movement back into the park. But information is necessary to effect such changes. The BLA will require special consideration and careful monitoring because of the elk hunting outside and the broad overlap in winter distribution of four ungulate species. Here, if anywhere, the ungulate–vegetation equilibria or the interspecies relationships could first come unstuck.

Research

Research needs have been mentioned throughout the text. Information is needed on the effects of grazing on ecosystem dynamics (Chap. 9). The natality and mortality rates of elk should be sampled from herd segments at ecological carrying capacity to better understand their dynamics at high densities. The nature and extent of resource division among the smaller ungulates require more work. Should wolves be restored to the park, then, without question, detailed studies of their effects upon prey and upon other carnivores must accompany studies of the wolves.

Understandably, studies of the "heroic mammals" have dominated park research. Consequently, comparatively little is known about other components of the system. The ecology of small mammals and birds needs examination, as does that of the invertebrate fauna. These are real research needs, not diversions for scientists and students, because the goal of park research should be a synthesis of information that includes models of the interactions of major species and ecosystem processes [the recent volume on Serengeti Park (Sinclair and Norton-Griffiths 1979) is a fine example]. Realistic models not only identify deficiencies in information, but one could hope that their progressive refinement would allow managers to predict the outcome of future natural or man-induced disturbances to the system and, for the latter, initiate sound corrective management.

Yellowstone is not only the first national park, but by any measure, it must be counted still among the world's finest. Undeniably, some changes from the pristine ecology have occurred. Modern man has altered the distribution and abundance of certain native species through fire suppression, by limited construction, by hunting and reduction programs, and by the introduction of some exotic plants and animals. Still in all, my lasting impression of the park is that it is remarkably intact ecologically and the potential for further restoration is very great.

APPENDIX I

Reports of Elk 1836–86, Yellowstone Park and Vicinity

Russell (in Haines 1965a)

19 Aug. 1836. "This valley [Yellowstone Lake outlet area] is interspersed with scattering groves of tall pines forming shady retreats for the numerous Elk and Deer during the heat of the day."

Aug. 1837. ". . . we hunted the branches of this stream then crossed the divide [Sylvan Pass] to the waters of the Yellowstone Lake where we found the whole country swarming with Elk we killed a fat Buck for supper . . ."

Aug. 1837. After ascending the highest mountain surrounding the Hoodoo Basin on headwaters of Lamar River. "But on the contrary those stupendous rocks whose surface is formed into irregular benches rising one above another from the vale to the snow dotted here and there with low pines and covered with green herbages intermingled with flowers with the scattered flocks of Sheep and Elk carelessly feeding or thoughtlessly reposing. . . . I descended to the camp where I found my companions had killed a fat Buck Elk. . . ."

29 Aug. 1839. "[Indians] commenced shooting at a large band of elk that was swimming in the [Yellowstone] lake killed 4 of them. . . ."

1 Sept. 1839 Traveling along the south shore of Heart Lake, "fell in with a large band of Elk killed two fat Does and took some of the meat."

Delacy 1876

13 Sept. 1863. Probably on the Gallatin-Madison divide from Grayling to Specimen Cr. "We saw many elks and one was killed near camp. . . ."

15 Sept. 1863. On headwaters of Gallatin River from Specimen Cr. north for 8–9 miles. "We encountered many bands of elk today, who like the bear, were not accustomed to the sight of men, and would stand within thirty yards of us without fear."

Henderson 1867

2 Sept. 1867. Between Yellowstone Lake and Hayden Valley. "The trail is thro open pine timber with game trails running in all directions. We found several open parks covered with fine bunch grass & elk everywhere. They all seemed to be making their way out of the mountains." Snow had fallen the previous night.

3 Sept. 1867. Vicinity of Tower Falls. "Plenty elk, deer antelope & bear"

4 Sept. 1867. Blacktail Plateau area. "Elk everywhere. . . . Camped near the river. . . . Elk deer & antelope in abundance."

Folsom et al. 1869 (in Haines 1965b)

16 Sept. 1869. Camped in Lamar Valley below Cache Cr. "We hear the elk whistling in every direction."

17 Sept. 1869. Traveled up Flint Cr. "We saw a great many deer today, and judging . . . tracks, elk are . . . abundant."

Henderson, 1870

20 June 1870. On Hellroaring Creek perhaps 10 miles above junction with Yellowstone River. "Killed a fine bull elk, out of which we got several pounds tallow, camped in a beautiful flat—fine grass, game plenty, but no gold."

21 June 1870. On Buffalo Plateau. "This flat is something like 10 miles by 6, with numerous lakes scattered over it, & the finest range in the world. Here we found all manner of wild game—buffalo, elk blacktail deer, bear & moose."

23 June 1870. ". . . up the East Fork [of Buffalo Cr. north of the Park] to foot of mountain, where we camped. Grass scarce, but snow, buffalo, elk & bear plenty."

27 June 1870. "Camped on waters of Buffalo Cr. [Henderson comments that this stream flows south 25 miles into East Fork of Yellowstone.]. . . Fine grass game plenty—buffalo elk deer & bear, mosquitos & ants."

24 July 1870. In Specimen Ridge area. "Buffalo, elk & bear, while deer are more plentiful than we have seen on the trip."

26 July 1870. In Upper Lamar area. "Game trails everywhere, no gold but thousands of elk & deer."

27 July 1870. Upper Lamar Area. "No gold; elk & sheep plenty . . . "

Doane (in Bonney 1970)

29 Aug. 1870. Sulphur Cr. area south of Mt. Washburn and west of the Grand Canyon of the Yellowstone River. "The ground was everywhere tracked by the passage of herds of elk and mountain sheep. Bear signs were everywhere visible."

1 Sept. 1870. After entering the Hayden Valley. "Elk were feeding in small bands on the other side of the valley. . . ."

6 Sept. 1870. In the valley of the Upper Yellowstone River on the southeast corner of Yellowstone Lake. "The ground was trodden by thousands of elk and sheep."

Barlow and Heap, 1872

2 Aug. 1871. Rush Lake in Lower Geyser Basin. "Here tracks of deer, elk and buffalo in great abundance were seen."

16 Aug. 1871. Two Ocean Plateau area. "Signs of game abound, among which were found tracks of the grizzly & the black bear, mountain sheep, elk and deer."

25 Aug. 1871. Mirror Plateau area. "[The] wood abounded with game-tracks, several elk and deer being seen. . . ."

Blackmore, 1872

30 July 1872. Traveling from Blacktail Cr. to Elk Cr. "Elk horns in abundance." Evidence for wintering elk.

Bradley 1873

Summer 1872. In Yellowstone canyon area. "This is evidently a favorite grazing-ground of deer and elk, whose tracks abounded even on the steepest slopes."

Upper Snake River, Mt. Hancock, Chicken Ridge area. "To avoid traveling in the bed of the stream, we followed some of the numerous game-trails. . . ."

Two Ocean Plateau area. "This is mostly fine grazing ground, and the numerous game-trails give evidence that it is frequented by deer and elk; indeed we found two herds of elk, of about twenty each, among the groves on the top of the ridge."

Doane (in Bonney 1970)

1874. After attempting to cross the densely forested headwaters of Tower Cr. from Canyon. "Late in the afternoon we reached the summit of the mountain toward Mammoth Springs. [probably the Upper Blacktail Plateau area in the vicinity of Prospect Peak], coming out in an open space where there were thousands of Elk horns. There are many such places in the Park, where these animals have gone for centuries to drop their horns in the early winter." Evidence of wintering elk.

Strong 1875

1875. Strong condemns the market hunting of game in the park during the winter and the slaughter of elk for their hides. Most of this seems to be second-hand information from either G. Doane or J. Baronette: "When the snow falls and the fierce winter storms begin in November and December, the elk, deer and sheep leave the summits of the snowy ranges and come in great bands to the foot-hills and valleys [of the park], where they are met and shot down shamefully by those merciless human vultures."

Reports "over four thousand" elk killed in previous winter, i.e., winter 1874–75 in the Mammoth Springs Basin alone. Compare this estimate with those of Ludlow and Grinnell for this same winter. Suggests that this slaughter has "thinned out" the "great herds" west of the Yellowstone but that plenty still exists, and that the area east of the Yellowstone River still abounds with wildlife. "Jack Baronette can point out and name the men who glide up to bands of elk on snowshoes and shoot them down when too poor and weak to run away, or when the snow lies on the ground to such great depth that they are unable to travel. . . ."

Ludlow 1876

Aug.–Sept. 1875. After a reconnaissance of the park. "Hunters have for years devoted themselves to the slaughter of the game, until within the limits of the park it is hardly to be found. I was credibly informed by people on the spot, and personally cognizant of the facts, that during the winter of 1874 and 1875, at which season the heavy snows render the elk an easy prey, no less than from 1500 to 2000 of these, the largest and finest game animals in the country, were thus destroyed within the radius of 15 miles of the Mammoth Springs. From this large number, representing an immense supply of the best food, the skins only were taken, netting to the hunter some $2.50 or $3 apiece, the frozen carcasses being left in the snow to feed wolves or to decay in the spring." Ludlow recommends that troops be stationed in the park to provide protection from vandals and hunters and that killing of game be forbidden. Compare Ludlow's comments on wildlife abundance to those of Grinnell on the same trip.

Grinnell 1876

Aug.–Sept. 1875. "It is estimated that during the winter of 1874–'75 not less than 3,000 elk were killed for their hides alone in the valley of the Yellowstone, between the mouth of Trail Creek [now Tom Miner Cr.] and the [Mammoth] Hot Springs."

"Elk were rather abundant all through the country which we traversed. They were seen in considerable numbers along the Missouri River, among the Bridger Mountains, and in the Yellowstone Park."

Doane (in Bonney 1970)

23 Oct. 1876. Hayden Valley Area. ". . . I had ridden close up to a herd of at least two thousand elk. They had been lying in the snow, and had all sprung up together frightening my horse. . . . It was a magnificant sight as the bulls were in full growth of horns, and the calves all large enough to run freely with the herd."

29 Oct. 1876. Heart Lake area. "Driving out a large herd of Elk resting there, we went into camp."

Server 1876–77

29 Oct. 1876. Trail from Yellowstone Lake to Heart Lake. "Saw one bear and a herd of elk."

Norris 1877 Supt. Ann. Rept., YNP

1877. "Hence in no other portion of the West or of the world was there such an abundance of elk, moose, deer, mountain sheep, and other beautiful and valuable animals, fish and fowl, nor as ignorant, or as fearless of and easily slaughtered by man as in this secluded and unknown park but 7 years ago. Most of the larger animals would stupidly gaze at man stalking erect as an added wonder in the "wonderland" until too often wantonly slaughtered, while the utter want of salary prevented my worthy predecessor, Hon. N. P. Langford, from residing there or seriously checking." Norris was present in the Park during summer to late autumn periods.

"From the unquestioned fact that over 2,000 hides of the huge Rocky Mountain elk, nearly as many each of the big horn, deer and antelope, and scores if not hundreds of moose and bison were taken out of the park in spring of 1875, probably 7000, or an annual average of 1000 of them [elk?] and hundreds if not thousands of each of these other animals have been thus killed since its discovery in 1870."

Animals were "often run down on snow-shoes and tomahawked when their carcasses were least valuable."

Considered game in much of the park decimated. "But the wild eastern portion between them [Yellowstone Lake, River and Grand Canyon] and the impassable snowy crests of the Shoshone Sierra or Yellowstone Range, from the base, say thirty miles, along the East Fork of the Yellowstone south, say fifty miles, to apex of a triangle at the head of the lake, contains fewer prominent wonders and more large valuable game animals than other portions of the park or of the mountains."

"Here is still a herd of three hundred or four hundred of the curly, nearly black bison, or mountain buffalo, with thousands of elk, deer, moose, antelope, bighorn and wooly sheep, beaver, and other beautiful and rare animals valuable for food, pelts and furs, while inclosed by impassable natural barriers elsewhere, only during the deep snows of winter occasionally visit the deep-sheltered grassy valley of the East Fork—from two to five miles wide."

Norris 1880 Supt. Ann. Rept., YNP

1879. "I have not allowed the killing of bison, and so checked the wanton slaughter of elk, deer, sheep and antelope, mainly for their pelts and tongues. . . . I have . . . seldom failed to find . . . game for our largest parties. . . . I am confident these choice animals have increased, rather than diminished, in numbers within the park since my management thereof."

Norris 1881

1880. "A good and well-located house was also constructed for the gamekeeper at the mouth of Soda Butte, a branch of the East Fork of the Yellowstone, and a favorite winter haunt of elk and bison."

"Elk, deer, and other game being driven by storms into the sheltered glens and valley, we were enabled to secure an abundant winter's supply of fresh meat, and also fine hides of the bear, wolf and wolverine."

". . . I would add that there are now in the park abundance of bison, moose, elk, deer antelope and bighorn sheep; besides fine summer pasturage, there are winter haunts for these animals. . . ."

"As stated in my first report, at least 7,000 of these valuable animals [elk] were slaughtered between 1875 and 1877 for their hides, or perhaps for their carcasses. . . . [Elk] have not seriously diminished, and but for the unprecedented severity of the past winter would have greatly increased. . . ." [Elk] frequent all portions of the park, often high up amid the mountain snows in summer, and in the most sheltered valleys in winter, in herds of a hundred or more."

Yount 1881a (in Norris, 1881)

1880. Appendix A. Report of Gamekeeper Harry Yount. "[I] constructed a cabin for my winters quarters at a good spring on the terrace commanding a fine view of both the East Fork and the Soda Butte valleys. Here I purpose wintering so as to protect the game, especially elk and bison, in their sheltered chosen winter haunts, from the Clarke's Fork and other miners. . . . I have, during the season found elk deer and bear in all portions of the park. . . ."

Yount 1881b (in Norris, 1881)

1881. Report of Gamekeeper Harry Yount. Yount remained at cabin ''during the entire winter, the early part of which was so severe that there were no mountain hunters. . . . The snowfall was unusually great and remained very deep high in the mountains, but the winds and hot vapors from the Fire Hole Basin at the foot of Mt. Norris kept the snow pretty clear along its western slopes; where there were abundance of mountain sheep and some elk, all winter Elk to the number of about 400 wintered in small bands in the valleys of the East Fork [presumably that part of the drainage around Yount's cabin] and Soda Butte, where the snow was about knee deep''

''I found that very few of the deer or antelope wintered anywhere in the park; that a small band of bison wintered on Alum Creek and another on the South Fork of the Madison; that there were elk in nearly all of the warm valleys and moose around the Shoshone and the fingers of the Yellowstone lakes; bighorn sheep on all the mountain slopes. . . .'' Apparently a very severe winter as Yount's own weather records show snow falling on 66 of 90 days from December 1880 to February 1881.

Tolhurst 1926

Summer 1882. ''On the trip through Yellowstone park we had meat all the time; game was plentiful. . . . Elk and deer were plentiful. . . . I have seen elk hides taken out of the park by the wagonload; and have seen all kinds of hides stretched out drying. . . . We saw bears, elk, deer, mountain sheep and lots of antelope on Swan lake flat. Most of the elk were seen early in the morning or late in the evening.''

Conger 1883 Supt. Ann. Rept., YNP

1883. ''. . . I returned to my post, where I arrived on the 1st of March, 1883, you [The Secretary of Interior] deeming my presence in the park necessary that early in the season by reason of reports reaching you of the slaughter of game within the Park. Upon investigating these rumors, I ascertained that a few elk and deer had been killed by parties contracting to furnish meat for the hotel company. . . . I am glad I can assure you that the reports which reached you last winter relative to the slaughter of game in the Park were greatly exaggerated.'' The report of the Superintendent for the year 1885 by D. W. Wear suggests otherwise.

Wear 1885 Supt. Ann. Rept., YNP

1885. ''The game in the Park had been shot with impunity and marketed at the hotels without any interference on the part of the officers whose sworn duty it was to protect & prevent its destruction. . . . I am glad to be able to say that the park is full of game of all kinds. . . . the elk in large numbers. . . .''

Wear 1886 Supt. Ann. Rept., YNP

1886. "There is more game in the Park now of every kind than was ever known before. Elk, antelope, deer and mountain sheep are here in large bands, and within less than four miles of Mammoth Hot Springs." Wear considered that he and a force of eight assistant superintendents had curtailed much of the "wholesale slaughter" of game.

Reports of Elk 1886–1910, Yellowstone Park and Vicinity

Harris 1886 Supt. Ann. Rept., YNP

1886. "From the reports of reliable scouts, familiar with the ranges of the elk, the deer, and the buffalo, there can be but little doubt that there is an abundance of game in the Park."

Harris 1887 Supt. Ann. Rept., YNP

1887. ". . . immense herds of elk have passed the winter along the traveled road from Gardiner to Cook City. . . . It is difficult to form any accurate estimate concerning the numbers of elk that passed the winter in the Park; certain it is that the number that wintered in the valley of Lamar River and on its tributaries have been estimated by all who saw them at several thousands. . . . The elk are accustomed, when driven out of the mountains by the snows of winter, to follow down the course of the mountain streams into the lower valleys. For this reason but little efficient protection can be afforded to this species of large game in the Park except upon the Yellowstone River and its tributaries."

"The elk which follow down the outward slopes of the mountains surrounding the Park along the tributaries of the Madison and the Gallatin on the west, or the Snake River on the south, pass beyond the Park limits before the hunting season permitted by the

Territorial laws has closed, and fall an easy prey to the hunters who are in wait for them.''

Hofer 1887

Winter 1887. Source of information was six-day February and early March snowshoe trip from Canyon to Yanceys to Gardiner. Hofer estimated numbers of elk and considered them to be low: ''Mt. Washburn area 150; [Tower] falls 50; On Specimen Ridge and the section of the Park to the north, at least 2000; on Blacktail, Lava, Elk and Lost Creeks and the country north of Tower Cr., some 1600; in the country between Mammoth and Madison [Gallatin] mountains some 500; . . . this would give us 4500 elk in the park this winter. A few of the best hunters, men who do not get excited when they see a hundred elk and say there are a thousand, think there are from 7000 to 8000 elk in all; but I cannot think so judging from the number I have counted in the country spoken of.'' Note: Hofer apparently did not go up the Lamar from Tower Falls or Junction Butte.

Harris 1888 Supt. Ann. Rept., YNP

1888. Commenting on a winter ski patrol: ''Immense bands of elk were encountered in every portion of the Park visited [Lamar Valley, Pelican Valley, Hayden Valley]. . . . there can be no doubt that many thousands of elk deer and mountain sheep winter in the Park every year, and that their numbers are constantly increasing.''

Crocker 1893

Probably late 1880s. Sheridan Lake area. ''[A] fine band of elk came out on the mossy shores of the pond. . . . on the trail to the outlet of Yellowstone Lake [from Thumb] I saw several bands of elk, and rode within thirty yards of them.''

Boutelle 1890 Supt. Ann. Rept., YNP

1890. ''The number of elk in the Park is something wonderful. In the neighborhood of Soda Butte herds were seen last winter estimated at from 2,000 to 3,000.''

Anderson 1891 Supt. Ann. Rept., YNP

1891. ''As the killing of the elk in Montana is absoultely prohibited by law for a term of years . . . [the] elk have increased enormously, and most convervative estimates place their numbers at 25,000, and I have no doubts of the presence of that many. . . . Their continuance in the Park is assured, and their overflow into adjoining territory will furnish abundant sport for the hunter.''

Anderson assumed charge of the Yellowstone Timber Reserve on April 14, 1891. This was a strip of land 25 miles wide on the eastern side and 8 miles wide on the southern side of the Park. This was referred to as "Extension of the Park," and it is unclear whether or not Anderson's estimates of summer elk numbers include these areas.

Anderson 1892 Supt. Ann. Rept., YNP

1892. "The elk are extremely numerous, and I am not disposed to revise in the least my estimate of 25,000 made last year. The very severe winter was extremely hard on them, and I judge that from 2,000 to 5,000 perished. This is not an alarming mortality among so many when it is considered that the deaths the previous winter were unusually few. The worst feature of it is that owing to the starved condition of the mothers this spring a very large proportion of the calves perished. There are still as many as the winter grazing will accommodate and loss of the old ones is not to be considered an evil."

Anderson 1893 Supt. Ann. Rept., YNP

1893. "Elk—For some reason the elk did not winter in the Hayden Valley in the same numbers as formerly. There were abundant signs of them in the autumn and they reappeared again in the spring. Perhaps many of them staid in the open valley of the Pelican. The usual large herd wintered in the valley of the East Fork, between Yancey's and Soda Butte. I still believe there are 25,000 in the park."

Hague 1893

1893. Note: Hague studied the geology of Yellowstone from about 1883 to 1896. He considered the park an ideal game reserve. "In winter they [elk] descend to the broad valley bottoms where food is accessible and shelter easily obtained. . . . That there are several thousand elk in the Park and adjoining country is quite certain. . . . Their number may vary from year to year, depending upon the severity of the winter and other causes. Exceptionally severe seasons would naturally cause an increased death rate."

Anderson 1894 Acting Supt. Rept., YNP

1894. "Elk—The elk wintered well and all reports show a large number of young this spring. A party sent out to Yancey's to investigate the subject in March last saw at least 3,000 of them at one time from a single point of view. This is also in the portion of the Park to be cut off by the segregation bill. The valley of the East Fork of the Yellowstone winters more of them than any other portion of the park, and should it be cut off, it is safe to say that their numbers would be diminished by at least one-half."

Guptill 1894

March 1894. Describes a winter tour of the park in March 1894 made by F. J. Haynes and Army personnel. Exploring Hayden valley, they found ''numerous small groups of elk aggregating fully 300. . . . Elk were found on the foothills of Mt. Washburn, on Specimen Ridge along the east fork of the Yellowstone, on Slough Creek and along the Yellowstone to Mount Everts in great numbers. Fully 5,000 have wintered in the above country.'' This is probably second-hand information.

Anderson 1895 Acting Supt. Rept., YNP

1895. ''Last winter there was less snow than ever before known within the Park. It was possible for the larger game, such as bison and elk, to pass at will over most parts of it during the entire winter. . . . The elk have quite held their own or increased in numbers. . . . They exist within the Park in such great numbers that the question of their preservation is not one that causes any concern. A succession of open winters like the last would possibly make them more numerous than the food supply could well support. That they breed and winter within the Park and wander outside of it to furnish sport for hunters is not an evil, and is perhaps one of the very excuses for game protection within its limits.''

Anderson 1896 Acting Supt. Ann. Rept., NYP

1896. ''During the spring months the elk are found in their several winter ranges in herds of thousands.''

Lindsley 1897 (in Young 1897)

1897. Elmer Lindsley, Second Lt. Fourth Cavalry: ''Elk—Not withstanding the hard winter of 1896–97, which killed many elk and drove many more out of the park, there is no perceptible diminution in their number. I believe that more than 5000 winter in the park, and that at least 15,000 leave the park in the autumn to winter in the lower country. . . . The country about Jackson Lake was literally alive with elk [Oct. 1897], and from the best estimates I believe that 10,000 crossed the south boundary this fall. Many go down the Madison to winter; some down the Gallatin, and some down the Yellowstone. All that survive the winter return to the park to raise their young, as soon as the snow will permit their return. Of those that winter in the park, the largest herd ranges north of the Yellowstone River, in the country that it has been so often proposed to cut off from the park. I doubt if any more would ever winter in the park under any circumstances, if this should happen. The park furnishes an ideal summer range for 40,000 elk, but there is not enough winter range for one-fourth that number.''

Young 1897 Acting Supt. Rept., YNP

1897. Note: Young was present from June 23 to Aug. 30, 1897. "Knowing the futility of attempting to give adequate protection to the greatest game park in the world, in which are located the greatest wonders of the world, an area including annexed timber reserve of 5000 square miles. . . ." "The prevailing impression is that game, buffalo excepted, is increasing in numbers."

Erwin 1898 Acting Supt. Rept., YNP

1898. "Elk—Numerous, and are increasing. The park is their breeding place in spring and feeding ground in winter. Immense herds can be seen in nearly any direction in winter, and in certain localities in summer."

Brown 1899 Acting Supt. Rept., YNP

1899. "Elk—Are more numerous than any other animal in the park. The scouts frequently report seeing herds of a thousand or more. While a great many died last winter, due to the unusually cold weather, yet they are without doubt rapidly increasing. Some of the scouts, from the number of dead ones seen by them, estimate that as many as 5000 died during the past winter. It is estimated that there are at present from 35,000 to 60,000 in the Park."

Goode 1900 Acting Supt. Rept., YNP

1900. Goode was present from July 24, 1900. "I have the assurance of the scouts, who have seen the game at all seasons, that, with the exception of the bison, American buffalo, all varieties, including . . . elk . . . are increasing, notwithstanding that the antelope range in winter over the north boundary and the elk in the fall over the south boundary, where many of them are killed."

Pitcher 1901 Acting Supt. Rept., YNP

1901. "The large game in the park, with the exception of the buffalo, seems to be even more numerous than ever; at least more has been seen this year by the tourists than ever before. . . ."

"The elk are very numerous, but unless something is done to prevent the encroachment of settlers on their winter range *south* [my emphasis] of the park and the slaughter of them merely for their tusks, it is possible that they will soon be reduced to the number that can live entirely within the limits of the park and this number I believe to be about 25,000. It is reported to me that the Teton Forest Reserve is the winter range for the elk that live in the southern part of the park during the summer; it is therefore to be hoped that this reserve will never be thrown open for settlement. . . .'' This is incorrect—these elk did not winter in the Timber Reserve.

Pitcher 1902 Supt. Ann. Rept., YNP

1902. ''The chief winter range for the elk that summer in the southern part of the park is located in or about the Teton Forest Reserve.''

Pitcher 1903 Supt. Ann. Rept., YNP

1903. ''Many startling reports were sent out from the country south of the park concerning the great loss of elk in that section through starvation, but from information received from one of the park scouts, who was located there during the entire winter, I am of the opinion that the reports were greatly exaggerated and that the loss was very slight.'' Pitcher reports that the danger of starvation losses increased because of settlements on winter ranges—north and south of the park.

Pitcher 1905 Supt. Ann. Rept., YNP

1905. ''The elk are by far the most numerous of all the large game which we have in the park, and it is a very difficult matter to determine exactly, or even approximately how many there are. . . . During the summer nearly all of the elk pertaining to the neighboring states of Wyoming, Idaho and Montana range entirely within the limits of the park, but during the winter it is probable that at least one half of this entire number goes out into the neighboring States. . . .''

Pitcher 1906 Supt. Ann. Rept., YNP

1906. ''In spite of the heavy fall of snow in the park last winter, the large game pulled thru in good shape, and the percentage of losses very small.''

Young 1907 Supt. Ann. Rept., YNP

1907. ''The number of elk in the park is estimated by persons of some experience at 40,000. From personal observation and information received from reliable scouts, also the daily reports of patrols and guards, 25,000 seems to be a safe estimate.''

Young 1908 Supt. Ann. Rept., YNP

1908. ''Information from all available sources seems to justify a conservative estimate of between 25,000 and 30,000 elk in the park. Mr. Wells in charge of the buffalo farm . . . estimates the number to be between 40,000 and 50,000. The winter storms and deep snows cause large bands to drift out of the park down the valleys of the Snake, Madison, Gallatin and Yellowstone Rivers where many are properly taken by the licensed hunters. . . .''

''There is no provision for feeding the elk in winter. They seem to do fairly well in the ordinary winter but when the snow falls to an unusual depth—say one winter in four— many perish.''

Benson 1909 Supt. Ann. Rept., YNP

1909. ''A conservative estimate would place the number of elk in the park at between 30,000 and 40,000.''

Benson 1910 Supt. Ann. Rept., YNP

1910. ''Although the past winter was a severe one, all game seemed to have wintered well. Quite a number of deaths were reported among the elk calves, due to the severe weather, but otherwise the deaths were about as usual.''

''The estimated number of elk in the park is from 30,000 to 40,000. Many of these elk wander out of the park into the adjoining states and a few of them are there killed during the hunting season.''

Letter to editors of Forest and Stream March 14, 1910. ''On my return from leave, I heard that large numbers of elk were dying, both in and without the park. A personal investigation by me since my return from leave, of the country in this vicinity, and investigations by reports from various outposts and patroling parties establishes the fact that but very few elk have died within the park—fewer than died last year, and last year the death rate was not excessive—in fact very few elk have died within the park this year.''

APPENDIX III

Reports of Elk 1911–20, Yellowstone Park and Vicinity

Brett 1911 Supt. Ann. Rept., YNP

1911. ''Elk in certain portions of the park are very numerous, and are numbered by thousands both in winter and summer. Last winter the deep snows drove them down in large herds from the latter part of November on, and many of them drifted into Montana, where they did much damage to haystacks, fields and fences on the ranches near the park.''

Shore 1912

1912. Reference to 15,000 elk in the upper Yellowstone Valley area. Shore was part owner of the Yellowstone Park Campers Co. and guide and outfitter from Cody, Wyo., but the source of his information is not clear.

Brett 1912 Supt. Ann. Rept., YNP

1912. ''During last April an approximate accurate census was taken of the elk that winter along the northern border of the park. Twenty-seven thousand eight hundred and one animals were counted inside of the park and 2,300 were observed just outside and therefore belonging to the same herd, making a total of 30,101 that actually belonged to the winter herd of the park.''

"About 600 elk were killed in the State of Montana near the park line. . . ."

Note: A "Superintendent's Journal" in the park archives shows that Brett was often on duty in Washington, D.C. or on leave from December to March or April periods. His accounts of wintering elk did not represent first-hand observation.

Scout Diaries 1912 YNP Archives

Elk Census, 3–22 APRIL 1912

DATE	AREA	TRISCHMAN	LITTLE	MCBRIDE
3	Mammoth to Blacktail	28	75	200
4	Blacktail area	180	1500	1050
5	(Stormy)			
6	Blacktail to Tower	1084	800	
	Blacktail–Hellroaring			1820
7	Tower to Mammoth	208		
	Tower to Hellroaring		1200	4000
8	Hellroaring to Cottonwood Basin		1000	2375
9	Hellroaring Area			600
10	Hellroaring Area			200
11	Hellroaring Area			3000
12	Hellroaring to Tower		100	2000
13	W. side of Yellowstone (Tower)		3000	50
14	S. side Lamar R.		1500	500
	Tower Area			
15	Tower to Rose Cr.		200	1700
16	Rose Cr. area			20
	S. of Lamar		250	
17	Rose Cr. to Tower		1000	
18	Tower to Mammoth		300	
19	Mammoth Area [apparently toward Gardiner]			825
20	Mammoth Area			155
21	Mammoth Area			158
	Mammoth to Swan Lake Flats		200	
22	Mammoth Area			18
		1500	11,125	18,671

(Apparently independent estimates—see text.)

Brett 1913 Supt. Ann. Rept., YNP

1913. "A census of elk in and along the north line of the park was taken between April 9 and May 1. The count showed 32,229, after having shipped 738, as noted below, making a total of 32,967, or an increase of 2,866 over the number found by the count of 1912. The elk were in excellent condition all winter, and but few dead ones were found, of 337 dead elk noted by the men making the count, 90 per cent were yearlings."

"Hunters were fairly successful west of the park in Montana last fall, but the slaughter of the preceding year on Crevice Mountain just at the end of the open season was not repeated."

Scout Diaries 1913 YNP Archives

Elk Census, 9 APRIL–1 MAY 1913

DATE	AREA	TRISCHMAN	LITTLE	McBRIDE
9	Mammoth to Blacktail	100	159	McBride reports
10	Blacktail		127	spending most
11	Blacktail		81	of April on elk
12	East of Blacktail		1075	census and
13	Blacktail to Yellowstone Ford			covering same
	and Return (12 mi.)		130	route as other
14	Cottonwood		150	men.
15	Granite Cr. & return (10 mi.)	48	114	Numbers of elk
16	Hellroaring	50	50	not recorded in
17	Hellroaring	581	4000	diary.
18	Slough Cr.		2000	
	Hellroaring to Headquarters	150		
19	Slough Cr.		2000	
20	Lamar River Country		1005	
22	Cache Cr.	25	1000	
23	Soda Butte Cr. + Pebble Cr.		40	
	Cache Cr. to Miller Cr.	1		
24	Cache Cr.		?	
25	Cache Cr.-Upper Lamar River	48	3	
26	Moved camp from Cache to			
	Tower Falls	187	2000	
27	Elk Cr.		209	
	Vicinity of Tower Falls	47		
28	Tower to Headquarters	0	600	
29	Headquarters to Reese Cr. &			
	return	300		
30	Headquarters to Glen Cr. &			
	return		411	
	Vicinity of upper Gardner			
	River	101		
1	Upper Gardner R.	157		
		1695	15,154	

Brett 1914 Supt. Ann. Rept., YNP

1914. "A census was again made of the elk, comprising the northern herd in the park, between April 11 and May 2 and showed a total of 35,209 in this herd. . . . Ninety-nine were shipped away before the census was taken, making a total of 35,308, an increase of 3,079 over the total number found the previous year. In making this count only 30 dead elk were found."

Scout Diaries 1914 YNP Archives

Elk Census, 11 APRIL–2 MAY 1914

DATE	AREA	TRISCHMAN	LITTLE	McBRIDE
11	?	Reports census		Census began on
13	?	began on 11th.		11th
14	Mammoth to Blacktail	Same route as	32	Elk nos. were
16	Blacktail to Cottonwood	Little		not recorded in
17	Cottonwood Basin	No. of elk not	187	diary.
18	Cottonwood to Hellroaring	recorded in	550	
19	Hellroaring to Slough Cr.	diary.	400	
20	Lamar River		489	
21	"at Slough Cr."			
22	Specimen Ridge		1500	
23	Move camp to Lamar		1200	
24	Soda Butte		119	
25	Cache Cr.		34	
26	Camp moved to Tower Falls		600	
27	"at Tower Falls"			
28	Antelope Cr.		82	
29	Moving camp to Headquarters		560	
30	N. of Headquarters (12 mi.)		488	
1	Mammoth Area		5	
	End of Census?			
			6246	

Brett 1915 Supt. Ann. Rept., YNP

1915. "The weather was so mild and there was so little snow in March and April that the elk went up to high ground earlier than usual, and it was impractical to take an accurate census of them. They were all in splendid condition, however, and careful estimates by experienced men placed the increase in the northern herd at 10 per cent and the decrease from natural causes at 3 per cent. Taking this into consideration, and deducting 375 elk shipped out of the park under authority of the department during the winter of 1914–15 leaves an estimated total of 37,192 in the herd."

Simpson and Bailey 1915 U.S. Forest Service and U.S. Biol. Survey

1915. Discussed nomenclature of Northern and Southern herds and showed that "northern herd" included those elk on Madison, Gallatin, Clarks Fork, North and South Forks of Shoshone and Yellowstone and Lamar Rivers—also listed are Grey Bull, Wyo. elk. Authors then discussed southern herd and commented: "At best these estimates are inaccurate and in many cases it is impossible to tell just how many belong to one herd or if the same animals are included in estimates of different herds." Authors quoted Superintendent YNP for estimate of 27,800 for winter herd in Lamar and Yellowstone River Valleys.

Bailey 1916 U.S. Biol. Survey

2–14 March 1916. Concerning March 1916 cooperative elk census: "Elk (*Cervus canadensis*)—In counting the elk five men (two scouts, two Forest Rangers and myself) began on March 8 at the Miller Creek Snowshoe cabin on Lamar River, above the Soda Butte soldier station, and at the Park line on Slough Cr and worked back against the drift of the elk herds and finished below Gardiner March 14. We spread out so as to cover practically all of the area occupied by the elk at that time.

"Elk Census

In the Lamar, Slough Creek and Specimen Ridge area	2247
North of the Yellowstone River in the Park	3118
Blacktail Basin to River and Yanceys	1859
Mt. Everts and slopes	856
Gardiner River Valley	428
Jardine Basin and vicinity	881
Cedar Creek Basin	130
Slopes back of Electric	45
	9564
Each of the men engaged in the count considers a liberal estimate of those not found to be	2000
making a total of	11,564"

U.S. For. Serv. and Bur. Biol. Surv. (unpubl.)

1916. Discussed cooperative studies and listed a March 16 count of the northern herd as follows: ". . . and made an actual count in the park of 9789 elk [includes Gallatin and Madison elk in park, see below]; in the Gardiner region north of the park line, 1056; in the west Gallatin Valley below the park line, 605; while on the Madison River below the park line 65 elk were reported, making a total of 11,515 elk in what is generally referred to as the northern herd. On the east or Big Horn Valley slope of the park region Forest Service officials counted 940 elk on the Shoshone Natl Forest, and as these are in reality a part of the northern herd they bring the total up to 12,455 elk actually counted. At the time when the count was made a few elk, especially old bulls, were scattered in the timber and higher mountain valleys, allowing a possible 10 per cent addition for these the total for the northern herd approximates 13,700 elk, instead of 35,000 previously reported."

Brett 1916 Special Rept. of Supt., YNP

1916. Subject of report is the elk census conducted by park personnel in spring of 1916 following earlier cooperative census organized by Bailey. "The work was done in the usual manner, by a crew of men consisting of regular scouts and rangers. . . . The work began on April 5th, and completed with the exception of the Gallatin herd . . . [on April 27]."

Elk ''counted inside of the park by regular employees and men hired for the purpose, 24,924 . . . outside of the park in the vicinity of Gardiner Crevice and Sheep mountains, 464.''

''Total actually counted by park employees 25,388.'' Note: These figures are actual counts plus large estimates. Superintendent attempts in this report to discredit Biol. Surv. and USFS count made in March 1916.

Lindsley 1916 Supt. Ann. Rept., YNP

1916. ''In accordance with instructions from the department beginning April 5, 1916 a very careful census was made of the elk belonging to the northern herd in the park and just along its borders outside on the north and northeast; 29,544 elk were found in this herd and 1,958 more were accounted for—namely 1000 estimated killed in adjoining States during the open hunting season, 611 shipped from the park under authority of the department, 90 shipped from just outside of the park by authorities of Montana to other points in the State, and 257 counted that had been killed for their teeth in the State of Montana not far from the park line after the close of the open hunting season. An unusual increase in the Jackson Hole herd south of the park, as found by the representatives of the Department of Agriculture referred to above, indicated that a number of the northern herd had probably migrated to the southern herd during the past year.'' Hunting season in Montana closed 12/15/15.

Simpson 1916 U.S. Forest Service

1916. Letter to Chief Forester, U.S. Forest Service reviewing procedures used by park authorities to make the elk census.

''The plan of making the census was about as follows:

''The Scouts would commence at Blacktail Creek and count everything between there and Gardiner the first day; the second day the count would extend as far up the Yellowstone River as the number of men would allow, and the third day it was expected to finish as far as Tower Falls. Camp would then be moved and the same procedure repeated upon the north side of the River, counting always with the drift. Dr. Bailey and I assisted in the count on April 6 and 7, and on the evening of the 6th, I told Dr. Bailey that as far as the Forest Service was concerned that I did not feel that I could represent them officially upon the count, since if I continued with the party it would be necessary for me to make an objection as to the method upon which the count was being made, and if no objection was offered and I continued with the party, it would give it official weight from the Forest Service that this count was entirely under the direction of the local employees of the Interior Department, and that I did not care to either offer an objection to their method or to give it official weight on the part of the Forest Service. Mr. Bailey agreed with me that this should not be done although he desired to continue a few days longer if possible, but I felt that it was simply a waste of money on the part of the Forest Service, and since I had a Forest to consider I left the party upon the evening of April 7. Dr. Bailey also joined me in leaving.

"In regard to the method under which the Park count is being taken by the Scouts, there is no possibility for an accurate count to be made. The outfit consisted of four Scouts, two Hunters, three packers, a cook, and twelve head of Government pack mules. Practically the entire count is made on horseback. The snow has left the country so that it is almost impossible to find the elk herds and they are scattered through the timber so that it is impracticable to make an accurate count after they are found. On top of this the count is being made with the drift, with the natural result that each day's count will bring increased totals that have been counted the day before.

"I talked with Supervisor Shaw who had spent a week last fall observing the herds when they came onto their winter range. He is under the impression that Dr. Bailey's count, which was participated in by the Rangers from the Absaroka Forest, is almost absolutely correct, and that there is nowhere near the reported number of elk in the Yellowstone Park herd that the Park authorities have been officially reporting in their annual reports to the Secretary. It was said that when the large herd of elk were first reported that it was the result of a wager that there was over 25,000 head of elk in the National Park, and the result was a count of some 27,000 head. Since then the figures will show that a 10% increase has been added each year." Simpson was a U.S. Forest Service employee responsible for conducting a number of elk censuses in the western United States.

Anon. 1916 YNP Archives

Abstract of Elk Counts by Area, 1912–1916

	1912	1913			1914		
		Dead	*Calves*	*Total*	*Total*	*Dead*	*Calves*
"Inside of Park, along Northern Line"							
"Count by main crew, Cooke to Electric Peak"		330	2,617	25,610	29,793	29	1,095
[Gallatin and Madison Firehole included here and account for difference]							
"Totals found inside Park:"	27,801	337	3,359	28,729	32,209	30	1,191
"Observed outside Park on Hellroaring, Slough Cr. etc."	500						
"Gardiner, Crevice Sheep Mt. etc" [also Gallatin Area]							
"Totals observed outside"	2,300		400	3,500	3,000		1,191
"Grand Totals belonging to Northern Herd"	30,101	337	3,759	32,229	35,209	30	

Not clear if "calves" and "dead" are included in "total." No count made in 1915. In 1916 a total of 24,924 was reported counted between Cooke and Electric Peak, with 28,332 reported for totals found inside park; 748 reported outside park in Gardiner, Crevice, Sheep Mt. area, with 1,212 reported for "Totals observed outside." Grand total for "northern herd" reported at 29,544.

Lindsley and Nelson 1917 Special Rept. Supt., YNP and Supv. Gallatin NF

1917. Cooperative census of 1917 was conducted from 5/26/17–6/9/17. Men worked from upper part of range down to Dailey Lake area. Numbers reported may have included calves of year. "In other words, the 20 percent increase should be applied to 10,769 elk that were actually counted, making a total of 12,922. To this should be added the 4500 head deducted for purposes just explained [2500 estimated for one group partially observed on Hellroaring Cr.; 2000 that had already gone to the summer range], making a grand total of 17,422 head or the number in the Gardiner herd at the present time." The individual daily reports of the census teams are vague here but suggest that at least part of the groups estimated to be on Hellroaring Cr. was subsequently counted by others.

Actual number of dead elk tallied from counter's daily reports was 1,888. This may have included over 600 dead on feedgrounds. This count was increased to 3,068 estimated dead.

Nelson 1917

1917. ". . . two great elk herds now centering there [around Yellowstone Park], and containing some 40,000 of these splendid animals. . . . [The Jackson Hole herd] numbers over 20,000."

Graves and Nelson 1919

1917–1919. This was an administrative report by Nelson, who was chief of Biological Survey, and Graves, Chief Forester of U.S. Forest Service. "The northern group [of elk] comprises slightly more than 19,000 animals, the number having been determined by actual count conducted in the spring of 1917. . . . This herd summers in the Yellowstone Park at the headwaters of the Yellowstone, Gallatin and Madison Rivers, and drifts northward to the northern part of the park and nearby national forests for the winter. . . . Approximately 85 percent of the more than 19,000 animals in the northern group ranges during the summer on the mountains & slopes of the main upper Yellowstone River within the Yellowstone National Park. A limited number, possibly 5 percent, summer on the Absaroka National Forest immediately north of the park. The remainder of the northern group range during the summer months in the north western portion of the park and on the Madison and Gallatin National Forests."

Lindsley 1917 Supt. Mo. Rept., YNP

Dec. 1917. "Scouts reported about 5000 elk on the north side of the Yellowstone River, and large numbers on Blacktail, near Tower Falls, and on Lamar River. The weather was not severe enough to drive them outside during the hunting season, which closed in Montana with Dec. 15th. . . . About 12,000 elk were reported in all during the month, without any special effort being made to look them up. . . . About 150 (elk) were killed on the Gallatin slope and 31 on the Madison River slope along the west line. . . . About 68 were killed along the north line, of which 64 were on Boulder and Buffalo Fork, several miles outside of the park where the hunting was difficult."

Lindsley 1918a Supt. Mo. Rept., YNP

Jan. 1918. "Game animals were reported during the month as follows: (Numbers approximate) . . .

Vicinity of Gardiner—within four miles—of same, inside the park	4000
Vicinity of Mammoth Hot Springs country	500
adjacent to Tower Falls and the Buffalo Farm	5000
Seen by patrols from Soda Butte Station	1200
North of the Yellowstone River between mouth of Bear Cr. and Valley of Slough Cr.	7000
Outside of the Park down Yellowstone Valley, left during January	2000
Totals (including 1000 on Gallatin)	20,700"

Not clear, see Lindsley, 1918d, below.

Lindsley 1918b Supt. Mo. Rept., YNP

Feb. 1918. "Scout Anderson patrolled, mounted, between Gardiner and the mouth of Buffalo Fork, along the north line, both inside and outside of the park. . . . He saw 5,000 to 6,000 elk in all in that district north of the Yellowstone River, all in fair condition, except that some of the calves and a few crippled elk are getting weak."

"Scout Lacombe remained on duty at Tower Falls. . . . He reported 22 inches of snow at the station. Also about 2000 elk . . . in that district."

"About 3,500 elk . . . were fed hay during the month" [presumably in the Gardiner Mammoth area, since he also reports on numbers of antelope, sheep, and deer].

"Reports of the Forest Rangers indicate that there are probably between 3,000 and 4000 [elk] outside of the park, extending down the Yellowstone Valley for several miles."

"Total dead elk reported, 19" [for Feb.].

These may again represent several estimates of the same elk—see April 1918 monthly report, below.

Lindsley 1918c Supt. Mo. Rept., YNP

March 1918. "Elk: Many of those reported outside of the park down the Yellowstone Valley, returned during the latter part of the month, but there are still quite a large number reported outside."

Remains of 50 elk found poached outside park in Yellowstone Valley.

Lindsley 1918d Supt. Mo. Rept., YNP

April 1918. "Elk: There are still about 1,500 elk outside of the park, down the valley of the Yellowstone River, as nearly as I can determine from reports of the forest rangers stationed there. Scout Dewing reports about 7000 seen on his patrols up Yellowstone River from Gardiner to Soda Butte. . . ."

"Steve Elkins, who was hunting lions, and Donald Stevenson . . . reported about 2500 elk between Hellroaring and Slough Creeks. . . ."

"Scout Lacombe reports slightly over 4000 elk in his district at Tower Falls."

These are probably three reports of the same elk groups.

Lindsley 1918e Supt. Mo. Rept., YNP

May 1918. "Scout Dewing estimates about 8000 [elk] in the country which was patrolled by him during the month, from Blacktail to Soda Butte."

Lindsley 1918f Supt. Ann. Rept., YNP

Winter 1917–18. From ". . . 3,000 to 4,000 [elk] again left the park and went down the Yellowstone Valley for several miles. . . ."

"At least 3,500 of them [elk] came down to the feeding grounds around headquarters and the northern entrance. . . ."

"While no accurate count was made of the herds of elk during the past year, more than 20,000 were seen in the park in the month of January, with no special effort having been made to count all of them."

Lindsley 1919a Supt. Mo. Rept., YNP

Jan. 1919. "Ranger Anderson reports about 3,500 elk. . . . Ranger Dewing reports having seen about 4000 elk. . . . The rangers at Crevice station report about 3000 elk in that District."

Hill 1919 Acting Supt. Mo. Rept., YNP

March 1919. "*Elk:* A few thousand elk which left the park earlier in the winter are reported still to be ranging outside of the park, down the Yellowstone Valley in the Absaroka Forest. . ."

"In connection with their patrols, the rangers in the most important districts during March made a count of the elk. The total number of elk seen, not including those in Gallatin and Riverside districts nor those now ranging outside of the park, amounted to 18,694."

I have been unable to locate any records of the methods employed in this count, but it was probably similar to those of 1912–16.

Albright 1919a Supt. Ann. Rept., YNP

Winter 1918–19. Oct. 1, 1918 The ranger force relieved soldiers of wildlife duties.

"The Elk . . . wintered in splendid condition [winter 1918–19]. . . . several thousand elk left the park and went into the Absaroka National Forest and down the Yellowstone River Valley. . . ."

Judkins 1919 Wyo. Game & Fish Comm. Ann. Rept.

1919. "Reports of Assistant & Deputy Game Wardens & of officials of the Yellowstone National Park on counts and conservative estimates show the following number of wild game as to counties. . . . Yell. Natl. Park—Elk 10,000." Presumably winter herd figures, as they give an estimate of 16,000 for "Lincoln Co.," which would have included present Teton county. This represents a very different estimate of elk in the northern herd compared to that of park officials.

Albright 1919b Supt. Mo. Rept., YNP

Oct. 1919. The following accounts concern the winter of 1919–20. "Elk: The storms of the month already referred to placed the elk herds of Yellowstone National Park in the gravest peril. . . . On October 28 several hundred head of elk had left the park, most of them going out in the vicinity of Crevice Gulch. Many of them were killed immediately upon leaving the park boundary. Acting Chief Ranger McBride reports there are now approximately 3,000 head on Crevice Creek which will probably leave the park in the early future. Every effort is being made, however, to hold these animals back, and it may be possible to hold them in the park for some weeks."

"Before the end of the month at least two large herds left the park at the mouth of Bear Cr. . . . In order to stop the drifting of the elk out of the park at this point the feeding of hay was begun."

The hunting season is described in emotional detail [p. 20]: "There is a possibility, however, that we may lose all of the animals [elk]. I repeat, the elk are facing the most serious winter in the history of the park."

Lindsley 1919b Acting Supt. Mo. Rept., YNP

Nov. 1919. "On account of the lack of forage on the range, and the exceptional winter conditions, the elk and deer continued to leave the Park during November. . . ."

"The prediction that our northern herd of elk, which for several years has numbered twenty to thirty thousand . . . would be in grave peril this winter due to shortage of grass on the range, is being rapidly fulfilled."

"Grazing has been fairly good on Blacktail and in the vicinity of Headquarters, and such elk and deer as have remained on these ranges have seemed to get enough to eat."

Lindsley 1919c Acting Supt. Mo. Rept., YNP

Dec. 1919. "The apparent serious conditions for wintering our wild animals continued with the severe weather up to about the middle of December, but the moderation of the weather to a nearly normal status has been such a relief that prospects seem much more encouraging."

"*Elk:* The situation regarding the elk and the probability of their extermination has been considerably improved with the milder condition of the weather. Since it moderated about the middle of December, the elk have seemed less anxious to go down, and in fact towards the end of the month they seem to be in many cases working back towards the park. . . . Chief Ranger McBride's estimates as to the number of elk lost to the herd during the fall to include the end of the hunting season is 7000 head, of which he thinks 4000 were killed by hunters and shipped out by express; about 1000 killed by hunters who live in Jardine, Gardiner, and the Yellowstone Valley as far north as Pray, Montana, and 2000 wounded by hunters and died later from their wounds." Compare this to actual counts reported by Shaw and Clark (1920).

"The elk seen and reported during the month were about as follows: 4500 at Gardiner being fed; 1200 at headquarters and vicinity; 1200 between Lava Cr and Tower Falls; 200 between Tower Falls and Lamar Bridge; 500–1500 between Lamar Bridge and the park line on Slough Creek; and 35 on Cache Cr. . . ."

An attachment to this monthly report, which may be Chief Rangers Report, shows 200 elk shipped to Canada.

"Chief Ranger McBride, Assistant Chief Ranger Trischman and Ranger Dupuis, spent the last week of the month [December] patrolling the country North of the park line in the vicinity of Gardiner, Jardine, Electric and Crevice. They report 1,678 elk all in good condition in this country, and that the elk are returning to the park in large numbers. They counted 199 dead elk all having died of wounds, caused by gun shot. They did not find one winter killed elk."

The hay crew at Gardiner ". . . fed between 3,000 and 4,000 head of elk."

Lindsley 1920a Acting Supt. Mo. Rept., YNP

Jan. 1920. "With the exception of 1896 and 1914 the month was the warmest January since the beginning of the record in 1887. . . . Light snows occurred on several days but the total fall was only 2.9″, which is the least total for January in 33 years record."

"No storms of consequence occurred and taking the month as a whole it may be considered one of the most pleasant midwinter months of which there is record."

"The mild weather and slight snowfall was a most welcome change from the severe weather of the early winter, and gives our deer, mountain sheep, antelope and large herds of elk, which are wintering on both sides of the north line of the park, a good chance to get through the winter without the serious loss predicted. . . . As the weather moderated . . . the number of elk on the feeding grounds diminished to about 1500 at the end of the month [in Gardiner area]."

"The antelope were fed daily, with the elk, near the northern entrance, but the warm weather also had its effects upon them and they did not care much for the hay."

"The deer scattered on account of the warmer weather, even more than did the other animals."

"*Elk:* With the moderation of the weather, continued throughout the month, the situation as regards the possible heavy loss of elk has improved wonderfully, and if the spring comes reasonably early, as indicated at present by all signs, we hope for a slight loss only. At the beginning of the month, about the usual number were being fed at Mammoth and Gardiner, but as the weather got warmer, they began to find food in the foothills, and began going back, until by the end of January there were not over 1500 taking hay at Gardiner. The condition of these animals is fair, except that quite a number of the calves appear to be getting weak, and quite a number have died, even those that have been at the feeding grounds all winter, and the reasons for this are doubtful. While the elk were scattered during January more than they were in December and therefore not easy to count, there is no reason why the numbers should be very much less, as not a great number have died. . . . The total number of elk found dead during the month near the feeding grounds at Gardiner and Mammoth was 122, of which six were killed while catching elk for shipment. Of these 98 were calves, 20 cows and 4 bulls. The older animals were mostly in bad condition because of their . . . age. Most of the calves that died appeared to be in fairly good flesh, and the cause of their death is uncertain."

"An estimate of the number of elk that spent most of the month of January outside of the park on the west side of the Yellowstone River is 700 to 1000 head, and these appear to be finding plenty to eat. . . . One park ranger was stationed at Electric, to patrol this part of the game preserve, during the month. . . . [He] reported having found 17 dead elk in this district during the month all of which had died of gunshot wounds, probably received during the hunting season. . . ."

"As to the elk outside the park east of the Yellowstone River. This range has the undivided attention of six forest rangers. . . . [McBride, Trischman and Dupuis] spent the last week of January patrolling this country and came back with the report that they saw 1,676 elk in good condition, and that they found 199 dead ones, all of which had died as a result of gunshot wounds. . . . They did not find a single elk that had died on account of the hard winter; also that all elk were moving up higher on account of the mild weather. . . ." Ernest Shaw, Supervisor of Absaroka Forest indicated "that on the last day of January there were approximately 1,350 head of elk on the area from Bear Cr. to Six Mile . . . [and] about 1,000 head on the west side of the river. . . ."

Total of 210 elk shipped during Jan. 1920.

Lindsley 1920b Acting Supt. Mo. Rept., YNP

Feb. 1920. "The temperature [for Feb.] was almost continually above normal during the first 19 days; the remainder of the month was moderately cold. . . . As a whole the weather conditions that prevailed throughout the month were favorable to the wild animals which are undergoing one of their hardest winters. . . ."

"The mild weather which characterized the month of February was favorable to our elk, deer, antelope and mountain sheep and its continuance will mean that they will get through the winter without serious losses. . . ." Lindsley's account is in agreement with weather records for this period. Elk returned to feedgrounds at Gardiner & Mammoth—estimated 5,000 fed.

"*Elk:* The conditions which effect the possible heavy loss of elk were encouraging throughout the month and with a reasonably early spring it now seems as if the loss might not be much more than normal."

"23 elk mostly calves died on feeding grounds at Mammoth during the month and 180 died on the feeding grounds near Gardiner, mostly calves and very old cows. This is not a heavy percentage of loss for February. Generally speaking it is considered that the herd is in fair condition."

Lindsley 1920c Acting Supt. Mo. Rept., YNP

March 1920. "As a whole, the weather conditions that prevailed throughout the month were not favorable to the wild animals, and the feeding of hay had to be kept up throughout the month."

"While the weather which was slightly more severe than normal in March was not especially encouraging . . . the situation [with respect to wildlife] has not yet become serious."

About 2,000 elk reported fed at Gardiner; 800 at Mammoth. "As will be noted, the number remaining on the feedgrounds at Headquarters was about the same as for February, but at Gardiner it was only about half the same number as many of the stronger animals went back to the hills and did not come down again."

Condition of deer and antelope reported as fairly good. "The elk are holding their own fully as well as could be expected under the severe winter conditions of March . . . generally speaking they are in poor condition as compared with normal winters." Lindsley's reference point is apparently those animals on feedgrounds: ". . . . the number of elk taking the hay during the month varied from 1500 to 3000 . . . . 272 elk died on feedgrounds during the month. . . . Those that remained further up on the range seemed to have fared better, as but few dead ones are reported." Ninety-eight elk shipped during the month.

Lindsley 1920d Acting Supt. Mo. Rept., YNP

April 1920. "The general conditions of the weather throughout the month were disappointing to everyone interested in the welfare of the wild animals dependent upon grass for subsistence . . . and while there was some advancement [i.e., growth of forage] from the beginning to the end of the month, and some green grass was available at the end of the month for the animals, it was far from being enough to relieve the situation, and feeding had to be continued throughout the month and into May.''

''. . . month was an especially trying one for all of our wild animals.'' Discusses the need to feed into April and mentions that $4703.00 was solicited from private individuals and organizations to buy hay. Compare this account to that in paragraph below.

''The timely receipt of funds donated by citizens for hay for the elk saved a heavy loss among the northern herds. The number fed during the month in the vicinity of Gardiner dwindled from about a thousand the first of the month, to a hundred the last of the month, as they gradually left the feeding grounds and went up as the grass became more abundant. At Mammoth the number varied from about 400 the first of the month to 100 at the close.'' These accounts suggest that rather insignificant numbers of elk were being fed.

Ninety-five dead elk on feedgrounds. ''The rangers making patrols from Gardiner reported 124 dead elk noted on patrols from that station, of which 30 were just outside the park line, which makes a total of 219 dead ones reported for the month of April, but of course there are many more that have died in the foothills that have not yet been discovered, though the general situation is very encouraging and we do not look for much further loss among them. . . . The proposed elk count has been abandoned for this season.''

''At the end of April there was an appreciable amount of grass available for the elk, and most of them had left the feeding grounds. By May 4th practically all of the elk had left the feeding grounds and there was enough grazing to warrant turning out the horse herd and the tame buffalo.''

Albright 1920a Supt. Mo. Rpt., YNP

May 1920. ''[It] was no longer necessary to feed wild animals [after May 5]. . . . The 100 tons of hay purchased with the $4703 donated by private subscription just lasted through, and served to save many thousands of the elk which were not strong enough to get through the last few hard weeks of winter without being fed.'' Compare this to Lindsley's account of elk on feedgrounds.

''While the losses have been considerable, they were not as bad as feared and we still have a goodly number of elk, deer, and antelope in the northern herds.''

''There were 284 carcasses found by ranger Anderson on his patrols along the north line east of Gardiner, but these died mostly in March and April [and may have been reported previously]. Conservative estimates place the number of elk remaining in the northern herd, including those of the Madison River and on the West Gallatin, at around 11,000. . . .''

Albright 1920a Chief Ranger McBride's Mo. Rept.

May 1920. ''Ranger Anderson reports that between the mouth of Bear Cr. and Hellroaring Cr. he counted during the month 211 dead elk, 5 dead buffalo and 19 dead deer. In the Blacktail district he counted 73 dead elk, one dead buffalo and 14 dead deer.'' These may be some of the same animals mentioned in the April report.

Albright 1920b Supt. Ann. Rept., YNP

1920. Review of history of elk from Superintendents' reports. Assumed 19,345 elk in northern herd in June 1917. ''[It] would not seem improbable that there were 25,000 in the herd a year ago [an estimate for the fall of 1919 including elk on Gallatin and Madison Rivers]. Last June, after the most disastrous winter which our wild animals have ever had to face, our rangers estimated the survivors of the northern herd of elk at 11,000, and I am reliably informed that the southern herd fared but little if any better. This loss of nearly 60 per cent in one winter is alarming and indicates most forcibly the possible danger of complete extermination of this most noble race of animals.''

''What became of 14,000 elk which were missing in our northern herd on June 1st last? Our records indicate that 449 were shipped out alive. . . . It has been estimated that 8000 were killed during the hunting season in Montana. . . . Reports have it that about 400 were killed in the west Gallatin country from the small part of the northern herd known as the Gallatin herd. . . . It is hard to believe that the balance of those missing died of sheer starvation and exposure, yet such was probably the case *if* [my emphasis] the number in the herd last fall was not greatly overestimated.''

''The winter storms and accompanying cold weather did not have such a quick effect on the deer. . . . Large numbers left the Park in October, November & December and many were killed by hunters. In spite of this and of the fact that 49 mule deer and 2 white tails were found dead, I do not believe that they suffered any serious dimunition [sic] in numbers. Most of those that did leave the Park returned when the proper season arrived. It is interesting to note that with the deer more than any other animal small bands were cut off by the early storms in remote sections of the Park and managed to survive the winter.''

''The usual herd of mountain sheep came down to Gardiner canyon during the October storm and remained in the vicinity all winter. . . . Only a few dead bodies [sheep] were found during the winter and it is evident that our estimated number of 200 in the Park is too low if anything. . . . The majority of the mountain sheep spent the winter at low altitudes where they were able to pick up a fair living.''

Note: Albright was not present in the park from about Nov. to April. His account should be compared to those of Lindsley (1919b,c; 1920a–d) and Shaw and Clark (1920).

Shaw and Clark 1920 Special Rept. Supv. Absaroka and Gallatin Natl. Forests

1920. Intense winter patrols were made in an attempt to suppress tusk hunting and delimit winter ranges. They describe weather conditions that blocked roads. The only access into the Gardiner area was by train.

Shaw Provides This Detailed Record of Express Shipments of Elk Carcasses Killed by Hunters

POINTS OF SHIPMENT	OCT. AND NOV.			DEC.			TOTAL	EST. LOCAL KILL	TOTAL
	to 10	*11–20*	*21–30*	*1–10*	*11–20*	*21–30*			
Gardiner	491	629	115	147	102	133	1617	188	1805
Corwin	264	285	90	59	66	88	853	18	871
Sphinx	2	17	8	4	15	6	52	4	56
Carbella	53	59	7	10	10	24	163	36	199
Dailey	11	18	4	—	—	6	39 ⎫	59	130
Emigrant	6	19	7	—	—	—	32 ⎭		
Pray	—	4	—	—	—	—	4	100	104
Totals	827	1032	231	220	193	257	2760	405	3165

In addition USFS ranger patrols "found, killed dressed but not taken or died of wounds—41. Total kill outside of Park—3206. About 100 head died of wounds in the Park and are tallied with the Park losses further on."

"It is indeed gratifying to know that the wild estimates of the elk killed and of those dying of wounds has been grossly exaggerated. . . . There will no doubt, be those who will forever maintain that the number of elk which died of wounds in the hills and were never found, equal or nearly so the number actually taken out. Investigations made during the hunt and immediately after it, by Forest officers contradicts that theory. As a matter of fact there were a great many elk wounded that were not taken by the hunter originally hitting them, but men were so thickly scattered over the area, that a wounded elk did not travel far before running into some other hunter who killed it or found it dead and claimed it. . . . A thorough search by our men after the hunt, only revealed a total of 41 elk that had been wounded and died without being found and taken. It is believed that 50 head would be a liberal estimate for this number."

"The number of animals using the usual winter range [outside the park] varied at times from less than 1,000 head to as many as 2,500 or 3,000 head. Accurate figures could not be obtained because of the continual drift back and forth to the Park."

"The remarkable thing featuring the season's observations is the fact that the elk that remained on the winter range area during the entire season were, as a whole, in much better condition at all times than those that occupied both Park and outside. They were also in better shape than those fed in the Park. There was a less proportionate loss in the former than in the latter."

"Many of us who thought we knew something about elk, were early in the season confident that there would be a very heavy loss on the drought denuded winter range; but the fact remains that a careful count of those which died from starvation places that number at not more than 340 head. This allows a margin for safety in excess of the tally. Ranger Johns who covered the entire area, and kept in close touch with all the patrolmen and their reports, places the loss on the winter range outside of the Park, including the Gallatin side of the River, at not to exceed 350 head. This total includes those killed for tusks. There were actually known to have been killed for their teeth or otherwise, subsequent to the close of the hunting season, 32 head; and, 14 of these were killed in Hellroaring.'' These are probably the best data on elk mortality during the winter 1919–20.

Shaw believed that a ''shrinkage'' in elk numbers in the northern herd had occurred between the 1917 count and 1920.

''Count of live elk in spring of 1917: Yellowstone herd 17,422 Gallatin 1,670

Madison 253	19,345
Increase @ 2,500 per year fall 1917 to fall 1919	7,500
Total numbers without deduction for loss, rounded off.	26,850

''Known and Estimated Losses Fall 1917 to Spring 1920

YELLOWSTONE HERD	1917	1918	1919	TOTAL
Hunting Kill (Absaroka) estimate	25	50	3206	3281
Killed for teeth (Absaroka) estimate	100	6	25	131
Starvation & Natural causes estimate	15	—	300	315
Losses in Yellowstone Park estimate	100	50	1500	1650
Live shipments Yellowstone Park (Gallatin)	?	?	?	500
Shipped from State Game Preserve	?	?	?	150
Starvation & natural causes	—	—	25	25
Killed for teeth	—	—	15	15
Total Losses Yellowstone Herd				6,067

Losses for Gallatin herd computed at 1,170; for Madison 67.	
Total losses of Northern Herd for period	7,304
The Northern herd should contain at this time	19,550 head
Estimated numbers at present time:	
Yellowstone herd at	10 to 12,000 head
Gallatin herd	1,300 head
Madison herd	200 head
Total Northern Herd	13,500
Unexplained difference or loss in this herd 6050 head''	

''Estimate placed on the present numbers of the Yellowstone herd are those stated by Chief Ranger James McBride. . . .''

''They check very closely the estimate of the present number made by Absaroka Forest officers. . . . It is realized that differences of opinion may exist as to the reliability of the foregoing figures, and that others in a position to express an opinion may offer figures that might show an entirely different status of the herd.''

Methods used to arrive at a 2,500 net annual increase are described. These were questionable calculations based upon the proportion of calves among elk found dead in 1917.

''The loss on the feedground in the Park during the past winter is believed to be greater than on any previous year.'' First-person reports by U.S. Forest Service Rangers are also included in Shaw's account of the winter of 1919–20.

DeHart 1920 Mont. Fish and Game Comm.

1920. DeHart reports 4,000 elk taken during the winter of 1919–20 from a herd of 10,000. His source of the 10,000 figure is a report from the Wyoming Game and Fish Commission giving overall winter losses at 700–1,000 elk.

"Regarding the statements relative to the elk starving to death in Montana, I desire to say that game wardens and forest rangers report finding less than 100 dead elk through-out the northern herds territory [presumably outside the park], and this loss was caused where drifting herds sought winter shelter."

State of Montana was also trying to get the area from Dome Mt. to Slough Cr. set aside for elk—i.e., restrict livestock use and development on these lands.

Henderson 1920 U.S. Biol. Surv.

Feb. 1920. Henderson conducted a personal review of the conditions on the northern winter range. He commented on the mild weather since mid-December and that elk and other ungulates were moving off winter ranges. Elk on feedgrounds "are in fair condition with 100–150 lost, mostly calves that were still in fair flesh." No winter losses reported among those wintering in outlying areas. No snow at Gardiner or on surrounding hills. This represents another independent assessment of winter conditions for 1919–20.

Anon. 1920

1920. "Park authorities and others agree that the estimate which had been made of the number of elk in Yellowstone Park was greatly exaggerated. Instead of the northern herd containing 20,000 elk it now develops that it numbered prior to last winter only about 12,000 of which some 8000 or 9000 succumbed either to cold or to bullets of hunters. Thus only 3000 or 4000 elk remain in the herd it is estimated." Subsequent counts showed this estimate of "survivors" to be much too low.

Note: This press release was made during a period when intense efforts were underway to acquire more elk winter range outside the park and to expand the park.

There are a variety of other reports on the status of the elk from 1911 to 1920 that appear in the popular press. Information used in all seems to have been either drawn from the sources listed here or are so garbled it is impossible to determine whether or not they dealt with the northern herd, southern herd, or both.

Calculations and Analyses of Population Dynamics

Natality

The December–March winter indexes at $t - 1$ for the yearling pregnancy samples of Table 5.1 were 13, -9, 4, 2, -7, 5, 1, 2, 6, -2 (i.e., 13 represents the 1934 index as it affected the 1935 pregnancy). Population size at $t - 1$ was calculated from Figure 3.2 or Table 3.2. Values for two-year-olds were the same as for yearlings.

Yearling pregnancy (arcsine transformation of pregnancy rates regressed on elk numbers [N_{t-1}] and winter index [I_{t-1}]).

$$\hat{Y} = .195482 - .000058961 \, (N_{t-1}) - .0535713 \, (I_{t-1}).$$

	Anova				
Source	df	SS	MS	F	P
Total	9	1.60540	1.78378		
Regression	2	1.21081	.605403	10.74	.005 < P < .01
$R(N\vert I)^a$	1	.246851	.246851	4.38	.05 < P < .10
$R(I\vert N)$	1	1.043712	1.043712	18.52	P < .005
Error	7	.394598	.563711		

[a]Regression sum of squares for N_{t-1} given I_{t-1} already in the model was calculated by using the "extra sum of squares" principle described by Neter and Wasserman (1974).

$$R^2 = .75, \ r^2_{N \cdot I} = .38 \ r^2_{I \cdot N} = .73$$

Two-Year-Old Pregnancy

$$\hat{Y} = 2.11660 - .0000631986\ (N_{t-1}) - .0374844\ (I_{t-1})$$

ANOVA

SOURCE	df	SS	MS	F	P
Total	7	.874015	.124859		
Regression	2	.682732	.341366	8.92	.01 < P < .025
$R(N|I)$	1	.152031	.152031	3.97	P < .10
$R(I|N)$	1	.247795	.247795	6.48	.05 < P < .10
Error	5	.191283	.038256		

$$R^2 = .78,\ r^2_{N \cdot I} = .44,\ r^2_{I \cdot N} = .56$$

Recruitment

Proportion of young in winter populations on elk numbers and winter severity at $t - 1$ (arcsine transformation).

$$\hat{Y} = -.488158 - .0000239073\ (N_{t-1}) - .00480188\ (I_{t-1}).$$

ANOVA

SOURCE	df	SS	MS	F	P
Total	22	.170194	.00773608		
Regression	2	.100422	.0502108	14.39	P < .001
$R(N|I)$	1	.0916508	.0916508	26.27	P < .001
$R(I|N)$	1	.0105332	.0105332	3.01	P < .10
Error	20	.0697722	.00348861		

$$R^2 = .59,\ r^2_{N \cdot I} = .57\ r^2_{I \cdot N} = .13$$

Proportion of females with young at heel (arcsine transformation)

$$\hat{Y} = .0641056 - .0000539566\ (N_{t-1}) - .00518382\ (I_{t-1}).$$

ANOVA

SOURCE	df	SS	MS	F	P
Total	22	.771673	.0350760		
Regression	2	.475022	.237511	16.01	P < .001
$R(N|I)$	1	.466837	.466837	31.47	P < .001
$R(I|N)$	1	.012276	.012276	.83	P > .10
Error	20	.296651	.0148326		

$$R^2 = .62,\ r^2_{N \cdot I} = .61,\ r^2_{I \cdot N} = .04$$

Proportion of females with yearling males "at heel" on elk numbers at $t - 1$ (arcsine transformation).

$$\hat{Y} = -.665004 - .0000323287 \; (N_{t-1})$$

ANOVA

Source	df	SS	MS	F	P
Total	19	.410118	.0215851		
Regression	1	.158457	.158457	11.33	P < .005
Error	18	.251661	.0139812		

$$r^2 = .39$$

Mortality Patterns

Comparisons of standing age distributions over time

Sex	Distributions Compared	χ^2	df	P
Females	1950–1951[a]	19.82	2	P < .005
	1951–1962	73.45	10	P < .005
	1962–1963	69.11	10	P < .005
	1963–1964	19.69	10	.025 < P < .05
	1964–1965	9.91	10	P > .10
	1965–1966	9.25	10	P > .10
Males[b]	1951–1963	8.25	3	.025 < P < .05
	1963–1964	3.11	3	P > .10
	1964–1965	9.71	3	.01 < P < .025

[a] Partial distributions with yearlings and two-year-olds separated from adults.
[b] Yearlings omitted and the age distribution collapsed into four classes as age 2, 3, 4–6, and 7+.

TABLE IV.1.
Calculated Elk Numbers by Sex and Age Class 1968–76

Period		Numbers							
		Yg	YrF	AF	YrM	AM	TF	TYr	TA
1968–69	PrH[a]	993	(444)[c]	(1,668)	305	945	2,112	(749)	(2,613)
	PoH	986[b]	(438)	(1,650)	301	934	2,088	(739)	(2,584)
1969–70	PrH	1,230	(537)	(2,149)	447	1230	2,686	(984)	(3,379)
	PoH	1,219	(532)	(2,129)	443	1220	2,661	(975)	(3,349)
1970–71	PrH	1,553	(620)	(3,029)	593	1531	3,649	(1213)	(4,560)
	PoH	1,544	(616)	(3,010)	590	1522	3,626	(1206)	(4,532)
1971–72	PrH	1,567	(713)	(3,747)	597	1666	4,460	(1310)	(5,413)
	PoH	1,553	(707)	(3,713)	591	1651	4,420	(1298)	(5,364)

(continued)

TABLE IV.1. (*Continued*)

Period		Yg	YrF	AF	YrM	AM	TF	TYr	TA
1972–73	PrH	1,895	(748)	(5,009)	476	2007	5,757	(1224)	(7,016)
	PoH	1,866	(737)	(4,932)	469	1976	5,669	(1206)	(6,908)
1973–74	PrH	1,826	(738)	(5,415)	709	2051	6,153	(1447)	(7,466)
	PoH	1,790	(724)	(5,309)	695	2011	6,033	(1419)	(7,320)
1974–75	PrH	1,939	(685)	(6,928)	804	2398	7,613	(1489)	(9,326)
	PoH	1,916	(677)	(6,850)	794	2370	7,527	(1471)	(9,220)
1975–76	PrH	2,162	(700)	(7,043)	408	2001	7,783	(1108)	(9,044)
	PoH	1,957	(649)	(6,558)	288	1355	7,207	(937)	(7,913)

[a] PrH = prehunt population numbers (mid-October); PoH = posthunt population numbers (usually mid-December) except for 1976, when hunting continued to mid-February.
[b] Numbers without parentheses calculated directly as winter herd classification × winter census (Table 3.2). PrH numbers calculated as winter census + numbers killed by hunting.
[c] Yearling females estimated as 21, 20, 17, 16, 13, 12, 9, and 9% of total females from 1968–69 to 1975–76, respectively. These based upon regression of percent yearling females in shot samples for 1950–67 on population size. All numbers in parentheses affected by these estimates.

TABLE IV.2.
Calculated Mortality of Calves 1969–75[a]

Time	Initial No. Calves (A)	Final No. Calves (B)	Percent Dying		Initial No. Calves Plus Adults (E)
			Total (C)	Natural Mortality (D)	
1969	1,401	984	29.76	29.26	4,763
1970	1,764	1,213	31.12	30.61	6,127
1971	2,487	1,310	47.33	47.00	8,260
1972	3,076	1,224	60.21	59.75	9,799
1973	4,112	1,447	64.81	64.11	12,352
1974	4,446	1,489	66.51	65.70	13,359
1975	5,688	1,471	74.14	73.73	16,503

[a] Calculated as follows:
(A) = Number of adult females in autumn populations × reduction in fertility of .84 for 1969 and .82 for 1970–75.
(B) = Number yearling males plus calculated number yearling females in autumn populations at $t + 1$, assuming negligible summer mortality of yearlings.
(C) = $A - B/A \times 100$.
(D) = C − known hunting mortality.
(E) = Calculated birth pulse population = (A) + autumn populations of adults and yearlings.

Natural mortality of calves on birth pulse population (N_I)

$$\hat{Y} = .116075 + .000040598 \, (N_I).$$

Anova

Source	df	SS	MS	F	P
Total	6	.186082	.0310136		
Regression	1	.172080	.172080	61.45	<.001
Error	5	.014002	.002800		

$$r^2 = .93$$

TABLE IV.3.
Calculated Mortality of Males 17 Months and Older, 1969–75[a]

Time	Initial No. Males (A)	Final No. Males (B)	Percent Dying		Initial Total Population (E)
			Total (C)	Natural Mortality (D)	
1969	1,250	1,230	1.60	0.01	4,305
1970	1,677	1,531	8.71	7.87	5,543
1971	2,124	1,666	21.56	20.99	7,281
1972	2,263	2,007	11.31	10.38	8,215
1973	2,488	2,051	17.40	15.87	9,981
1974	2,760	2,398	13.12	11.16	10,529
1975	3,202	2,001	37.51	36.32	12,607

[a]Calculated from autumn prehunt populations as follows:
(A) = Calculated number of adult and yearling males in prehunt populations.
(B) = Number of adult males in prehunt population at $t + 1$ assuming negligible mortality of males over summer periods.
(C) = $A - B/A \times 100$.
(D) = $C -$ known hunting mortality.
(E) = Posthunt populations assuming all natural mortality occurred over winter.

Natural mortality of males on initial population (N_I)

$$\hat{Y} = -11.3638 + .00311578 (N_I)$$

Anova

Source	df	SS	MS	F	P
Total	6	802.26	133.71		
Regression	1	494.46	494.46	8.03	< .025
Error	5	307.80	61.56		

$$r^2 = .62$$

TABLE IV.4.
Mortality of Calves and k-Factors, 1969–75[a]

Source		1969	1970	1971	1972	1973	1974	1975
Max. potential calves (A)		1,668	2,149	3,029	3,747	5,009	5,415	6,928
	$\hat{k}_0$	.0758	.0857	.0856	.0856	.0857	.0856	.0856
Calves produced (B)		1,401	1,764	2,487	3,076	4,112	4,446	5,688
	$\hat{k}_1$	.1495	.1566	.2045	.2929	.3365	.3865	.4674
Calves alive 6 Mo. (C)		993	1,230	1,553	1,567	1,895	1,826	1,939
	$\hat{k}_2$	.0030	.0039	.0026	.0033	.0067	.0087	.0052
Calves alive 9 Mo. (D)		986	1,219	1,544	1,553	1,866	1,790	1,916
	$\hat{k}_3$	.0009	.0022	.0714	.1040	.1105	.0799	.1148
Calves alive 12 Mo. (E)		984	1,213	1,310	1,224	1,447	1,489	1,471
	$\hat{K}$	.2292	.2484	.3641	.4858	.5394	.5607	.6730

Time

[a]Calculated from Table IV.1 as follows:

(A) = Calculated adult females in autumn populations.
(B) = (A) × reduction in fertility of .84 in 1969, .82 for 1970–75.
(C) = Calves in autumn populations.
(D) = Calves in early winter populations.
(E) = Yearlings in autumn populations at $t + 1$, assuming negligible summer mortality of yearlings.
$\hat{k}_0$ (reduction in fertility) = $\log A - \log B$
$\hat{k}_1$ (neonatal mortality) = $\log B - \log C$
$\hat{k}_2$ (hunting mortality) = $\log C - \log D$
$\hat{k}_3$ (winter mortality) = $\log D - \log E$
$\hat{K}$ (total reduction) = $\hat{k}_0 + \hat{k}_1 + \hat{k}_2 + \hat{k}_3$

243

Mortality of calves $\hat{k}_1$ on log initial total population (log N_I)

$$\hat{Y} = -2.12253 + .605991 \ (\log N_I)$$

ANOVA

SOURCE	df	SS	MS	F	P
Total	6	.0876136	.0146023		
Regression	1	.0816403	.0816403	68.34	< .001
Error	5	.0059733	.0011946		

$$r^2 = .93, \quad s_b = .073305$$

Proof of density-dependence for $\hat{k}_1$

Log initial on log final numbers:

$$\hat{Y} = -2.85589 + 1.98589(X), \quad F = 68.33, \quad P < .001, \quad s_b = .24024$$

Log final on log initial numbers:

$$\hat{Y} = 1.55725 + .469220 \ (X), \quad F = 68.33, \quad P < .001, \quad s_b = .05676$$

FIGURE IV.1.

Calf mortality. "Proof of density dependence" test for $\hat{k}_1$.

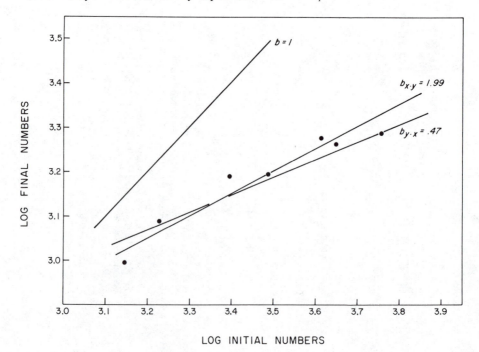

LOG INITIAL NUMBERS

Mortality of calves $\hat{k}_3$ on log initial total population (log N_I)

$$\hat{Y} = -.981221 + .269543 \ (\log N_I)$$

ANOVA

SOURCE	df	SS	MS	F	P
Total	6	.0142692	.0023782		
Regression	1	.0117561	.0117561	23.39	< .001
Error	5	.0025132	.000503		

$$r^2 = .82, \quad s_b = .055734$$

Proof of density-dependence for $\hat{k}_3$
   Log initial numbers on log final:

$$\hat{Y} = -1.74252 + 1.58214 \ (X), \quad F = 52.84, \quad P < .001, \quad s_b = .21766$$

Log final numbers on log initial:

$$\hat{Y} = 1.27518 + .577414(X), \quad F = 52.84, \quad P < .001, \quad s_b = .079437$$

FIGURE IV.2.
Calf mortality. "Proof of density dependence" test for $\hat{k}_3$.

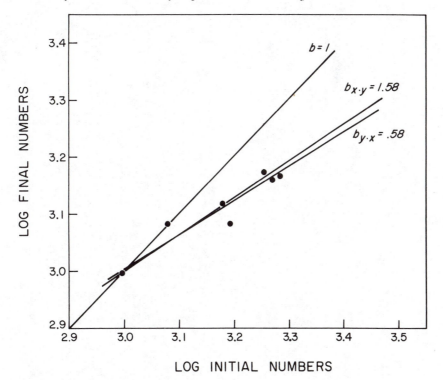

TABLE IV.5.
Mortality of Males and k-Factors, 1969–75[a]

Source	Time						
	1969	1970	1971	1972	1973	1974	1975
Initial No. males (A)	1,250	1,677	2,124	2,263	2,483	2,760	3,202
k_1	.0052	.0036	.0025	.0041	.0067	.0086	.0052
Posthunt males (B)	1,235	1,663	2,112	2,242	2,445	2,706	3,164
k_2	.0018	.0359	.1030	.0481	.0763	.0525	.1990
Final No. males (C)	1,230	1,531	1,666	2,007	2,051	2,398	2,001
K	.0070	.0395	.1055	.0522	.0830	.0611	.2042

[a]Calculated from Table IV.1 as follows:

(A) = Number yearling and adult males in autumn population.

(B) = Number yearling and adult males in early winter (posthunt) population.

(C) = Number of adult males in autumn population at $t + 1$ assuming all natural mortality occurred during winter.

k_1 (hunting mortality) = $\log A - \log B$

k_2 (natural winter mortality) = $\log B - \log C$

$K = k_1 + k_2$

Mortality of males k_2 on log initial total population (log N_I)

$$\hat{Y} = -1.04249 + .286473 \; (\log N_I)$$

Anova

Source	df	SS	MS	F	P
Total	6	.0242685	.0040448		
Regression	1	.0132792	.013279	6.04	.10 > P > .05
Error	5	.109893	.0021978		

$$r^2 = .55, \quad s_b = .11655$$

FIGURE IV.3.

Male mortality as k_2 on log initial total population.

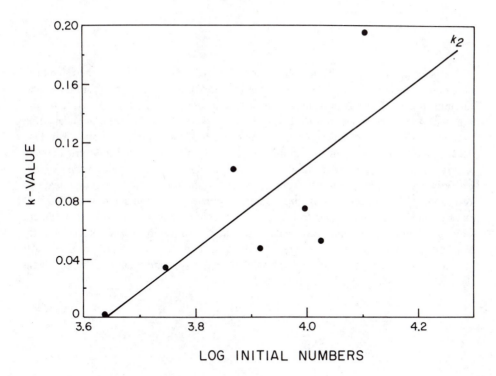

LOG INITIAL NUMBERS

APPENDIX V

Comparative Photographs

A sample of 51 comparative photos of the seasonal ranges of the northern Yellowstone elk is included in this Appendix. Photo plates 1–21 are of spring, summer, and autumn ranges. The location of each is shown in Fig. V.1. Plates 22–51 are on the northern winter range, with 49–51 outside the park, and 45–48 in the boundary line area (BLA) within the park. The locations of each of these plates are shown in Fig. V.2, as well as the locations of additional photos on file. Note that this series covers nearly the entire winter range. In all cases the *upper photo* of each plate is the *original* or early photo. Camera points were recorded as *similar* when foreground features (e.g., rocks, trees) were exactly duplicated; as *approximate* when details of middle and backgrounds were duplicated (this was within a few meters of the original camera point.) When camera points were moved for the retake (often several meters, usually because of increased forest cover), the distance and direction were recorded. All photos are on file at Yellowstone National Park. All sites are identified by Universal Transverse Mercator (UTM) coordinates.

FIGURE V.1.
Approximate camera point locations for Plates 1–21 on spring, summer, and autumn ranges of the northern Yellowstone elk.

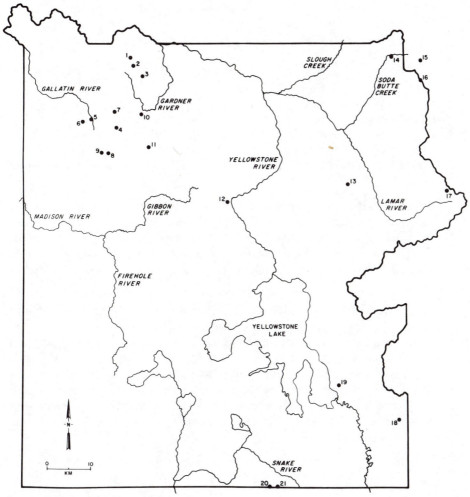

See p. 352 for locations of Plates 22–51.

PLATE 1

LOCATION: View southeast to summit of Sepulcher Mt. across headwaters of Stephens Creek (516.6 E, 4983.6 N; elev. 2,530 m).

PHOTOGRAPHERS: J. P. Iddings ~ 1885 (USGS No. 321).
                 D. B. Houston, September 1, 1971.

VEGETATIVE CHANGES: Approximate interval of 87 years (camera points similar).

Middleground shows some increase in size and density of whitebark pine and subalpine fir. Grassland in retake was dominated by slender bluebunch wheatgrass and Idaho fescue, with bluebunch wheatgrass, Junegrass, and bluegrasses increasingly important on the sparsely vegetated ridgetop sites. Certain poorly vegetated snowbank sites in retake were dominated by herbs such as mountain dandelion.

Background suggests a small increase in coniferous forest. Little vegetative change. The harsh-appearing ridgetop and snowbank areas present in original are present in the retake (they are more pronounced in original because the photo was probably taken in late July or early August, judging from snowbanks). This ridgetop is a wintering area for small groups of bull elk, and the area receives spring, summer, and fall use by elk. A major elk trail crosses the divide area in foreground but is not visible in this photo. The sparsely vegetated swale sites represent snowbank areas. The appearance of several conifers in both photos suggest ungulate browsing.

PLATE 2

LOCATION: Upper Glen Creek view northwest to Electric Peak (517.7 E, 4980.6 N; elev 2350 m).

PHOTOGRAPHERS: J. P. Iddings, ~ 1885 (USGS No. 305).
D. B. Houston, September 1, 1971.

VEGETATIVE CHANGES: Approximate interval of 87 years (camera points similar).

Foreground shows change from a sagebrush grassland to grassland containing mountain brome, slender bluebunch wheatgrass, and Idaho fescue.

Middle ground shows a decrease in willow in the meadow (arrow in retake). Present vegetation is dominated by sedges, reedgrass, hairgrass, with Idaho fescue in more xeric sites. The extensive stand of aspen at right in the original has been nearly completely replaced by lodgepole pine.

Background shows an increase in coniferous forest (whitebark pine, subalpine fir, lodgepole pine) on lower slopes of Electric Peak.

The area receives light grazing from migratory groups of elk and other ungulates during spring, summer, and fall.

PLATE 3

LOCATION: Gardner's Hole area view southwest across Glen Creek to Gallatin Range (519.3 E, 4978.9 N; elev. 2,380 m).

PHOTOGRAPHERS: J. P. Iddings, ~ 1885 (USGS No. 246).
D. B. Houston, August 23, 1971.

VEGETATIVE CHANGES: Approximate interval of 87 years (camera point moved 50 m west because of increase in conifers).

Foreground suggests an increase in big sage and perhaps a decrease in aspen. A small decline in willow has occurred in the Glen Creek bottom.

Middle ground shows an increase in big sagebrush (note that glacial erratic boulders visible on the ridge in original are obscured by sage in retake, arrow). A small increase in area occupied by forest and a definite change in species composition in the forest has occurred. Aspen has declined and Douglas-fir, lodgepole pine, and subalpine fir have increased. Dead conifers on left suggest a fire or insect attack. Trees along forest–grassland ecotones show three to four fire scars. Idaho fescue is a dominant grass in the retake. This area is on the periphery of the northern winter range and receives some use by elk in early winter and spring. Small groups of elk and some moose spend the entire winter on the area.

PLATE 4

LOCATION: Indian Creek, view southwest to Dome Mountain (513.4 E, 4967.1 N; elev. 2,350 m).

PHOTOGRAPHERS: J. P. Iddings, ~ 1885 (USGS No. 250).
                 D. B. Houston, August 17, 1972.

VEGETATIVE CHANGES: Approximate interval of 87 years (camera points similar—note rock at arrow).

Foreground is now dominated by Idaho fescue, hairgrass, slender bluebunch wheatgrass, and alpine timothy, with Gairdner's yampah, yarrow, and elk thistle as dominant forbs. Vegetation in the original appears to be dominated by marsh-marigold, which was not present in the retake, suggesting a change in soil moisture.

Middle ground shows a decline in willow and an increase in lodgepole pine, subalpine fir, and Engelmann spruce. Western coneflower occurs in a dense stand at the base of the trees.

Background shows an increase in lodgepole pine and subalpine fir on the slopes of Dome Mt. Charred snags suggest that the opening was created by a fire that burned down the south side of Indian Creek. A sample from a fire-scarred tree indicated an approximate fire date of 1856.

Moderate summer elk use presently occurs in this meadow.

PLATE 5

LOCATION: Bighorn Pass from the west across Gallatin River (509.8 E, 4968.5 N; elev. 2,560 m).

PHOTOGRAPHERS: J. P. Iddings, ~ 1885 (USGS No. 133).
                D. B. Houston, August 30, 1972.

VEGETATIVE CHANGES: Approximate interval of 87 years (camera points similar).

Foreground shows little change in the subalpine fir–whitebark pine forest. The original shows what appears to be a substantial willow community along the Gallatin River. Willows were essentially gone from this portion of the Gallatin at the time of the retake.

Middle ground shows a subalpine herbland dominated by slender bluebunch wheatgrass, mountain brome, mountain dandelion, tall mountain larkspur, Douglas' clematis, and many-flowered stickseed. Swale vegetation was dominated by cow-parsnip and western coneflower. The light-colored areas of sparse vegetation in original were in a similar condition in retake, with 70–80% bare ground due to pocket gopher burrowing. These areas are not as conspicuous in retake because of differences in lighting and vegetation (many gopher mounds supported a sparse cover of Douglas' knotweed at retake). The subalpine fir groves show minor increases.

Background shows very little difference in the distribution of subalpine fir on the talus and cliff areas of Madison limestone.

Herbland in middle ground showed moderate summer elk grazing on mountain dandelion and the seedheads of tall mountain larkspur.

PLATE 6

LOCATION: Gallatin mountain range view west to Crowfoot Ridge (506.6 E, 4968.5 N; Elev. 2,650 m).

PHOTOGRAPHERS: J. P. Iddings, ~ 1885 (USGS No. 268).
D. B. Houston, August 14, 1972.

VEGETATIVE CHANGES: Approximate interval of 87 years (camera point moved 6m north due to increase in subalpine fir).

Foreground shows an increase in subalpine fir and whitebark pine into a wet meadow. Present herbaceous vegetation in the wet meadow is dominated by rushes, sedges, hairgrass, bluegrasses, alpine timothy, cinquefoil, mountain dandelion, and bistort. Substantial pocket gopher activity occurred in the original and was conspicuous at the time of the retake.

Middle ground shows an increase in subalpine fir and whitebark pine at right.

Background shows little or no change in subalpine fir on Crowfoot Ridge.

The area is elk summer range, and the wet meadow showed substantial elk use at the time of the retake.

PLATE 7

LOCATION: Panther Creek view northwest to Bannock Peak (513.0 E, 4970.2 N; elev. 2,440 m).

PHOTOGRAPHERS: J. P. Iddings, ~ 1885 (USGS No. 173).
D. B. Houston, July 23, 1974.

VEGETATIVE CHANGES: Approximate interval of 89 years (camera points approximate—note boulder in middle-ground meadow [arrow]).

Foreground shows a shift in channel of Panther Creek to an area 50 m farther north. Original photo suggests an abundance of willows along the stream. These were absent along both the "original" streambed and new channel at the time of retake. Foreground meadow in retake was dominated by alpine timothy grass, slender bluebunch wheatgrass, oniongrass, and mountain brome, with stickseed, mountain dandelion, and western coneflower.

Middle ground shows a decline in big sagebrush and an increase in subalpine fir, whitebark pine, and some lodgepole pine. Meadow vegetation was dominated by slender bluebunch wheatgrass, arnica, mountain brome, and oniongrass with scattered big sagebrush.

Background subalpine fir thickets show little change on Bannock Peak.

263

PLATE 8

LOCATION: Upper Winter Creek view NW to Mt. Holmes in left background (513.6 E, 4962.0 N; elev. 2,590 m).

PHOTOGRAPHERS: J. P. Iddings, ~ 1885 (USGS No. 56).
D. B. Houston, September 16, 1971.

VEGETATIVE CHANGES: Approximate interval of 86 years (camera point moved 15 m NW because of increase in conifers).

Foreground and *middle ground:* A subalpine herbland dominated by slender bluebunch wheatgrass, mountain brome, stickseed, aster, and mountain dandelion. Big sage, Rocky Mountain sage, coneflower, tall mountain larkspur, and lupine also present. Little change appears to have occurred, except for some decrease in big sage. The showy flowers around the horse in original are probably a lupine, which is still present, but not in bloom in retake. The sparsely vegetated area in right middle ground is a snowbank area dominated by mountain dandelion and shows no change. Some increase in subalpine fir and whitebark pine has occurred. Original shows evidence of tree mortality from forest insects.

Little vegetative change. The area is an elk summer range.

PLATE 9

LOCATION: Winter Creek view NE across flank of Mt. Holmes (512.0 E, 4962.0 N; elev. 2,680 m).

PHOTOGRAPHERS: J. P. Iddings, ~ 1885 (USGS No. 53).
D. B. Houston, August 25, 1972.

VEGETATIVE CHANGES: Approximate interval of 87 years (camera points similar—note small stump in foreground).

Foreground shows little change in a subalpine grassland dominated by slender bluebunch wheatgrass, Idaho fescue, mountain brome, dandelion, and buckwheat. The small shrub present in both photos is mountain gooseberry. This site is located on an exposed ridgetop and receives heavy summer elk use. Elk apparently concentrate on this windy ridgetop to seek relief from molesting insects. Area at time of retake also showed extensive burrowing by pocket gophers.

Middle ground shows increase in density of subalpine fir and whitebark pine. Meadow areas are subalpine herbland, developed on limestone, and show extensive pocket gopher burrowing at time of retake (and very probably in original). Vegetation was dominated by slender bluebunch wheatgrass, Idaho fescue, mountain dandelion, yarrow, blue flax, aster, paintbrush, and harebell.

Background shows subalpine herbland and minor increases in density of subalpine fir and whitebark pine. Ridgetop areas show little change in density of whitebark pine groves. Detailed descriptions and comparative photos of the herbland in background will be found in Pl. 8.

PLATE 10

LOCATION: Indian Creek view SW to Antler Peak (519.3 E, 4970.2 N; elev. 2,260 m).

PHOTOGRAPHERS: J. P. Iddings, ~ 1885 (USGS No. 251).
D. B. Houston, July 25, 1971.

VEGETATIVE CHANGES: Approximate interval of 86 years (camera points similar).

Foreground and *middle ground* show no apparent change in distribution or density of the willow community. The lodgepole pine forest has recolonized the glacial moraine at rear of meadow, apparently following a fire.

Background shows an increase in subalpine fir and whitebark pine on the slopes of Antler Peak.

The area receives light year-round grazing by both elk and moose but is primarily a spring, summer, and autumn range.

PLATE 11

LOCATION: Beaver Lake and Obsidian Cliff view north down Obsidian Creek (521.5 E, 4963.7 N; elev. 2,260 m).

PHOTOGRAPHERS: J. E. Haynes, ~ 1885–1900 (photo No. 9281).
D. B. Houston, July 16, 1971.

VEGETATIVE CHANGES: Interval of 71–86 years (camera points similar).

Foreground and *middle ground* show succession from an open water pond–lily stage to a beaked sedge meadow.

Background suggests an increase in density of lodgepole pine at left. Evidence for past fires occurs as scarred trees around Obsidian Cliff.

PLATE 12

LOCATION: East side of Chittenden Bridge, south of road across from parking lot from Uncle Tom's trail, looking north toward Mt. Washburn (539.5 E, 4951.0 N; elev. 2,370 m).

PHOTOGRAPHERS: W. H. Jackson, ~ early September 1890s (State Historical Society of Colorado Library).
M. Meagher, September 19, 1975.

VEGETATIVE CHANGES: Interval of 80–85 years

Foreground of silver sagebrush has decreased in density. Seasonal differences in forbs and grasses account for some differences in appearance. Species composition has changed somewhat. Nonnative timothy is now prevalent, although annual variation in growing seasons probably accounts for differences in grass height (1975 was a very wet year).

Middle ground forest at canyon rim appears less in center, probably due to development (road, trail, etc.). Note double-crowned lodgepole at right in both photos.

This site may have been subject to limited summer horse grazing during some period of the old Canyon Lodge operation. There is one deeply entrenched trail crossing the meadow.

PLATE 13

LOCATION: Mirror Plateau, head of the north fork of the Mirror Fork of Timothy Creek, looking southeast. (567.5 E, 4955.1 N; elev. 2,590 m).

PHOTOGRAPHERS: J. E. Haynes, 1916 (No. 16202).
M. Meagher, September 6, 1973.

VEGETATIVE CHANGES: Interval of 57 years.

Invasion of meadow edges by lodgepole pine apparent. Ground cover appears essentially the same, allowing for changes in phenology because of season of year. Lupine in the Haynes photo indicates an earlier time of year, probably July.

This is major elk and bison summer–autumn range.

PLATE 14

LOCATION: Soda Butte Creek view west to Barronette Peak (575.0 E, 4983.9 N; elev. 2,260 m).

PHOTOGRAPHERS: J. P. Iddings, ~ 1885 (USGS No. 347).
D. B. Houston, August 25, 1970.

VEGETATIVE CHANGES: Interval of 85 years (camera point on retake moved about 15–30 m to the north because of development of forest).

Foreground shows that an extensive willow thicket on the flood plain of Soda Butte Creek has been replaced by various conifers and by mesic grassland. A charred snag provides evidence of past fires.

Middle ground shows that conifers (mostly subalpine fir and lodgepole pine, but including some spruce) have expanded into forest parks. The original photo shows some evidence of fire, insects, or disease in the conifers. The road in the original has filled in, but one of the tree stumps visible above the road (arrow) was found at the time of the retake.

Background shows little overall change in the distribution of forest cover on Barronette Peak, although one stand present at the forest border in the original is not present in the retake.

The seral nature of willow communities to both grassland and forest is graphically demonstrated in these photos. Changes in the activity of the stream on its flood plain are also suggested. Since this is a deep-snow area, and is well outside the usual winter range of elk, it seems unlikely that native ungulates were primarily responsible for the replacement of willow. Low densities of moose occur year round in this area.

PLATE 15

LOCATION: Republic Creek, Shoshone National Forest. View north to Beartooth Plateau (582.7 E, 4982.3 N; elev. 2,530 m).

PHOTOGRAPHERS: J. P. Iddings, ~ 1885 (USGS No. 342).
D. B. Houston, August 20, 1972.

VEGETATIVE CHANGES: Approximate interval of 87 years (camera points similar).

Foreground and *middle ground* show substantial decreases in willow. Dominant grasses in the foreground meadow are presently hairgrass, mountain brome, alpine timothy, and sedges; dominant forbs were broad-leafed bluebells, diverse-leaved cinquefoil, fleabane, butterweed groundsel, and cow-parsnip. Scattered willow persist on the lowest flood plain of the stream (below the forked tree at right [arrow]), but even here lodgepole pine is invading willows. Forest shows some increase and is dominated by lodgepole pine, subalpine fir, and Engelmann spruce.

This area receives very light summer foraging from elk and moose.

PLATE 16

LOCATION: Republic Pass view west toward Amphitheater Mt. (582.8 E, 4978.0 N; elev. 3,050 m).

PHOTOGRAPHERS: J. P. Iddings, ~ 1885 (USGS No. 345).
D. B. Houston, August 16, 1970.

VEGETATIVE CHANGES: Interval of 87 years (camera points similar).

Foreground shows little change in vegetation. The vegetation in 1970 could be characterized as subalpine meadow with sedges and bluegrass the dominant cover, with small lupines and mountain dandelion also present. This area showed moderate to abundant elk use in the form of beds, droppings, and feeding areas in 1970. Bighorn sheep sign and pocket gopher mounds were also present.

Middle ground is a steep southeast facing slope composed of Absaroka volcanics that show little change in vegetation (mostly whitebark pine stands) or in patterns of erosion. Ungulate trails were visible on portions of this ridge, outside of photo, in 1970. Large snowbanks lasting until early to midsummer occur on portions of this ridge. Vegetation on snowbank areas was dominated by mountain dandelion with sparse grasses and sedges.

Background shows some increase of coniferous forests on Amphitheater Peak.

Little or no change has occurred on this elk summer range during the 87-year interval. The patterns of erosion from harsh volcanic substrates show little change.

PLATE 17

LOCATION: East–west escarpment north of main Parker Peak, looking northwest (586.5 E, 4953.3 N: elev. 2,930 m).

PHOTOGRAPHERS: J. P. Iddings, ~ 1885 (USGS No. 348–9).
M. Meagher, August 14, 1972.

VEGETATIVE CHANGES: Interval of 87 years. Camera point altered somewhat because of erosion at edge of ridge. Forest (lodgepole pine at lower elevations, spruce–fir and a small amount of whitebark pine at higher elevations) has increased. Note presence of what may be forest insect attack on trees to right in earlier photo.

Slopes are similar except for erosion at edge. Substrate of exposed Absaroka volcanics, mainly breccias, is readily eroded.

The Parker Peak area is elk summer range.

PLATE 18

LOCATION: Looking north at Eagle Peak from Mountain Creek (576.9 E, 4901.9 N; elev. 2,560 m).

PHOTOGRAPHERS: J. P. Iddings, 1889–90 (No. 273).
                 M. Meagher, August 8, 1973.

VEGETATIVE CHANGES: Interval of 83–84 years.

Forest has increased on suitable sites on Eagle Peak.

The foreground meadow may be less wet now. Willow had disappeared—present vegetation is predominately sedges and rushes, with some grasses and forbs.

This area receives limited elk use summer–autumn.

PLATE 19

LOCATION: Southeast Arm from Langford Cairn, looking southeast (563.5 E, 4909.5 N; elev. 2,700 m).

PHOTOGRAPHERS: W. H. Jackson, Hayden Survey, 1871.
M. Meagher, August 7, 1973.

VEGETATIVE CHANGES: Interval of 102 years.

Forest cover—mainly lodgepole—has increased only slightly at all elevations. Meadow invasion by trees is apparent on the flats at right rear.

Sagebrush and bunchgrass have both increased on the Cairn in foreground.

Meadow areas receive some summer–autumn elk use.

PLATE 20

LOCATION: Big Game Ridge, looking at Mt. Hancock (548.9 E; 4887.0 N; elev. 3,020 m).

PHOTOGRAPHERS: Steven Leek, ~ 1900 (Library, U. of Wyoming).
M. Meagher, July 16, 1973.

VEGETATIVE CHANGES: Interval of approximately 73 years.

The forest on Mt. Hancock shows a slight increase in density and area. Vegetation of the foreground is within a snowbank site. Some decrease in plant density is apparent on selected sites—such as right center (arrow). Other sites show an increase in density. Much of this is forb vegetation. The appearance of the foreground vegetation probably varies annually in response to time and rate of snow melt, temperature variation, summer precipitation, stage of growing season for that particular year, and intensities of elk grazing.

This is elk summer range.

PLATE 21

LOCATION: Big Game Ridge, view northeast to base of Chicken Ridge (549.3 E, 4887.3 N; elev. 2,770 m).

PHOTOGRAPHERS: Vernon Bailey, August 19, 1915 (Natl. Archives No. 22-WB-16076).
George Gruell, USFS, August 13, 1969.

VEGETATIVE CHANGES: Interval of 54 years (camera points similar).

Foreground and *middle ground* show little change in subalpine herbland. Some increase in herbaceous vegetation may have occurred on deeper soils. Subalpine fir has increased in density.

Background shows little change in distribution of subalpine fir and whitebark pine. Little change has occurred in appearance of subalpine herbland. Sparsely vegetated areas occur on steep snowbank areas and on talus slopes with little soil development. The area is an elk summer range.

PLATE 22

LOCATION: About 1.6 km north of Mammoth on Mammoth–Gardiner road (424.5 E, 4981.0 N; elev. 1,800 m).

PHOTOGRAPHERS: YNP library files 1900–1915 (?) (neg. no. 4360).
D. B. Houston, June 29, 1971.

VEGETATIVE CHANGES: Interval of 56–71 years (camera points similar).

A bunchgrass community presently dominated by bluebunch wheatgrass, but also containing Junegrass, ricegrass, needle-and-thread, and Sandberg's bluegrass. Big sage has declined. Present sage stands in swales contain all age classes and are in excellent condition. Plants on slopes are heavily grazed. An increase in grass cover is suggested, but this probably reflects differences in precipitation or season of photos. Livestock grazing may have occurred on this site at the time of the original photo and for perhaps 20 years before.

PLATE 23

LOCATION: Mammoth Hot Springs, view east to Mt. Everts (523.5 E, 4979.1 N; elev. 1,950 m).

PHOTOGRAPHERS: W. H. Jackson, 1871.
                 D. B. Houston, July 19, 1971.

VEGETATIVE CHANGES: Interval of 100 years (camera points similar).

Foreground shows some substantial changes in hot spring deposits.

Middle ground has been variously altered by human activities. Vegetation in the retake is primarily bluebunch wheatgrass grassland with stands of big sage in swales. Dark areas are marshes, which show no change. Other early Jackson photos suggest no change in this sagebrush grassland and show sage and common rabbitbrush as dominant shrubs in swales.

Background shows little change in herbaceous vegetation on west and southwest slopes on Mt. Everts. Erosion rills and channels appear similar after 100 years. Vegetation on bare south slopes is ricegrass, greasewood, and saltbush, with 60–80% bare ground. Some increase in conifers, mostly Douglas-fir, has occurred on upper slopes and on top of Mt. Everts.

Mt. Everts is a bighorn sheep, mule deer, and elk winter range. Soils on these steep slopes have developed from Cretaceous sediments and contain a high percentage of clays. Vegetative cover on the slopes is considered to be the result of peculiar topoedaphic conditions and grazing by native ungulates.

PLATE 24

LOCATION: Mammoth Hot Springs, view south to Bunsen Peak (524.1 E, 4978.9 N; elev. 1,950 m).

PHOTOGRAPHERS: Homer Shantz, 1907 (print is on file at University of Arizona at Tucson).
D. B. Houston, July 7, 1972.

VEGETATIVE CHANGES: Interval of 65 years (camera points similar).

Foreground swale shows an increase in big sagebrush. The conspicuous large grass in the original was probably giant wild rye and is present in the retake. Idaho fescue is also abundant in retake.

Middle ground shows a substantial increase in Douglas–fir on a sagebrush grassland (previously a forest which was burned). The lower arrow in both photos marks the same tree as a point of reference. The low, shrubby-appearing vegetation behind the conspicuous dead tree at left center was a combination of aspen and willow. This was largely gone at the time of the retake.

Background arrow marks the 1886 fire boundary on Bunsen Peak. The burned area has been reforested with lodgepole pine as the dominant conifer. Douglas-fir and subalpine fir also occur on this forested north slope.

The photo shows the influence of past fire and the entire scene may have been burned during an 1886 fire.

PLATE 25

LOCATION: South slopes of Mt. Everts (527.3 E, 4977.3 N; elev. 2, 010 m).

PHOTOGRAPHERS: J. P. Iddings, ~ 1885 (USGS No. 170).
                 D. B. Houston, September 18, 1970.

VEGETATIVE CHANGES: Interval of 85 years (camera point moved 30–60 m east because of increased height of conifers.)

Foreground shows little change in the dense coniferous vegetation on the steep north-facing slope above Lava Creek.

Background shows a substantial increase of conifers on lower slopes, upper slopes, and on the summit of Mt. Everts. Comparatively little change has occurred in vegetation on the steep slopes, and some shrubby groups of Rocky Mountain juniper have retained the same configuration. Gully erosion has continued. There is a suggestion of an insect attack, disease, or fire on the edge of a grove of conifers in the original photo (upper left). This area is winter range for elk, mule deer, bighorn, and moose.

Relatively little change has occurred on the harsh south slopes, but an increase in conifers has occurred over the area.

PLATE 26

LOCATION: Lower Blacktail Creek, view east across the Blacktail Plateau (532.0 E, 4980.6 N; elev. 1,950 m).

PHOTOGRAPHERS: C. P. Russell, 1929 (YNP Neg. 2711).
D. B. Houston, August 9, 1972.

VEGETATIVE CHANGES: Interval of 43 years (camera points approximate).

Foreground vegetation shows little change except for minor increases in the shrubs, rubber rabbitbrush, and horsebrush. Dominant herbaceous vegetation is Idaho fescue, bluebunch wheatgrass, needlegrasses, with hairgrass, and aster in more mesic sites.

Middle ground and *background* show a decline in aspen and suggest an increase in big sagebrush. Dominant grasses in the more mesic sites are Idaho fescue and hairgrass; in the xeric sites, bluebunch wheatgrass, and Junegrass. The bare-appearing slope sites are essentially unchanged. Vegetation on these sites is dominated by bluebunch wheatgrass and Junegrass (sites appear less harsh in retake, but this is due primarily to differences in lighting). The arrow marks an erosion site that is part of a complex of mineral licks used by ungulates. A minor decline in shrubs, possibly shrubby cinquefoil or willow, has occurred in the swale to the left of the arrow.

PLATE 27

LOCATION: Blacktail Plateau view north (535.2 E, 4978.9 N; elev. 2,110 m).

PHOTOGRAPHERS: B. H. Thompson, September 17, 1933 (Neg. No. 3274).
D. B. Houston, September 11, 1972.

VEGETATIVE CHANGES: Interval of 39 years (camera points similar—same lichen-covered stone at arrows?).

Photo shows vegetation on a steep south-facing ridgetop that receives heavy winter grazing by elk. This site is not typical of most of the surrounding Blacktail Plateau but does give an excellent comparison of vegetation on a harsh site. The original photo was taken during the severe drought of the 1930s. In addition to the drought, Thompson's notes indicate grasshoppers had cropped much of the vegetation in this area by the late summer of 1933. Movements of rocks show that some erosion has occurred on this steep slope in the 39 years, aided by extensive burrowings of pocket gophers and Uinta ground squirrels. Vegetation at the time of retake was dominated by bluebunch wheatgrass, with Junegrass, Sandberg bluegrass, fringed sage, toadflax, phlox, goldenweed, and cutleaf fleabane also present.

PLATE 28

LOCATION: Upper Geode Creek, view north to Hellroaring Mt. at right (539.9 E, 4977.1 N; elev. 2,230 m).

PHOTOGRAPHERS: USFS Photo No. 3957A, August 1918.
D. B. Houston, August 2, 1971.

VEGETATIVE CHANGES: Interval of 53 years (camera points similar).

Foreground now contains a dense stand of needlegrasses, Idaho fescue, and bluegrasses and shows little change from original.

Middle ground shows little change in the bunchgrass (Idaho fescue, bluebunch wheatgrass) Douglas–fir areas. Note that the area of sparse vegetation in retake (arrow) was present in original.

Background shows little change in distribution of Douglas-fir and grassland areas.

This area is in the heart of the northern winter range, receives consistent use by elk, and shows little change in 53 years.

PLATE 29

LOCATION: Elk Creek, view west (544.7 E, 4975.4 N; elev. 1,950 m).

PHOTOGRAPHERS: E. R. Warren (Beaver in YNP, *Roosevelt Wildl. Bull.* No. 1), July 23, 1921 (Neg. No. 5072).
D. B. Houston, August 14, 1971.

VEGETATIVE CHANGES: Interval of 50 years (camera points similar).

Foreground shows an active beaver pond in 1921, ringed by aspen and containing scattered willow. Warren described the willows "as mostly dead with a few living." The dam is in the upper right corner of the pond partially obscured by aspen. The pond was deserted by 1923. Retake shows a sedge meadow with hairgrass on drier sites. Remnants of the lodge are present but are difficult to observe in the retake. Engelmann spruce are invading the far edge of the sedge meadow. Substantial spruce invasion of the meadow is occurring just out of the picture on the left.

Middle ground shows a sagebrush grassland in original; some invasion of Douglas-fir has occurred. A substantial increase in Douglas-fir has occurred in the retake, with fir invading the grassland and nearly replacing the aspen grove at left.

Background shows an increase in conifers on the east-facing slopes and ridgetops (appearance of vegetation suggests this is recolonization of burned area). These are mostly Douglas-fir but include lodgepole pine and subalpine fir.

Many of the changes are considered to reflect secondary succession following fire and show a change in frequency of natural fires. A fire-scarred tree cut in this vicinity in 1971 showed a mean interval between fires of 51 years for the last 303 years. The construction and foraging activities of beaver have contributed to vegetative changes.

PLATE 30

LOCATION: Lower Hellroaring slope, view northeast (544.7 E, 4978.9 N; elev. 1,830 m).

PHOTOGRAPHERS: McDougall and Grimm, August 27, 1943 (43–230).
D. B. Houston, August 26, 1974.

VEGETATIVE CHANGES: Interval of 31 years (camera points similar).

Vegetation in original was described as green rabbitbrush, Idaho fescue, and needle-and-thread grass and was similar at retake.

This ridgetop area has been consistently heavily grazed by wintering elk.

PLATE 31

LOCATION: Lower Hellroaring slope, view north (544.7 E, 4978.9 N; elev. 1,830 m).

PHOTOGRAPHERS: McDougall and Grimm, August 27, 1943 (43–199).
D. B. Houston, August 26, 1974.

VEGETATIVE CHANGES: Interval of 31 years (camera points similar).

Foreground swale was dominated by a highly productive stand of introduced timothy grass in both photos, with components of sedge, giant wildrye, and bluegrass.

Background slopes were dominated by needle-and-thread, bluebunch wheatgrass, and Junegrass.

This area receives consistent heavy winter grazing by elk.

PLATE 32

LOCATION: View west down Yellowstone River canyon, 1.5 km below confluence with Elk Creek (541.5 E, 4978.9 N; elev. 1,800 m).

PHOTOGRAPHERS: J. P. Iddings, ~ 1885 (USGS No. 335).
          D. B. Houston, August 11, 1971.

VEGETATIVE CHANGES: Approximate interval of 86 years (camera points exact).

Foreground shows a sparsely vegetated ridgetop above a steep cliff on the Yellowstone River. Bluebunch wheatgrass is the dominant grass on the ridgetop. Some increase in Rocky Mountain juniper has occurred.

Middle ground shows some increase in big sagebrush in the grassland at left.

Background shows an increase in Douglas-fir forest. Fir have almost completely replaced an aspen stand at right (arrow).

The change in forest cover probably reflects a change in frequency of natural fires. The ridgetop site with sparse vegetation at right foreground is part of a heavily used bighorn sheep–elk winter range and is little changed.

PLATE 33

LOCATION: View east across Yellowstone River to Junction Butte (547.9 E, 4973.7 N; elev. 1,980 m).

PHOTOGRAPHERS: U.S. Army Engineers, 1900.
                 D. B. Houston, July 15, 1972.

VEGETATIVE CHANGES: Interval of 72 years (camera point moved 15 m west and uphill because of increase in height of aspen).

Foreground of original shows a low, dense stand of aspen (probably 3–5 m high, based on size of rock at left). Stand in retake has matured, shows no reproduction, and big sagebrush dominates the understory.

Middle ground shows an increase in Douglas-fir and possibly big sagebrush on Idaho fescue–bluebunch wheatgrass steppes.

Background shows increase in Douglas-fir, probably in sagebrush, and a decline in aspen. Aspen in original had an appearance similar to foreground stand; i.e., dense reproduction with no large overstory trees. Remnant stands in retake show no reproduction. Aspen stands in original show the effects of ungulate browsing on stand margins.

Fire-scarred trees cut in this area suggest a mean fire frequency historically of 20–25 years, and the photos indicate a reduction in fire frequency.

PLATE 34

LOCATION: Tower Junction area, view south through a field of glacial erratic boulders (546.3 E, 4973.7 N; elev. 1,920 m).

PHOTOGRAPHERS: J. P. Iddings, ~ 1885 (USGS No. 152).
D. B. Houston, August 25, 1970.

VEGETATIVE CHANGES: Approximate interval of 85 years (camera points similar).

Foreground shows the addition of a big sagebrush canopy to the former bunchgrass–rabbitbrush community. Perennial grasses under the present canopy are Idaho fescue and needle-and-thread.

Background shows a grassland community with two young aspen stands (the boulder adjacent to the aspen on the right is about 3m in height) without an overstory of older trees. Scattered Douglas-fir of various sizes were present in the original. The recent photo shows the replacement of the aspen by sagebrush and Douglas-fir, the addition of a sagebrush canopy to the former grassland, an increase in Douglas-fir density, an invasion of Douglas-fir into the sagebrush grassland, and the highlining of many of the larger Douglas-fir trees.

The addition of a sagebrush overstory to the grassland may reflect the development of a climatic climax vegetation. The presence of sagebrush, the increase in Douglas-fir, and the decline in aspen suggest a reduced fire frequency. Fire-scarred trees cut in this area suggest a historic fire frequency of one fire every 20–25 years for the past 300–400 years.

PLATE 35

LOCATION: Tower Junction, view north toward the Little Buffalo Creek drainage (546.3 E, 4973.7 N; elev. 1,920 m).

PHOTOGRAPHERS: J. P. Iddings, ~ 1885 (USGS No. 154).
                D. B. Houston, August 25, 1970.

VEGETATIVE CHANGES: Interval of 85 years (camera points similar).

Foreground shows the development of a sagebrush overstory on a former grassland community (which appears to have contained scattered rabbitbrush plants). There has been an increase in conifers beyond the boulder.

Middle ground shows benches across the Yellowstone that are presently a sagebrush grassland. They may have lacked big sage in the early photo, although this is difficult to determine (see extreme left of benches in both photos). An increase in conifers has occurred on the knob in left center.

Background shows an increase in conifers on the southwest-facing slopes at the expense of grassland and some of the aspen stands. Some of the aspen stands in the center background now have conifers (mostly Douglas-fir) in the understory.

The sagebrush canopy contains a variety of age classes. The sagebrush steppe may represent the development of climatic climax vegetation as influenced by reduced fire frequency.

PLATE 36

LOCATION: Aspen stand, Tower Junction area (546.3 E, 4973.7 N; elev. 1,920 m).

PHOTOGRAPHERS: E. R. Warren, August 26, 1921.
                 D. B. Houston, August 14, 1971.

VEGETATIVE CHANGES: Interval of 50 years (camera point moved 20 m south).

Vegetation in foreground has been altered by road construction. Original shows an aspen stand heavily utilized by beaver. The beaver trail in original is still visible in retake but difficult to distinguish. Aspen stand in retake shows no successful reproduction, and understory contains many small Douglas-fir.

PLATE 37

LOCATION: View up the Yellowstone River canyon in Bumpus Butte area (547.5 E, 4972.2 N; elev. 1,980 m).

PHOTOGRAPHERS: W. H. Jackson, 1871.
D. B. Houston, July 19, 1971.

VEGETATIVE CHANGES: Interval of 100 years (camera points approximate).

Middle ground shows relatively little change in distribution of vegetation on steep slopes above river. Conifers are Douglas-fir, grasses at present are mainly Indian ricegrass and bluebunch wheatgrass. Ephemeral erosion rills occur on this slope following intense rains. Ridgetop in retake showed 60% bare ground and was probably in the same condition in the early photo.

Background shows some increase in Douglas-fir forest. Area of sparse vegetation at left (arrow) was present in both photos. These ridgetops receive heavy winter grazing by elk and bighorn.

PLATE 38

LOCATION: Tower Fall area, view east across the Yellowstone River canyon (547.9 E, 4970.2 N; elev. 2,010 m).

PHOTOGRAPHERS: J. P. Iddings, ~ 1885 (USGS No. 142).
D. B. Houston, July 19, 1971.

VEGETATIVE CHANGES: Interval of approximately 86 years (camera points similar).

The pattern of herbaceous vegetation on the west-facing ridge is essentially unchanged. Grasses present in the retake are bluebunch wheatgrass, Indian ricegrass, Junegrass, and Sandberg's bluegrass. Some increase in density of conifers, mostly Douglas-fir, has occurred on the ridgetop at right and between the outcrops of columnar basalt. Note that some of the dead trees present in original are present in the retake. The appearance of several trees in both photos suggests "high-lining" from ungulate browsing. The ridge top receives heavy winter grazing by bighorn and elk.

PLATE 39

LOCATION: About 1.6 km east of Junction Butte, view east to Druid Peak (551.0 E, 4973.7 N; elev. 1,890 m).

PHOTOGRAPHERS: USFS Neg. No. 39576A, August 1918.
                 D. B. Houston, August 2, 1971.

VEGETATIVE CHANGES: Interval of 53 years (camera points similar).

Foreground is a bunchgrass community dominated by Idaho fescue and needle-grasses. Shrubs are green rabbitbrush and big sage. Shrubs in original were probably rabbitbrush. There may have been a decline in this species, although it is abundant in the retake but obscured by grass production.

Middle ground shows little change in Idaho fescue grassland. Conifers in both photos show ungulate use.

Background shows little change except for an increase in Douglas-fir forest. Aspen (to left of foreground boulder) shows little change.

This site is a climax grassland in the heart of the northern winter range that shows little change in 53 years.

PLATE 40

LOCATION: Lamar River, view southwest to Prospect Peak (552.6 E, 4973.7 N; elev. 1,890 m).

PHOTOGRAPHERS: U.S. Army Engineers, 1905 (No. 1818).
D. B. Houston, July 17, 1973.

VEGETATIVE CHANGES: Interval of 68 years (camera points approximate).

Foreground shows little change in the sagebrush grassland except for local increases in the density of big sage. Dominant grasses in retake were Idaho fescue and needle-and-thread.

Middle ground across the Lamar River shows little change except for a decrease in willow around a seep. Dominant grasses are currently Idaho fescue and needle-and-thread; dominant shrubs, rubber and green rabbitbrushes and big sage.

Background shows some increase in Douglas-fir and a decline in aspen on Specimen Ridge at left and at lower elevations in the Prospect Peak area.

PLATE 41

LOCATION: View north on lower Slough Creek (554.2 E, 4975.4 N; elev. 1,890 m).

PHOTOGRAPHERS: E. R. Warren, August 7, 1923.
D. B. Houston, July 17, 1973.

VEGETATIVE CHANGES: Interval of 50 years (camera points approximate).

Foreground shows a reduction in willow (note that the willows appear to be dying in the original, but the dead branches do not have the hedged appearance of shrubs that have received heavy browsing by ungulates). Dominant herbaceous vegetation in the foreground includes bluegrasses, hairgrass, and giant wildrye (note that the same clumps of this grass occur at left in both photos) with sedges dominating the marshy area along the oxbow (above the arrow).

Middle ground also shows a small decline in willow and aspen. Herbaceous vegetation is somewhat similar to that described for foreground except that the introduced timothy grass dominates certain sites.

Background shows little change in the sagebrush grassland. Dominant grass in this type is Idaho fescue with bluebunch wheatgrass and Junegrass on more xeric sites. A decline in aspen has occurred in swale areas, and the understories of present stands are dominated by timothy. Some increase in Douglas-fir has occurred on upland areas.

Warren's notes suggest that extensive beaver activity had occurred at this site just prior to the 1920s. Remnants of beaver dams occur throughout this area. Note beaver cuttings in foreground of original.

PLATE 42

LOCATION: Lamar River valley looking south to Specimen Ridge (561.8 E, 4969.8 N; elev. 1,980 m).

PHOTOGRAPHERS   A. Nelson, 1898 (U. of Wyoming Western History Research Center collection).
D. B. Houston, July 10, 1970.

VEGETATIVE CHANGES: Interval of 72 years (camera points approximate).

Foreground shows relatively little change in the distribution of sagebrush or the mesic grassland type.

Middle ground shows relatively little change in the sagebrush grassland, with the exception of the replacement of a willow community by a mesic grassland on an old channel of the Lamar River. Remnants of the willow community (to the left of the photo) suggest that it was composed of species such as Geyer willow and mountain alder.

Background shows that coniferous forests on the north-facing slopes of Specimen Ridge have increased. Sagebrush grassland and aspen (arrow) on the lower slopes and xeric grasslands on the upper slopes and summit have declined. Aspen in the original photo appears to have contained a variety of size classes. Recent examination shows no successful reproduction of aspen and the occurrence of Douglas-fir, spruce, and lodgepole pine in the understory of aspen stands. One of the large trees in the aspen above the edge of the willow thicket in the original photo was a Douglas-fir (the tree is now dead) showing multiple fire scars.

The successional relationships between willow and grassland, coniferous forest and aspen, and coniferous forest and sagebrush grasslands are shown. The increase in conifers on the upper slopes and the top of Specimen Ridge has occurred on a bighorn sheep range.

PLATE 43

LOCATION: Druid Peak, view north across the Lamar River from Specimen Ridge (560.2 E, 4968.0 N; elev. 2,070 m).

PHOTOGRAPHERS: J. P. Iddings, ~ 1885 (USGS No. 331).
D. B. Houston, August 27, 1970.

VEGETATIVE CHANGES: Interval of 85 years (camera point probably 50–60 m higher in retake because of increase in conifers).

Foreground shows an increase in conifers . There has been erosion from the exposed areas, and one of the petrified logs present in the Iddings photo is gone.

Middle ground shows some changes in the channel of the Lamar River with consequent changes in the location of the small cottonwood and willow communities. An Idaho fescue–big sagebrush steppe dominates the valley bottom.

Background shows some increase in conifers on the south slopes of Druid Peak. Little change is detectable in the Idaho fescue and bluebunch wheatgrass steppe because of the quality of the original photo. Certain of the ridgetops and upper slopes in this area showed 60% or more bare ground in 1970. These same sites showed low densities of vegetation in the original (arrow, lower photo). The area of sparse trees on the left center of the original also suggests a considerable amount of bare ground, and it is in that condition at present. Aspen stands (arrow, upper photo) show a slight decrease in area. Small size of conifers and aspen suggest a recent fire in the original—which in turn suggests that less big sagebrush would have been present on the bunchgrass steppe.

PLATE 44

LOCATION: Soda Butte, view north up Soda Butte Creek (566.9 E, 4968.5 N; elev. 2,030 m).

PHOTOGRAPHERS: W. H. Jackson, 1871 (No. 307).
                 D. B. Houston, July 20, 1971.

VEGETATIVE CHANGES: Interval of 100 years (camera points approximate).

Foreground and *middle ground* show a willow and alder community on Soda Butte flood plain in original. Density of willow in background might be exaggerated because of angle of photo. Willow has declined in retake, and meadow vegetation consists of rushes, sedges, hairgrass, and reedgrass. (Note cast elk antlers in original.) Beavers had constructed an extensive series of ponds on the flood plain by 1900 that remained flooded until the early 1920s. Area at left is a sagebrush grassland showing disturbance along a trail. Other Jackson photos show a sagebrush steppe around Soda Butte on this upper terrace. The formerly bare, harsh-looking flood plain terrace is completely vegetated in retake. (''Soda Spring'' in foreground may have been excavated for purposes of photo.) Hay was cut in this area in the 1920s, and willows may have been removed.

Background shows little evidence of change in forest distribution except at right, where revegetation of a burned forest area has occurred.

PLATE 45

LOCATION: Reese Creek view southwest to Electric Peak (517.7 E, 4989.8 N; elev. 1580 m).

PHOTOGRAPHERS: Jack E. Haynes, May 13, 1941 (permission to use photo granted by Mrs. J. E. Haynes).
D. B. Houston, May 13, 1971.

VEGETATIVE CHANGES: Interval of 30 years (camera points similar).

Foreground shows change from a sagebrush grassland to a grassland dominated by bluebunch wheatgrass and needle-and-thread. An increase in grass cover is suggested, although grass densities may be underestimated in both photos because of the early spring dates.

Middle ground beyond fence shows comparatively little change in distribution of sagebrush.

Background shows little change in forest distribution.

Foreground and middle ground areas were added to the park in 1932. Cattle may have continued to graze the foreground thereafter but were progressively excluded. The middle ground was still grazed heavily by cattle from spring through fall in 1971 even though it is within the park. Both areas receive winter grazing by elk, mule deer, and smaller numbers of antelope and bighorn sheep. Other photos from 1871 in adjacent areas suggest that the foreground in retake may be closer to pristine conditions, and that the dense stands of big sagebrush in the upland sites of the original represent a disclimax condition resulting from livestock grazing and fire suppression.

PLATE 46

LOCATION: View southwest to Electric Peak from Gardiner–Stevens Creek Road (521.5 E, 4986.8 N; elev. 1,620 m).

PHOTOGRAPHERS: NPS Files No. 298, taken about 1893.
D. B. Houston, June 17, 1971.

VEGETATIVE CHANGES: Approximate interval of 78 years (camera points similar).

Foreground is a mudflow substrate with clay soils. Vegetation in swale is now greasewood with scattered big sage, bluegrasses, cheatgrass, and foxtail barley. Vegetation on slopes dominated by Sandberg bluegrass, Junegrass with scattered bluebunch wheatgrass, and phlox. A decline in shrubs, probably big sage, has occurred. An increase in grass cover is suggested, but annual variations in the appearance of grasses are spectacular at this elevation.

Background shows some increase in Douglas-fir on lower slopes.

A very complex site. The condition of the original suggests that the bentonite soils (note a ''pavement'' of small stones) have a low site potential. Terraces in the retake suggest heavy grazing by livestock until the area was added to the park in 1932. The area is also heavily used by native ungulates (elk, deer, pronghorn) and may have received unnaturally high concentrations of elk because of conditioned avoidance behavior along the boundary. A change in frequency of natural fires has probably also influenced vegetative changes.

PLATE 47

LOCATION: Gardiner cemetary, view west to Electric Peak (521.5 E, 4986.9 N; elev. 1,610 m).

PHOTOGRAPHERS: U.S. Forest Service, 1917 (Photo No. 32077A).
D. B. Houston, July 14, 1971.

VEGETATIVE CHANGES: Interval of 54 years (camera points similar).

Foreground shows a reduction in big sagebrush in the swale with present vegetation containing some greasewood, with saltbush, and spiny hopsage. Robust bluebunch wheatgrass occurs in swales with cheatgrass. Grassland beyond swale dominated by Junegrass and fringed sage. A decline in big sage has occurred in the next swale, but shrub cover is now dominated by spiny hopsage. Cheatgrass is dominant grass.

Middle ground shows some reduction in big sagebrush. Grazing trails present in the original are not so conspicuous in retake. Grasses are primarily Sandberg bluegrass, Junegrass with bluebunch wheatgrass, and cheatgrass in swales. Most of the vegetation in retake is inside two exclosures.

Background shows some increase in Douglas-fir forest.

A very complex site. The area was outside the park in 1917 (added in 1932) and was probably subjected to very intense grazing by livestock. The area is also a mudflow substrate with high component of clay in soils. Additionally, a conditioned avoidance behavior among elk may have caused unnaturally high winter concentrations along this boundary area.

PLATE 48

LOCATION: View northwest down the Rescue Creek trail across the Yellowstone River to the foothills of Sheep Mountain. Gardiner is visible below the quarry. (527.0 E, 4985,0 N; elev. 1,770 m).

PHOTOGRAPHERS: R. Smith, August 1918, USFS Neg. No. 39574A.
D. B. Houston, September 18, 1970.

VEGETATIVE CHANGES: Interval of 52 years (camera points similar).

Foreground shows a sagebrush grassland on the south-facing slope at right, a mesic grassland dominated by giant wildrye grass in the swale, and a xeric grassland dominated by bluebunch wheatgrass and associates on left. Scattered Douglas-fir and some Rocky Mountain juniper occur along the ridgetop. Major elk trails appear unchanged. There may have been an increase in the number of trails since 1918, but this might be due to differences in lighting, as there is a hint of additional trails in the original. Relatively little change is apparent in the vegetation. The vegetation on the ridgetop above the large outcrop was sparse in 1918 and remains so in the retake.

Background suggests little change in the sagebrush grassland communities. Some increase in conifers has occurred on the slopes of Sheep Mt. Vegetation on the bare-appearing Cretaceous deposits in both photos is primarily a ricegrass community with more than 80% bare ground, on a highly unstable substrate.

Little change has occurred in this area, which is 0.4 km from the north park boundary. The vegetation on the ridgetop in center foreground above horses had an understory of more than 60% bare ground in 1970, showing little change in 52 years. The sparse vegetation on the background slopes occurs on a harsh mudstone formation similar to Mt. Everts (Pl. 23).

PLATE 49

LOCATION: Yellowstone River, view North to Dome Mountain (513 E, 500.0 N; elev. 1,590 m).

PHOTOGRAPHERS: W. H. Jackson, 1871 (No. 207).
D. B. Houston, July 21, 1971.

VEGETATIVE CHANGES: Interval of 100 years (camera points approximate).

Foreground of original shows a bunchgrass–big sagebrush community in a swale that has been altered by road construction.

Middle ground. Characteristics of original are obscure, but it may also have been a sagebrush grassland; area is presently a pasture and hayfield.

Background shows an increase in Douglas-fir on upper Dome Mt. and increases in fir and Rocky Mountain juniper at lower elevations. Character of original grassland is not discernable.

The character of historical vegetation is shown, but the area has been altered by modern man.

PLATE 50

LOCATION: Cutler Lake, view south to Cinnabar Mountain (513.5 E, 4999.8 N; elev. 1,590 m)

PHOTOGRAPHERS: W. H. Jackson, 1871 (No. 209).
D. B. Houston, July 16, 1973.

VEGETATIVE CHANGES: Interval of 102 years (camera points moved 5 m south).

Foreground in original shows a bunchgrass community (probably bluebunch wheatgrass and needle-and-thread) with scattered big sagebrush. Winterfat and fringed sage also occur in original. Vegetation in retake was dominated by needle-and-thread, ricegrass, bluegrasses, and phlox.

Middle ground shows a bunchgrass–sagebrush community. Grasses at present were needle-and-thread, bluegrasses, and cheatgrass. Some increase in big sage and common rabbitbrush has occurred in retake. Middle ground shows evidence for very heavy grazing by livestock (note trail system across lake).

Background suggests an increase in Douglas-fir forest and in big sage.

PLATE 51

LOCATION: Devil's Slide, view west (517 E, 4993 N; elev. 1,590 m).

PHOTOGRAPHERS: W. H. Jackson, 1871 (No. 211).
D. B. Houston, July 16, 1973.

VEGETATIVE CHANGES: Interval of 102 years (camera points similar—the conspicuous rock in left foreground of original is the pile of rubble in retake).

Foreground and *middle ground* of original show a bunchgrass community, very probably bluebunch wheatgrass and needle-and-thread, with winterfat, and prickly pear. Scattered shrubs in middle ground are probably rabbitbrushes and big sagebrush. Grasses in retake were Junegrass, Sandberg's bluegrass, cheatgrass, some needlegrass, and bluebunch wheatgrass, with a marked increase in rabbitbrushes and big sagebrush.

Background suggests an increase in Douglas-fir and Rocky Mountain juniper.

The change in vegetation on this area, outside the present park boundaries, has probably been influenced by heavy livestock grazing for 90 or so years. The area is heavily grazed at present by cattle. A change in frequency of natural fires probably has contributed to observed changes. Mule deer also browse shrubs in this area during winter months.

FIGURE V.2.

Northern winter range showing approximate camera points of comparative photos. Locations are given for photos presented in this report (Pls. 22–51; ●) and those additional photos on file (○). Arrows (---→) show direction of views that were especially useful in estimating the amount of change of various vegetation types. Boundary line area of the park is shaded.

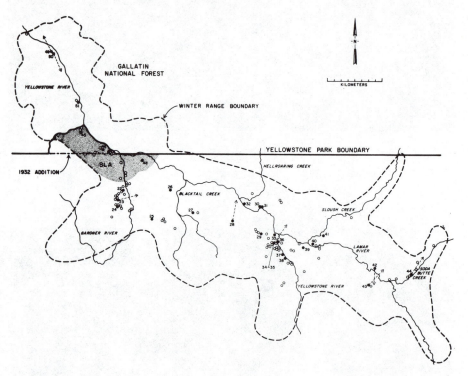

APPENDIX VI

Vegetation Measurements

Descriptive Measurements

Grasslands of the Northern Winter Range

Measurements at 41 sites and reconnaissance over eight years were used to describe the grassland vegetation on the northern winter range. Mueggler and Stewart (1980) provided both a useful perspective from which to interpret results of sampling and a nomenclature for grassland types. For convenience of discussion, I have separated measurements made on grassland types representative of large areas from measurements made on ridgetop and upper-slope sites that received heavy grazing by native ungulates. The appearance of these latter sites has long been of concern.

The combination of extensive reconnaissance, studies of past human activities, and maps of surficial geology (U.S.G.S. Scale 1:62,500) was used to divide the range into broad physiographic areas and vegetation types in preparation for descriptive sampling (e.g., Lamar valley floor—sagebrush grasslands on Pinedale till and mesic grasslands on ice-dammed lake deposits). A site within each area considered broadly representative in slope, exposure, soils, and composition was chosen for sampling (Fig. VI.1) using a Daubenmire (1959) canopy coverage transect ($\sim$ 80 m long with 40 sample plots). The sampled sites often had well-developed soils and received moderate ungulate grazing, some xeric grasslands excepted. Each site was photographed. A brief description of the soil and the frequency of ungulate pellet groups were also recorded. Areas disturbed by human activities (e.g., cultivation, extensive haycutting) and sites showing substantial invasion of exotic species (e.g., timothy in some swales) were not sampled. Plant communities on ridgetop and upper-slope sites with 60% or more bare ground also were sampled using Daubenmire plots (25–40 sample plots/transect). These sites were characterized by very heavy winter grazing, comparatively less-well-developed soils, and harsh microclimates (high winds, little snow accumulation, needle ice, frost heaving of soils, etc.).

FIGURE VI.1.

Northern winter range showing locations of 44 transects used to describe grassland vegetation. Numbers 1–27 sampled extensive grassland and shrub steppe types; numbers WM 1–5 sampled wet meadows; numbers I–IX sampled grasslands on ridgetops and upper slopes. Three sites sampled by Mueggler and Handl (MH) are also shown.

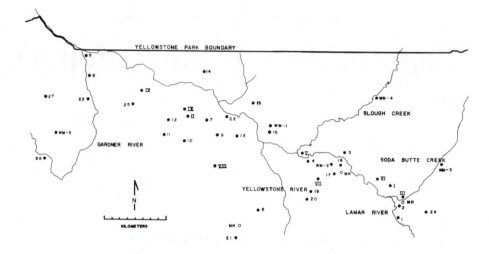

EXTENSIVE GRASSLANDS AND SHRUB GRASSLANDS

The 41 sample units were separated into a sagebrush grassland group, a wet meadow group, and mesic and xeric grassland groups. In most cases, the vegetation existing on the sampled sites appeared to represent potential climatic climax conditions (see below). Thus the term *association* (existing climax vegetation) also represented a *habitat type* (potential climax vegetation) as used by Mueggler and Stewart (1980), and the terms are treated here as synonyms. Throughout most of the text I wished to avoid the connotation of describing a potential vegetation and therefore used the term *association*.

Eight of nine sites sampled in the sagebrush group were identified as *big sagebrush/Idaho fescue* habitat type (ht) or association (Table VI.1). This is by far the most abundant sagebrush grassland on the area and occurs on sites with thin cobble soils to well-developed loams at higher elevations. Big sage dominates the shrub canopy and Idaho fescue is the most abundant grass. Total number of species and forb cover increased on lower slopes and at higher elevations to the point that a *big sage/Idaho fescue ht–sticky geranium phase* was recognized (Table VI.1). Most of these types received substantial winter grazing by native ungulates. There appeared to be little relationship between an index of grazing (pellet groups) and either total cover, cover of big sage, or number of plant species. Mueggler and Stewart also sampled a *big sage/Idaho fescue* site on the area (Fig. VI.1) (Handl pers. commun. to Despain 1973). A *big sage/bluebunch wheatgrass ht* was identified in the Gardner River Canyon (Table VI.1). Big sage at this particular site received considerable browsing from native ungulates and the shrub canopies were reduced in size. This habitat type occurs in small zones throughout the area on south or west slopes, often between a lower *big sage/Idaho fescue ht* and other grasslands on ridgetops and upper slopes. The type was heavily grazed in winter by ungulates. In addition to these major sage types, small

TABLE VI.1.
Canopy Cover and Frequency (CC/F) of Plant Taxa at Nine Sagebrush Grassland Sites[a]

TAXA	2	3	5	8	14	16	22	24	26
					SITES				
Bluebunch wheatgrass		8/63	1/10	31/98	13/60		1/18	7/60	3/18
Bearded wheatgrass			10/70					1/10	2/25
Junegrass	1/25	1/28	*/8	4/58	*/5	*/5	3/30	2/15	
Idaho fescue	35/93	14/73	18/78		32/78	71/100	37/95	38/98	34/13
Bluegrass	*/8		2/28					2/13	
Sandberg bluegrass	*/18	1/40	3/23	1/30			1/23	3/10	12/60
Western needlegrass					*/3	*/5			
Needle-and-thread					*/3	1/15			
Timber oatgrass					*/3	*/3			5/33
Sedges	1/28	1/15			*/3	*/8	*/5	*/10	
Other grasses	1		2	1	1	2		1	*
Total grasses	38	25	36	37	47	74	42	55	56
Yellow owl clover	1/38	*/3			*/5	*/5	*/15	*/3	
Lupine			5/40		*/3				
Silky lupine	14/93	3/28				10/55	2/30	9/50	2/8
Ballhead sandwort	1/45		*/5		*/3			*/5	
Sulfur buckwheat	3/30	1/10			1/8	9/35	1/5	7/40	3/25
Phlox	1/15				*/18	*/10	3/28	1/8	2/15
Hood's phlox	1/35			*/5			1/35		
Pussytoes	*/3	1/25		*/5					*/3
Yarrow			*/20	1/5	1/28	*/5		2/30	1/25
Sticky geranium			9/50		1/20				
Fleabane			1/10			1/15	*/15	1/10	2/25
Showy fleabane					3/33				

(continued)

355

TABLE VI.1. (Continued)

TAXA				Sites					
	2	3	5	8	14	16	22	24	26
Graceful cinquefoil			*/5					8/28	
Field chickweed			*/10		4/55			2/25	3/50
Arrowleaf balsamroot								1/10	
Other forbs	*	2	3	1	*	*	*	2	3
Total forbs	21	7	19	2	10	20	7	33	16
Big sagebrush	32/85	29/80	13/53	19/45	35/75	32/63	31/75	34/78	37/68
Fringed sagebrush				1/15					
Green rabbitbrush		1/10	2/18	2/8			1/18		
Rose		*/3							
Common snowberry								1/10	
Other shrubs		*							
Total shrubs	32	30	15	22	35	32	32	35	37
Mosses and soil lichens	2/25			3/18			6/45		
Total bare ground	2/16	15/23	3/10	16/50		1/18	4/23	2/10	1/8
Total plant species	14	16	27	15	22	17	16	24	18
Elk pellet groups	/25	/10		/15[b]	/28	/28	/18	/20	
Exposure/slope (%)	40	S/40	SE/25	W/35	W/10		L/0	SW/20	L/0
Parent material/soil[c]	4/2	1/3	2/1	5/4	1/2	1/2	1/3	3/1	1/2
Elevation (m)	2,040	2,070	2,320	1,710	2,200	2,040	1,830	2,440	2,350
Habitat type[b]	1	1	2	3	1	1	1	2	1

[a] Asterisks indicate species showing less than 1% canopy coverage.

[b] Also deer and bighorn pellets show a frequency of 18%.

[c] Parent material: 1, Pinedale glacial till; 2, Pinedale kame deposit sand and gravel; 3, Pinedale rubble veneer; 4, Pinedale outwash alluvium; 5, proglacial flood deposit—clays and gravel. Soils: 1, sandy loam; 2, sandy loam in gravel or stone matrix; 3, silt loam in gravel matrix; 4, clay loam in gravel.

[d] 1, *big sagebrush/Idaho fescue habitat type*; 2, *big sage/Idaho fescue–sticky geranium phase*; 3, *big sage/bluebunch wheatgrass ht.*

amounts of *silver sage/Idaho fescue ht* and a *low sage/Idaho fescue ht* (Mueggler and Stewart 1980) occurred on the winter range.

A consideration of species abundance and composition suggests that vegetation sampled by these transects represents examples of climatic climax plant communities. This interpretation would apply to most of the big sage communities on the area. Exceptions included sites where sagebrush has been greatly reduced or eliminated or where coniferous forests were invading *big sage/Idaho fescue* communities (discussed elsewhere). Fire suppression probably has resulted in a greater expression of these shrub steppes than would otherwise occur.

Five wet meadow sites were sampled on humic soils (Table VI.2). These highly productive sites were characterized by relatively few species and were dominated by sedges, mostly beaked or inflated sedge. Some types seemed related to the *tufted hairgrass/sedge ht* described by Mueggler and Stewart (1980), but evidence presented elsewhere showed changes in composition and distribution over time. This suggested that some of these sites were seral to forests and mesic grasslands. Species composition of wet meadows varied greatly, from those dominated by sedges and rushes to those with many species characteristic of mesic grasslands. Other small wet meadows with alkaline soils had considerable amounts of alkali-grass; still others that had been cut for hay now have a large component of timothy. Wet meadows received substantial winter grazing by elk and especially bison.

Eight of ten transects established in relatively more mesic grasslands were identi-

TABLE VI.2.
Canopy Cover and Frequency (CC/F) of Plant Taxa at Five Wet Meadow Sites[a]

Taxa	Sites				
	WM-1	WM-2	WM-3	WM-4	WM-5
Tufted hairgrass	25/88	1/23	*/25	7/28	
Bluejoint reedgrass	3/21			*/5	
Sedges (mostly beaked or inflated sedge)	35/85	96/100	95/100	87/100	95/100
Spikerush	9/43				
Other grasses	*	1	1	1	
Total grasses	72	98	96	95	95
Aster	3/38	*/10	*/3	1/8	
Cinquefoil	2/18	*/8			
Thick-leaf groundsel				2/13	
Onion				1/15	
Other forbs	1	2		1	
Total forbs	6	2	*	5	
Willow	1/5	*/13			
Total shrubs	1	*			
Total plant species (N)	13	9	5	9	1
Parent material/soil[a]	1/1	1/1	1/1	1/1	1/1
Elevation (m)	2040	2100	2100	2010	2230

[a] Asterisks indicate less than 1% canopy coverage.
[b] Parent materials: 1, fine-grained humic alluvium. Soils: 1, humic.

fied as *Idaho fescue/bearded wheatgrass ht* (Table VI.3, Fig. VI.2). These highly productive grasslands of great species diversity occurred on well-developed soils throughout the area. Idaho fescue in combinations with wheatgrasses and needlegrasses dominated the types. Forb cover and species abundance sometimes increased in swales and lower slopes, and an *Idaho fescue/bearded wheatgrass ht–sticky geranium phase* was recognized (Table VI.3). Occasionally forbs dominated in swales (Transect 25); sometimes this condition was associated with substantial burrowing by pocket gophers in the deep loam soils. Mueggler and Stewart sampled two additional *Idaho fescue/bearded wheatgrass* stands on the area (Handl pers. commun. to Despain 1973). Two other sites were considered to represent *Idaho fescue/Richardson's needlegrass ht* (Table VI.3). This type commonly occurred in swales throughout the area. These types received substantial winter grazing by native ungulates. Four transects did not fit well into established categories (Nos. 1, 10, 13, 18). This was usually because of a low amount of one key species, but the occurrence of other species suggested type affinities. Transect 1 is a good example. This luxuriant stand of Idaho fescue occurs on a sandy loam derived from an ice-dammed lake deposit. The type seems most closely related to the *Idaho fescue/bearded wheatgrass* type even though bearded wheatgrass did not occur on the transect. A consideration of species abundance and composition suggested that the "poor fit" of some sites into discrete categories was mainly an indication of the great diversity of grasslands and the occurrence of vegetative continua. Mueggler and Stewart (1980) also recognized great variation in types and found stands that could not be categorized easily. The sites sampled seemed representative of climatic climax grasslands. Exceptions included the periodic disturbance of some sites by gophers, but this was considered to represent a natural biotic influence.

Five of eight transects established in relatively more xeric grasslands were identified as *Idaho fescue/bluebunch wheatgrass ht* (Table VI.4). This was the most common xeric grassland on the area. Grasses dominated this vegetation, with bluebunch wheatgrass and Idaho fescue making up much of the cover. I found it useful to recognize a xeric phase of this type on upper slopes where bluebunch wheatgrass cover usually exceeded that of Idaho fescue and where Junegrass, green rabbitbrush, and phlox were relatively more abundant (Fig. VI.3). A *bluebunch wheatgrass/Sandberg bluegrass ht* occurred in small amounts throughout the area, often on gravelly soils of steep south slopes. Bluebunch wheatgrass usually dominated with Junegrass and Sandberg bluegrass. Shrub and forb cover was low. At 1,620-m elevation near the mouth of the Gardner River, a grassland occurred on a sandy soil that seemed most closely related to the *needle-and-thread/blue grama ht,* even though blue grama was not encountered on the transect. This type was limited in occurrence to the BLA and upstream to the Black Canyon of the Yellowstone River. Compared to communities sampled in the sagebrush and mesic grassland groups (Tables VI.1, VI.3), the xeric grasslands in Table VI.4 shared the similarities of more bare ground, thinner soils, harsher microclimates, and heavier winter and spring grazing by native ungulates. Vigor of grasses and cover of shrubs was suppressed on some sites because of this grazing. Despite these influences, the species composition and abundance suggested that the sampled xeric grasslands represented climatic climax plant communities. Exceptions include the most extreme sites (not included in Table VI.4) on the thinnest soils with the heaviest grazing. These sites are discussed below.

The grasslands and shrublands described here are characteristic of most of the unforested areas of the winter range in the park. They appear to represent good examples of climatic climax plant communities. It is impossible to sample all their

TABLE VI.3.
Canopy Cover and Frequency (CC/F) of Plant Taxa at 10 Mesic Grassland Sites

Taxa	\	\	\	\	Sites	\	\	\	\	\
	1	7	10	12	13	15	17	18	20	25
Bluebunch wheatgrass			1/13				1/3			
Bearded wheatgrass		2/13	1/18				2/15	*/18	1/13	1/18
Thick-spiked wheatgrass		*/28	1/20			*/3	*/3			
Junegrass	1/25	1/8	1/18			*/8	*/8	1/8		
Idaho fescue	61/100	41/90	58/100	8/58	34/95	60/100	39/100	47/95	51/98	18/48
Bluegrass	3/8			2/10	1/3	*/5	1/10	1/15	*/8	3/23
Wheeler's bluegrass		1/10	*/3				2/10		*/8	
Western needlegrass	1/25	8/33	6/35	*/5	2/8	*/8	6/25	*/3		2/13
Richardson's needlegrass				57/98	13/53			11/40	9/40	
Needle-and-thread						1/20				
Nodding brome	2/20	1/10		1/15	1/23	*/3	4/40	3/33	3/33	3/33
Fringed brome										1/15
Timber oatgrass			1/10	2/28	2/38	*/8	1/8	11/70	6/43	
Sedges	*/5	*/8	*/3	*	*	1/8	1/13	1/15	1/30	
Other grasses	*	*	*			*	*	*	*	1
Total grasses	68	56	68	70	53	63	57	75	69	29
Mountain dandelion	3/48		*/5	*/3	*/3	*/10		*/18		
Lupine										
Silky lupine	5/48	2/13	2/23		*/3	4/35	4/35	1/53		
Yarrow	1/40	1/35	1/43	*/3	*/15	*/13	1/28	1/18	1/43	5/53
Flax	*/8				2/13	*/10	*/3		*/3	
Graceful cinquefoil	1/5	3/30	*/3	1/5	3/33	5/23	16/83		13/88	14/65
Buckwheat						*/3		1/10		
Sulfur buckwheat	1/5	9/50	4/30	1/13	1/8		*/3			
Sticky geranium		3/23			11/78					3/13

(continued)

TABLE VI.3. (*Continued*)

Taxa	Sites									
	1	7	10	12	13	15	17	18	20	25
Field chickweed					*/10					2/15
Milk vetch		2/55	*/13		2/35					
Weedy milk vetch		*/3	*/10			1/23				
Fleabane		*/5			2/25			1/15	1/18	
Showy fleabane		1/33			2/38		2/45			
Prairiesmoke		*/3	*/3	13/83	*/3			3/25	*/13	
Elk thistle								1/18	4/50	1/10
Fireweed				*/5	*/3					1/5
Hall's groundsel								3/40		
Tall groundsel										1/13
Rocky Mountain helianthella										20/65
Western larkspur										2/8
Other forbs	3	2	1	1	*	1	2	3	*	*
Total forbs	14	23	9	17	23	12	25	14	19	49
Total bare ground	4/38	*/8	1/10			3/18	*/3			5/18
Total plant species (N)	19	23	23	16	22	24	28	22	22	22
Elk pellet groups	/13	/8	/30			/43	/13	/23	/23	/3
Exposure/slope (%)	L/0	NW/10	NW/15	L/0	E/15	W/12	N/12	N/5	L/0	E/10
Parent material/soil[b]	2/2	1/1	1/2	1/1	1/2	1/2	1/1	1/3	2/3	1/1
Elevation (m)	2040	2130	2320	2380	2100	2040	2130	2040	2320	2200
Habitat type[c]	1?	2	1?	3	2?	1	3?	3?	1	2

[a] Asterisks indicate less than 1% canopy coverage.

[b] Parent materials: 1, Pinedale glacial till; 2, Pinedale ice-dammed lake deposits—silt and sand. Soils: 1, deep loam; 2, deep sandy loam; 3, deep silt loam.

[c] 1, *Idaho fescue/bearded wheatgrass*; 2, *Idaho fescue/bearded wheatgrass—sticky geranium phase*; 3, *Idaho fescue/Richardson's needlegrass*. ?, poor fit in recognized habitat type (see text).

FIGURE VI.2.

An *Idaho fescue/bearded wheatgrass ht.* on a deep loam soil derived from a Pinedale ice-dammed lake deposit (Transect 20.)

variations. The transects describe seemingly discrete packages of vegetation; this is, of course, an abstraction from reality—vegetation types occur on the area as complex continua.

Despain (pers. commun. 1978) independently surveyed the grasslands on the northern range as part of a study to describe nonforested vegetation of the park. His results generally agree with those described here.

RIDGETOP AND STEEP-SLOPE GRASSLANDS

Measurements of composition and canopy cover for nine representative ridgetop and steep-slope grasslands are shown in Table VI.5. The vegetation was dominated by low densities of native species, and the number of plant species encountered was sometimes low. Frequency of ungulate pellet groups was often high. On heavier soils the composition might be considered a subclimax or a highly modified version of the *Idaho fescue/bluebunch wheatgrass ht.* Species composition, low densities of plants and litter, and large areas of bare ground at sites on steep south slopes with coarse soils were somewhat similar to pristine grasslands in central Idaho (Mueggler and Harris 1969).

Data presented elsewhere in this report suggested that such low-density vegetation occurred historically on these sites that are here called zootic climax vegetation. Autumn standing crop of herbage on six sites averaged 236 kg/ha air-dried weight

TABLE VI.4.
Canopy Cover and Frequency (CC/F) of Plant Taxa at Eight Xeric Grassland Sites[a]

Taxa	Sites							
	4	6	9	11	19	21	23	27
Bluebunch wheatgrass	*/5	3/33	37/98	30/90	27/98	12/78	18/95	30/93
Thick-spiked wheatgrass	*/18				*/3	*/8		
Junegrass	1/40	*/25	*/3	1/35	2/23	3/38	18/98	6/53
Idaho fescue	58/98			38/85	21/100	22/85		28/93
Sandberg bluegrass	*/8	*/3	1/43	*/3	6/63	1/20	1/25	*/8
Needle-and-thread	1/13	83/100						
Ricegrass		1/8						
Sedges	4/63		2/18	*/3	2/13	10/68	*/5	*/5
Other grasses	1	*				*		
Total grasses	65	48	40	69	59	48	37	64
Mountain dandelion								1/25
Lupine			1/10					
Silky lupine	10/95			5/50	2/10			7/33
Sulfur buckwheat	*/3		*/8	2/23	*/5	*/3		3/18
Hood's phlox	1/28				2/38			
Many-flowered phlox					4/38	1/23		1/13
Pussytoes	*/13		*/3	*/13	*/5	2/23		*/5
Prickly pear		2/8						
Field chickweed			1/45					
Fleabane			1/10					5/60

	1	2	3	4	5	6	7	8
Showy fleabane						5/38		6/43
Weedy milk vetch		*/10	1/40	12/60	2/35	6/60		
Prairiesmoke							3/60	
Goldenweed		*		1	*	*		*
Other forbs	2	*	2	1	*	*	2	*
Total forbs	12	2	6	10	21	15	5	23
Fringed sagebrush	2/15	1/8	1/13			3/53		*/3
Green rabbitbrush	4/30				10/48	2/20	1/10	4/23
Winterfat		4/30			*		*/8	
Other shrubs		1	2					
Total shrubs	2	5	2		10	5	1	4
Mosses and soil lichens				2/10	2/10	3/23		
Total bare ground	4/40	23/93	26/78	5/30	7/35	1/8	29/10	6/38
Total plant species (N)	13	11	22	12	17	15	12	19
Elk pellet groups	/50[b]	/10[b]	/25	/25	/48	/28	/10[b]	/25
Exposure/slope (%)	L/0	L/0	W/70	L/0	W/29	W/28	W/5	S/25
Parent material/soil[c]	2/1	3/1	4/2	1/4	1/3	5/1	2/5	5/2
Elevation (m)	1950	1620	2320	2100	2380	2620	1890	2530
Habitat type[d]	1?	2?[e]	3	1a	1a	1	3	1a

[a] Asterisks indicate less than 1% canopy coverage.

[b] Bison droppings had a frequency of 3 on Site 4; deer, pronghorn, and bighorn had a combined frequency of 60 on Site 6 and 5 on Site 23.

[c] Parent material: 1, Pinedale glacial till; 2, Pinedale kame deposit sand and gravel; 3, alluvium; 4, talus deposit; 5, Pinedale rubble veneer. Soils: 1, sandy loam; 2, sandy loam in gravel matrix; 3, silt loam in gravel matrix; 4, clay loam; 5, clay loam in gravel matrix.

[d] 1, Idaho fescue/bluebunch wheatgrass; 1a, a xeric phase where bluebunch wheatgrass cover exceeded Idaho fescue and where substantial cover of green rabbitbrush and phlox was often present; 2, needle-and-thread/blue grama; 3, bluebunch wheatgrass/Sandberg bluegrass.

[e] Blue grama not encountered on transect but present in the immediate area.

FIGURE VI.3.
An example of the *Idaho fescue/bluebunch wheatgrass ht.* – xeric phase (Transect 19.)

(range, 144–368) in 1970; 180 kg/ha (101–213) in 1971. Measurements in this appendix that showed the effects of precipitation on production suggest that 40–60 kg/ha might occur on such sites during a drought. Buechner (1960) and Oldemeyer (1966) provided additional samples of vegetation characteristic of some ridgetop sites.

In addition to heavy winter foraging and trampling by ungulates, these windswept ridgetops and steep south slopes represented extremely harsh microclimates for plant communities. These sites were often snow free in winter, and alternate freezing and thawing subjected sites to frost upheaval (Kittams 1950:11). Patten (unpubl.) found that the average maximum summer soil temperatures on upper slopes on the Gallatin elk winter range were 3–9°C higher than adjacent sagebrush grassland sites. Winter minimum soil temperatures were 2–9°C colder on exposed ridgetop and slope sites. Patten also characterized soils on these sites as comparatively shallow, with high bulk density, low water holding capacity, higher pH, lower nitrogen and potassium, and less humus or decaying matter when compared to adjacent sites.

GRASSLANDS IN THE BOUNDARY LINE AREA

The grasslands of the BLA added to the park in 1932 were such an enigma that some quantitative measurements were necessary to understand the elk, livestock, and soil interrelationships (Table VI.6). Sites I and II were on similar soils and received winter grazing by elk, pronghorn, and mule deer (see Pl. 45, Appendix V). Site II was an inholding (private land) within the park boundaries that received heavy spring and

TABLE VI.5.
Canopy Cover and Frequency (CC/F) of Plant Taxa on Nine Selected Zootic Climax Sites[a]

Taxa					Sites				
	I	II	III	IV	V	VI	VII	VIII	IX
Bluebunch wheatgrass	5/68	15/64	1/12	9/64	12/80	2/8		19/93	4/65
Thick-spiked wheatgrass			5/60			4/12			
Idaho fescue	5/80								5/55
Junegrass				*/4	14/100	15/80	6/76		10/90
Sandberg bluegrass	4/76			*/12	4/76		14/80		2/58
Inland bluegrass	*/16							1/18	
Bluegrass						3/6			
Ricegrass		8/40	1/24	2/28	1/24				
Idaho fescue	9/100					10/70	6/60		
Other grasses	2		2			3			
Total grasses	25	23	9	12	31	37	26	20	21
Phlox	6/72					4/10		*/5	3/60
Pussytoes	*/12						10/44		*/8
Goldenweed	2/28		*/4		22/92				2/10
Milk vetch	3/44			6/32	*/16			*/13	
Fleabane	2/44		*/8	1/28					
Cutleaf fleabane								*/5	1/43
Rockcress	*/20								
Onion	*/8								

(continued)

TABLE VI.5. (*Continued*)

Taxa					Sites				
	I	II	III	IV	V	VI	VII	VIII	IX
Groundsel	1/32								
Toadflax			7/80				*/16	*/3	
Field chickweed			9/72	*/4	*/4			2/35	*
Other forbs	5	2	12	2		2	3	3	
Total forbs	19	2	28	9	22	6	13	6	6
Fringed sagebrush	*/12	2/8	5/56	2/16	4/44				
Green rabbitbrush						1/16			
Serviceberry	*/4							1/13	1/28
Other shrubs	*		1	5	1/8		2	*	*
Total shrubs		2	6	7	5	1	2	1	1
Total plant species (N)	25	8	18	15	14	11	20	15	17
Total bare ground[b]	64	70	67	71	56	64	60	72	58
Pellet groups	/52	/44	/12	/32	/12	/40	/44	/13	/60
Exposure/slope (%)	S/60	S/100	S/100	S/90	W/65	N/30	N/30	S/70	N/5
Soil[c]	1	2	3	3	2	1	1	2	2

[a] Measured and calculated using Daubenmire (1959) with 25–40 plots/transect. Asterisks indicate less than 1% canopy coverage.
[b] A separate estimate made; therefore, total vegetation plus bareground sometimes does not equal 100.
[c] Clay loam (1), loam in gravels (2), sandy loam (3).

TABLE VI.6.
Canopy Cover and Frequency (CC/F) of Plant Taxa on Ridgetop Grasslands of Different Types in the BLA[a]

Taxa	Sites[b]			
	I	II	III	IV
Bluebunch wheatgrass	19/90	5/57	*/3	9/37
Junegrass	12/90	15/80	15/93	9/80
Sandberg bluegrass	1/37	2/30	2/70	3/67
Needle-and-thread	2/13			23/80
Ricegrass			*/13	
Foxtail barley			1/33	
Cheatgrass	*/3			*/3
Other grasses	*		*	
Total grasses	34	22	19	44
Fleabane	*/17			*/10
Phlox	*/20	*/17		*/7
Pussytoes	*/7	*/3	*/3	*/10
Prickly pear	1/3	2/10		*/3
Aster			11/73	
Other forbs		*		
Total forbs	2	3	12	2
Big sagebrush	*/3	25/73		
Fringed sagebrush	9/70	1/23	8/53	8/87
Saltbush			1/17	
Total shrubs	9	26	9	8
Soil lichens		*	6/23	*/13
Bare ground[c]	15	33	47	18
Litter	17	3	*	15

[a] Asterisks indicate less than 1% canopy coverage.
[b] Sites and treatment: Each transect had 30 sample plots; technique followed Daubenmire (1959). I. Alluvial deposit: level; winter grazing by elk, deer, pronghorn; no livestock grazing since 1930s. II. Alluvial deposit: level; winter grazing by elk, deer, pronghorn; heavy spring and summer livestock grazing. III. Mudflow: level; winter grazing by elk, deer, pronghorn; no livestock since 1930s. IV. Alluvial deposit: level; adjacent to mudflow; grazing history same as III.
[c] Separate estimates, totals may exceed 100.

summer grazing by cattle through 1972. The canopy cover and frequency (CC/F) of big sagebrush were much greater at site II, and the CC/F of bluebunch wheatgrass and of total grasses was lower. Additionally, bluebunch wheatgrass showed 50% of 64 plants ≥ 3 cm diameter at site I. Wheatgrass mortality apparently was higher at site II, with only 8% of 36 plants ≥ 3 cm. I attributed these differences to a long history of heavy grazing by cattle during the spring and summer. These transects and Pl. 45 provided a test of the effects of grazing by native ungulates and livestock in the BLA where the decrease in big sagebrush has been of concern. These data showed that with the present climate and reduced frequency of natural fires, big sagebrush could withstand browsing by native ungulates on slopes so long as the native grasses were heavily grazed by livestock. Sagebrush decreased on upland sites grazed only by native ungulates when competition from vigorous native grasses increased. Similar changes in big sagebrush apparently also have occurred outside the park in the Little Trail Creek area.

The vegetation on a ridgetop mudflow (site III) was compared to an alluvial substrate that was immediately adjacent (site IV) and that had a similar grazing history. The CC/F of grasses was much higher on the alluvial deposits and the amount of bare ground was much lower. Mudflows supported more forbs and Junegrass. Soil lichens were common on mudflows. Some physical and chemical characteristics of mudflow and alluvial soils at the sites of vegetation measurements are compared in Table VI.7. The heavy clay soils of mudflows were derived from parent material described as "fragments of shale, sandstone, basalt, and volcanic breccia in a plastic bentonitic clay matrix" (Waldrop and Hyden 1963). Soils derived from alluvial parent materials were considered to be fine loam over sandy or sandy skeletal (Brownfield pers. commun. 1973). The permeability, organic nitrogen, and phosphorus levels were lower in clay soils. Clay soils contained more water than alluvial soils, but measurements showed much lower densities of vegetation and observations showed earlier dessication and curing of vegetation on clays, indicating that water was less available. This also was indicated by the comparatively high amounts of water in clay soils long after vegetation growth had ceased. Clay soils are especially harsh habitats in more arid regions (Walter 1973:99). Additionally, clay soils often were covered with a pavement of small stones, A horizons were still present, and small stones were virtually absent from the soil profile. Surface erosion doubtless occurs from these mudlfows, but these pavements may have resulted from movement of stones upward through the profile with alternate freezing and thawing (an interpretation suggested by D. G. Despain; see also Bales and Péwé 1979). These data and the comparative photos showing luxurious stands of climax grasses on alluvial soils and impoverished-appearing stands on adjacent mudflows suggested that differences in vegetation between these sites resulted from soil characteristics that were largely inherent. They did not clearly support the interpretation of range deterioration due to winter grazing of native ungulates.

ADDITIONAL DESCRIPTIVE MEASUREMENTS

Buechner (1960) sampled vegetation on areas of the winter range used by bighorn. The description of the sites (Buechner 1960:133) and the vegetation (Buechner, unpubl., Table 43, Document No. 6145, ADF Auxiliary Publication Project, Library of Congress) suggested that samples were from harsh ridgetop and upper-slope sites that were grazed heavily by ungulates and comparable to those referred to as zootic climax sites in this paper. Oldemeyer (1966) also described vegetation on heavily used ridgetop and upper-slope bighorn areas. These writers generally viewed the vegetation of these sites as having retrogressed from a former climax condition. An 11-day range site and condition survey of the vegetation was conducted in 1963 using criteria developed for domestic livestock (Soil Conservation Service 1963). The assumptions (e.g., the presence of big sagebrush in grasslands was always interpreted as an unnatural retrogressed condition due to grazing) and the approach used were appropriate for assessing the conditions of a livestock range but seemed inappropriate for native ungulates in a national park.

Measurements Repeated Over Time

Vegetation measurements on the northern winter range for 1930–78 are compiled and compared to indices of climate and ungulate grazing. Measurements that used ex-

TABLE VI.7.
Characteristics of Soils from Mudflows and Alluvial Deposits in the BLA

SITE	SOIL CLASSIFICATION	HORIZONS SAMPLED	PERCENT Sand	PERCENT Silt	PERCENT Clay	P[a]	N[b]	PERM.[c]	SOIL MOISTURE (%) 1/3 A	SOIL MOISTURE (%) 15A	Weeks 1	Weeks 5	Weeks 10
1. Mudflows	Borollic haplargids[d]	A	6	35	59	12	67	.08	37.8	16.1	34[e]	19	17
		B	12	36	52	11	54	.09	41.7	18.2			
2. Mudflows	Borollic haplargids	A	34	25	41	8	76	.13	31.3	14.5	30	25	18
		B	45	20	35	1	58	.17	26.8	13.1			
3. Alluvial deposits	Borollic camborthids	A	45	29	26	28	105	.25	10.2	5.3	14	8	5
		B	45	31	24	2	65	.28	21.1	11.0			
4. Alluvial deposits	Borollic camborthids	A	45	31	24	34	94	.30	13.9	7.3	11	9	4
		B	40	38	22	5	67	.33	21.6	11.3			

[a]ppm
[b]Organic N (kg/ha).
[c]Permeability (cm/hour).
[d]Tentative classification (S. Brownfield, Soil Conserv. Serv.).
[e]Soil moisture at ca. 10 cm on 5/9, 6/8, and 7/13/73.

closures all compared grazing with no grazing by native ungulates. Studies without exclosure comparisons are described below as being on the open range. Measurements generally are discussed in chronological order by category. Those sample units located in the BLA are usually discussed separately. Terms used to describe quantitative attributes of vegetation generally followed the National Academy of Science (1962). Many of the early samples were recorded in English units of measurement—all are converted here to metric forms.

It was necessary to examine the relationships of these measurements to climate and ungulate grazing. Barmore (1975) reviewed the conflicting results from studies that attempted to correlate climatic measurements with some attribute of plant communities. No consistent relationships to the usually available climatic information were apparent. Several indices of climate from 1930 to 1978 are shown in Fig. VI.4. These included precipitation for the October–September water year at Mammoth Hot Springs as the departure from the period mean of 40.6 cm. The Mammoth data were used because they were more complete than other stations on the winter range. The mean monthly Palmer drought index (PDI; Palmer 1965) for May–September periods was also used to summarize growing conditions. Some extremely severe drought conditions were obscured by using the mean values. PDIs below −3.00 indicate severe drought (Palmer 1965:28); some monthly values in the 1934–37 growing seasons were less than −5.00!

In addition to the precipitation measurements in Fig. VI.4, recall that a conspicuous decrease in frequency of large-scale precipitation (i.e., ≥ 1.27 cm/day) occurred

FIGURE VI.4.

Water year precipitation for Mammoth Hot Springs shown as centimeters of departure from the 1930–78 mean. A tree ring index (--o--) is shown as the departure from the mean index of 100. The mean monthly Palmer drought index (–●–) for May–September periods at Mammoth Hot Springs is also shown.

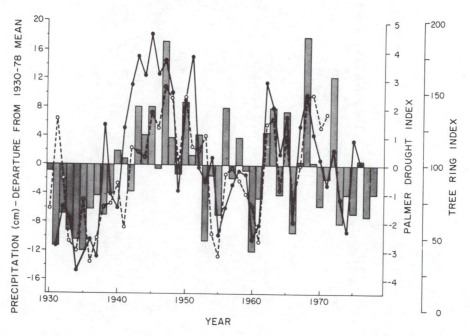

from 1946 to 1954 (see climatic trends Chap. 8). A comparison of relative widths of annual growth rings of Douglas-fir trees ("tree ring index," TRI) also was used to reflect climatic variation. The sampling and computations of the TRI and its interpretation are discussed by Stockton (1973). Trees were sampled from a climatically sensitive site between Mammoth Hot Springs and Gardiner at 1,800 m. Stockton determined that about 68% of the variance in ring widths could be attributed to climatic variations. The seasonal climatic conditions necessary for maximum ring growth included a wet (more important), cool (less important—these descriptions are based upon departures from normals) July and August the year before a specific ring was developed, followed by a moist, cool September and October, a wet or moist and warm January–March, a cool, moist April–June, and a normal July. The value of the TRI to this study is that it is "output" from living organisms that is, in part, an integrated expression of climatic "input." Certainly the herbaceous plant species measured on sample units would respond to somewhat different climatic inputs, would integrate these differently, and would show different lag times to fluctuations in climate. Also, the TRI responds to other inputs, e.g., insect defoliation. A precise correlation between the TRI and measurements of basal area of perennial grasses, for example, should not be expected.

In general, these various indices suggest extremely poor growing conditions during most of the 1930s, very good conditions during the 1940s, variably poor conditions during the 1950s, and variable, but mostly good conditions during the 1960s into the 1970s.

The calculated winter elk numbers (Fig. 3.2) were used to represent general trends over time. As discussed below, numbers can be a deceptive index of grazing intensities because some range areas were heavily grazed even with low elk numbers; others were lightly grazed at high numbers.

Herbaceous Vegetation

Standing Crop: Open Range, 1935–63

The autumn standing crop of herbaceous vegetation on the northern range was sampled by clipping 4–15 quadrats at the end of the growing seasons from 1935 to 1950 (Table VI.8). Fourteen quadrats were established on "representative areas" of native bunchgrass communities in 1935 (Grimm 1936), with an additional quadrat (No. 15) established on a flood plain sedge meadow in 1937. Photos of the plots showed most of them to be on upper-slope or ridgetop sites (Gammill 1939b). Most quadrats contained 9.3 m^2 (100 ft^2). Contiguous quadrats were clipped on alternate years to avoid repeated annual clipping of the same plants. Four quadrats were located in the BLA. The original purpose of the quadrats seems to have been to establish the variation in annual standing crop for calculations of carrying capacity for the northern elk herd. These attempts were abandoned when the number of other recognized variables became formidable, but the plots were of interest nonetheless.

Standing crop on the 14 quadrats showed significant annual variation [analysis of variance (ANOVA), F = 14.56] from 1935 to 1947. Autumn standing crop on 10 quadrats on the main winter range for 1935–47 averaged about 750 kg/ha and ranged from about 360 kg/ha during the most severe part of the drought to about 1,200 kg/ha. Standing crop on the sedge meadow averaged about 4,700 kg/ha and ranged from

TABLE VI.8.
Autumn Standing Crop of Herbage, 1935–50

VEGETATION CLASS	HERBAGE (KG/HA, AIR-DRIED WT., MEAN + SE)									
	1935	1936	1937	1938	1939	1940	1941	1947	1949	1950
Bunchgrass steppe 10 quads	467 ± 69	356 ± 82[a]	583 ± 94	964 ± 148	706 ± 133[a]	893 ± 118	1,200 ± 148	855 ± 166	166 ± 10[b]	445 ± 25[b]
Bunchgrass steppe BLA 4 quads	363 ± 49	141 ± 12[a]	447 ± 76[a]	474 ± 49	578 ± 108[c]	1,152 ± 632[c]	731 ± 96[c]	628 ± 118	296 ± 59[b]	554 ± 225[b]
Sedge meadow			3,750	4,304	4,574	4,994	5,950	4,779		

[a] Grasshoppers reduced standing crop on one–two quadrats.
[b] Only two quadrats.
[c] Includes substantial weights of *Salsola kali* on one plot.

372

about 3,750 to 8,950 kg/ha for 1937–47. Combined standing crop from the four quadrats in the BLA, 1935–47, showed the greatest variation and averaged about 540 kg/ha with a range of 130–1,150. Part of the variation in this area reflected the variable occurrence of annual species; part probably reflected range improvement following removal of livestock.

Annual variation was attributed primarily to differences in weather during the growing season (see Appendix VII), which was especially unfavorable during the drought of the mid-1930s and which became increasingly favorable in the early 1940s. Standing crop was tested for association with water year precipitation, PDI, and elk numbers in multiple-regression models. Standing crop was also tested for correlation with the TRI. Complex models that tested for interaction or lag effects (e.g., elk numbers for two winters prior to herbage production or precipitation for the two prior years) usually did not improve simpler models. Standing crop on the 10 quadrats from 1935 to 1947 was positively associated with water year precipitation ($r^2 = .89$, P $< .001$), as was production on the sedge meadow ($r^2 = .85$, P $< .005$). Standing crop on the four quadrats in the BLA was weakly associated with water year precipitation ($r^2 = .49$, P $< .10$). Associations between standing crop and the PDI and TRI were low and not significant (e.g., regression of production from the 10 quadrats on PDI gave $r^2 = .43$, P $< .10$). Elk numbers did not improve any model significantly, suggesting that much of the variation in crop was not associated with elk population size. (Models using these same independent variables are used below to test associations with other early vegetation measurements. Only the strongest associations are reported hereafter.) Changes in autumn standing crop of the magnitude shown here appear to be common in grasslands over drought periods (Blaisdell 1958, Passey et al. 1964).

Kittams (1950–58) assessed relative autumn standing crop of herbaceous vegetation from 1949 to 1957 by using several series of photos taken at established photo points (see below). Many plots were on ridgetop and upper-slope sites. This approach was more subjective than clipping studies but afforded wider coverage. Kittams considered overall production of herbaceous vegetation to be especially poor in 1949; especially good in 1950, 1956, and 1957. These estimates continued to show wide annual variation in standing crop, as well as variations at different elevations on the winter range. Again, much of this variation can probably be attributed to growing conditions. Bergstrom (1964) reported autumn standing crops of 1,021; 3,153; 3,213 kg/ha (air dry weight) for an Idaho fescue grassland on deep soils in the Lamar Valley for 1961, 1962, and 1963, respectively. These differences also seemed to be related to growing conditions, as precipitation, PDI, and TRI were all below average in 1961 and above average in 1962 and 1963 (Fig. VI.4).

Exclosure Studies: m² Quadrats, 1930–40

Fifteen small (~ 6 m × 6 m) ungulate exclosures were established on herbaceous vegetation from 1930 to 1936 (5 in 1930, 7 in 1934, 2 in 1935, 1 in 1936). Paired square-meter quadrats were established inside and outside the exclosures in an attempt to measure plant succession in relation to climate and ungulate grazing. The basal area of grasses and forbs and crown area of shrubs were charted from 1930 to 1940. Two to four exclosures were located in the BLA. All are used in this analysis, but one straddled the 1932 boundary addition and another was located on a clay substrate adjacent to an ungulate mineral lick—both were of questionable relevance to overall conditions. No measurements ever were made in 2 of the 11 remaining exclosures located away from the BLA, data for another have been lost, and I excluded 2 more as being wholly unrepresentative of the range (in pastures used by horses and bison). This left six pairs of quadrats available for analysis (three measured 1930–40; two, 1935–40; one, 1937–40).

Analyses were difficult, because of design problems and sampling errors. Some errors in species identification occurred throughout the study (these were detected by comparing locations of characteristically shaped plants over time and were partly the result of difficult plant identification under drought conditions). Such errors were frequent enough from 1930 to 1933 that only total area measurements (basal area plus crown area) were potentially useful. However, sometime between 1930 and 1935 definitions of basal area were changed; measurements for 1930–33 appear to have overestimated area. The season in which measurements were made changed from late spring or early summer to late summer after about 1935. The data suggested that some initial differences in vegetation occurred between quadrat pairs that persisted throughout the study. This probably resulted from subjective selection of quadrat sites.

Measurements of three to six paired quadrats on the main winter range spanned the drought of the 1930s (Table VI.9). From 1930 to 1936, the vegetation of both protected and grazed quadrats generally showed decreases in mean total area (the amount of the decrease is distorted, because measurement methods changed after 1933). Perennial grass and forbs decreased from 1935 to 1936. This retrogressive succession reversed and seemed to be associated with increased precipitation (Fig. VI.4). Succession proceeded toward more climax conditions in both protected and unprotected quadrats. This is best illustrated by two species of perennial grasses important in climax communities. Total area of bluebunch wheatgrass on five quadrats was about 5, 3, 8, and 14 dm^2 on outside quadrats in 1935, 1936, 1937, and 1940, respectively, and 2, 2, 5, and 9 on inside quadrats. Regressions suggested significant positive association of grass area with water year precipitation for both inside ($r^2 = .95$, P $< .025$) and outside quadrats ($r^2 = .96$, P $< .025$). Idaho fescue showed about 7, 6, 14, and 32 dm^2 on outside quadrats; and 37, 29, 23, and 72 dm^2 on inside quadrats for these same years. Regression showed a significant positive association of area with PDI on inside ($r^2 = .94$, P $< .05$) but not outside quadrats ($r^2 = .83$, P $< .10$). (Note also that what may have been partly inherent differences in basal area of grasses between inside and outside quadrats persisted throughout this period.) Basal area of grasses doubled by 1940 after the 1936 lows. The quadrats in the BLA showed similar trends in mean total area except that in some cases the decreases continued through 1937 (Table VI.9).

Differences between grazed and protected quadrats in mean total area of all vegetation usually were 1–3 dm^2 but up to 8 dm^2 in 1940. This was due largely to greater forb area in protected plots and to an apparently temporary increase in shrub area (Table VI.9). Similar differences in mean basal area of perennial grasses were often 1 or 2 dm^2 up to 3 or 4 dm^2.

These differences might have been attributed to the biotic effects of ungulate grazing (plus some unknown but inherent differences in plot selection) if it were not for other influences that invalidate this interpretation. Observations by Grimm and Kittams (Appendix VII) showed that these small exclosures, in addition to eliminating ungulate grazing, also changed microclimates by altering the interception of precipitation. Effects of these differences in moisture interception still can be observed. For example, in 1971 the exclosure on Hellroaring slope, established in 1935, showed about 100%

TABLE VI.9.
Plant Area on Protected and Grazed Square-Meter Quadrats, 1930–40

Vegetation	1930		1932		1933		1935		1936		1937		1940	
	Out[a]	In	Out	In	Out	In	Out	In	Out	In	Out	In	Out	In
Excluding BLA[b]														
Mean perennial grass							12.0	13.1	8.2	8.6	9.4	10.1	17.3	19.9
Mean forbs							2.0	4.3	1.6	2.9	3.6	2.1	9.2	14.1
Mean shrubs							1.2	1.4	0.7	2.7	1.0	2.8	2.3	1.5
Mean total area[c]	28.2	32.1	25.8	32.5	28.7	26.2	17.0	19.2	10.6	14.2	14.2	15.1	29.4	35.6
BLA Only[d]														
Mean perennial grass							10.1	12.7	5.4	6.6	6.3	7.6	12.4	15.6
Mean forbs							0.9	2.4	0.5	0.7	0.3	1.6	0.7	7.1
Mean shrubs							1.7	0.7	1.8	1.3	1.2	1.3	4.3	1.3
Mean total area[c]	21.6	18.7	14.8	24.1	15.4	26.3	13.9	18.4	7.7	9.5	7.8	10.6	17.4	24.8

[a] dm² basal area for grasses and forbs, crown area of shrubs, out = grazed, in = protected.
[b] Mean for three pairs quadrats for 1930–33; five pairs, 1935–36; six pairs, 1937–40.
[c] Includes unknown species, totals overestimated 1930–33 (see text).
[d] Two pairs quads, 1930–33; four pairs, 1935–40.

canopy coverage for vegetation with total perennial grasses at 72% and Idaho fescue at 70% with a frequency of 100%. An outside transect showed corresponding values of 80, 56, and 41% canopy cover, respectively, and 100% frequency. Vegetation characteristic of the exclosure extended outside for about 1 m on the lee side. Similar conditions occurred at other exclosure sites. Finally, some of the grazed plots were located too close to the exclosure fence and exaggerated the grazing influence by attracting animals to the fences for rubbing, etc. Daubenmire (1940) has discussed some of these and other exclosure effects.

Design errors (no initial measurements of plots, effects of exclosures on microclimate and grazing) and sampling or mechanical errors (plants misidentified or unidentified, changed criteria for basal area, etc.) preclude more detailed analysis. Some of these difficulties were recognized at the time of the earlier studies and led to abandonment of the plots. The futility of extrapolating measures of plant succession on these few plots—which required considerable manhours to measure and tabulate—to an area as large and diverse as the northern range was also appreciated. The declines in area of vegetation, with retrogressive succession, and subsequent recoveries on grazed and ungrazed areas were probably associated with annual growing conditions. Similar findings were reported on other grasslands during and after the drought of the 1930s (Weaver et al. 1936, 1940, Robertson 1939, Ellison and Woolfolk 1937, Pechanec et al. 1937).

SQUARE-FOOT-DENSITY TRANSECTS: OPEN RANGE, 1938–43

Results from measuring 11 square-foot-density transects (Stewart and Hutchings 1936) from 1938 to 1943 are shown in Table VI.10. This range technique involved estimating foliage area (National Academy of Sciences 1962) in square feet by species on a transect composed of 10 circular plots each 100 ft² (9.3 m²) in area. This provided somewhat lower estimates of plant cover than Daubenmire's (1959) canopy coverage. Transects were established on native grasslands, often extending for several miles; the species recorded show that the transects crossed a variety of different plant communities. The starting point of each transect was the same between years, but individual sample plots were located by pacing (65 or 440 paces between plots) along a designated compass bearing. A comparison of perennial shrub species encountered suggested that the location of individual plots varied considerably from year to year. The technique itself provides a fairly subjective estimate that could vary substantially among observers (National Academy of Sciences 1962). Four transects were in the BLA; the others were located between Blacktail Creek and Rose Creek (Table VI.10).

The average cover of perennial grasses and total cover generally increased from 1938 to 1943, with largest increases between 1939 and 1941. Shrub and forb cover showed either no change, or minor increases, followed by a decrease in 1943 (Table VI.10). Parallel changes generally occurred in the BLA and other range areas. The increase in total plant cover was statistically significant on the combined 11 transects for 1938, 1939, and 1943 (ANOVA Random Blocks F = 10.49) and on 6 transects for 1938, 1939, 1941, and 1943 (F = 11.74) (data were grouped this way because 5 transects had incomplete data for 1941). The changes appeared to have been due mostly to the increased cover of perennial grasses. R. Grimm made measurements in 1938 and 1943 (in conjunction with W. McDougall); W. Gammill made those of 1939 and 1941. It seems unlikely that changes in cover could be attributed entirely to differences among observers. The design of this study and limitations in the technique

TABLE VI.10.
Plant Cover on 11 Square-Foot-Density Transects, 1938–43

Vegetation Class	Plant Cover (dm², mean + SE[a])			
	1938	*1939*	*1941*	*1943*
Excludes BLA[b]				
Perennial grasses	864 ± 87	687 ± 32	1,012 ± 172	1,086 ± 49
Forbs	204 ± 33	242 ± 32	390 ± 184	242 ± 17
Shrubs	186 ± 23	158 ± 33	158 ± 60	195 ± 49
Total cover[c]	1,254 ± 129	1,086 ± 80	1,560 ± 296	1,524 ± 40
BLA only[d]				
Perennial grasses	632 ± 91	613 ± 96	929 ± 72	1,106 ± 66
Forbs	18 ± 8	46 ± 12	120 ± 49	84 ± 28
Shrubs	186 ± 20	269 ± 22	288 ± 32	130 ± 36
Total cover	854 ± 72	938 ± 94	1,366 ± 99	1,477 ± 192

[a] Standard error.
[b] Seven transects 1938, 1939, 1943; 2 only in 1941.
[c] Includes small amounts of annual grasses and forbs.
[d] Four transects.

precluded detailed analyses (and make even these questionable), but changes generally paralleled those recorded in the exclosure and forage production studies made during this same period. Changes seemed related to precipitation or overall growing conditions (the TRI and PDI), which were more favorable during 1941 and 1943 than during the late 1930s (Fig. VI.4).

Photo Transects: Open Range, 1949–58

Ten photo transects (Y1–Y10) were established in 1949 or 1950 and photographed in spring and autumn through 1958 with 35-mm color film. Each transect contained 2–12 photo points marked by iron rods; the total number of points was 69. Six transects with 35 photo points were located in the BLA. Three of these were of herbaceous vegetation on mudflow sites, and 3 were to document the condition of big sagebrush. One transect, with 2 photo points, was located on zootic climax sites on the Blacktail Plateau; another, with 12 points, was located on various ridgetop and swale grasslands between Oxbow and Geode Creeks. The remaining 2 transects, with 20 points, were also in a wide variety of grassland types (many on ridgetops and steep slopes) on Hellroaring Slope. The original purpose of the transects was to assess relative autumn standing crop and its utilization.

All photos are on file at Yellowstone National Park. I have examined them for possible consistent changes in species composition or density over time. The photos of extremely harsh mudflow sites in the BLA showed annual variations in production of sagebrush and grasses (similar to spot plots 6 and 7 described below) but showed no consistent changes in composition or density. Substantial annual variation in standing crop occurred on harsh sites on interior range areas (Fig. VI.5), but this was generally less spectacular than on lower elevation sites along the boundary. No consistent or obvious changes in composition or density were apparent on interior areas (except for the variable presence of annual forbs). Individual shrub and grass plants persisted throughout the entire study period, often with consistent heavy winter grazing by

FIGURE VI.5.
Autumn photos of bunchgrass plot 5–Y7 in 1951 (upper) and 1958 on a ridgetop on Hellroaring slope. No changes in density or composition were noted over the years of measurement, but standing crop of herbage varied annually.

1951

1958

ungulates. Annual variations in standing crop may have been related more to growing conditions than ungulate grazing and were more apparent on harsh ridgetop and upper-slope sites than in swales or lower slopes (Fig. VI.6).

PHOTO POINTS: OPEN RANGE, 1949–58

Ten photo points (spot plots) were established in 1949 and photographed in spring and autumn with 35mm color film through 1958 (Kittams 1958). Nine photo points were in the BLA; five of these were on previously cultivated fields containing a variety of introduced grass species. The remaining plot was located on a ridgetop grassland site near Mammoth. The original purpose of these plots was to illustrate "range condition, utilization, and growth," and range trend (Kittams 1950). Subsequently, they were used to assess relative standing crop and its utilization.

These photos also are on file in Yellowstone National Park. Photos taken in the autumn showed very large annual variations in standing crop; two plots in needle-and-thread grassland were of special interest (Figs. VI.7 and VI.8). Except for the presence or absence of annual species, no sites showed changes in species composition, or such changes were masked by annual variations in production of herbage. In several cases, individual perennial plants appeared to have survived the entire study period, even through years of extremely poor growing conditions. Annual differences in standing crop and density seemed best attributed to growing conditions, although overall elk densities were reduced after about 1955. The extreme difficulty of making short-term assessments of range condition and trend is well illustrated by Figs. VI.7 and VI.8. Indeed, the annual variations in standing crop, cover, biomass, and density (reflecting primarily variations in growing conditions) were so great that conventional techniques used to assess the influence of grazing on range trend seemed quite inadequate.

I located and rephotographed spot plots 6 and 7 in the autumn of 1978, 29 years after they were established (Figs. VI.7, VI.8). These photos continued to show little change in the needle-and-thread grasslands.

PARKER TRANSECTS AND CHART QUADRATS ASSOCIATED WITH EXCLOSURES, 1958–74

Five 5-acre (2-ha) ungulate exclosures were established on the northern range in 1957; five more were established in 1962 (four adjacent to 1957 exclosures). The measurements from these exclosure studies were especially interesting because they covered a period of extensive reductions in ungulate numbers (through 1968) and a subsequent increase (Chaps. 3, 10). Transects and quadrats established inside exclosures were matched with grazed plots outside. For four of the 1962 exclosures the outside plots were the same ones established in 1957.

The Parker three-step method (Parker 1954, Parker and Harris 1959) as variously modified (USDA Forest Service 1969) was used to record frequency of hits on basal portions of plants, litter, and abiotic elements (bare ground, erosion pavement, rock). Frequency was recorded within a loop 0.75 inches (1.9 cm) in diameter at 1-ft ($\sim$ 0.3-m) intervals along a 100-ft (30.5-m) steel tape. Frequency of hits on shrub canopies was recorded separately. A close-up and an oblique transect photo complemented measurements (see Fig. VI.9). A comparison of the recording techniques used over time (Denton 1958, Bergstrom 1962, Lambertson 1967, and USDA Forest Service

FIGURE VI.6.

Autumn photos of swale grassland plot 5–Y6 in 1951 (upper) and 1958 on Hellroaring slope. No changes in density or composition were noted over time (arrows indicate location of plot stake).

1951

1958

FIGURE VI.7.

Autumn photos of "spot plot" No. 6 in 1949 (upper), 1950, 1954, 1958, and 1978 on an alluvial soil in the BLA. Vegetation is dominated by needle-and-thread and bluebunch wheatgrass with fringed sage and prickly pear. Photos illustrate the great annual differences in standing herbage, which reflect variations in growing conditions. Remains of dead sagebrush plants visible in 1949 are interpreted as a return to more pristine conditions following elimination of livestock when the area was added to the park in 1932.

1949

1950

(continued)

FIGURE VI.7. (*Continued*)

1954

1958

(*continued*)

FIGURE VI.7. (*Continued*)

1978

1969) showed that some changes have occurred. Hits on perennial species under shrub canopies were not tabulated in the 1958 measurements; they were tallied as ''½ hit'' in 1962 and as whole hits in 1967 and 1974. Some minor differences in investigator's interpretation of particle size for abiotic hits also appears to have occurred over time. These changes probably would have made little difference on transects with low densities of shrubs and should not have influenced measurements in and out of exclosures made in any one year. They may have influenced differences among years. All transects were located in the field, and a determination was made of their proximity to exclosure fences prior to the 1974 measurements. Those that did not meet minimum standards (USDA Forest Service 1969) were omitted from this analysis to avoid the exclosure effects on microclimate or the exaggerated heavy grazing on outside plots adjacent to fences.

Plant frequency recorded by this technique is a nonabsolute measure influenced by plant density, shape, size, and size class distribution, and is very difficult to interpret (Hutchings and Holmgren 1959, Reppert and Francis 1973). Reppert and Francis (1973) concluded that when used with care, and supplemented with the photos, a change in frequency might be used to determine trend, but they cautioned that changes in frequency could be influenced by any one or combination of the attributes listed above. They also described the difficulties in interpreting results, which included failure to document potential trend-causing agents during the intervals between measurements.

A series of 81 cm × 81 cm chart quadrats also was used in these studies. The basal area of grasses and forbs and aerial cover of shrubs were mapped at the same time as Parker transects were measured from 1958 to 1967. Inflorescence height and leaf

FIGURE VI.8.

Autumn photos of "spot plot" No. 7 in 1949 (upper), 1950, 1954, 1958, and 1978. Great annual differences in standing herbage and basal area of needle-and-thread and fringed sage paralleled fluctuations in growing conditions. A comparison of annual photos suggested that individual perennial plants persisted over the 1949–58 period.

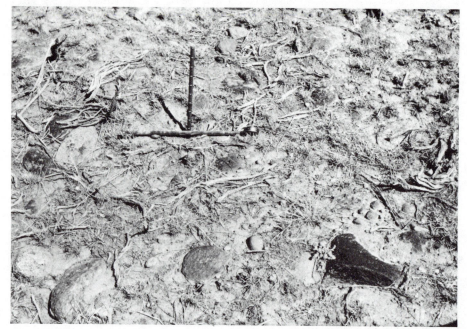

1949

1950

FIGURE VI.8. (*Continued*)

1954

1958

(*continued*)

FIGURE VI.8. (*Continued*)

1978

length for selected grasses were measured on transect sites in the autumn of 1962, 1965, and 1967 (Barmore 1975).

Barmore (1975) discussed the difficulties of statistical analysis of the present study design and the rationale for using a factorial ANOVA that compared the responses of 10 dependent variables (perennial grasses, forbs, bare ground, etc.) to two treatments (grazing and nongrazing by native ungulates) with 11 pairs of plots and four years of measurements. Briefly, this ANOVA provided a method for analyzing the variance among sample means and isolating variances that might be attributed to treatments. The analysis measured the effects of one factor upon another (interaction), such as the effects of grazing and nongrazing over time. In this analysis the ANOVA tables showed that the variation among pairs of plots was sometimes significant. This was known in advance, because pairs were located deliberately on different vegetation types and is of no concern here. This variance source was isolated to evaluate the effects due to treatments and years (Barmore 1975). Significant differences for *years* were interpreted as indicating that mean frequency (MF) of some dependent variable for grazed and ungrazed plots was significantly different from one or more other means. As discussed by Barmore (1975), inspection of tabular data was used to determine the time(s) and direction of changes. Significant differences in *treatment* (grazing and nongrazing) per se do not necessarily imply a cause-and-effect relationship, since significant differences between plots of a pair may have been present initially when they were established. Significant differences in *interaction* of treatments × years was interpreted as meaning that a dependent variable was affected by differences in treatments. It was then necessary to interpret the ecological significance of the statistical analyses. ANOVA was restricted to vegetation categories, because the

FIGURE IV.9.

Parker transect C1T1 inside the Blacktail exclosure in 1958 and 1974. Comparable photos for transect MC1T1 outside the exclosure are also shown. Both transects sampled the *Idaho fescue/bluebunch wheatgrass assn.*–xeric phase on an upper slope.

1958

1974

(*continued*)

FIGURE VI.9. (*Continued*)

1958

1974

frequency of hits on individual species usually was too small. Changes in major species are described in the text.

Barmore (1975) provided a detailed description of location and vegetation types sampled in these studies. He also made an exhaustive analysis of individual transects and quadrats measured for 1958–67, as well as various combinations. This included tabular information on frequencies with standard deviations by forage class, individual species, etc. No purpose is served by repeating this information here. The 1974 measurements are on file at Yellowstone National Park.

Five Parker transects inside the 1957 Blacktail and Lamar exclosures, and their matched outside transects were measured in 1958, 1962, 1967, and 1974 (seven transect pairs were potentially available, but two were eliminated because of proximity to exclosure fences). Three pairs of transects were located on ridgetop or upper-slope bluebunch wheatgrass sites; two pairs on lower-slope or swale Idaho fescue or big sagebrush/Idaho fescue sites.

Grazing versus nongrazing had no significant effect from 1957 to 1974 (i.e., treatment × year interaction was not significant) on the *MF* of perennial grasses, forbs, shrubs, total perennial vegetation, bare ground, or litter (Table VI.11, Fig. VI.10). Treatment × year interactions were significant for pavement and overstory shrubs. The decrease in pavement was greater inside exclosures (Fig. VI.10), due in part to a greater accumulation of litter (nonsignificant). Although differences in shrub overstory were present on transects when they were established (Fig. VI.10), the MF increased to a greater extent inside exclosures. Examinations of individual transect data and photos showed that this was due mostly to a greater increase in canopy size and density for big sagebrush on the lower slope transect at the Blacktail exclosure (MF of big sagebrush for all inside transects was 1.9 in 1958, 8.0 in 1974; MF outside was 1.4 and 6.4). Photos showed that this significant difference in overstory shrubs was also influenced by a decrease in MF of green rabbitbrush crowns on outside ridgetop transects (MF: 1958, 1.4; 1974, 0.2) and an increased canopy size inside exclosures (MF: 1958, 2.3; 1974, 3.4).

ANOVA showed significant differences among years for all dependent variables except shrubs (Table VI.11). This was due mostly to an increase in perennial grasses and forbs and a decrease in MF of abiotic measurements, which showed no significant relation to grazing. The significant differences in abiotic measurements may have also been influenced by observer's interpretations of particle size categories (rock, pavement, bare ground) over time (Fig. VI.10). The increased MF in perennial grasses over time was influenced mostly by Idaho fescue (MF inside: 1958, 2.6; 1974, 12.1; outside 1958, 2.7; 1974, 16.6). The increase in perennial forbs was due mostly to pussytoes (MF inside: 1958, 0.2; 1974, 3.2; outside: 1958, 0.5; 1974, 0.9); silky lupine (MF inside: 1958, 0.2; 1974, 1.4; outside: 0.4 and 2.4); and phlox (MF inside: 1958, 0.6; 1974, 5.9; outside: 0.5 and 2.4). Transect photos suggested that increased MF of grasses resulted from growth in basal size of those originally present, rather than increased density. Perennial forbs increased in size and density over time. Photos also suggested that some individual perennial forbs and grasses persisted over the entire measurement period on ridgetop sites inside and outside exclosures. Note that the MF of perennial grasses decreased under protection from ungulate grazing compared to grazed transects.

Eight pairs of 81 cm × 81 cm quadrats at the 1957 Mammoth ($N = 1$ pair), Blacktail ($N = 4$), and Lamar ($N = 3$) exclosures were measured in 1958, 1962, and 1967. Results of these measurements are presented and discussed in detail by Barmore

TABLE VI.11.
Analysis of Variance 1957 Parker Transects (N = 5 Pairs) Blacktail and Lamar Exclosures, 1958–74

		MEAN SQUARES[a]							
SOURCE OF VARIATION	df[b]	Perennial		SHRUBS	Total Perennials	Overstory Shrubs	Bare Ground	Pavement	Litter
		GRASSES	FORBS						
Pairs	4	285.9*	106.8	16.6	128.1	611.7*	31.6	1290.5**	621.9*
Treatments	1	84.7	69.9	119.4	0.5	155.6	19.2	76.2	61.5
Error (A)[c]	4	34.8	32.3	34.3	26.2	44.7	43.8	26.6	87.5
Years	3	315.8**	205.3**	11.2	568.2**	161.4**	727.4**	318.8**	88.3**
Error (B)	12	22.7	11.9	8.2	26.6	25.2	87.3	16.3	13.1
Trt × year	3	30.9	23.8	21.8	7.1	40.9*	24.6	45.2*	21.2
Error (C)	12	16.7	22.4	6.5	30.6	7.5	26.5	11.9	22.7

[a] Values represent arc-sine transformations as described by Barmore (1975). Significant at .05(*) or .01(**) levels.
[b] Degrees of freedom.
[c] F values calculated by dividing pairs and treatments by error (A), years by error (B), treatment (Trt) × year interaction by error (C).

FIGURE VI.10.

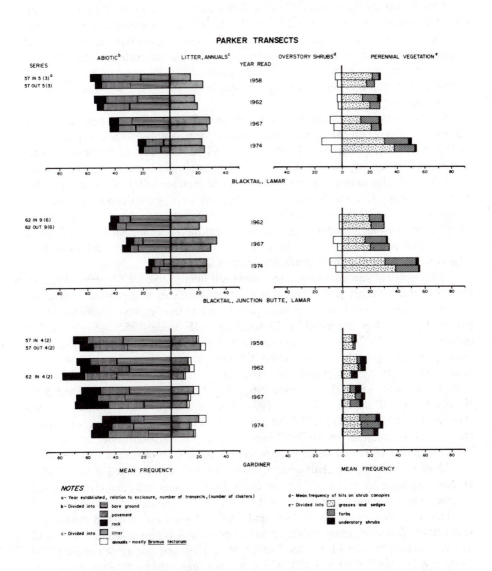

PARKER TRANSECTS

NOTES

a– Year established, relation to exclosure, number of transects, (number of clusters)

b– Divided into ▦ bare ground
　　　　　　　 ▦ pavement
　　　　　　　 ■ rock

c– Divided into ▒ litter
　　　　　　　 ☐ annuals – mostly <u>Bromus tectorum</u>

d– Mean frequency of hits on shrub canopies

e– Divided into ▩ grasses and sedges
　　　　　　　 ▨ forbs
　　　　　　　 ■ understory shrubs

(1975). In general, ANOVA of these measurements showed that grasses, forbs, and shrubs responded similarly inside and outside exclosures; i.e., grazing by ungulates had no measurable effects. Percent cover for grasses decreased significantly between 1958 and 1967 inside and outside exclosures. Forbs showed no significant differences among years. Aerial cover of shrubs differed significantly between years due mostly to an increase in big sagebrush inside and outside exclosures between 1962 and 1967. Barmore (1975:145) compared these measurements to corresponding Parker transects and found that neither data set showed consistent significant differences in vegetation responses inside versus outside exclosures. Both sets suggested differences among years, which included decreases in perennial grasses inside exclosures (significant only for quadrats), and either no such changes outside (transects) or a decrease (quadrats).

Aerial cover of big sagebrush increased both inside and outside exclosures but was significantly greater inside only for the transects.

Nine Parker transects inside the 1962 Blacktail ($N = 3$), Junction Butte ($N = 5$), and Lamar exclosures ($N = 1$) and matched outside transects were measured in 1962, 1967, and 1974 (12 transect pairs were potentially available, but three were eliminated because of proximity to exclosure fences). The outside transects for Blacktail and Lamar were the same as for the 1958 exclosure analysis. Six pairs of transects were located on ridgetop bluebunch wheatgrass sites, three pairs on lower slope or swale Idaho fescue sites.

Grazing versus nongrazing had no significant effect (treatment × year interaction was not significant) on MF of perennial grasses, forbs, shrubs, total perennials, bare ground, pavement, or litter over 12 years (Table VI.12, Fig. VI.10). Treatment × year interaction for overstory shrubs was significant. Measurements and photos showed that this was mostly due to an apparently greater rate of increase in MF of shrubs on inside transects. Canopy size and density of big sagebrush increased on two inside transects on lower slope sites (MF inside: 1958, 1.4; 1974, 6.1; outside: 1.2 and 3.9). Overstory shrubs apparently increased at a greater rate inside than outside. An increased crown size of common and green rabbitbrushes on several inside transects located on ridgetops contributed to this significant difference.

All dependent variables except pavement and litter (Table VI.12) showed significant differences among years. This resulted from increases in perennial grasses and forbs from 1967 to 1974 and an associated decrease in bare ground. Increased MF of perennial grasses was due mostly to Idaho fescue (MF inside: 1962, 3.8; 1974, 19.3; outside: 6.8 and 20.2). Again note that the MF of perennial grasses decreased after initial protection from ungulate grazing. Changes in perennial forbs over time were influenced mostly by pussytoes (MF inside: 1962, 1.1; 1974, 2.9; outside: 1.8 and 1.3), weedy milk vetch (MF inside: 1962, 0.1; 1974, 1.6; outside: 0.9 and 5.4), Hood's phlox (MF inside: 1962, 2.7; 1974, 6.8; outside: 2.7 and 2.8) and stonecrop (MF inside: 1962, 1.7; 1974, 4.5; outside: 1.2 and 1.9). Interpretation of transect photos was the same as for the 1957 series, except for Junction Butte, which sometimes suggested increased density of perennial grasses on protected ridgetop sites.

Eight 81 cm × 81 cm chart quadrats were established in the 1962 Blacktail ($N = 4$), Junction Butte ($N = 1$), and Lamar ($N = 3$) exclosures and compared to outside quadrats (same outside quadrats as for the 1957 exclosures at Blacktail and Lamar). Quadrats were measured only in 1962 and 1967 and were not analyzed statistically. Tabulations (Barmore, unpubl.) suggested a decrease in perennial grass cover inside (percent cover: 1962, 10.84 ± 5.65; 1967, 5.81 ± 2.79) and a decrease outside (1962, 10.06 ± 4.86; 1967, 6.66 ± 1.82), which was not suggested by the Parker transects. Shrub aerial cover, mostly big sagebrush, increased both inside (1962, 3.67 ± 2.39; 1967, 13.47 ± 11.01) and outside exclosures (1962, 1.72 ± 2.49; 1967, 8.16 ± 11.45) on several quadrats, i.e., measurements similar to those suggested by Parker transects.

These data from Parker transects and chart quadrats can be compared imprecisely with measurements of elk numbers and growing conditions (Figs. 3.2 and VI.4). Overall winter elk numbers were 7,000–8,000 just prior to establishment of the 1957 exclosures. Further reductions in the 1960s led to overall winter populations of about 4,000. For the seven years from the 1967 measurements until 1974, the elk population more than doubled. Bison numbers were mostly around 200 in the late 1950s and early 1960s, were reduced to less than 100 in the mid-1960s, and increased to about 140 by

TABLE VI.12.
Analysis of Variance 1962 Parker Transects ($N = 9$ pairs) Blacktail, Junction Butte, and Lamar Exclosures, 1962–74

SOURCE OF VARIATION	df^b	MEAN SQUARES[a]							
		Perennial			Total Perennials	Overstory Shrubs	Bare Ground	Pavement	Litter
		GRASSES	FORBS	SHRUBS					
Pairs	8	94.8	165.9*	20.6*	50.6	382.6**	184.9	579.6*	313.7*
Treatment	1	103.9	71.2	22.0	2.8	225.3**	134.1	8.8	36.0
Error (A)^c	8	33.7	30.4	4.3	67.9	14.0	62.7	59.6	52.3
Years	2	643.2**	292.3**	52.6*	1216.7**	182.8**	1796.3*	22.3	126.5
Error (B)	16	23.5	34.2	10.1	46.3	19.1	63.6	16.7	49.8
Trt × year	2	21.3	11.4	3.1	0.8	73.1**	4.4	11.8	13.4
Error (C)	16	18.0	16.1	6.5	24.1	11.2	41.9	13.1	28.6

[a]Values represent arc-sine transformations as described by Barmore (1975). Significant at .05 (*) or .01 (**) levels.

[b]Degrees of freedom.

[c]F values calculated by dividing pairs and treatments by error (A), years by error (B), treatment (Trt) × year interaction by error (C).

1974 (Meagher 1973 and unpubl.). Overall numbers of ungulates can be misleading, since some sites remained heavily grazed at the lowest ungulate densities; other sites showed light grazing at high densities. Barmore (1975:147) found that mean winter utilization of cured grasses on transects outside the Mammoth, Blacktail, and Lamar exclosures was 10–30% from 1964 to 1969, but up to 50–70% for bluebunch wheatgrass in 1966–67. Mean percentage of grass plants grazed in spring ranged from 12 to 27%, with highs of 21% on Idaho fescue and 62% on bluebunch wheatgrass in 1967. Big sagebrush was lightly browsed (mean 9% leader use) at these sites from 1965 to 1969; green rabbitbrush was grazed moderately on ridgetop sites even at low elk densities. Winter and spring utilization of grasses on ridgetop and slope sites increased from 1971 to 1974 in roadside areas (see Forage Utilization, Chap. 9). Utilization of big sagebrush has remained low. Observations suggested that use of rabbitbrushes has been heavy on ridgetop sites.

Precipitation was below normal for four of five years prior to the 1958 measurements (Fig. VI.4), and as Barmore (1975) pointed out, precipitation was generally above normal for 1962–67, when some ungulate populations were low. Precipitation was highly variable during 1967–74 as some ungulate populations increased. Both 1973 and 1974 had below normal annual precipitation. Note, especially, that while annual precipitation exceeding 50 cm has occurred only three years since 1930, two of these years (1968, 1972) occurred between the 1967 and 1974 measurements. The TRI and PDI were low in the late 1950s and generally increased into the early 1970s.

These data covering the period of major elk reductions and subsequent increases suggested little consistent difference between the treatments of nongrazing and grazing by native ungulates on species abundance, basal cover, and composition of these grasslands. Differences appeared to have been related more to fluctuations in growing conditions. For example, the increased frequency of Idaho fescue for 1967–74 may be related to the two years of unusually high annual precipitation. Some perennial grasses decreased with protection from ungulate grazing, although at these lower plant densities the maximum inflorescence height or leaf length was sometimes significantly greater (Barmore 1975:154), especially on ridgetop and upper-slope sites. This was attributed either to the absence of spring grazing (Barmore 1975:162) or perhaps to the increased vigor of surviving plants upon reduction in density. Ungulate browsing did influence crown size and possibly density of certain shrubs, especially on ridgetop and upper-slope sites. Accumulations of litter sometimes were greater on protected plots, but litter did not accumulate on some ridgetops even with protection.

Maximum leaf length was measured on three bunchgrass species inside and outside four of the 1962 exclosures during October 1977. One hundred plants were measured on or adjacent to permanently established Parker 3 step transects using a "closest plant" sampling technique (Cole 1963). The grasses measured were by far the most abundant bunchgrass species at each site. A ridgetop or upper-slope site and a lower-slope site were measured in each exclosure and compared to corresponding outside transects after 15 years of protection from ungulate grazing. The exclosures established in 1957 showed a great deal of accumulated litter and were not used. The 1962 exclosures also showed heavy litter accumulations around grasses in some sites.

Variability often was high within each sample, but maximum leaf lengths were significantly shorter outside when compared to paired inside transects on three of four upper-slope sites (P < .05) and on one of four lower slope sites (Table VI.13). The physiography of the lower-slope sites at Junction Butte, where differences were significant, is different from the other sites. The exclosure is located on an undulating

TABLE VI.13.
Comparisons of Maximum Leaf Lengths of Three Bunchgrass Species Inside and Outside of Four Exclosures Established in 1962[a]

Exclosure	Site[b]		Grass Species	Maximum Leaf Length (mm, mean + SD)
Gardiner	US	In	3[c]	71 ± 15
		Out	3	66 ± 14[d]
	LS	In	1	236 ± 53
		Out	1	229 ± 47
Blacktail	US	In	1	253 ± 48
		Out	1	201 ± 36[d]
	LS	In	2	170 ± 50
		Out	2	178 ± 51
Junction Butte	US	In	2	121 ± 31
		Out	2	92 ± 23[d]
	LS	In	2	154 ± 30
		Out	2	142 ± 31[d]
Lamar	US	In	1	241 ± 55
		Out	1	230 ± 45
	LS	In	2	143 ± 34
		Out	2	145 ± 40

[a]Measurements made in autumn 1977 after 15 years of protection from grazing by ungulates.
[b]US, upper-slope or ridgetop site; LS, lower slope site. $N = 100$ plants/transect.
[c]Plant species: bluebunch wheatgrass (1), Idaho fescue (2), Junegrass (3).
[d]Significant difference between leaf length inside versus outside exclosures, t-test, $P < .05$.

moraine, and differences in relief between upper and lower slopes are less pronounced than at other sites. The differences in maximum leaf length between paired transects were small. For example, the four outside transects located on upper slopes showed a difference in leaf length that averaged 14% (7–24%) shorter than their respective inside transects. The three pairs showing significantly different leaf lengths averaged 17% shorter. As reported above, Barmore (1975) measured differences in leaf length of about the same magnitude in the same general areas (his samples were far more extensive than mine) during the 1960s.

Interpretations of these and earlier measurements of leaf length are difficult. The most obvious is that ungulate grazing maintains less vigorous appearing plants on some ridgetop and upper-slope sites; i.e., plants with comparatively shorter leaves, fewer and shorter flower stalks, and possibly smaller standing autumn crops of herbage. However, as mentioned above, earlier measurements at these sites also showed that perennial grasses declined under protection from grazing. Surviving plants may be simply more vigorous because of reduced competition for resources. It does seem likely, however, that grazing (particularly spring grazing) contributes to less vigorous appearing plants on upper-slope sites. The relationship between this index of autumn plant vigor and annual net primary productivity is not clear.

Four Parker transects inside the 1957 Gardiner exclosure and their matched outside transects were measured in 1958, 1962, 1967, and 1974. These transects were located in the BLA and are discussed separately. All transects were on mudflow substrates. Two pairs were on ridgetop Junegrass communities; two, on swale bluebunch wheatgrass communities.

Grazing versus nongrazing had no significant effect over 17 years (treatment × year interaction was not significant) on MF of perennial grasses, forbs, shrubs, total perennials, annuals, pavement, or litter (Table VI.14, Fig. VI.10). Interaction for overstory shrubs was statistically significant but of questionable ecological significance, since the MF for inside and outside transects ranged from 0.0 to 0.8. Interaction for bare ground was significant because of greater decrease under protection (Fig. VI.10). This appears to have been due to an increase in litter and annuals (cheatgrass) on inside swale transects.

ANOVA showed significant differences among years for perennial grasses, forbs, total perennials, and overstory shrubs (Table VI.14). These variables generally increased from 1958 to 1974. Changes in perennial grasses were due mostly to bluebunch wheatgrass (MF inside: 1958, 1.5; 1974, 4.0; outside: 2.3 and 2.0) and Junegrass (MF inside: 1958, 0.8; 1974, 3.9; outside: 2.3 and 5.6). Changes in perennial forbs were due to fringed sagebrush (MF inside: 1958, 0.0; 1974, 8.9; outside: 0.0 and 11.9) and prickly pear (MF inside: 1958, 0.0; 1974, 1.3; outside: 0.0 and 1.4). Changes in understory shrubs (not significant, but contributed to changes in total perennials) involved minor and inconsistent changes in saltsage and winterfat. Transect photos (inside and outside) suggested that the basal area of perennial grasses increased over time and contributed most to MF rather than increased density. Some perennial forbs increased in size and density, others decreased. Individual perennial forbs and possibly grasses appeared to have persisted for the entire period of measurement.

Four Parker transects inside the 1962 Gardiner exclosure and matched outside transects (which were the same as for the 1958 series) were measured in 1962, 1967, and 1974. All transects were on mudflow substrates, with two pairs on ridgetop sites and the remaining two pairs on swale sites.

Grazing versus nongrazing had no measurable effects over 12 years (treatment × year interaction was not significant) on MF of perennial grasses, forbs, shrubs, total perennials, annuals, overstory shrubs, pavement, or litter. Treatment × year interaction for bare ground showed significant differences. This occurred with a somewhat greater rate of accumulation of litter on inside swale transects, but the result may have been influenced by interpretations of abiotic particle sizes over time (Fig. VI.10).

ANOVA showed significant differences among years for perennial grasses, forbs, and total perennials (Table VI.14). The species and changes in MF involved over time were similar to those described for the 1958 exclosure series. Interpretations of associated photos were generally the same, although the density of some perennial grasses decreased on protected plots.

Barmore (1975) analyzed four pairs of 81 cm × 81 cm chart quadrats at the 1957 Gardiner exclosure that were measured in 1958, 1962, and 1967. ANOVA showed treatment × year interaction was not significant for any variable, nor were there significant differences among years (Barmore 1975:106). Some changes over time were suggested. These included an increase in perennial forbs on outside quadrats between 1958 and 1962 and a decrease inside. Aerial cover of big sagebrush and fringed sagebrush increased inside but remained relatively stable outside; winterfat showed the reverse trend. A comparison of quadrats and Parker transects for 1958–67 suggested an increase in perennial grasses outside exclosures (significant only for transects) and a decrease inside. Few other comparisons were possible. An additional four quadrats were measured only in 1962 and 1967 (tabulated by Barmore, unpubl.) and suggested changes somewhat similar to the 1957 series. The 1962 quadrats were not analyzed statistically since only two measurements were made. However, mean

TABLE VI.14.
Analysis of Variance for 1957 and 1962 Parker Transects ($N = 4$ pairs) Gardiner Exclosures, 1958–74

SOURCE OF VARIATION	df^b	MEAN SQUARES^a								
		Perennial			Total Perennials	Annuals	Overstory Shrubs	Bare Ground	Pavement	Litter
		GRASSES	FORBS	SHRUBS						
1957 Series										
Pairs	3	151.5*	71.9	53.9	46.3	68.8	1.0	133.8	117.7	455.6**
Treatment	1	29.1	1.3	55.1	6.8	0.3	9.1	0.7	2.3	17.9
Error (A)	3	12.2	8.8	27.6	8.3	96.5	1.0	99.2	16.4	5.8
Years	3	53.4**	320.7**	73.0	261.6**	4.4	9.1**	89.4	37.1	51.1
Error (B)	9	5.9	30.6	22.7	13.2	25.4	1.0	33.4	10.0	26.7
Trt × years	3	5.5	1.1	13.6	4.8	33.1	9.1**	39.3*	4.8	18.7
Error (C)	9	4.2	17.9	6.0	10.3	32.3	1.0	6.9	12.0	7.2
1962 Series										
Pairs	3	64.9	42.2	156.5*	1.8	2.9	12.2	159.1	59.5	162.4
Treatment	1	54.3	4.5	7.7	49.9	43.2	12.2	87.4	128.8	0.9
Error (A)	3	53.3	7.6	5.3	26.3	17.0	12.2	76.4	52.8	40.1
Years	2	76.0**	310.6**	11.1	238.2*	11.8	0.0	145.3	0.4	30.2
Error (B)	6	3.7	19.3	3.1	6.8	14.2	0.0	35.8	7.4	24.1
Trt × years	2	20.2	28.2	2.9	8.3	17.1	0.0	116.8**	34.3	20.4
Error (C)	6	5.1	57.8	16.3	25.5	21.7	0.1	7.6	14.1	18.3

^{a}See footnotes Table VI.11 for methods of calculation.

perennial grasses remained the same inside [basal area (%): 1962, 7.04 ± 3.76 SD; 1967, 7.09 ± 3.18) and increased outside (1962, 8.44 ± 7.27; 1967, 10.72 ± 11.18). Mean aerial cover of shrubs (mostly big sagebrush and winterfat) increased inside (1962, 3.09 ± 2.25; 1967, 17.61 ± 24.05) and was essentially stable outside (1962, 2.56 ± 3.07; 1967, 2.90 ± 0.87). As reported earlier, maximum leaf length of Junegrass plants inside the 1962 exclosure was greater than outside when measured in 1977.

Data from Parker transects and chart quadrats on mudflows in the BLA may also be compared to ungulate numbers and climate. Overall elk numbers and climatic fluctuations have been discussed above. Recall that annual precipitation is much lower and temperatures higher in the BLA than at Mammoth Hot Springs. Numbers of elk wintering in the BLA were reduced in the late 1950s through mid-1960s but increased from 1968 to 1974 (see Chap. 4, Seasonal Distribution). Mule deer numbers did not change over this period (Barmore 1975); pronghorn numbers in this area of the BLA were reduced by 200 to 300 in the mid-1950s and have remained insignificant (20–40) for 1968–74 (Barmore 1975:114). Winter utilization of bluebunch wheatgrass averaged 28% but was 50–70% in 1967. A mean of 8% of perennial grasses was grazed in spring, but 28% of the bluebunch wheatgrass plants was grazed in 1967 (Barmore 1975). Winter use of grasses on ridgetop mudflows has been 70% or more since 1971; spring percent of plants grazed has ranged from 40 to 70%. Big sagebrush remained heavily browsed from 1964–69 (88%) and to 1974 (see Chap. 9, Forage Utilization) even at lower ungulate densities.

Little or no consistent differences were measured between treatments of grazing and nongrazing by native ungulates on the abundance and composition of perennial grasses and forbs on these mudflows over 17 years, even at greatly changed ungulate levels. Litter accumulations were greater on some protected plots (usually in swales—not on ridgetops). By contrast big sagebrush increased in canopy size and density with a treatment of no browsing; it remained stable but heavily browsed outside exclosures. Differences over time seem best interpreted as responses to climatic fluctuations, except for big sagebrush.

PARKER TRANSECTS: OPEN RANGE, 1954–74

Seventeen Parker transects were established on the open range from 1954 to 1958 (Figs. VI.11 and VI.12). Transects were located in clusters of two or three per site. The loop frequency measurements and their limitations were similar to those described for the 1957 and 1962 exclosure series. ANOVA was used to test for differences among transects and years as described by Barmore (1975). Significant differences for *transects* were interpreted as indicating possible site confounding among transects (Reppert and Francis 1973). It then was necessary to determine the cause (e.g., transects were located initially on very different types of sites) and to evaluate these effects. As before, significant differences between years meant that the MF of a dependent variable changed over time. Barmore (1975) provided a description of transect sites and detailed analysis of individual and combined transects from 1954 to 1967. None of this is repeated here.

Eleven Parker transects were established on the open range outside of the BLA. Five transects (clusters Y1, Y5) were measured in 1954 (Y1) and 1955 (Y5) and 1963, 1967, and 1974. Barmore (1975:226) described in detail the rationale for combining the initial 1954 and 1955 measurements for purposes of statistical analysis. Cluster Y1

FIGURE VI.11.

Parker transect No. Y1–1 on the open range at Geode Creek in 1954 and 1974.

1954

1974

FIGURE VI.12.
Parker transect No. Y6–2 on the open range at Specimen Ridge in 1956 and 1974.

1956

1974

at Geode Creek was in Idaho fescue grassland; Y5 was located between Junction Butte and Crystal Creek and sampled a ridgetop needle-and-thread grassland.

ANOVA showed significant differences among transects for both perennial forbs and total perennials (due mostly to forbs) (Table VI.15). This was due mainly to field chickweed on cluster Y1. Overstory shrubs were significantly different due to rabbitbrush (MF: 1954 and 1955, 0.3; 1974, 1.2) on transect Y5. Bare ground and pavement differed significantly due mostly to the variable influence of pocket gophers on transect Y1. These differences appear to have been present when the transect clusters were established and persisted throughout.

ANOVA showed significant differences among years for total perennials; these generally increased from 1954 and 1955 to 1974 (Table VI.16) due to field chickweed (MF: 1954 and 1955, 5.0; 1974, 11.7), Sandberg bluegrass (MF: 1954 and 1955, 5.6; 1974, 10.0), and needle-and-thread (MF: 1954 and 1955, 3.1; 1974, 7.9). The significant decreases in bare ground and pavement were associated with an increase in perennials (again, field chickweed constituted most of the difference—related to pocket gopher burrowing). Also, litter increased significantly from 1954 and 1955 to 1963, followed by a decrease. Note that changes shown on these transects from 1963 to 1974 roughly paralleled those shown in the 1957 and 1962 exclosure series. Analysis of transect photos suggested no consistent changes in perennial forb or grass density.

Two Parker transects (cluster Y6) located in Idaho fescue grassland on Specimen Ridge at 2,500 m were measured in 1956, 1963, and 1974 (Fig. VI.13). ANOVA showed no significant differences among transects or years for any dependent variable (Table VI.16). Changes in MF of some perennial grasses occurred among years. Idaho fescue (MF: 1956, 6.8; 1974, 19.5) and thick-spiked wheatgrass (MF: 1956, 4.5; 1974, 12.3) increased; bluegrasses decreased (MF: 1956, 30.8; 1974, 11.6). Perennial forbs showed no large or consistent changes. Transect photos suggested no change in density of perennials, but variations occurred in standing crop of perennial grasses.

Two Parker transects (cluster Y2) were established in 1954 in the Blacktail Creek area on an Idaho fescue grassland. These transects were measured in 1954 and 1963 but were discontinued when construction activities destroyed one transect. Some measurements for 1954–63 paralleled those for clusters Y1 and Y5, with a significant increase in perennial grasses, mostly Idaho fescue (Barmore 1975:191). Other variables showed no significant change. Transect photos of cluster Y2 for 1954–74 suggested no change in density of perennial species but showed annual differences in standing crop of grasses.

Two Parker transects were established outside the 1957 Mammoth exclosure in Idaho fescue grassland and measured in 1958, 1962, 1967, and 1974 (the two inside transects adjacent to the lee side of the exclosure fence were omitted). Results were not analyzed statistically. Mean frequency of perennial grasses (mostly Idaho fescue) showed an initial decrease for 1958–62, followed by a subsequent increase to 1974 (Fig. VI.13). Perennial forbs (mostly pussytoes and phlox) showed little change in 1958–62, a decrease in 1967, and an increase by 1974. Transect photos suggested no changes in density of perennial grasses or forbs but showed increased density and crown size for big sagebrush. Overstory shrubs, mainly big sagebrush, increased. Mean frequency of litter was generally inverse to hits on perennial vegetation; bare ground showed a decrease from 1958 to 1974. Changes in perennial vegetation, overstory shrubs, and bare ground appeared to parallel those recorded at the 1957 Blacktail and Lamar exclosures and the 1962 Blacktail, Junction Butte, and Lamar exclosures.

Data from these transects also may be related to ungulate numbers and growing

TABLE VI.15.
Analysis of Variance for Open-Range Parker Transects Y1 and Y5, 1954–74

SOURCE OF VARIATION	df^b	MEAN SQUARES^a							
		Perennial			Total Perennials	Overstory Shrubs	Bare Ground	Pavement	Litter
		GRASSES	FORBS	SHRUBS					
Years	3	74.2	127.9	5.4	282.3**	20.3	318.8**	111.1*	100.1*
Transects	4	14.9	153.2*	7.3	48.8*	55.3**	167.8***	106.8***	51.5
Error	12	61.2	44.8	4.4	121.2	9.0	25.3	7.7	20.0

^{a}See footnotes Table VI.11 for methods of calculations.

TABLE VI.16.
Analysis of Variance for Parker Transects on Specimen Ridge, 1956–74

SOURCE OF VARIATION	df^b	MEAN SQUARES^a							
		Perennial			Total Perennials	Overstory Shrubs	Bare Ground	Pavement	Litter
		GRASSES	FORBS	SHRUBS					
Years	2	19.2	1.2	2.8	22.0	10.0	11.9	5.4	14.8
Transects	1	26.0	91.3	2.8	4.0	18.0	16.7	0.4	31.7
Error	2	3.1	20.7	2.8	5.4	10.0	17.8	16.2	3.2

^{a}See footnotes Table VI.11 for calculations.

FIGURE VI.13.

Summary of mean frequency of "hits" on vegetation and abiotic elements for Parker transects on the open range, 1954–74 (excluding BLA).

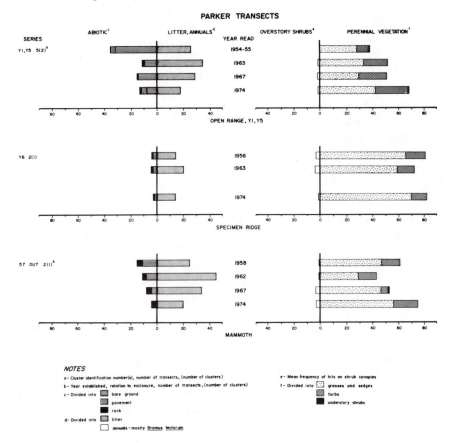

conditions. Overall winter elk numbers were around 10,000–12,000 prior to and during establishment of the first of these transects. Trends for elk and bison since 1958 have been discussed elsewhere. Barmore (1975) reviewed the grazing on these transects in detail. Winter and spring utilization of perennial grasses on cluster Y1 was very light (0–10%), mostly by rodents, for 1963–69. This continued during the 1970s. Leader use on green rabbitbrush was 68 and 32% in 1966 and 1969, "mostly or entirely due to pocket gophers." The overwhelming biotic influence on this cluster appears to have been periodic burrowing by pocket gophers. Utilization of grasses was very light (0–10%) on Y2 for 1964–68 but was possibly higher in 1954. Winter utilization of Idaho fescue on Y5 remained moderate to heavy (50–100%) in 1965–69, even at lower ungulate densities. The number of Idaho fescue plants grazed in spring averaged 29 (range, 7–46). Winter and spring utilization of perennial grasses remained high on ridgetops in this area during 1971–74 (see Chap. 9, Forage Utilization). Use of green rabbitbrush increased from very light to heavy on such sites. Utilization on the transects outside the Mammoth exclosure has been discussed above. Winter utilization of Idaho fescue on Y6 at 2,500 m was estimated at 70–100% in 1967, with 32% of the plants grazed in spring. My observations in the spring of 1974 suggested similar levels of utilization.

Trends in precipitation during this period of measurement were discussed above. Initial measurements were made during a period of below normal precipitation. This also is reflected in the TRI and PDI. Analysis of these measurements, comparisons with those of the 1957 and 1962 exclosure series, and data on ungulate numbers and forage utilization suggested that changes in abundance and composition of perennial grasses and forbs measured over 20 years were related less to ungulate densities than to climatic fluctuations or other herbivores such as pocket gophers. Exceptions related to increased crown size of some shrubs on ridgetop sites.

Six Parker transects (clusters Y3, Y4) located in the BLA were measured in 1955, 1964, 1967, and 1974 (Fig. VI.14). Cluster Y3 was located on mudflow substrates where Junegrass and bluebunch wheatgrass predominated; Y4, on alluvial deposits where needle-and-thread predominated.

ANOVA showed significant differences among transects for shrubs, pavement, and litter. Photos and records for individual transects suggested that in most cases differences were present when the transects were initially established.

ANOVA showed significant differences among years for perennial grasses and forbs, total perennials, and annuals (Table VI.17). Mean frequency of perennial grasses and forbs increased from 1955–74 (Fig. VI.14). Changes in MF of grasses were influenced mostly by Junegrass (MF: 1955, 0.4; 1974, 10.3) and needle-and-thread (MF: 1955, 0.5; 1974, 4.9). Perennial forbs were influenced by fringed sagebrush (MF: 1955, 0.3; 1974, 3.5). Overstory shrubs showed statistically significant differences in increased crown size (also shown by photos) of common rabbitbrush (MF: 1955, 0.0; 1967, 0.7; 1974, 0.3) and winterfat (MF: 1955, 0.0; 1967, 0.7; 1974, 0.0). The significant decrease in bare ground and pavement reflected increased hits on perennial species, the variable production of litter, and the highly variable occurrence of annuals (mostly cheatgrass). Changes in 1967–74 paralleled those shown by the 1958 and 1962 exclosure studies in the BLA. Photos suggested that the greater MF of perennials mainly reflected increased size of grasses present in 1955, but also included increases in density. Tremendous annual variation in standing crop of perennials and of cheatgrass was shown.

FIGURE VI.14.

Summary of mean frequency of "hits" on vegetation and abiotic elements for Parker transects on the open range in the BLA, 1955–74.

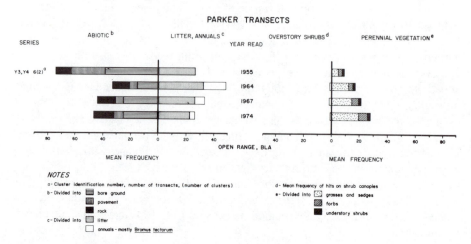

TABLE VI.17.

Analysis of Variance for Open-Range Parker Transects in the BLA, 1955–74

Source of Variation	df^b	Mean Squares[a]								
		Perennial			Total Perennials	Annuals	Overstory Shrubs	Bare Ground	Pavement	Litter
		GRASSES	FORBS	SHRUBS						
Years	3	194.5***	72.0*	18.0	212.9**	413**	43.2*	257.5***	146.9**	33.5
Transects	5	15.5	19.2	57.1*	24.4	234.8	35.2	67.2	650.8***	409.2***
Error	15	12.2	17.6	8.6	17.5	56.1	8.3	25.0	13.1	23.5

[a] See footnotes Table VI.11 for calculations.

Trends in ungulate numbers and climate affecting these six transects have been discussed above. Winter utilization of perennial grasses on cluster Y3 was "no more than 30 to 50%" for 1964–69 and "no more than 10 to 30% on most transects most years" (Barmore 1975:201). Fewer than 20% of the Sandberg bluegrass plants were spring-grazed on most years (up to 64% in 1967). From 1971 to 1974 winter utilization of perennial grasses on ridgetop sites in the transect areas often exceeded 70%; over 50% of the plants were spring-grazed. Swale sites showed lighter grazing (see Chap. 9, Forage Utilization). Leader use on winterfat was low in 1966–69 (Barmore 1975:203). Cluster Y4 showed mean winter utilization of bluebunch wheatgrass of 25–33% and of needle-and-thread of 18–33% for 1965–69, with mean spring grazing of no more than 2–8% (maximum of 44% for needle-and-thread in 1967) (Barmore 1975:211). From 1971 to 1974 winter use on perennial grasses often exceeded 70%; more than 50% of the plants were grazed in spring. Utilization of winterfat and scattered big sagebrush averaged about 80% for 1967–69 but was somewhat lower in 1965–66 (Barmore 1975:210). Scattered big sagebrush in the area of these transects was browsed heavily 1970–74.

The initial 1955 measurements were made following three years of below normal precipitation, and as Barmore (1975:203) pointed out, photos showed a low standing crop of perennials and also of annuals—which was further evidence of drought conditions. The TRI and PDI also suggested poor growing conditions when transects were first measured (Fig. VI.4). Note again that these measurements tended to parallel exclosure studies in the BLA.

Herbaceous Vegetation—Harsh Physiographic Sites

SQUARE-FOOT-DENSITY TRANSECTS: OPEN RANGE, 1943–47

Nine square-foot-density transects were established in 1943 on some of the most "severely utilized" sites (ridgetops, etc.), which were not considered to be representative of the range as a whole (Grimm 1943) (Table VI.18). This range technique has been described previously; measurements were similar except that each of the 10 sample plots per transect was staked for subsequent relocation. Two or three transects apparently were in the BLA but could not be located exactly; all were combined for analysis. Transects were remeasured once in 1947 and then discontinued. Mean total cover, mean forb cover, and mean shrub cover increased somewhat between 1943 and 1947. Mean grass cover decreased. Although the small but consistent increases in total cover were statistically significant (ANOVA random blocks, $F = 8.07$), Kittams (1948) cautioned that at least part of this change could have been due to differences in technique between observers. Annual precipitation was above normal during this period, the TRI increased steadily, and elk numbers were around 12,000 (Figs. VI.4 and 3.2).

SQUARE-YARD QUADRATS: OPEN RANGE, 1948–78

Kittams (1949) established 19 yd^2 (0.84 m^2) quadrats in the autumn of 1948 (Nos. 1–11) and 1949 (12–19) to study plant succession, forage production, and utilization (Kittams 1950:16). Quadrats were photographed semiannually in the autumn and spring through 1967 (few photos for 1959–62) and again in autumn 1973, 1975, and

TABLE VI.18.
Summary of Plant Cover on Nine Square-Foot-Density Transects, 1943 and 1947

Vegetation Class	Plant Cover (DM^2, mean + S.E.[a])	
	1943	*1947*
Perennial grasses	956 ± 98	929 ± 68
Forbs	139 ± 35	242 ± 61
Shrubs	158 ± 20	214 ± 25
Total cover[b]	1,272 ± 136	1,394 ± 122

[a] Standard error.
[b] Includes small amounts of annual grasses and forbs.

1978. A sample photo series is shown in Fig. VI.15. The photographic record of the vegetation on 13 of these quadrats covers 29–30 years (one quadrat was vandalized by 1973; four more by 1978; one could not be relocated). The basal area of perennial grasses and forbs and aerial cover of shrubs were mapped in 1949, 1952 (11 plots only), 1955, 1962, and 1967.

Most quadrats were established on sites where the topoedaphic, climatic, and biotic influences on vegetation were extremely severe and were not representative of overall range conditions. Five of 17 quadrats were on slopes of 50–68%, two on slopes of 35–40%, two on slopes of 10–15%, and eight on harsh, windswept ridgetops. Movements of stones on the soil surface shown in the serial photos were judged arbitrarily to be high on six quadrats, medium or low on four, and undetectable on seven. Quadrat 15 straddled an erosion rill on a steep slope. Most quadrats were subjected to strong winds with potential for wind erosion. Six quadrats (Nos. 2, 3, 7, 9, 10, 11) were on soils derived from harsh mudflows. Eleven quadrats located for the first time by me in 1973 fell in areas that I mapped in 1970 as zootic climax vegetation because of intense grazing and heavy trampling by ungulates. Five quadrats (2–5, 12) were adjacent to major ungulate trails; quadrat 12 was adjacent to a mineral lick. Quadrats 12 and 16 also showed periodic disturbance of vegetation by pocket gophers. Seven quadrats were located in the BLA; six plots were in roadside areas.

Barmore (1975:176) analyzed the measurements of quadrats made in 1949, 1952, 1955, 1962, and 1967 in great detail after first separating them into higher elevation (Nos. 12 and 15–19) and lower elevation (Nos. 1–11) sites (7 of which were in the BLA). He concluded, after ANOVA, that "the main differences in plant responses at low and high elevations were (1) the large and consistent increase in aerial cover of several shrubs at high, but no change at low elevations, and (2) no evidence at high elevation of a decline in basal area of grasses between 1949 and 1955 such as apparently occurred at low elevation. In fact, basal area of grasses may have increased between 1949 and 1955 on quadrats at high elevations." Barmore also analyzed photos and climatic information for 1949–67 and concluded that reduction in plant cover on some sites in the mid-1950s reflected primarily climatic fluctuations rather than ungulate grazing and that a change in either biotic or climatic influences could have caused changes in cover and herbage production.

I tallied individual plants of recognizable species for each autumn photo for 1948–78 in an attempt to evaluate changes in density (plants/yd^2), longevity, and species composition. Individual perennial grasses were tallied on 12 quadrats (recogni-

FIGURE VI.15.
Autumn photos of yd^2 plot No. NY4 in 1948, 1958, and 1978. This plot is located on a steep south slope (54%) at MacMinn Bench within 5 m of a major ungulate trail and received heavy winter grazing by elk and bighorn. Large annual variations in herbage production were apparent over the 30 years of observation. Some bluebunch wheatgrass and needle-and-thread plants appear to have persisted over the entire period.

1948

1958

(continued)

FIGURE VI.15. (*Continued*)

1978

tion of individuals was sometimes questionable on five of these quadrats); this was not possible on five others because grasses lacked a discrete bunch-form. Grasses other than bluebunch wheatgrass were not tallied individually. Relative changes in autumn standing crop also were estimated.

Overall density of recognizable perennial vegetation was considered to show no change, or changes could not be detected, from 1948 or 1949 to 1973 on 11 quadrats; a possible decrease in overall density occurred on quadrat 4; a decrease in perennial grass density was suggested on 3 quadrats; a temporary decrease in grasses for the 1950s was noted on 4 quadrats; and a decrease in density of grasses with a corresponding increase in other species occurred on quadrat 18 (Table VI.19).

Species composition showed no change, or changes could not be detected, on 13 quadrats; this estimation was complicated by difficulties in recognition of perennial grasses. Examinations of chart quadrats supported these interpretations. Changes were detected on four quadrats: a substitution of one or more species for others on Nos. 15 and 18, a decrease in the number of species on No. 14, and a possible increase in species on No. 4.

Standing crop or plant vigor showed annual variations on 13 quadrats and was less apparent on 4 others. Ten quadrats showed apparent increases in standing crop in 1963–67 photos, but the appearance of some plants suggested that this also represented the accumulation of two or more years of herbage on grasses. As Barmore (1975:183) pointed out, photos showed standing crop to be higher in 1962 (when elk populations were comparatively high) than any other year until 1967.

Fourteen quadrats rephotographed in 1975 and 12 rephotographed in 1978 continued to show no significant changes in composition, density, or longevity. One plot

TABLE VI.19.
Photo Interpretation of Vegetation on 17 Square-Yard Quadrats, 1948 or 1949 to 1973

PLOT NUMBER AND LOCATION	PLANT DENSITY	SPECIES COMPOSITION	ANNUAL HERBAGE PRODUCTION	PLANT LONGEVITY
1	0[a]	0[b]	±*[c]	+[d]
2	0*	0	±*	+
6	−*	0	±	+
8	0	0	±*	+
12	0	0	0	+
14	0	−	±*	+
15	0	±	0	+
16	0	0	+*	+
18	±	±	±	+
19	−	0	0	+
BLA				
3	0*	0	±*	+
4	−*	+	±*	+
5	−*	0	+*	+
7	0	0	0	+
9	0	0	±*	+
10	0	0	+*	
11	0	0	±	+

[a]No consistent change (0), decrease (−), variable change (±), temporary decline in 1950s (*).
[b]No change in composition (0), decrease (−), or increase (+) in number, species substitution (±).
[c]Variable (±), increased (+), decreased (−), or no change (0), temporary increase 1963–67 (*).
[d]One or more perennial species persisting for the entire period (+).

(No. 1) was being driven upon by trucks in the summer of 1978 and showed considerable change!

Although the aboveground size of plants varied annually, and mortality of plants can be observed in the photos, most of the quadrats appeared to have one to several plants (shrubs and grasses) that survived for the 29–30 year period.

As an aside, ungulate droppings appeared to have persisted for four or five years on three quadrats. This might confound short-term studies seeking to establish relative ungulate densities on certain sites by using pellet groups as an index of relative abundance.

Barmore (1975:177) found that average winter utilization of cured perennial grasses was high (66–100%) over 1952–58 for two years on low-elevation quadrats and for four years at high elevations. Mean utilization was significantly less during 1963–69. The mean percentage of bluebunch wheatgrass plants grazed in spring from 1965–69 was 5–18 at high elevations, 1–19 at low elevations. About 23–57% of the Idaho fescue plants were grazed in spring at higher elevation sites. Leader use on two rabbitbrush species averaged 46–54% at both high and low elevations in 1963–69. Utilization of big sagebrush and winterfat, two sites for each species, averaged 55% in 1965–69 (sagebrush use averaged 24% at one site and 88% at another). These quadrats did not show progressive changes in density, composition, or basal area over the study period. The changes in composition that did occur were not inconsistent with what might be expected in dynamic plant communities over 30 years. Increases in standing crop reflected some combination of grazing and climatic influences. Litter did not accumulate on most sites even with reduced grazing.

LINE INTERCEPT TRANSECTS: OPEN RANGE, 1948–52

Nineteen line intercept transects, each 150 ft (45.7 m) in total length, were established in 1948, remeasured in 1952, and then discontinued (Kittams 1954). Transects were composed of three adjacent 50-ft (15.2-m) sections along which basal intercept of all plants was recorded. Thirteen of these transects were located in the BLA; six on interior range areas. Most transects appear to have been located on harsh topoedaphic sites, i.e., steep slopes or ridgetops, with six or seven located on mudflows and one on an active alluvial fan derived from Cretaceous sandstones and mudstones. In addition to other biotic influences, these sites received heavy winter and spring grazing by ungulates [13 transects were adjacent to the square-yard quadrats discussed above (Kittams 1954:20)]. In sum, these transects sampled very harsh sites because of topoedaphic conditions and biotic influences.

Changes between 1948 and 1952 were generally similar on both BLA and interior areas; total intercept decreased about 27%, mostly because of decreases of 30–37% on perennial grasses (Table VI.20). The decreases in total intercept and in perennial grasses were significant for the 19 combined transects (ANOVA random blocks, F = 31.14 and 36.23, respectively). No substantial changes in frequency of occurrence were suggested for species on any transect, but some showed large changes in intercept. Bluebunch wheatgrass and Sandburg bluegrass both occurred on 17 transects, and their total intercepts declined about 46 and 37%, respectively, between readings. Analysis of adjacent square-yard quadrats (discussed above) over a longer time period suggested that these changes were short-term fluctuations rather than continued changes, probably reflecting the poor growing conditions of 1949. Overall elk numbers probably decreased during this period (Fig. 3.2). These measurements were valuable because they showed the magnitude of short-term changes that occurred on harsh sites

TABLE VI.20.
Summary of Plant Basal Intercept on 19 Line Transects, 1948 and 1952

VEGETATION CLASS	INTERCEPT (CM, MEAN + S.E.[a])	
	1948	*1952*
Excludes BLA[b]		
Perennial grasses	81 ± 24.1	51 ± 15.0
Forbs	25 ± 9.6	22 ± 8.6
Shrubs	8 ± 2.8	10 ± 2.0
Total intercept[c]	114 ± 33.3	84 ± 21.6
BLA Only[d]		
Perennial grasses	109 ± 15.0	76 ± 10.9
Forbs	18 ± 4.3	15 ± 3.6
Shrubs	10 ± 3.8	10 ± 2.8
Total intercept	137 ± 16.3	107 ± 11.4

[a] Standard error.
[b] Six transects.
[c] Includes small amounts of annual grasses.
[d] Thirteen transects.

that were heavily grazed. Short-term fluctuations much greater than this were typical of a number of bunchgrass communities even without grazing (Blaisdell 1958).

Kittams (1954:20) interpreted these data as showing downward trends on 10 transects, slightly down on 7, static on 1, and upward on 1, but suggested that differences in growing seasons "accentuated this apparent decline of vegetation." He suggested that "check plots" on less harsh sites and in exclosures would be necessary to evaluate these changes. There was little correlation in indicated trends of vegetation between these transects and adjacent square-yard quadrats—in fact, the majority of quadrats suggested "improvement" when adjacent transects suggested "decline."

AGRONOMY CAGES YD² QUADRATS, 1949–54

Steppe vegetation on five quadrats each 1 yd² was protected in 1949 with wire mesh agronomy cages and compared photographically to adjacent unprotected square-yard quadrats in 1954 (Kittams 1955). Quadrats were located on harsh ridgetop and upper-slope sites in the Mammoth area (3 quadrats) and in the BLA (2 quadrats).

Little change in plant density or species composition was evident between grazed and protected quadrats after protection for five growing seasons. The standing crop of vegetation appeared to be somewhat greater in several protected plots. This was due to accumulation of several years annual growth on perennial grasses and possibly some increase in vigor associated with protection. Greater differences in the appearance of vegetation occurred as a result of very different annual growing conditions, with 1949 judged by Kittams to be especially poor; 1954, fair at higher elevations. These differences did span a period of improved growing conditions in the early 1950s (Fig. VI.4). Just as with the small exclosures, agronomy cages left in place for five years probably altered microclimates on protected quadrats and made further comparisons impossible (Owensby 1969, Daubenmire 1940). Quadrats were apparently abandoned in 1954.

Trees and Shrubs

EXCLOSURE STUDIES: ASPEN, 1935–65

The number of aspen suckers (i.e., vegetative reproduction from established stands) inside two small range exclosures (37 m², 45 m²) were tabulated for nine years, 1935–65, and compared with numbers on two adjacent unprotected plots. One exclosure (No. 10) was established in 1935 on small aspen suckers in the Mammoth area, with the unprotected plot immediately adjacent to the exclosure fence. The other exclosure (No. 25) was established on a small stand of aspen of about 12 years of age that grew up within the protection of a hay corral near Tower Junction. Horses and probably some elk were fed at this site well into the 1930s. The unprotected plot also was immediately adjacent to the fence.

Tabulations (Table VI.21) showed an initial increase in number of trees, followed by a slow decrease in one protected plot (No. 10) (probably related to greatly increased height and diameter of individual trees inside the exclosure) and a general slow increase in numbers followed by a decrease in the other protected plot (No. 25). Trees inside both exclosures increased greatly in height (Barmore 1975). Both outside plots showed a decrease in the numbers of suckers and small trees to 1943. One plot showed

TABLE VI.21.
Numbers of Aspen Inside and Outside Two Exclosures, 1935–65[a]

PLOT NUMBER	NUMBER OF LIVING ASPEN								
	1935	*1936*	*1937*	*1938*	*1939*	*1940*	*1941*	*1943*	*1965*
10 protected	187	238	243	219	215	202	183	173	41
10 unprotected	97	86	82	32	12	6	2	0	5
25 protected	—	99	114	112	108	121	154	133	90
25 unprotected	—	86	80	43	23	33	22	17	75

[a]From Grimm (1943) and Barmore (1975); suckers under 3.7m only.

an increase in small suckers by 1965. The aspen mortality on unprotected plots was attributed to browsing by ungulates, primarily elk, but all plots showed substantial mortality due to the foraging by insects (aphids or plant lice) in 1938 (Grimm 1938). Grimm (1943; see Appendix VII) pointed out that the exclosure fences greatly altered the microclimate inside the plot and that unprotected plots adjacent to the fence received exaggerated heavy browsing as a result of the attraction of ungulates to the fence. Elk also suppressed aspen sprouts in areas away from the fence during this period. Barmore (1975:275) pointed out that when part of the enclosed stand at site 25 was exposed to browsing in 1936, most exposed trees were dead from browsing by 1941. Barmore (1975) reexamined these plots in 1965; no increased height had occurred on outside plots.

Recently, Mueggler and Bartos (1977) demonstrated the difficulty of interpreting the findings from small study plots and exclosures in aspen. Deer suppressed aspen regeneration in small (0.05 ha) clear-cuts in southern Utah, whereas aspen reproduced successfully inside exclosures. However, large burned stands of aspen regenerated successfully with deer browsing in adjacent areas. Interpretations of ungulate–vegetation relationships from a few small plots can be quite misleading.

ASPEN REPRODUCTION, 1948–52

The condition, height, current growth, and mortality of 20 marked aspen suckers in each of 20 stands were tabulated for five years, 1948–52 (Kittams 1948–55). New suckers (only six of the trees exceeded 1.8 m in height) were added annually to compensate for mortality and to maintain a total of 400 trees. About 43, 49, and 68% of 1,221, 1,326, and 1,108 twigs on the 400 suckers were browsed in 1948, 1949, and 1950, respectively. Mortality and reduction in twig length were attributed primarily to browsing, secondarily to weather, disease, rodents, or unclassified. Data for the remaining years and other measurements (except photos of individual stands) are not available. The original purpose of the measurements was to determine the factors that limit reproduction "perhaps to establish an index for use in management of the range" (Kittams 1948). The study was terminated, and Kittams (1955) commented, upon completion of tabulations, that "thus far no success has been had in determining the critical point at which browsing results in tree loss."

These aspen stands did provide additional information on mortality of overstory stems. I counted the number of stems standing in five scenes photographed in 1947 or 1948 and compared these to numbers present in 1964 (photographed by W. J. Barmore). The stands were considered suitable when the 1964 retake closely duplicated the original photograph and when live trees could be readily distinguished from dead. Recruitment to the number of mature stems was nil in all stands. Stands showed an average mortality of .30 (.16–.51), or mean $\bar{r} = -.022$, for the period.

Two other stands located on belt transects photographed outside 2-ha exclosures (see below) were suitable for similar calculations. Mean mortality was .34 (.31 and .36) with $\bar{r} = -.069$ during 1958–65.

These samples were too small for additional analysis, but they did give an indication of the rate of attrition of parent stems in the overmature stands.

Aspen Reproduction, 1963–69

Barmore (1975) measured the height and number of aspen suckers in relation to ungulate browsing for 1963–69 in 4–20 aspen stands. In general, sucker height and number did not differ significantly during these years. Browsing remained high (mean of 75% leader use) on aspen suckers in this period, even with low elk numbers. Means for transects established in 1964 and 1965 (some sampled aspen stands on the periphery of the winter range) suggested a "slight but consistent" increase in sucker height by 1969 (Barmore 1975). These increases represented mean gains in height of 8 or 10 cm (Barmore 1975:282, 283). Barmore also showed that ungulate browsing was an important factor in determining height loss of suckers from autumn to spring and that "high levels of utilization occurred at relatively low levels of elk use as indicated by pellet group counts."

Aspen Survey, 1970

During 1970, I tallied the condition of vegetative reproduction in 203 aspen stands during a reconnaissance of the range (Table VI.22). Stands were tallied as encountered and probably were biased toward those that occurred along trails and roadsides. Vegetative reproduction was low in most stands: only about 11% showed reproduction over 25,000 stems/ha. Only 10% of all stands showed escapement from browsing. Within the park, 9 of the 12 escaped stands were adjacent to roadsides and elk traps. The combined area of the nine roadside stands was less than 0.4 ha. The three other stands had been burned in 1939 (see Chap. 8, Fire). Successful escapement occurred in some roadside stands in the Eagle Creek drainage outside the park. This demonstrated that in the virtual absence of elk, moose, and fire some stands could reproduce successfully.

TABLE VI.22.
Aspen Reproduction in 203 Stands on the Northern Winter Range, 1970

Location	Vegetative Reproduction[a]			Number Stands Showing Escapement from Browsing[b]
	0–2,500	2,600–25,000	>25,000	
In park	29	127	19	12
Outside park	7	18	3	8
Total	36	145	22	20[c]

[a] Approximate stems/ha categories estimated from samples of density measured in 10 stands by belt transects of 3 m × 30 m.
[b] Considered as any suckers over about 60 cm high.
[c] Mostly less than .4 km from roads or elk traps.

The role of fire in the regeneration of some of the Eagle Creek stands has not been determined, but a fire and cutting of several other stands did occur in the drainage in the 1930s (Tanascu pers. commun. 1976). Escapement of roadside stands in and out of the park seems best explained by virtual elimination of elk groups that frequented these areas. (The height of roadside willows also increased in some areas following the elk reduction for this same reason.) About 70% of 203 stands showed substantial invasion by conifers (mostly Douglas-fir) and in the absence of fire were clearly seral. Exotic timothy grass dominated about 17% of the understories.

EXCLOSURE STUDIES: WILLOW, 1930s

A small willow exclosure was established in the Tower Junction area sometime in the 1930s. The protected area was refenced in 1935 (Gammill 1939) and possibly enlarged to about 6 m × 12 m. The canopy cover of willows in the exclosure was mapped once (date and species of willow were not recorded) and was of little value. Periodic photos through 1943 showed an increase in height of individual protected shrubs and no change on unprotected sites. It is unclear if any change in willow density (increased number of shrubs) or species composition occurred. The original protected plot was incorporated into a larger 2-ha exclosure established in 1957.

PHOTO POINTS: BIG SAGEBRUSH, 1950–58

Twenty-one tagged big sagebrush plants were photographed in spring and fall from 1950 to 1957 in the BLA (Kittams 1958). Seven of the 21 had died by 1957. Additionally, three marked sagebrush plants were photographed semiannually with 35mm color film from 1954 to 1958 in this same area. One plant appeared to have died during this period. All photos are on file at Yellowstone National Park. Plants were in areas previously grazed by livestock. Utilization of big sagebrush by wintering ungulates was consistently heavy, and sagebrush was being replaced by herbaceous vegetation.

BELT TRANSECTS: ASPEN, WILLOW, SAGE, MISC. SHRUBS. EXCLOSURE STUDIES, 1958–74

The crown cover and density of selected shrubs were measured on 27 belt transects, each containing 76 or 152 m², inside and outside 2-ha exclosures from 1958 to 1974. The exclosures and study design were the same as described above for Parker transects in the 1957 and 1962 exclosures. Measurements were robust and involved drawing in the approximate outline of shrub canopies on graph paper and sometimes counting the number of individuals or measuring shrub height (Denton 1958). I omitted six other transects from calculations because I considered them to be too close to exclosure fences.

Results from 10 sagebrush transects are shown in Table VI.23. Crown cover increased both inside and outside exclosures at Mammoth, Blacktail, and Junction Butte. Numbers of plants recorded over time were variable but decreased as individuals increased in size in the Mammoth exclosure. Sagebrush in the BLA Gardiner transect showed increased cover under protection; cover decreased on the outside unit. Plant numbers decreased outside and showed a slight increase inside. These changes generally were similar to those suggested by some Parker transects and chart quadrats at these sites.

TABLE VI.23.
Big Sagebrush Belt Transects on the Northern Range, 1958–74

LOCATION	RELATIVE TO EXCLOSURE	YEAR[a]			
		1958	1962	1967	1974
Gardiner[b]	Out	0.9 (21)[c]	0.9 (15)	0.6 (14)	0.7 (12)
	In	1.6 (33)	1.9 (36)	5.0 (37)	10.2 (39)
	In		0.5	2.0	4.4
Mammoth	Out	0.7 (133)	1.1 (56)	1.3 (100)	1.5
	In	2.0 (169)	3.3 (171)	6.0 (100)	10.2
Blacktail	Out	1.9	1.9	3.2	5.5
	In	2.8	2.9	5.2	6.9
	In		1.9	2.8	4.5
Junction Butte	Out		0.9	1.7	3.4
	In		1.0	2.3	4.2

[a] 1958–67 data from Barmore (1975).
[b] Located in the BLA.
[c] m^2 crown cover (No. plants).

Interpretation of changes was difficult. Denton (1958) purposely established these transects across ecotones between sagebrush steppe and bunchgrass communities (Fig. VI.16). Barmore (1975) found that average leader use at exclosures, other than at Gardiner, was 10% or less in 1963–69. Utilization also was light when examined in 1974, although some plants along ecotones were heavily browsed. Sagebrush utilization around the Gardiner exclosure was intense (mean leader use 88% in 1963–69) throughout the period of measurement, even at reduced elk and pronghorn densities. Mule deer densities were not reduced during this period.

Three–six shrub species were measured on Lamar transects from 1958 to 1974 (Table VI.24). Big sagebrush showed an increase in numbers and cover on one inside unit, no change on another, and little change on the outside unit. Serviceberry showed a decrease in numbers on one outside and one inside unit, and no change on the other inside unit. Rose showed a decrease in number of plants on both outside and inside units. Green rabbitbrush showed no change in cover on outside units but a decrease in number of plants. Inside units showed an increase in crown cover but no consistent changes in number. Horsebrush showed no change in cover or number outside; and a minor increase in cover with no consistent change in numbers inside. Chokecherry showed a reduction in numbers of plants outside. As Barmore (1975:154) pointed out, the crown area of rabbitbrush and serviceberry on this steep slope continued to be suppressed, when compared to inside transects, even at low ungulate densities from 1958 to 1967.

Results from nine willow transects are given in Table VI.25. The willow species generally were not recorded separately but were species commonly found in marsh areas (see footnote, Table VI.25). Transects inside exclosures showed large increases in crown cover and in height but usually no substantial changes in the density (recognition of individual willow plants was often difficult). Willows outside showed no consistent changes in crown area and densities generally remained unchanged. An increase in density occurred on one inside Tower transect, but this may have been due in part to separation of individual species in clumps of willow that formerly were mapped as a single plant.

FIGURE VI.16.

Big sagebrush belt transect inside the Blacktail exclosure in 1958 and 1974, and comparable photos for the outside transect. Transects were established on upper slopes across ecotones between *Idaho fescue/bluebunch wheatgrass assn.*–xeric phase and *big sagebrush/bluebunch wheatgrass assn.* An increase in distribution and density of big sagebrush occurred inside and outside exclosures.

1958

1974

(continued)

417

FIGURE VI.16. *(Continued)*

1958

1974

418

TABLE VI.24.
Lamar Exclosure, Browse Transect Measurements, 1958–74

SPECIES	RELATIVE TO EXCLOSURE	YEAR			
		1958	*1962*	*1967*	*1974*
Serviceberry	Out	(63)	(45)	(44)	0.7 (23)[a]
	In	(38)	(27)	(45)	(18)
	In	—	(56)	(64)	1.2 (53)
Rose	Out	(30)	(28)	(28)	0.3 (16)
	In	(16)	(18)	(21)	0.2 (4)
Green rabbitbrush	Out	0.1 (5)	0.1 (4)	0.1 (2)	0.1 (1)
	In	0.3 (7)	0.3 (8)	0.7 (9)	0.6 (9)
	In	—	0.3 (28)	0.9 (52)	1.5 (28)
Horsebrush	Out	0.1 (5)	0.1 (5)	0.2 (5)	0.2 (4)
	In	0.2 (4)	0.4 (8)	0.8 (7)	0.6 (5)
Chokecherry	Out	(28)	(22)	(20)	0.3 (16)
	In	?	?	?	0.2 (1)
Big sagebrush	Out	0.1 (2)	0.2 (2)	0.2 (2)	0.3 (6)
	In	0.7 (29)	1.0 (22)	3.0 (29)	4.6 (81)
	In	—	0.1 (2)	0.1 (2)	0.2 (3)

[a] m^2 crown cover (No. plants). Data from 1958–65 were compiled by Barmore.

ANOVA suggested that aerial cover of willow responded similarly with and without ungulate browsing during 1958–65 at the Tower Junction, Lamar, and Mammoth exclosures (Barmore 1975:261). Barmore attributed this lack of significance in part to high variation in cover between transects inside exclosures. ANOVA showed that willow on some transects responded differently with and without browsing; i.e., plants inside exclosures became taller than those outside during 1958–65 at the Tower Junction, Lamar, and Mammoth exclosures (Barmore 1975:264). These differences were still apparent in 1974. Photos suggested heavy browsing of outside transects prior

TABLE VI.25.
Willow Belt Transects on the Northern Range, 1958–74[a]

LOCATION	RELATIVE TO EXCLOSURE	YEAR			
		1958	*1962*	*1965*	*1974*
Lamar	Out	2.8 (38)[b]	2.5 (38)	2.9 (36)	4.4 (38)
	In	3.8 (11)	6.6 (12)	10.8 (14)	13.2 (16)
	In		0.8	2.6	7.7 (24)
Tower[c]	Out	1.2 (4)	1.4 (4)	2.0 (7)	
	Out	3.5 (19)	5.6 (22)	4.5 (40)	
	In	0.6 (4)	1.8 (4)	2.8 (3)	
	In	3.0 (21)	9.9 (15)	16.3 (19)	
	In		6.1 (10)	17.9 (7)	
	In		1.3 (9)	6.5 (10)	

[a] Willow species were often not distinguished, but included *Salix bebbiana, S. geyeriana, S. monticola,* and *S. novae-angliae.*
[b] m^2 crown cover (No. of plants).
[c] Proximity to exclosure fence for inside units is unknown.

TABLE VI.26.
Aspen Belt Transects on the Northern Range, 1958–74[a]

LOCATION	RELATIVE TO EXCLOSURE	YEAR			
		1958	*1962*	*1965*	*1974*
Mammoth	Out	19	0	3	10
	In	38	25	19	18
Lamar	Out	4	5	13	1
	In	23	36	30	25
	In	—	1	1	3

[a]Number of stems over 60 cm high.

to 1958, but hedging appeared to be less in 1962 and 1965 (Barmore 1975:271). Plants were browsed heavily in 1974.

Tabulations of aspen suckers over 60 cm tall from five transects are shown in Table VI.26. Aspen outside exclosures generally showed that little or no escapement of the low-density aspen reproduction or increase in density occurred following a reduction in ungulate populations. The number of aspen shoots inside the Mammoth exclosure showed a decrease as individuals increased substantially in height (Barmore 1975:278). At Lamar no change in numbers occurred on one inside unit as individuals increased in height; no substantial changes of any kind occurred on the other protected unit. These measurements showed that two aspen stands reproduced successfully given complete protection from browsing; another showed no response. Density of regenerated aspen stands did not approach the density of the parent stand, and as Barmore (1975:277) pointed out, growth of protected shoots was far below that common to vigorous clones. Utilization remained high on outside transects even following ungulate reductions (Barmore 1975:277); i.e., there was no measurable relationship between ungulate population levels and utilization.

MISCELLANEOUS MEASUREMENTS

Small-scale plant-clipping studies were conducted periodically to determine utilization of big sagebrush and common rabbitbrush in the BLA from 1937 to 1940 (Gammill 1940). These showed 60–70% of the annual growth of forage browsed from seven big sagebrush plots; two small plots of rabbitbrush showed variable but lighter utilization.

Other measurements known to have been made but which I considered to be unusable included 18-m^2 chart quadrats mapped once in the BLA in 1936. We have no data on location, objectives, etc. Measurements of grass vigor inside and outside range exclosures were made once in 1941. I considered that selection of specific plants and exclosure effects precluded analysis. Ten line transects were established on harsh ridgetop sites in 1943; data have been lost. Seventeen roadside photo points of aspen and willow established in 1962 have not been rephotographed.

APPENDIX VII

Narrative Reports of Range Conditions

Rush 1932a Mont. Fish and Game Comm.

"In September 1914, the writer rode over the range on Blacktail Creek, Hellroaring to Slough Creek, Lamar Valley near specimen Ridge and up Slough Creek. . . . At that time none of the range showed heavy use except that part of Blacktail Creek used by the horse herd, and a small area north of Specimen Ridge known as the Horseshoe which had had heavy use in the spring by buffalo." This ride was apparently the basis for Rush's later assessment of conditions. Rush also mentions that prior to 1905 livestock grazed the area between Mammoth and the north boundary of the park without any restrictions as to season of use, numbers or class of stock. He reports as many as 3,000 horses grazed in the summer on upper Blacktail Cr. until 1916—and that 200–300 park horses were grazed there during the 1930s. Army records do not confirm the large numbers of horses on the Blacktail Plateau (see Chap. 8, Human Developments and Activities). Sheep and cattle used as a meat supply were also grazed in the park—small numbers in the Mammoth–Gardner's Hole area.

All of the winter range outside the park was used for stockraising, and the entire area was grazed by cattle and horses. "It was an overgrazed range in 1914 and by 1926 hardly enough forage existed to give hope of this range ever recovering without extensive artificial reseeding." This proved to be an overly pessimistic assessment. He considered that the range area outside the park was deteriorated due to livestock use and "is covered with sagebrush. . . . Exclusive of the cultivated lands, the soil is of rather poor grade, with a high rock or gravel content. However, on areas from which all stock has been excluded the forage has rejuvenated to a most unexpected degree."

Range conditions in 1930–32:

"Mammoth to Gardiner west to Sepulcher [mostly the BLA]. . . . Overgrazed. Erosion of top soil occurring. . . . Heavily used by domestic stock (cattle and horses) prior to 1905."

"Blacktail. . . . West of creek to slope of Everts north of road. . . . Acreage winter range, average winter 2,000 acres. . . . Badly overgrazed—erosion of top soil occurring. Antelope and horse summer range. Used by elk and saddle horses in spring."

"Lamar Valley. . . . Above Junction Butte, south of river. . . . Elevation 6,000 to 6,500 feet. Much used winter range. Gravelly soil, rather poor grade. Overgrazed. Erosion of top soil occurring. Antelope summer range. Used to limited extent by saddle horses in summer. Used by buffalo in fall, winter, and spring. Practically all of this winter range is badly overgrazed to the extent that sheet erosion has occurred the past few years and much of the rich top soil has washed away. The original stand of grass is badly disturbed and weakened and the reduction of root competition by the grasses for moisture has allowed such undesirable plants as Yellowbush (*Chrysothamnus* sp.) to become prevalent. Other plant indicators of overgrazing are Western wheatgrass (*Agropyron smithii*), dwarf Muhlenbergia (*Muhlenbergia* sp.), and several species of weeds." Recommended removal of saddle horses and change in grazing pattern of bison.

These are the only areas Rush mentions specifically as being in poor condition—due apparently to livestock and a semidomestic bison herd. He goes on to report (p. 64), "The winter range, *as has been mentioned before* [my emphasis] deteriorated fully 50 per cent since 1914 [Rush's earlier horseback trip. This interpretation may have been based upon the assumption that over 35,000 elk occurred on the area about 1914—which is incorrect.] due to overgrazing [by livestock and bison?] and drought. [Rush may also have been referring primarily to ridgetop sites.] On more than half of the range sheet erosion has taken place to a depth of one or two inches which in soil of this type is a serious loss. [Rush is unclear here—he may be again referring to those three areas described above.] In some few minor areas gully erosion has begun. . . . All browse species are heavily overgrazed by elk and will eventually disappear from the range unless improvement is shown in the next few years [aspen and willow?]. Even the sagebrush on the Mammoth to Gardiner section is nearly all dead, due in some measure to browsing by antelope."

"The writer depended a great deal upon his experience in dealing with domestic stock on mountain ranges and his familiarity with the northern Yellowstone and Sun River elk herds and their ranges for his conclusions regarding what is taking place on the elk ranges. This is not the scientific method of range study and was adopted only for the sake of expediency—to allow more time for other phases of the project." Rush also believed that the area was not historical elk winter range.

Roemer 1933 Range Survey

Range Notes: "Sheet erosion is occurring especially along the lower Gardiner Range [Mt. Everts mudstone and mudflows?] and the range along the lower Lamar River. Generally the tops of ridges and the sides of hills exposed during the winter by the prevailing south and southwest winds are usually badly overgrazed, and some erosion is taking place in these areas.''

"Overgrazing is especially noticeable in the Gardiner Range and the range along the lower Lamar River. Much of the overgrazing along the lower Lamar River is due to the fact that the buffalo use this area early in spring for calving.''

Childs 1935 Winter Elk Range and Game Studies

"For the past few years the volume of forage available for game animals in Yellowstone National Park, during the winter months, has shown a marked annual decrease. The primary cause being due to insufficient annual precipitation.''

An attempt was made to determine carrying capacity. Two estimates of carrying capacity of 5,300 and 6,600 elk were made and herd reductions were recommended using criteria developed for livestock. It was also stated that elk were using sheep and mule deer range and that competition was occurring, although no data were provided.

"The elk were in comparatively good condition all winter'' (Ranger Aiton).

Grimm 1935 Range and Game Studies

"Climatic conditions, as represented by lack of precipitation, have for the last 6 years very adversely affected the vegetation cover of the winter elk range; while no decrease in the number of animals using this range, primarily elk, has occurred.''

"Precipitation is the largest single factor governing the growth of vegetation. . . . The direct result of this moisture deficiency was the reduced amount of forage grown.''

"Outstanding examples of erosion may be seen in the Mammoth–Gardiner region [Mt. Everts and mudflows?] where considerable areas are denuded of all forage cover. While erosion is not an unnatural condition, having been observed where there was little or no grazing, it has been greatly aggravated by the overly large numbers of elk using the winter range.''

Grimm suggests an increase had occurred in "indicator plants'' denoting overgrazing = *Chrysothamnus* spp., *Achillea, Gutierrezia* sp., *Muhlenbergia* sp., *Agropyron smithii*. *Bromus tectorum* was established in Gardiner area and was spreading south.

Estimated a 40% increase in forage production over the previous year. Comments on decline of sage in Gardiner area.

"Grasshoppers and crickets also were responsible for a considerable amount of damage to the range this summer. Rangers stationed on the winter range area report that the damage done by these insects this year has been greater than normal.''

Condition of elk excellent until late Feb. Condition declined and 514 dead animals found.

Condition of aspen and willow discussed at length.

Whitlock and Hayes 1935–36 Absaroka Winter Game Studies

Reported heavy grazing by livestock on that portion of Slough Cr. outside park boundaries. They go on to say that "a large percent of the willows in the meadows were dead largely due to drouth conditions coupled with heavy grazing and probably some frost kill." It is unclear if the reported heavy grazing of willows was from domestic livestock or native ungulates.

Grimm 1936 YNP Range Studies

Elk reported to have wintered in good condition without major "loss."

Surface acres of range available to wintering elk were mapped—carrying capacity estimated at 6,500 using techniques for livestock.

"The northern Yellowstone Game Range is now in the most depleted condition of the writer's experience."

"The immediate cause of the decline of the volume of forage produced this year as compared to that produced in 1935 may be found in the climatic conditions that prevailed during the growth season this year."

Concern was expressed over condition of aspen, willow, and sage along northern boundary: "the precipitation for the months March–May, when moisture is most vital to the plants, amounted to 1.82 inches more in 1935 than for the same period in 1936. Also rainfall during all months of the growing season of 1936 was maldistributed, and large amounts falling within a short time resulted in a large percentage of runoff. The heavy rains of June and July came too late to benefit the range materially."

"July of 1936 has the highest mean temperature on record." This was still true as of 1980.

Grimm 1937 YNP Range Studies

A very mild winter—elk apparently wintered in good condition.

Monthly estimates of available winter range were made. Carrying capacity estimated at 8,100—based on *1933* range reconnaissance.

"The plant cover on the winter range made remarkably good growth during the spring and summer of 1937. This increased growth was brought about by numerous rains well distributed over the growing period of the plants and by favorable temperatures."

Height of grasses averaged 53% greater in 1937 than for 1936 and an "ample" seed crop was produced—first time in several years.

"Decrease in plant density for the years 1930 to 1937 in protected plots amounted to 42.6% while the decrease in plant density for average unprotected plot during the same period was 59%." No individual measurements given. Goes on to calculate that 72.2%

of the total loss in density was due to climate, 27.8% due to "abusive use of the range." Compare these comments to those in 1943–45 reports.

Grimm 1938 YNP Range Studies

Icing caused by rain on top of snow resulted in substantial elk movements—tremendous annual variation in winter conditions is first reported. Amount of winter range was tabulated by months—carrying capacity estimated at 7,200.

"The marked improvement in forage plant growth that took place during the growing season of 1937 failed to prevent an acute forage shortage during the following winter on the winter range within Yellowstone Park."

"There was a marked general improvement in the plant growth on the winter range as a whole during the summer of 1938."

Concern is again expressed over the status of big sagebrush along the north boundary and of aspen throughout the range.

Bauer 1938 Yellowstone Nature Notes

"Assistant Naturalist Oberhansley has also pointed out that during the drouth period large areas of sagebrush have been killed off. . . . Whether the sagebrush was actually killed by grubs, rodents or some other agent is not definitely known, but there is no doubt that the drouth which persisted more or less from 1933 to 1936 had a definite adverse effect on it. Some large patches are cut off just below the ground level." Much of this mortality must have occurred along the north boundary because there is reference to its importance as winter forage for pronghorn.

Gammill 1939 YNP Range Studies

Suggests that an increase of "better forage grasses" was occurring as a result of more favorable growing conditions. Concern over status of aspen is expressed.

Bauer 1939 Yellowstone Nature Notes

Bauer tabulated 1,362 living and 1,297 recently dead aspen (large trees) in four stands on the northern range in August 1939. This was a 49% mortality. He commented on the scarring of aspen trunks by elk and the absence of living "saplings." Bauer attributed the condition of aspen to the elk but does not mention the recent drought. Elk browsing of aspen may have increased during the drought, but mortality of overstory trees to this extent seems more likely due to the effects of the drought plus the effects of herbivores. This illustrates the severity of drought conditions.

Gammill 1940 YNP Range Studies

"Forage plants have shown only about 50% recovery in density from the damage done during the drought period."

"A very good growth of forage was produced over all of the winter range. This was especially noticeable on the lower winter range where the *Stipa* and *Agropyron* were more than knee high. A good seed crop was produced by most species."

Concern expressed over aspen mortality and sagebrush utilization along the north boundary.

Gammill 1941 YNP Range Studies

A wide variety of range measurements was made. Concern expressed over the status of aspen on the range.

Grimm 1943 YNP Winter Range Studies

Discussion of exclosures: "Also it was realized that the type of study plots used in these studies, consisting in part of small enclosures, did not represent natural conditions."

Snow cover: winter of 1942–43 was 64% greater than normal; also ice cover on snow led to substantial elk movements from the park and to winter mortality.

"Critical winter range may be defined as such areas on which the forage produced is available to game animals during the entire winter period."

"It has long been established and realized that weather conditions, as primarily expressed in the form of precipitation and temperatures, are the most important factors that affect the status of the range plant cover."

Discusses status of willow and aspen (p. 11): "The amount of forage available to game animals from these browse species [willows and aspen] now is too small to be considered a factor in connection with the forage requirements of a game population numbering even a fraction of the animals now using the winter range."

"When one views the vegetative cover of the northern Yellowstone winter range it is found that, aside from certain trees and shrubs, the soil in its present condition is producing nearly the maximum amount of plant growth that prevailing climatic conditions will permit it to support."

"When one considers the large acreage of all of the Northern Yellowstone Winter range the extent of intrusion of exotic plants, particularly *Bromus tectorum*, is comparatively light, but is reflected in an exaggerated form by the analysis of transect plots because two of these transects happen to coincide in location with areas of aforementioned man caused plant cover disturbances." (p. 12).

Grimm recognized the occurrence of limited zootic climax sites or "spot damage" to the range.

". . . the study plot [aspen] enclosure and the aspen trees contained therein served as a windbreak and in doing so were instrumental in forming a snow drift covering these young aspen [immediately outside the exclosure on the Mammoth–Gardiner road] and protected them from browsing animals."

"The growth of trees and plants within these aspen study plot areas of limited size, and this is also true of all other range study plots of small dimensions, is influenced by the unnatural conditions which such absolute protection affords. Moderate utilization and consequent thinning out of these plants by animals as would occur even on an under-stocked range is lacking and therefore a very dense stand of trees is permitted to grow up. Also, the enclosing fence and the trees contained therein will stop the blowing snow and cause it to pile up within the enclosure, thus providing greater than normal amount of moisture for plant growth. The combined effect of these two factors is to enhance plant growth within the protected study plot area to an unnatural extent." Grimm also pointed out that areas immediately outside the plots received unnaturally heavy grazing.

"A certain amount of soil erosion has occurred on the critical winter range area [mostly zootic climax sites?] in the past and largely during the drouth years."

"Intrusion of exotic grasses and weeds has occurred on some of the winter range. However, such plant intrusions were most pronounced on limited range sectors where man caused disturbances of the plant cover such as [where] formerly cultivated but now abandoned fields were located and former game feeding and elk trapping operations took place."

McDougall 1943 Winter Range Survey

Winter range in YNP was considered to be "typical Palouse Prairie." Pointed out that aspen may be fire dependent.

"It is impossible to tell from the studies of a single year whether the range is at present deteriorating or improving or neither. It is evident that some deterioration has taken place at some time in the past. This is shown especially by the presence in some places of *Bromus tectorum* . . . [and also because] *Stipa comata* is more prominant than the true dominants, *Agropyron* and *Festuca*."

"It would be practically an impossibility to determine the carrying capacity of the Yellowstone winter range. There are too many variable factors. . . . Indeed, climate seems to be a much more important factor in the fortunes of the range than numbers of elk, except that the numbers of elk is a controlable factor and climate is not."

Grimm 1944 YNP Winter Range Studies

Range work consisted primarily of reconnaissance and estimates of utilization due to reduced number of personnel during World War II.

"The status of the range plant cover in Yellowstone Park is primarily determined by weather conditions prevailing over that area throughout the entire year."

"A grasshopper and cricket infestation occurred on some sectors of the range on the lower Hellroaring slopes and of the lower Lamar drainage. Large numbers of ravens and crows as well as some other birds were observed feeding on these insects and the infestation ran its course without extensive damage to range plants."

Suggested that an increase in bluebunch wheatgrass and thick-spiked wheatgrass had occurred on the range. This was a general trend over those portions of the winter range that normally sustained the large numbers of game animals. Wheatgrasses increased due to increased precipitation since the 1930 drought and higher ground water levels.

"This higher ground water level is indicated by the many shallow ponds distributed over the range area which only a few years ago mostly dried up during each summer, but now retain water throughout the year. . . . This intrusion of wheatgrasses was also observed to have occurred on bare spots created by buffalo wallows and similar plant cover disturbance where all top soil had been lost."

"Range areas most notably and beneficially affected by the intrusion of wheatgrasses were sectors of the lower Lamar drainage [Horseshoe buffalo range], the Hellroaring slopes and the Gardiner–Game Ranch range."

Sagebrush was deteriorating in the Gardiner–Game Ranch area: "There is evidence on other range sectors of sagebrush deterioration caused by the competition of grasses and causes other than browsing."

Hellroaring slopes were examined in 1935 and "offered a most discouraging aspect. . . . In contrast to this there may now be observed on this range a vigorous growth of grasses and a diminishing occurrence of undesirable weeds. This condition existed despite the comparatively heavy utilization of that range."

"Elk came through the winter in good condition. . . ."

"Yellowbrush (*Chrysothamnus nauseosus* and *C. pumilus*) was browsed upon quite heavily and provided much of the winter browse for the game animals during the past winter."

"The reproductive growth of aspen . . . provided only insignificant amounts of forage. . . ."

Grimm 1945 YNP Range Studies

"The beginning of the winter 1944–45 found the Northern Yellowstone winter range covered with the most abundant amount of vegetation grown there since the drouth period of the 1930's."

Precipitation for Mar.–Aug. was 55.2% above normal.

"As in the preceding year, considerable numbers of grasshoppers and Mormon crickets made their appearance on the winter range during the summer of 1945, notably on the Hellroaring slopes and the grasslands of the lower Lamar drainage. . . . But it is noteworthy that, after a dormancy of 5 years, these insects are again occurring in increasing numbers."

". . . it appears that the lack of moisture on the lower range areas during the drouth period of the 1930's probably was a factor of equal importance to that of over utilization in bringing about the deterioration of sagebrush on the Gardiner–Game Ranch winter range.'' No mention of livestock or fire.

Grimm recommends (p. 13) that because of the annual variations in absolute abundance and relative availability of forage, visual range inspections are sufficient for management purposes; i.e., detailed determination of carrying capacity from range surveys was not feasible.

Grimm 1947 YNP Winter Range Studies

Adverse growing conditions during the summer of 1946 caused a ''setback'' in range conditions.

Grimm mentions his criteria that at least 50% of current plant growth must remain unconsumed on the ground to prevent soil depletion. Also mentions that ''overuse'' was heaviest on exposed ridgetops and southerly slopes (i.e., zootic climax sites?). Heavy use occurred on the range in the Gardiner–Game Ranch area.

Kittams 1948 Northern Winter Range Studies

''The condition of both ranges [northern range and Gallatin] in the spring of 1947 was much below that desired. Gross deterioration of vegetation had occurred, sheet erosion was widespread [no specific sites referred to] and small gullies were appearing on steep slopes [photos suggest Kittams was referring to ridgetop and steep-slope sites].'' Part of the contemporary condition was attributed to drought of 1930s.

''Management of the entire winter range should be based on the condition of the soil and vegetation on these sectors [i.e., windswept ridgetop and upper-slope sites and lower range areas].'' References to erosion and poor condition also refer to ridgetop sites (p. 30). Concern was expressed over status of aspen and willow, and of sagebrush along the north boundary.

Kittams 1949 Northern Winter Range Studies

Suggested 50% winter use of grasses as a trial utilization of supposed deteriorated sites (i.e., ridgetop and steep-slope sites).

Speculated that retrogressive succession was so extensive that carrying capacity was only a fraction of the original (p. 17), but no specific references were given. Referred to lower plant forms, general sheet erosion, occasional gullies, and numerous trails characteristic of critical portions of the range (i.e., zootic climax sites). ''Also the rather complete use of portions of the range, even with much reduced numbers of animals [i.e., zootic climaxes?] indicates the present limits of the range.'' Concern expressed over status of willow and aspen.

Kittams 1950 Northern Winter Range Studies

Growing season of 1949 was decidedly poor.

Grasshoppers "further reduced forage" on extreme lower range. Apparently elk wintered in good condition.

Kittams also interprets exclosures as the standard (p. 18) by which unprotected areas were to be compared. No mention is made of the difficulties of interpreting exclosures because of changes in microclimate that result from snow and rain accumulation, even though Kittams comments that "several times I have observed a snow cover within the plot [exclosure 11] after wind has drifted snow from most of the Flat [Coal mine flat in BLA]."

Vegetation of ridgetop and steep-slope sites was a major concern, as was condition of aspen and willow.

Kittams 1950b

Considered that physical disturbance, trampling and pawing, by elk and to a lesser extent bison, probably was responsible for decline of sagebrush on northern range above Mammoth. Considered that overbrowsing was responsible for decline on about 4,800 acres in BLA. Attributed decline primarily to pronghorn but suggested that deer and elk contributed. No mention is made of past influence of livestock grazing on distribution and abundance of big sagebrush. Recommends reduction of pronghorn.

Kittams 1952 Northern Winter Range Studies

The 1950 growing season was good. Elk in good condition through winter (p. 13). Concern expressed over ridgetop and upper-slope sites representing retrogressive succession and over status of aspen and willow and sagebrush along northern boundary. Considered that soil erosion had occurred on ridgetop and slope sites (p. 19)—photos show soil movement on very steep slope sites.

Concern was expressed over status of aspen, willow, sagebrush, and the vegetation on ridgetops.

"Erosion as described in previous reports, is continuing. During spring runoff and heavy showers, soil movement is readily apparent." Range measurements and photos indicate that this occurred on ridgetop and steep-slope sites and mudflows along the northern boundary.

Kittams 1954 Northern Winter Range Studies

"The downward trend on portions of the critical range appears to be unchanged [i.e., ridgetop sites]." Status of sagebrush along north boundary and of aspen and willow is of concern. "Heavy rains during summer of 1952 washed considerable soil and rock from steep portions of the critical range. Large deposits at the bases of slopes near the Gardner and Lamar rivers [mudflows and Mt. Everts?] represent an irreplaceable loss from late-winter range."

"Observations indicate that plant retrogression and soil loss on late winter range [ridgetop and slope sites?] and thinning and lessening of the aspen and willow types, as described in previous reports, are continuing."

Kittams 1955 Northern Winter Range Studies

Continued concern expressed over status of sagebrush, aspen, willow, and herbaceous vegetation on ridgetop sites.

Kittams 1957 Northern Winter Range Studies

Concern expressed over condition of vegetation on ridgetop sites. Considered that much of the topsoil had been lost from these sites.

Kittams 1958 Northern Winter Range Studies

"The deteriorated condition of the Yellowstone and Gallatin ranges in Yellowstone National Park has been recognized for decades." This apparently refers to condition of willow, aspen, herbaceous vegetation on ridgetops and upper slopes, and sagebrush along the north boundary.

Exclosures were set up to evaluate range trends following elk reduction—exclosures were again considered the standard by which outside areas were to be evaluated.

APPENDIX VIII

Forage Consumption

An estimate of winter forage removal by elk was required to assess their role in the dynamics of the vegetation on the northern range. Unfortunately, data on the daily forage consumption of free-ranging wild elk are virtually nonexistent; consumption rates from feeding trials and feedgrounds were used as first approximations (from Thorne and Butler 1976, Mereszczak 1978, Nelson and Leege 1979). Rates for body maintenance ranged mostly between 21 and 25 g (dry wt.)/kg/day, but varied with diet quality, age of the test animals, and test conditions. Most elk were inactive during tests, and Thorne and Butler (1976) suggest that 28.6 g/kg/day might be required for maintenance of active elk on feedgrounds with diets of alfalfa hay. Extrapolating these values to elk wintering on the northern range is difficult. Food consumption by free-ranging northern Yellowstone elk might be greater than for test animals because they (1) are more active, (2) occupy a harsher environment, and (3) have access to a greater variety of foods. However, diet quality is low on the northern range in winter, and elk reduce forage intake under these conditions (see Chap. 6). Also, intakes calculated to maintain body weight would be too high, because the elk in the northern herd lose considerable weight over winter. I have used 25 g/kg/day and consider this to be quite generous. This represents a daily consumption of 6 kg for a 240-kg female elk; consumption equivalent to 2.5% of body weight/day.

Daily food consumption for populations of 12,000 and 14,000 elk was calculated as 67,700 and 78,900 kg from mean live weights and the sex and age composition of winter populations. These elk populations would consume about 11,171,500 and 13,019,000 kg of food during the 165 days from mid-November to 1 May on the winter range. This would be 112–130 kg/ha if evenly distributed on the 100,000-ha winter range, which certainly was not the case (see Chaps. 4 and 9).

Autumn standing crop of herbage varied between years (Appendix VI), and data for several vegetation types were limited. However, an estimate of 126,980,000 kg of standing crop (Table VIII.1) present and within reach of elk in the absence of restrictive snow cover was produced from measurements made on the northern range and in adjacent areas (Mueggler 1972). I believe these estimates are conservative.

TABLE VIII.1.
Estimates of Mean Autumn Standing Crop by Vegetation Type on the Northern Winter Range (Air-Dried Weight)

VEGETATION	STANDING CROP (KG/HA)	RANGE AREA[a] (%)	STANDING CROP (KG × 10³)
Xeric steppe	670	7	4,690
Mesic steppe[b]	1,680	20	33,600
Wet meadows	4,490	4	17,960
Shrub steppe[c]	2,500	22	55,000
Coniferous forest[d]	350	41	14,350
Other[e]	230	6	1,380
Total			126,980

[a]No data available on vegetation types outside the park. The same percent as inside park was used in calculations.
[b]Includes swales and old fields.
[c]Despain (pers. commun. 1975) found that herbaceous vegetation in 10 sage steppe sites averaged 1,800 kg/ha, plus 900 kg/ha of twigs, leaves, and seed stalks of sagebrush. The estimate of 2,500 kg is conservative.
[d]Understories in six Douglas-fir stands produced 590 kg/ha (Despain: pers. commun. 1975), excluding forage from conifers. An estimate of 350 kg is conservative for all forest types.
[e]Included aspen and willow, miscellaneous vegetation, and areas unavailable to elk (3%) as rock, water, and developments.

The forage requirements of populations of 12,000 or 14,000 suggested that elk might consume about 9–10% of the average standing crop during winter. Portions, sometimes substantial, of this standing crop were periodically unavailable during winter because of snow cover; also, some species of plants were much less palatable or of less quality as forage. Barmore (1972) used a simulation model to calculate that a winter population of 10,000 elk would consume about 5% of the standing forage on the winter range inside the park. This model allowed over 800 animals to migrate outside the park for part of the winter. Even allowing for substantial error, these crude estimates provided a useful perspective on elk–vegetation relationships.

Zootic climax sites occur on 3% of the winter range and produce about 60–225 kg/ha of herbage (Appendix VI). Autumn standing herbage may total 180,000–675,000 kg on these sites. This herbage would supply about 1–6% of the winter food requirements of 12,000 or 14,000 elk.

APPENDIX IX

Ungulates Other Than Elk—Supporting Information

Mule Deer

TABLE IX.1.
Sex and Age Composition for Mule Deer: Winter Periods, 1971–79[a]

PERIOD		PERCENT COMPOSITION				RATIOS/F	
	N	F	Yg	Yr M	AM	Yg	Yr M
1971	264	44	41	3	12	.93	.07
1972	390	45	40	4	11	.89	.09
1973	411	41	39	3	17	.94	.08
1974	212	48	41	6	5	.86	.12
1975	276	43	41	3	13	.94	.08
1976	185	40	41	4	15	1.03	.11
1977	231	50	38	1	11	.76	.02
1978	309	44	40	8	11	.97	.20
1979	572	46	39	4	11	.84	.09

[a]Mostly December–January classifications. Abbreviations: F, female; Yg, young; Yr M, yearling male; AM, adult male.

Additional Yg/F ratios of .60, .84, .63, .74, and .79 for 1938, 1939, 1968–70, respectively, from Barmore (1980).

Regressions

1. Yg/F on elk numbers at $t - 1$ (E) and December–March winter severity index at $t - 1$ (I):

$$Yg = .701352 + .000011(E) + .00693(I)$$
$$P > .10, R^2 = .12$$

2. YrM/F on E and I:

$$YrM = .07860 + .0000033(E) - .00243(I)$$
$$P > .10, R^2 = .10$$

Appendix continues on p. 436

Bighorn Sheep

TABLE IX.2.
Winter Ground Counts and Reports of Bighorn Sheep on the Northern Winter Range, 1922–50

WINTER	BIGHORN COUNTED[a]	AREAS COUNTED[a]				SOURCES AND COMMENTS[b]
		1	2	3	4	
1923	142	×				SMR 12/22. "Many important sheep districts have not been investigated as yet and it would no doubt be easy to more than double the above number. All are in excellent condition and there is no sign of the scab that caused so much trouble several years ago."
	248		×?			SMR 4/23.
	233	×				SAR. Reported as those "actually seen," but no report of effort or areas covered.
1924	217			×?		SMR 1/24, SAR. May be a cumulative winter count. Greer (1931) observed about 90 bighorns in November 1924 or 1925 on Specimen Ridge. He also commented on extensive sheep mortality in late 1920s.
1925	185	×				SMR 2/25. Considered a very incomplete count.
	195		×			SMR 4/25. Not an organized effort, incomplete coverage.
1926	217		×			SAR.
1927	177	×				SMR 12/26. Not an organized effort, incomplete coverage.
						SMR 1/27. A ram was reported dead of scabies; this led to increased patrols of winter ranges.
	207		×			SMR 2/27. Included 11 sheep outside the park at Bear Cr.
	346				×	SMR 3/27. Thorough coverage of range, results reported in detail. Three dead sheep found and mortality was attributed to scabies.
						SMR 4/27. Six found dead of natural causes; 10 sheep reportedly taken by hunters outside the park before the 3/27 count.
1928	134	×				SMR 1/28.
	170		×?			SMR 2/28.
						SMR 5/28. 31 dead sheep found during winter, mortality attributed to scabies and lungworm.

Year	Count		Notes
1929	68	×	SMR 1/29.
	77	×	SMR 2/29. Methods and effort unreported.
	80	×	SMR 3/29. Cumulative over two months.
	77 (120?)	×	SAR. A very confusing report. "The herd has gradually dwindled from 346 animals in 1926 to only 77 in the spring of 1929. The losses for the winter of 1928–29 account for only 7 animals. The present status of the mountain sheep is very much better [?] than it has been for a number of years . . . . Deer and mountain sheep were fed during the past winter at Mammoth and Gardner River Canyon." AGR 1930 gives 120 sheep actually counted during the spring of 1929.
1930	125	×?	AGR. Four counts made with 83 tallied in January, 80 in February, 125 in March, 63 in April. "It is known that some mountain sheep do winter on Mt. Norris and other high peaks but no accurate counts of these herds have been possible." Sheep fed hay along Gardner River.
1931	101?	×	AGR. "In cases where the actual count [1931] of game is considerably below those counted last year [1930], last years figures were used [?] . . . . It is known that some sheep do winter on Mt. Norris, Abiathar Peak, Mt. Washburn and other high peaks but no counts of these bands have been possible." Sheep in Gardner Canyon fed cottonseed cake in December and January.
1932	66	×	SMR 2/32.
	79		SMR 4/32. Sheep counted during deer and antelope census in Gardner area only because "21 sheep are known to be wintering at Tower Falls. . . ."
	79 (86?)	×	AGR. "No counts available on sheep which winter on some of the inaccessible peaks." Hay and cake fed in Gardner Canyon. 86 sheep reported as actually counted for 1932 in the 1933 AGR.
1933	39		SMR 12/32. Only two areas counted, a casual effort.
	63		SMR 1/33. As above.
	86	×	SMR 4/33. Counted during elk census.
	82	×	AGR.
1934	125	×?	AGR.
1935	126	×	AGR and Mills (1935b).
1936	118	×?	AGR. Parsons (1936) reported, "It should be stressed that this count did not cover all of the sheep winter range in the park, especially in such an open winter as we had had up to that time, but only the more important areas."

(continued)

TABLE IX.2. (*Continued*)

Winter	Bighorn Counted	Areas Counted[a] 1	2	3	4	Sources and Comments[b]
1937	175		×			AGR. Attributed increased numbers to better counting conditions.
1938	181		×?			AGR. Included six on the Gallatin National Forest. Murie (1940) made 6 counts of sheep on Mt. Everts from 11/37–4/38: low count of 38 made 4/11/38, high of 123 observed on 1/18, 19/38.
1939	228			×		AGR. "This year bighorns were observed on Abiathar and Barronette Peaks and on Mt. Norris, while in previous counts these animals have been found only on Rose Creek and Druid Peak. . . . apparent increase in bighorn population must be credited to the discovery of additional animals wintering in the Lamar District." Counts made from 1935–37 also did not include sheep wintering on the Gallatin National Forest adjacent to the park. Murie (1940) also believed that annual increase in sheep numbers reported was due to increased effort.
1940	272				×	AGR. Included four sheep at Bootjack Gap. Gammill (1941) made 10 counts on Mt. Everts from 1/18/39–5/10/40 ranging from 41–103 sheep.
1941	200					SAR. Poor counting conditions for outlying areas.
1942	139		×?		×?	AGR. Poor counting conditions, incomplete count.
1943	134?				×	AGR. Very severe winter, some difficult counting conditions occurred.
1944	91					Memo, Mammoth District Ranger. These counted on Mt. Everts and Deckard Flat.
1945	185	—			×	AGR.
1946	176			×		AGR. Parts of Specimen Ridge not counted.
1947	140	×			×	AGR. "A number of areas where bighorn are regularly found were not visited." Also did not include winter range outside the park.
1948	176				×	Memo, Supt. YNP. Only 97 sheep counted on February 17–19, recount in late February and March gave 176.
1949	144				×?	AGR. All "well-known" areas reported covered, but these were not listed; 15 sheep counted outside the park.
1950	101		×			AGR.

[a] Areas: 1, unreported; 2, main winter areas in park mostly Mt. Everts, Black Canyon of Yellowstone, Junction Butte, Specimen Ridge, and occasionally one or more outlying areas; 3, in park including outlying peaks on the northern range; 4, all areas in 3 plus adjacent National Forest.

[b] Sources: SAR, Superintendent's Annual Reports; SMR, Superintendent's Monthly Reports; AGR, Annual Game Report. All are on file at Yellowstone Park.

TABLE IX.3.
Aerial Counts of Bighorn Sheep on Northern Winter Range, 1955–78

WINTER	BIGHORN COUNTED	SOURCE AND COMMENTS
1955	192	Buechner (1960). 189 counted from the air on 2/10/55, 3 more from ground on 2/11. Temperature, −17°C.
1956	121[a]	Kittams (1956). Count made 3/20–22 in conjunction with elk census.
1961	118[a]	Howe (1961). Count made 3/20–26 following elk reduction and in conjunction with elk census.
1962	148[a]	NPS census report. Count made 4/3–4 in conjunction with elk census; a very severe winter.
1965	227[a]	Barmore (1980). Count made 4/6–9, mostly in conjunction with elk census; flying conditions poor.
1966	229	Oldemeyer (1966). Helicopter count along Yellowstone River from Gardiner to Slough Cr., plus periodic ground counts.
1967	231[a]	Barmore (1980). March 22–27. Includes 11 counted on Cinnabar Mountain, an area not usually covered. Count made in conjunction with elk census.
1968	178 (257)	Barmore (1980) and April 1968 Flight Report. Eight flights made 12/16–4/22. Maximum count for any single flight was 178; 257 was considered maximum winter number.
1969	247 (295)	Barmore (1980) and May 1969 Flight Report. Nine flights from 11/4–5/2. Maximum single count was 247; 295 sheep considered maximum winter number. Included ground counts at Reese Creek and Druid Peaks.
1970	324 (384)	Barmore (1980). Sheep census made on 3/10 and /19; 12 additional sheep observed in the Republic Pass area; 384 sheep considered maximum winter number based on census plus seven additional flights. D. Stradley (pers. commun. 1972) considered that the March count was the most intensive ever made.
1971	227	This study. Maximum on 4/3 and /4 of five counts from 12/31–5/1 (see text); range, 128–227 sheep. Abiathar Peak and other areas in extreme NE corner of the park were not covered on these flights unless otherwise mentioned.
1972	373	This study. Maximum on 4/3 and /4 of five flights from 12/2–5/3; range, 169–373. One flight per year aimed to coincide with particular environmental conditions from this year through 1978 (see text).
1973	332	This study. Maximum on 4/26 and /27 of four flights from 12/9–4/27; range, 225–332.
1974	446	This study. Maximum on 4/22 and 23 of four flights from 1/3–4/23; range, 141–466.
1975[b]	404	This study. Maximum on 5/13 and 14 of four flights from 12/29–5/14; range, 152–404.
1976	426	This study. Maximum on 5/7 and 8 of four flights from 12/17–5/8; range, 110–426.
1977	430	This study. Maximum on 4/21 and 22 of three flights from 1/23–4/22; range, 130–430. An additional 10 sheep counted on Abiathar Peak on 3/16.
1978	471	This study. Maximum on 4/28 and 5/4 of four flights from 12/20–5/4. An additional 20 sheep counted on Abiathar Peak on 5/4.

[a] Helicopter flight. All others fixed-wing.
[b] In addition, I searched the Absaroka Mountains inside the east boundary of Yellowstone Park for sheep on 2/24, 3/14, and 4/17,18,21/75. None was observed.

Regressions: Aerial Sheep Censuses

1. Sheep numbers (S) 1970–78 ($N = 33$) on ground temperature (T) at Mammoth Hot Springs during aerial counts:

$$S = 296.77 + 7.696(T)$$
$$r^2 = .52, \quad P < .001$$

2. Sheep numbers on (T) and percent greenup of vegetation (G):

$$S = 250.494 + 4.04081(T) + 1.46219(G)$$
$$R^2 = .62, \quad P < .001$$

3. ln sheep numbers ($N = 25$) on time, 1955–78 winter counts only:

$$\ln S = -16.7654 + .0112(\text{Year})$$
$$r^2 = .04, \quad P > .10$$

4. ln sheep numbers ($N = 32$) on time 1955–78 with winter counts adjusted from relationship 2 above:

$$\ln S = -13.5907 + .0099(\text{Year})$$
$$r^2 = .09, \quad P = .10$$

5. ln sheep numbers ($N = 9$) on time 1971–78 April to mid-May counts only:

$$\ln S = -126.60 + .0671(\text{Year})$$
$$r^2 = .69, \quad P < .01$$

TABLE IX.4.
Sex and Age Composition for Bighorn Sheep, Mt. Everts and Vicinity, 1971–79[a]

| PERIOD | N | PERCENT COMPOSITION | | | | RATIOS/F |
		F	Yg	YrM	AM	Yg[b]
1971	87	60	21	7	13	.31
1972	101	55	18	8	19	.29
1973	101	54	17	6	23	.28
1974	133	50	21	4	25	.39
1975	129	51	11	13	25	.18
1976	137	47	16	4	33	.32
1977	147	57	6	7	29	.10
1978	101	59	19	4	19	.30
1979	169	51	12	5	31	.19

[a] Mostly December–January classifications, proportion of adult males highly variable and depended upon rutting intensity.
[b] Expressed as Yg/F + YrM to make them comparable to earlier data.

TABLE IX.5.
Sex and Age Composition, "Overall" Bighorn Sheep Population, 1972–79[a]

PERIOD	N	PERCENT COMPOSITION				RATIOS/F
		F	Yg	YrM	AM	Yg[b]
1972	163	56	18	6	20	.28
1974	235	49	23	6	22	.42
1975	269	51	14	12	23	.23
1977	222	56	10	6	27	.16
1978	172	59	20	4	17	.32
1979	242	54	14	5	28	.23

[a] Includes Mt. Everts and vicinity plus sheep from lower Specimen Ridge to Hellroaring Creek and Reese Creek to Cinnabar Mt.
[b] Expressed as Yg/F + YrM to make them comparable to earlier data.

Additional Yg/F + YrM ratios for Mt. Everts area of .28, .50, .25, .36, .36, .35, .42, and .51 for 1938–40, 1944, 1965, 1968–70 from Barmore (1980). Yg/F + YrM ratios for overall population of .31 and .41 for 1938 and 1939 were calculated from Murie (1940).

Regressions

1. Sheep numbers (from Fig. 10.8) on elk numbers at $t - 1$ (E) and winter severity index at $t - 1$ (I):

$$S = 447.85 - .004561(E) - 4.5339(I)$$
$$R^2 = .17, \quad P > .10$$

2. Yg/F + YrM Mt. Everts on I and E:

$$Yg_{Everts} = .45639 - .0000127(E) - .00420(I)$$
$$R^2 = .16, \quad P > .10$$

3. Yg/F + YrM Overall on I and E:

$$Yg_{overall} = .34237 - .00000045(E) - .009378(I)$$
$$R^2 = .14, \quad P > .10$$

4. Yg/F + YrM Overall on I, E, and sheep numbers at $t - 1$ (S):

$$Yg = .2052 - .0000109(E) + .002265(I) + .000379(S)$$
$$R^2 = .07, \quad P > .10$$

Bison

The proportion of calves in mixed herd groups during winter was .21, .19, .17, .20, .10, .12, .12, .14, .11, and .11 for 1969–79, respectively (Meagher pers. commun., 1980). A mixed herd group contained females, young, and some males.

Regressions

1. Bison numbers (B) on elk numbers at $t - 1(E)$ and winter index at $t - 1(I)$:

$$B = 30.2475 + .01665(E) - 4.22181(I)$$
$$R^2 = .83, \quad P < .001; \quad R^2_{E|I} = .74, \quad P < .001.$$

2. Yg/Adult on I and E:

$$Yg = .2424 + .00306(I) - .00001244(E)$$
$$R^2 = .85, \quad P < .001; \quad R^2_{E|I} = .81, \quad P < .001.$$

3. Yg/Adult on bison numbers at $t = 1(B)$:

$$Yg = .2193 - .000524(B_{t-1})$$
$$r^2 = .41, \quad P < .05$$

Moose

TABLE IX.6.
Sex and Age Composition for Moose, 1972–78[a]

Period	N	Percent Composition			Ratios/F
		F	Yg	M	Yg
1972	41	48	22	30	.46
1973	52	46	21	33	.46
1974	36	47	25	28	.24
1975	30	37	23	40	.64
1976	28	39	29	32	.73
1978	21	48	33	19	.70

[a]December classification from ground and air.

Additional Yg/F values of .76 and .71 for 1969–70 were available from Barmore (1980). Best May or early June moose/hour of flying time values were 2.94, 2.63, 1.49, 2.26, 3.84, 4.45, 4.94, 1.58, 3.18, 2.30, and 3.27 for 1968–78; the 1968–70 values calculated from Barmore (1980).

Regressions

1. Moose/hour (M) on winter severity index at $t - 1(I)$ and elk numbers at $t - 1(E)$:

$$M = 2.14512 + .02841(I) + .000083(E)$$
$$R^2 = .07, \quad P > .10$$

2. Yg/F on I and E:

$$Yg = .670524 + .00183(I) - .0000114(E)$$
$$R^2 = .06, \quad P > .10$$

Pronghorn

TABLE IX.7.
Sex and Age Composition for Pronghorn, 1971–79[a]

PERIOD	N	PERCENT COMPOSITION			RATIOS/F	MORTALITY OF YOUNG[b]
		F	Yg	M	Yg	
1971	63	54	18	28	.32	.84
1974	132	59	11	30	.18	.91
1975	106	48	17	35	.35	.82
1976	83	57	25	18	.45	.77
1977	94	56	12	32	.21	.89
1978	86	48	36	16	.76	.61
1979	179	48	26	26	.53	.73

[a]Mostly December classifications.
[b]From birth, and calculated from pregnancy rate of $(1.96 - Yg/F)/1.96$ (see Barmore 1980).

In addition Yg/F ratios of .36 and .32 for 1969–70 were taken from Barmore (1980).

Regressions

1. ln pronghorn (P) numbers ($N = 12$) on time 1969–80:

$$\ln P = 4.8802 + .0083(\text{Year}).$$
$$r^2 = .03, \quad P > .10.$$

2. Pronghorn numbers on winter index $t - 1(I)$ and elk numbers at $t - 1(E)$:

$$P = 142.8 - .1920(I) - .000519(E)$$
$$R^2 = .01, \quad P > .10$$

3. Yg/F on I and E:

$$Yg = .24223 - .008839(I) + .0000201(E)$$
$$R^2 = .14, \quad P > .10$$

4. Yg/F on pronghorn numbers $t - 1(P)$:

$$Yg = .3838 + .0000459(P)$$
$$r^2 = .005, \quad P > .10.$$

5. Yg/F on I, E, and P:

$$Yg = .08031 + .00002(E) + .00126(P) - .01169(I)$$
$$R^2 = .15, \quad P > .10.$$

APPENDIX X

Common and Scientific Names of Animals and Plants

COMMON NAME	SCIENTIFIC NAME
Mammals	
Bear, black	*Ursus americanus*
Bear, grizzly	*U. arctos*
Beaver	*Castor canadensis*
Bison	*Bison bison*
Buffalo, African	*Syncerus caffer*
Caribou	*Rangifer tarandus*
Cougar	*Felis concolor*
Coyote	*Canis latrans*
Deer, mule	*Odocoileus hemionus*
Deer, white-tailed	*O. virginianus*
Elk	*Cervus elaphus*
Goat, Rocky Mountain	*Oreamnos americanus*
Gopher, northern pocket	*Thomomys talpoides*
Moose	*Alces alces*
Pronghorn	*Antilocapra americana*
Sheep, bighorn	*Ovis canadensis*
Squirrel, Uinta ground	*Spermophilus armatus*
Wolf, gray	*Canis lupus*
Wolverine	*Gulo luscus*
Birds	
Eagle, bald	*Haliaeetus leucocephalus*
Eagle, golden	*Aquila chrysaetos*
Magpie, black-billed	*Pica pica*
Raven	*Corvus corax*

(continued)

COMMON NAME	SCIENTIFIC NAME
Invertebrates	
Grasshoppers	Orthoptera
Beetle, pine bark	*Dendroctonus ponderosae*
Budworm, western	*Choristoneura occidentalis*
Plants	
Alder	*Alnus* spp.
Alder, mountain	*A. incana* (tenuifolia)
Alkali grass	*Puccinellia* spp.
Arnica	*Arnica* spp.
Aspen	*Populus tremuloides*
Aster	*Aster* spp.
Aster, leafy	*A. foliaceus*
Balsamroot	*Balsamorhiza sagittata*
Barley, foxtail	*Hordeum jubatum*
Barley, meadow	*H. brachyantherum*
Bentgrass, creeping	*Agrostis alba*
Birch, red	*Betula occidentalis*
Bistort	*Polygonum bistortoides*
Bluebells, broad-leafed	*Mertensia ciliata*
Bluegrass	*Poa* spp.
Bluegrass, inland	*P. interior*
Bluegrass, Sandberg	*P. sandbergii*
Bluegrass, Wheeler's	*P. nervosa*
Brome, fringed	*Bromus ciliatus*
Brome, mountain	*B. carinatus*
Brome, nodding	*B. anomalus*
Brome, smooth	*B. inermis*
Buckwheat	*Eriogonum* spp.
Buckwheat, sulfur	*E. umbellatum*
Buffaloberry, russet	*Shepherdia canadensis*
Bulrush	*Scirpus* spp.
Cattail	*Typha* spp.
Cheatgrass	*Bromus tectorum*
Chickweed, field	*Cerastium arvense*
Chokecherry, common	*Prunus virginiana*
Cinquefoil	*Potentilla* spp.
Cinquefoil, diverse-leaved	*P. diversifolia*
Cinquefoil, graceful	*P. gracilis*
Cinquefoil, shrubby	*P. fruticosa*
Clematis, Douglas	*Clematis hirsutissima (douglasii)*
Clover, long-stalked (Rydberg)	*Trifolium, longipes (rydbergii)*
Clover, sweet-yellow	*Melilotus officinalis*
Coneflower, western	*Rudbeckia occidentalis*
Cottonwood	*Populus* spp.
Cow-parsnip	*Heracleum lanatum*
Dandelion, mountain	*Agoseris* spp.
Dogwood, red-osier	*Cornus stolonifera*
Douglas-fir	*Pseudotsuga menziesii*
Fescue, Idaho	*Festuca idahoensis*
Fir, subalpine	*Abies lasiocarpa*
Fireweed	*Epilobium angustifolium*
Flax, blue	*Linum perenne*
Fleabane	*Erigeron* spp.
Fleabane, cutleaf	*E. compositus*
Fleabane, showy	*E. speciosus*

(continued)

COMMON NAME	SCIENTIFIC NAME
Geranium, sticky	*Geranium viscosissimum*
Goldenweed	*Haplopappus* spp.
Gooseberry, mountain	*Ribes montigenum*
Grama, blue	*Bouteloua gracilis*
Greasewood	*Sarcobatus vermiculatus*
Groundsel	*Senecio* spp.
Groundsel, butterweed (tall)	*S. serra*
Groundsel, Hall's	*S. halli*
Groundsel, thickleaf	*S. crassulus*
Hairgrass	*Deschampsia* spp.
Hairgrass, tufted	*D. caespitosa*
Harebell	*Campanula rotundifolia*
Helianthella, Rocky Mtn.	*Helianthella uniflora*
Hopsage, Spiny	*Grayia spinosa*
Horsebrush	*Tetradymia canescens*
Junegrass	*Koeleria cristata*
Juniper, Rocky Mountain	*Juniperus scopulorum*
Knotweed, Douglas	*Polygonum douglasii*
Larkspur, little	*Delphinium bicolor*
Larkspur, tall mountain	*D. glaucum (scopulorum)*
Lupine	*Lupinus* spp.
Lupine, silky	*L. sericeus*
Marshmarigold	*Caltha leptosepala*
Milkvetch	*Astragalus* spp.
Milkvetch, weedy	*A. miser*
Needlegrass	*Stipa* spp.
Needle-and-thread	*S. comata*
Needlegrass, Richardson	*S. richardsonii*
Needlegrass, western	*S. occidentalis*
Oatgrass	*Danthonia* spp.
Oatgrass, timber	*D. intermedia*
Onion	*Allium* spp.
Oniongrass	*Melica bulbosa*
Owl-clover, yellow	*Orthocarpus luteus*
Paintbrush	*Castilleja* spp.
Phlox	*Phlox* spp.
Phlox, Hoods	*P. hoodii*
Phlox, many-flowered	*P. multiflora*
Phlox, prickly	*Leptodactylon pungens*
Pine, limber	*Pinus flexilis*
Pine, lodgepole	*P. contorta*
Pine, whitebark	*P. albicaulis*
Pinegrass	*Calamagrostis rubescens*
Pond-lily	*Nuphar polysepalum*
Prairiesmoke	*Geum triflorum*
Prickly pear	*Opuntia polyacantha*
Pussytoes	*Antennaria* spp.
Quackgrass	*Agropyron repens*
Rabbitbrush	*Chrysothamnus* spp.
Rabbitbrush, common	*C. nauseosus*
Rabbitbrush, green	*C. viscidiflorus*
Reedgrass	*Calamagrostis* spp.
Reedgrass, bluejoint	*C. canadensis*
Ricegrass	*Oryzopsis* spp.

(continued)

COMMON NAME	SCIENTIFIC NAME
Ricegrass, Indian	*O. hymenoides*
Rockcress	*Arabis* spp.
Rose	*Rosa* spp.
Rush	*Juncus* spp.
Sagebrush	*Artemisia* spp.
Sagebrush, big	*A. tridentata*
Sagebrush, fringed	*A. frigida*
Sagebrush, low	*A. arbuscula*
Sagebrush, Rocky Mtn.	*A. scopulorum*
Sagebrush, silver	*A. cana*
Saltbush	*Atriplex canescens*
Saltsage	*A. gardineri*
Sandwort, ballhead	*Arenaria congesta*
Sedge	*Carex* spp.
Sedge, beaked	*C. rostrata*
Serviceberry	*Amelanchier alnifolia*
Snowberry, common	*Symphoricarpos albus*
Snowbrush	*Ceanothus velutinus*
Spikerush	*Eleocharis* spp.
Spruce, Engelmann	*Picea engelmanii*
Stickseed	*Hackelia* spp.
Stickseed, many-flowered	*H. floribunda*
Stonecrop	*Sedum lanceolatum*
Strawberry	*Fragaria* spp.
Sumac, smooth	*Rhus trilobata*
Thistle, elk	*Cirsium scariosum*
Timothy, alpine	*Phleum alpinum*
Timothy, common	*P. pratense*
Toadflax	*Comandra umbellata*
Wheatgrass	*Agropyron* spp.
Wheatgrass, bluebunch	*A. spicatum*
Wheatgrass, crested	*A. cristatum*
Wheatgrass, bearded (slender bluebunch)	*A. caninum (trachycaulum)*
Wheatgrass, thickspiked	*A. dasystachyum*
Wildrye	*Elymus* spp.
Wildrye, giant	*E. cinereus*
Willow, Bebb's	*Salix bebbiana*
Willow, blueberry	*S. novae-angliae (myrtillifolia)*
Willow, Geyer's	*S. geyeriana*
Willow, interior	*S. fluviatilis*
Willow, mountain	*S. monticola*
Willow, Wolf's	*S. wolfii*
Winterfat	*Eurotia lanata*
Yampah, Gairdner	*Perideridia gairdneri*
Yarrow	*Achillea millefolium*

References

Abrams, P. 1980. Some comments on measuring niche overlap. *Ecology* **61**:44–49.

Albright, H. M. 1919a. Annual report of the superintendent, Yellowstone National Park. Yellowstone National Park library. 105 pp. Typewritten.

_____. 1919b. Monthly report of superintendent, Yellowstone National Park, October. Yellowstone National Park library. Typewritten.

_____. 1920a. Monthly report of the superintendent, Yellowstone National Park, May. Yellowstone National Park library. Typewritten.

_____. 1920b. Annual report of the superintendent, Yellowstone National Park. Yellowstone National Park library. 152 pp. Typewritten.

_____. 1926. Annual report of the superintendent, Yellowstone National Park. Yellowstone National Park library. 60 pp. Typewritten.

_____. 1928. Annual report of the superintendent, Yellowstone National Park. Yellowstone National Park library. Typewritten.

_____. 1932. Game conditions in western national parks. Yellowstone files. 10 pp. Typewritten.

Allred, W. J., R. C. Brown, and O. J. Murie. 1944. Disease kills feedground elk: Necrotic stomatitis takes toll of Jackson Herd. *Wyo. Wildl.* **9**: 1–8, 27.

Anderson, C. C. 1958. *The elk of Jackson Hole.* Wyoming Game and Fish Commission. Bulletin No. 10. 184 pp.

Anderson, E. 1974. A survey of the late Pleistocene and Holocene mammal fauna of Wyoming, pp. 79–87. In *The Holocene history of Wyoming.* M. Wilson (ed.). Geological Survey of Wyoming Report No. 10.

Anderson, G. S. 1891. *Annual report of the superintendent, Yellowstone National Park.* Washington, D.C.: U.S. Govt. Printing Office. 21 pp.

_____. 1892. *Annual report of the superintendent, Yellowstone National Park.* Washington, D.C.: U.S. Govt. Printing Office. 18 pp.

_____. 1893. *Annual report of the superintendent, Yellowstone National Park.* Washington, D.C.: U.S. Govt. Printing Office. 20 pp.

_____. 1894. *Annual report of the superintendent. Yellowstone National Park.* Washington, D.C.: U.S. Govt. Printing Office. 24 pp.

_____. 1895. *Annual report of the superintendent, Yellowstone National Park.* Washington, D.C.: U.S. Govt. Printing Office. 24 pp.

_____. 1896. *Annual report of the superintendent, Yellowstone National Park.* Washington, D.C.: U.S. Govt. Printing Office. 22 pp.

Anderson, R. M. 1978. The influence of parasitic infection on the dynamics of host population growth, pp. 245–281. In *Population Dynamics*. R. M. Anderson, B. D. Turner, and L. R. Taylor (eds.). Proceedings of the British Ecological Society Symposium. London: Blackwell.

Annison, E. F., and D. Lewis. 1959. *Metabolism in the rumen*. London: Methuen. 184 pp.

Anonymous. 1916. *Abstract of elk count by area*. Yellowstone National Park archive.

———. 1920. Article from the *Livingston Enterprise and Dillon Tribune*, November 26. Yellowstone National Park archive.

Appleby, M. C. 1980. Social rank and food access in red deer stags. *Behaviour* **74**:294–309.

Baggley, G. F. 1930. Wild game report, winter of 1929–30. Yellowstone files. 11 pp.

Bailey, V. 1916. Letter to superintendent, Yellowstone Park. Yellowstone National Park archive.

Baker, R. G. 1970. Pollen sequence from Late Quaternary sediments in Yellowstone Park. *Science* **168**:1449–1450.

Bales, J. T., and T. L. Péwé. 1979. Origin and rate of desert pavement formation—a progress report. *J. Ariz. Nev. Acad. Sci.* **14**:84.

Barlow, J. W., and D. B. Heap. 1872. An engineer report of a reconnaissance of the Yellowstone River in 1871. Exec. Doc. No. 66, U.S. Senate. Washington, D.C.: U.S. Govt. Printing Office. 43 pp.

Barmore, W. J. 1968. Aspen ecology in Yellowstone National Park, pp. 146–155. In *Annual report*, Office of Natural Science Studies, National Park Service.

———. 1969. Pronghorn-mule deer range relationships on the northern Yellowstone winter range, pp. 121–137. *Annual report*, Office of Natural Science Studies, National Park Service.

———. 1972. A computer simulation model of elk distribution, habitat use, and forage consumption on winter range in Yellowstone National Park. 27 pp. plus appendixes. Typewritten.

———. 1975. Population characteristics, distribution and habitat relationships of six ungulates in northern Yellowstone National Park. Preliminary report. Yellowstone files.

———. 1980. Population characteristics, distribution and habitat relationships of six ungulates in northern Yellowstone Park. Final report. Yellowstone files.

——— and D. Stradley. 1971. Predation by black bear on mature male elk. *J. Mammal.* **52**:199–202.

Barry, R. G., and R. J. Chorley. 1968. *Atmosphere, weather and climate*. London: Methuen. 319 pp.

Bauer, C. M. 1938. Climate and range. *Yellowstone Nature Notes* **15**:49–50. Mimeo.

Bauer, H. L. 1939. Elk vs. aspen. *Yellowstone Nature Notes* **16**:61–65.

Beetle, A. A. 1952. A 1951 survey of summer elk range in the Teton Wilderness Area. *Wyo. Range Manage.* **51**:1–6. Mimeo.

———. 1962. *Range survey in Teton County, Wyoming. Part 2. Utilization and condition classes*. University of Wyoming, Agricultural Experiment Station Bulletin 400. 38 pp.

Bell, R. H. V. 1969. The use of the herb layer by grazing ungulates in the Serengeti National Park, Tanzania. Ph.D. thesis, Manchester University.

———. 1971. A grazing ecosystem in the Serengeti. *Sci. Am.* **224**:86–93.

Benedict, J. B. 1968. Recent glacial history of an alpine area in the Colorado Front Range. U.S.A. II. Dating the glacial deposits. *J. Glaciol.* **7**:77–87.

Benson, H. C. 1909. *Annual report of the superintendent, Yellowstone National Park*. Washington, D.C.: U.S. Govt. Printing Office. 18 pp.

———. 1910. *Annual report of the superintendent, Yellowstone National Park*. Washington, D.C.: U.S. Govt. Printing Office. 18 pp.

Bergerud, A. T. 1967. Management of Labrador caribou. *J. Wildl. Manage.* **31**:621–642.

Bergstrom, R. C. 1962. A report of changes and trends of vegetation in and near six elk exclosures on the northern Yellowstone wildlife winter range. Yellowstone files. 13 pp. Typewritten.

_____. 1964. Competition between elk and phytophagus insects for food in the Lamar Valley, Yellowstone National Park. Ph.D. thesis, University of Wyoming. 107 pp.

_____. 1968. Parasites of ungulates in the Jackson Hole area. In *Annual report of Jackson Hole Biological Research Station*. University of Wyoming. Mimeo.

Bertram, B. C. R. 1979. Serengeti predators and their social systems, pp. 221–248. In *Serengeti-Dynamics of an ecosystem*. A. R. E. Sinclair and M. Norton-Griffiths (eds.). Chicago: University of Chicago Press.

Blackmore, W. 1872. *Diary*. Yellowstone National Park library. Photocopy.

Blaisdell, J. P. 1958. *Seasonal development and yield of native plants on the upper Snake River plains and their relation to certain climatic factors*. USDA Technical Bulletin 1190.

_____ and J. F. Pechanec. 1949. Effects of herbage removal at various dates on vigor of bluebunch wheatgrass and arrowleaf balsam root. *Ecology* **30**:298–305.

Blanchard, B. M., and R. R. Knight. 1980. Status of grizzly bears in the Yellowstone system. *Trans. North Am. Wildl. Conf.* 45. In press.

Bliss, L. C. 1975. Tundra grasslands, herblands, and shrublands and the role of herbivores. *Geosci. Man.* **10**:51–79.

Bonney, O. H., and L. Bonney. 1970. *Battle drums and geysers*. Chicago: Swallow. 622 pp.

Boutelle, F. A. 1890. *Annual report of the superintendent, Yellowstone National Park*. Washington, D.C.: U.S. Govt. Printing Office. 23 pp.

Boyce, M. S., and L. D. Hayden-Wing (eds.). 1979. *North American elk: Ecology, behavior and management*. Laramie: University of Wyoming. 294 pp.

Bradley, F. H. 1873. Report of F. H. Bradley, geologist, pp. 190–250. In *Annual report of the U.S. Geological Survey of the Territories*. F. V. Hayden (ed.). Washington, D.C.: U.S. Govt. Printing Office.

Bradley, R. S. 1974. Secular changes of precipitation in the Rocky Mountains and adjacent western states. Ph.D. thesis, University of Colorado. 444 p.

Bray, J. R. 1971. Vegetational distribution, tree growth and crop success in relation to recent climatic change, pp. 177–233. In *Advances in Ecological Research* Vol. 7. J. B. Cragg (ed.). New York: Academic.

Brazda, A. R. 1953. Elk migration patterns, and some of the factors affecting movements in the Gallatin River drainage, Montana. *J. Wildl. Manage.* **17**:9–29.

Brett, L. M. 1911. *Annual report of the superintendent, Yellowstone National Park*. Washington, D.C.: U.S. Govt. Printing Office. 20 pp.

_____. 1912. *Annual report of the superintendent, Yellowstone National Park*. Washington, D.C.: U.S. Govt. Printing Office. 22 pp.

_____. 1913. *Annual report of the superintendent, Yellowstone National Park*. Washington, D.C.: U.S. Govt. Printing Office. 20 pp.

_____. 1914. *Annual report of the superintendent, Yellowstone National Park*. Washington, D.C.: U.S. Govt. Printing Office. 29 pp.

_____. 1915. *Annual report of the superintendent, Yellowstone National Park*. Washington, D.C.: U.S. Govt. Printing Office. 39 pp.

_____. 1916. Special report, Superintendent, Yellowstone National Park to Secretary of Interior. Yellowstone National Park archive.

Brown, O. J. 1899. *Annual report of the superintendent, Yellowstone National Park*. Washington, D.C.: U.S. Govt. Printing Office. 20 pp.

Bryson, R. A. 1974. A perspective on climatic change. *Science* **184**:753–760.

_____ and F. K. Hare. 1974. The climates of North America, pp. 1–47. In *World survey of climatology. Vol. 11*. H. E. Lansberg (ed.). New York: Elsevier.

Buechner, H. K. 1960. *The bighorn sheep in the United States, its past, present and future*. Wildlife Monograph No. 4. 174 pp.

Bureau of Land Management, U.S. Department of Interior. 1965. *Upper Yellowstone River area—Montana and Wyoming—land planning report. Missouri River Basin Investigations*. 63 pp. + appendix.

———. 1969. *Middle Yellowstone River area—Land planning and classification report*. 56 pp. + appendix.

Cahalane, V. H. 1941. Wildlife surpluses in the national parks. *Trans. North Am. Wildl. Conf.* **6**:355–361.

———. 1943. Elk management and herd regulation—Yellowstone National Park. *Trans. North Am. Wildl. Conf.* **8**:95–101.

Camenzind, F. J. 1978. Behavioral ecology of coyotes on the National Elk Refuge, Jackson Wyoming, pp. 267–294. In *Coyotes: biology, behavior and management*. M. Bekoff (ed.). New York: Academic.

Carbyn, L. N. 1974. *Wolf predation and behavioral interactions with elk and other ungulates in an area of high prey density*. Canadian Wildlife Service. 233 pp.

Caughley, G. 1966. Mortality patterns in mammals. *Ecology* **47**:906–917.

———. 1967. Calculation of population mortality rate and life expectancy for thar and kangaroos from the ratio of juveniles to adults. *N. Z. J. Sci.* **10**:578–584.

———. 1970. Eruption of ungulate populations, with emphasis on Himalayan thar in New Zealand. *Ecology* **51**:53–72.

———. 1971. An investigation of hybridisation between free-ranging wapiti and red deer in New Zealand. *N. Z. J. Sci.* **14**:993–1008.

———. 1976a. Plant–herbivore systems, pp. 94–113. In *Theoretical ecology: principles and applications*. R. M. May (ed.). Philadelphia: Saunders.

———. 1976b. Wildlife management and the dynamics of ungulate populations, pp. 183–246. In *Applied Biology*. Vol. 1. T. H. Coaker (ed.). New York: Academic.

———. 1977. *Analysis of vertebrate populations*. New York: Wiley. 234 pp.

———. 1979. What is this thing called carrying capacity?, pp. 2–8. In *North American elk: ecology, behavior and management*. M. S. Boyce and L. D. Hayden-Wing (eds.). Laramie: University of Wyoming.

——— and L. C. Birch. 1971. Rate of increase. *J. Wildl. Manage.* **35**:658–663.

Childs, F. W. 1935. Winter range and game studies. Yellowstone files. 4 pp. Typewritten.

Cole, G. F. 1963. *Range survey guide*. Rev. ed. Grand Teton National Park Natural History Association. 22 pp.

———. 1969a. *The elk of Grand Teton and southern Yellowstone National Parks*. Yellowstone Library and Museum Association. 80 pp.

———. 1969b. *Elk and the Yellowstone ecosystem*. Research Note, Yellowstone National Park. 14 pp. Mimeo.

———. 1971a. An ecological rationale for the natural or artificial regulation of native ungulates in parks. *Trans. North Am. Wildl. Conf.* **36**:417–425.

———. 1971b. *Yellowstone wolves*. Research Note No. 4, Yellowstone National Park. 6 pp. Mimeo.

———. 1972. Grizzly bear–elk relationships in Yellowstone National Park. *J. Wildl. Manage.* **36**:556–561.

———. 1976. *Management involving grizzly and black bears in Yellowstone National Park, 1970–1975*. Natural Resources Report No. 9. U.S. National Park Service. 26 pp.

———. 1978. *A naturally regulated elk population. Symposium on Natural Regulation of Wildlife Populations*. New York: Academic. In press.

——— and B. T. Wilkins. 1958. *The pronghorn antelope: Its range use and food habits in central Montana with special reference to wheat*. Montana Fish and Game Department Technical Bulletin No. 2. 39 pp.

Conger, P. H. 1883. *Annual report of superintendent, Yellowstone Park*. Washington, D.C.: U.S. Govt. Printing Office. 10 pp.

Connell, J. H. 1975. Some mechanisms producing structure in natural communities: a model and evidence from field experiments, pp. 460–490. In *Ecology and evolution of communities*. M. L. Cody and J. M. Diamond (eds.). Cambridge: Harvard University Press.

Cook, C. W. 1972. Comparative nutritive values of forbs, grasses and shrubs, pp. 303–310. In

Wildland shrubs: their biology and utilization. C. M. McKeel, J. P. Blaisdell, and J. R. Goodin (eds.). U.S. For. Serv. Gen. Tech. Rep. INT-1.

Cooper, S. V. 1975. Forest habitat types of northwestern Wyoming and contiguous portions of Montana and Idaho. Ph.D. thesis, Washington State University. 190 pp.

Coupland, R. T., E. A. Ripley, and P. C. Robbins. 1973. *Architecture of the vegetative cover. Matador project.* University Saskatchewan and National Research Council of Canada. Technical Report No. 2. 54 pp.

Cowan, R. L., J. S. Jordan, J. L. Grimes, and J. D. Gill. 1970. Comparative nutritive values of forage species. In *Range and wildlife habitat evaluation—A research symposium,* U.S. Forest Service. Misc. Publication No. 1147. Washington, D.C.: U.S. Govt. Printing Office.

Craighead, J. J., G. Atwell, and B. W. O'Gara. 1972. *Elk migrations in and near Yellowstone National Park.* Wildlife Monograph No. 29. 48 pp.

_____ and F. C. Craighead, Jr., R. L. Ruff, and B. W. O'Gara. 1973. *Home ranges and activity patterns of non-migratory elk of the Madison drainage as determined by biotelemetry.* Wildlife Monograph No. 33. 50 pp.

_____ and F. C. Craighead, Jr. 1974. *A population analysis of the Yellowstone grizzly bears.* Montana Forest and Conservation Experiment Station Bulletin No. 40. 20 pp.

Crampton, E. W. and L. E. Harris. 1969. *Applied animal nutrition.* San Francisco: Freeman. 753 pp.

Crocker, F. C. 1893. After wapiti in Wyoming, pp. 140–154. In *American big game hunting, the book of the Boone and Crockett Club.* T. Roosevelt and G. B. Grinnell (ed.). New York: Forest and Stream.

Croft, R. A. and L. Ellison. 1960. *Watershed and range conditions on Big Game Ridge and vicinity.* U.S. Forest Service. 37 pp.

Daubenmire, R. F. 1940. Exclosure technique in ecology. *Ecology* 21:514–515.

_____. 1952. Forest vegetation of northern Idaho and adjacent Washington, and its bearings on concepts of vegetation classification. *Ecol. Monogr.* 22:301–330.

_____. 1959. A canopy coverage method of vegetation analysis. *Northwest Sci.* 33:43–64.

_____. 1968. *Plant communities: a textbook of plant synecology.* New York: Harper and Row. 300 pp.

Dean, R. E., E. T. Thorne, and I. J. Yorgason. 1976. Weights of Rocky Mountain Elk. *J. Mammal.* 57:186–189.

Dehart, J. 1920. *Biennial report of Montana Fish and Game Commission—preserving the game in Yellowstone Park.* Montana Fish and Game Department Publication.

DeLacy, W. W. 1876. A trip up the south Snake River in 1863. *Contrib. Hist. Soc. Mont.* 1:113–143.

Denton, G. B. 1958. Vegetational cover in and near five wildlife exclosures on the northern Yellowstone National Park winter game range. Yellowstone files. 5 pp. Typewritten.

Despain, D. G. 1972. *Forest insects and diseases.* Information Paper No. 18. Yellowstone National Park. Mimeo.

_____. 1973. *Major vegetation zones of Yellowstone National Park.* Information Paper No. 19. Yellowstone National Park. Mimeo.

_____. 1976. *Western spruce budworm in Yellowstone National Park.* Information Paper No. 31. Yellowstone National Park. Mimeo.

_____ and R. E. Sellers. 1977. Natural fire in Yellowstone National Park. *West. Wildlands* 4:20–24.

Dietz, D. R. 1970. Definition and components of forage quality, pp. 1–9. In *Range and wildlife habitat evaluation—A research symposium.* U.S. Forest Service. Misc. Publication No. 1147.

Dightman, R. A., and M. E. Beatty. 1952. Recent Montana glacier and climate trends. *Mont. Weather Rev.* 80:77–81.

Dirks, R. A. 1974. *Climatological studies of Yellowstone and Grand Teton National Parks.* Department of Atmospheric Sciences, University of Wyoming. 37 pp. + appendixes.

———. 1975. *Climatological studies of Yellowstone and Grand Teton National Parks—continuing studies.* Department of Atmospheric Sciences, University of Wyoming. 37 pp. + appendixes.

——— and B. E. Martner. 1978. *The climate of Yellowstone and Grand Teton National Parks.* Natural Resources Report, National Park Service. In press.

Douglas, A. V., and C. W. Stockton. 1975. *Long-term reconstruction of seasonal temperature and precipitation in the Yellowstone National Park region using dendroclimatic techniques.* Tucson: Laboratory of Tree-Ring Research, University of Arizona. 86 pp.

Ellis, R. I. 1964. Movements and concentrations of marked elk on the winter range (northern Yellowstone elk herd). M.S. thesis, University of Montana. 93 pp.

Ellison, R., and E. J. Woolfolk. 1937. Effects of drought on vegetation near Miles City, Montana. *Ecology* **18:**329–336.

Erwin, J. B. 1898. *Annual report of the superintendent, Yellowstone National Park.* Washington, D.C.: U.S. Govt. Printing Office. 59 pp.

Farnes, P. E. 1970. Mountain precipitation map. Soil Conservation Service. Yellowstone files. Unpublished memo.

———. 1974. Preliminary analysis of mean annual snowfall for Yellowstone National Park. Soil Conservation Service. Unpublished.

———. 1975. Mean annual precipitation for Yellowstone National Park. Soil Conservation Service. Unpublished map.

——— and B. A. Shafer. 1972. *Hydrology of the Gallatin River, Montana.* Soil Conservation Service, 27 pp.

Flook, D. R. 1970. *A study of sex differential in the survival of wapiti.* Canadian Wildlife Service Report Series, No. 11. 71 pp.

Forest Service and Biological Survey, U.S. Department of Agriculture. 1916. Elk herds in the Yellowstone region of Wyoming, Montana and Idaho. Yellowstone National Park archive. Unpublished manuscript. 4 pp.

Fowler, C. W. 1978. Non-linearity in population dynamics with special reference to large mammals. In *Dynamics of large mammal populations.* C. W. Fowler and T. D. Smith (eds.). New York: Wiley. [In press 1978; Published 1981.]

——— and W. J. Barmore. 1979. A population model of the northern Yellowstone elk herd. pp. 427–437. In *Proceedings of Scientific Research in the National Parks.* R. M. Linn (ed.). National Park Service Proceedings Series, No. 5.

Franklin, J. F. 1977. The biosphere reserve program in the United States. *Science* **195:**262–267.

———, W. H. Moir, G. W. Douglas, and C. Wiberg. 1971. Invasion of subalpine meadows by trees in the Cascade Range, Washington and Oregon. *Arct. Alp. Res.* **3:**215–224.

Franklin, W. L., A. S. Mossman, and M. Dole. 1975. Social organization and home range of Roosevelt elk. *J. Mammal.* **56:**102–118.

——— and J. W. Lieb. 1979. The social organization of a sedentary population of North American elk: a model for understanding other populations, pp. 185–198. In *North American elk: ecology, behavior and management.* M. S. Boyce and L. D. Hayden-Wing (eds.). Laramie: University of Wyoming.

Frazer, G. D., H. A. Waldrop, and H. J. Hyden. 1969. *Geology of the Gardiner area Park County, Montana.* Geological Survey Bulletin 1277. Washington, D.C.: U.S. Govt. Printing Office. 118 pp.

Fuller, P. R. 1976. Browse production and utilization on the Spotted Bear Mountain winter range and seasonal movement of the Spotted Bear elk herd. M.S. thesis. University of Montana. 66 pp.

Gammill, W. H. 1939–41. Yellowstone National Park range studies. Yellowstone files. Typewritten.

———. 1939b. Yellowstone National Park range study plots open history from 1930. Yellowstone files. 82 pp. Typewritten.

_____. 1941. Rocky Mountain bighorn studies, Yellowstone National Park. Yellowstone files. 31 pp. Typewritten.

Garrison, G. A. 1972. Carbohydrate reserves and response to use. pp. 271–278. In *Wildland shrubs: Their biology and utilization.* C. M. McKell, J. P. Blaisdell, and J. R. Goodin (eds.). U.S. Forest Service, General Technical Report INT-1.

Geist, V. 1966. Ethological observations on some North American cervids. *Zool. Beitr.* **12:**219–250.

_____. 1971a. The relation of social evolution and dispersal in ungulates during the Pleistocene with emphasis on the old world deer and the genus *Bison. Q. Res.* **1:**283–315.

_____. 1971b. *Mountain sheep—a study in behavior and evolution.* Chicago: University of Chicago Press. 383 pp.

_____. 1974. On the relationship of social evolution and ecology in ungulates. *Am. Zool.* **14:**205–220.

_____. 1979. Adaptive strategies in the behavior of elk. In *Elk of North America: Ecology and management.* J. W. Thomas (ed.). Harrisburg, Pa.: Stackpole. [In press, 1979; published 1982.]

Gennett, J. A. 1977. Palynology and paleocology of sediments from Black-Tail Ponds, northern Yellowstone Park, Wyoming. M.S. thesis. University of Iowa. 74 pp.

Gillette, W. C. 1870. Personal diary of 1870 expedition to Yellowstone Park area. Yellowstone National Park Library. 18 pp. Typewritten.

Goode, G. W. 1900. *Annual report of the superintendent, Yellowstone National Park.* Washington, D.C.: U.S. Govt. Printing Office. 20 pp.

Graves, H. S., and E. W. Nelson. 1919. *Our national elk herds: a program for conserving the elk on national forests about the Yellowstone National Park.* USDA Circular 51. Washington, D.C.: U.S. Govt. Printing Office. 34 pp.

Greer, J. 1931. An ecological study of wild game animals in Yellowstone National Park. Mountain Sheep. Yellowstone files. 10 pp. Typewritten.

Greer, K. R. 1965a. *Special collections—Yellowstone elk study. Job completion report.* Montana Fish and Game Department Project W-83-R-8. 3 pp.

_____. 1965b. *Collections from the Gardiner elk post season, 1965.* Montana Fish and Game Department Report W-83-R-8. 17 pp.

_____. 1966a. *Special collections—Yellowstone elk study. Job completion report.* Montana Fish and Game Department Project W-83-R-9. 3 pp.

_____. 1966b. *Fertility rates of the Northern Yellowstone elk populations.* Annual Conference of the Western Association of State Fish and Game Commissions. No. 46. 10 pp.

_____. 1967. *Special collections—Yellowstone elk study.* Montana Fish and Game Department Report W-83-R-10. 15 pp.

_____. 1968. *Special collections—Yellowstone elk study, 1967–68.* Montana Fish and Game Department Report W-83-R-11. 26 pp.

_____ and R. E. Howe. 1964. Winter weights of northern Yellowstone elk, 1961–62. *Trans. North Am. Wildl. Conf.* **29:**237–248.

_____, J. B. Kirsch, and H. W. Yeager. 1970. Seasonal food habits of the northern Yellowstone elk herds during 1957 and 1962–67 as determined from 793 rumen samples. Montana Department of Fish and Game Project W-83-R-12. 76 pp.

Grimm, R. L. 1935–38. Yellowstone Park range studies. Yellowstone National Park files. Typewritten.

_____. 1939. Northern Yellowstone winter range studies. *J. Wildl. Manage.* **3:**295–306.

_____. 1943–47. Yellowstone National Park range studies. Yellowstone files. Typewritten.

Grinnell, G. B. 1876. Zoological report. pp. 66–89. In *Reconnaissance from Carroll, Montana Territory on the upper Missouri to the Yellowstone National Park and return, made in the summer of 1876.* W. Ludlow (ed.). Washington, D.C.: U.S. Govt. Printing Office. 141 pp.

Gruell, G. E. 1973. *An ecological evaluation of Big Game Ridge.* U.S. Department of Agriculture Publication. U.S. Forest Service, Intermountain Region. 62 pp.

_____. 1980a. *Fire's influence on wildlife habitat on the Bridger–Teton National Forest,*

Wyoming. Vol. 1: Photographic record and analysis. USDA Forest Service Research Paper INT-235. 207 pp.

————. 1980b. *Fire's influence on wildlife habitat on the Bridger–Teton National Forest, Wyoming. Vol. 2. Changes and causes, management implications.* USDA Forest Service Research Paper INT-252. 35 pp.

————. 1982. Vegetative trends in the northern Rockies, 1871–1981: A photographic record. USDA Forest Service. Unpublished report.

———— and L. L. Loope. 1974. *Relationships among aspen, fire and ungulate browsing in Jackson Hole, Wyoming.* USDA Forest Service. 33 pp.

Guptill, A. B. 1894. *Yellowstone Park guide.* Published by F. J. Haynes. Yellowstone National Park library.

Guthrie, R. D. 1966. The extinct wapiti of Alaska and Yukon Territory. *Can. J. Zool.* **44:**47–57.

Hague, A. 1886. Vegetation of the Yellowstone Park. Monograph No. 32. Part 2. Draft manuscript. Washington, D.C.: National Archives.

————. 1893. The Yellowstone Park as a game reservation, pp. 240–270. In *American big game hunting, the book of the Boone and Crockett Club.* T. Roosevelt and G. B. Grinnell (eds.). New York: Forest and Stream.

Haines, A. L. 1962. The Bannock Indian trails of Yellowstone National Park. *Archeol. Mont.* **4:**1–8.

————. 1965a. *Osborne Russell's journal of a trapper.* Lincoln: University of Nebraska Press. 191 pp.

————. 1965b. *Valley of the upper Yellowstone.* Norman: University of Oklahoma Press. 79 pp.

————. 1977. *The Yellowstone story—a history of our first national park,* Vol. 1. Yellowstone Library and Museum Association and Colorado Association Press. 385 pp.

Hall, C. A. S. 1972. Migration and metabolism in a temperate stream ecosystem. *Ecology* **53:**585–604.

Halls, L. K. 1970. Nutrient requirements of livestock and game, pp. 10–18. In *Range and wildlife habitat evaluation—a research symposium.* U.S. Forest Service, Misc. Publication No. 1147.

Harper, J. L. 1977. *Population biology of plants.* New York: Academic. 892 pp.

Harris, M. 1886. *Annual report of superintendent, Yellowstone National Park.* Washington, D.C.: U.S. Govt. Printing Office. 13 pp.

————. 1887. *Annual report of the superintendent, Yellowstone National Park.* Washington, D.C.: U.S. Govt. Printing Office. 28 pp.

————. 1888. *Annual report of the superintendent, Yellowstone National Park.* Washington, D.C.: U.S. Govt. Printing Office. 30 pp.

Hastings, J. R. and R. M. Turner. 1965. *The changing mile.* Tucson: University of Arizona Press, 317 pp.

Henderson, A. B. 1867. A narrative of a prospecting trip in the summer of 1867. Yellowstone National Park library. Typewritten.

————. 1870. Narrative of a prospecting expedition to the East Fork and Clarkes Fork of the Yellowstone, 1870. Yellowstone National Park library. Typewritten.

Henderson, W. C. 1920. Letter to Chief of U.S. Biological Survey. Yellowstone National Park archive.

Hill, L. 1919. Monthly report of acting superintendent, Yellowstone National Park, March 1919. Yellowstone National Park library. Typewritten.

Hilborn, R., and A. R. E. Sinclair, 1979. A simulation of the wildebeest population, other ungulates, and their predators, pp. 287–309. In *Serengeti—Dynamics of an ecosystem.* A. R. E. Sinclair and M. Norton-Griffiths (eds.). Chicago: Univ. Chicago Press.

Hobbs. N. T., D. L. Baker, J. E. Ellis, and D. M. Swift. 1979. Composition and quality of elk diets during winter and summer: A preliminary analysis, pp. 47–53. In *North American elk: ecology, behavior and management.* M. S. Boyce and L. D. Hayden-Wing (eds.). Laramie: University of Wyoming.

_____. 1980. Botanical and chemical composition of elk winter diets in the upper montane zone, Colorado. *J. Wildl. Manage.* In press.

Hofer, E. 1887. Winter in wonderland. *Forest and Stream* 5 May 1887.

Holling, C. S. 1973. Resilience and stability of ecological systems. *Annu. Rev. Ecol. Syst.* **4**:1–23.

_____ (ed.). 1978. *Adaptive environmental assessment and management.* New York: Wiley. 377 pp.

Honess, R. F., and K. B. Winter. 1956. *Diseases of wildlife in Wyoming.* Wyoming Game and Fish Commission Bulletin No. 9. 279 pp.

Hopkins, D. M. 1967. The Cenozoic history of Berengia—a synthesis. pp. 451–484. In *The Bering land bridge.* D. M. Hopkins (ed.). Stanford University Press.

Hornocker, M. G. 1970. *An analysis of mountain lion predation upon mule deer and elk in the Idaho primitive area.* Wildlife Monograph 21. 39 pp.

Houston, D. B. 1968. *The shiras moose in Jackson Hole, Wyoming.* Technical Bulletin No. 1. Grand Teton Natural History Assocation. 110 pp.

_____. 1971. Ecosystems of national parks. *Science* **172**:648–651.

_____. 1973. Wildfires in northern Yellowstone National Park. *Ecology* **54**:1111–1117.

_____. 1974. The northern Yellowstone elk. Parts I and II: History and demography. Yellowstone National Park. 185 pp. Mimeo.

_____. 1976. Research on ungulates in northern Yellowstone National Park, pp. 11–27. In *Research in the parks. Transactions of the National Park Centennial Symposium, December 1971.* National Park Service Symposium Series No. 1.

_____. 1978a. *Cougar and wolverine in Yellowstone National Park.* Yellowstone Park Research Note No. 5. 2 pp.

_____. 1978b. Elk as winter-spring food for carnivores in northern Yellowstone National Park. *J. Appl. Ecol.* **15**:653–661.

_____. 1979. The northern Yellowstone elk—winter distribution and management, pp. 263–272. In *North American elk: ecology, behavior and management.* M. S. Boyce and L. D. Hayden-Wing (eds.). Laramie: University of Wyoming.

_____. 1980. The northern Yellowstone elk. Yellowstone National Park files, 605 pp. Unpublished report.

Howard, W. E. 1960. Innate and environmental dispersal of individual vertebrates. *Am. Midl. Nat.* **63**:152–161.

Howe, D. L. 1970. Miscellaneous bacterial diseases: Vibriosis, actinomycosis, blackleg and malignant edema, pp. 376–381. In *Infectious diseases of wild mammals.* J. W. Davis, L. H. Karstad, and D. O. Trainer (eds.). Ames: Iowa State University Press.

Howe, R. E. 1961. Census of bighorn sheep, northern winter range, Yellowstone National Park. Yellowstone files.

Hudson, R. J. 1976. Resource division within a community of large herbivores. *Nat. Can.* **103**:153–167.

Hutchings, S. S., and R. C. Holmgren. 1959. Interpretation of loop-frequency data as a measure of plant cover. *Ecology* **40**:668–677.

Jacobsen, R. H., D. E. Worley, and K. R. Greer. 1969. The fringed tapeworm (*Thysanosoma actinioides*) as a parasite of the Rocky Mountain elk in Yellowstone National Park. *Bull. Wild. Dis. Assoc.* **5**:95–98.

Janz, B., and D. Storr. 1977. *The climate of the contiguous mountain parks: Banff, Jasper, Yoho, Kootenay.* Project Report No. 30, Atmospheric Environment Service, Department of Environment, Can. 324 pp.

Jameson, D. A. 1963. Response of individual plants to harvesting. *Bot. Rev.* **29**:532–594.

Jarman, P. J. 1974. The social organization of antelope in relation to their ecology. *Behaviour* **48**:215–266.

_____ and A. R. E. Sinclair. 1979. Feeding strategy and the pattern of resource partitioning in ungulates, pp. 130–163. In *Serengeti—dynamics of an ecosystem.* A. R. E. Sinclair and M. Norton-Griffiths (eds.). Chicago: University of Chicago Press.

Jenkins, K. J. 1980. Home range and habitat use by Roosevelt elk in Olympic National Park, Washington. M.S. thesis. Oregon State University. 84 pp.

Jenkins, R. E., and W. B. Bedford. 1973. The use of natural areas to establish environmental baselines. *Biol. Conserv.* **5**:168–174.

Johnson, D. E. 1951. Biology of the elk calf, *Cervus canadensis* nelsoni. *J. Wildl. Manage.* **15**:396–410.

Jonas, R. J. 1955. A population and ecological study of the beaver (*Castor canadensis*) of Yellowstone National Park. M.S. thesis. University of Idaho. 193 pp.

Judkins, W. T. 1919. *Report of the state game wardens of the State of Wyoming, 1919*. State of Wyoming publication. 19 pp.

Keating, K. A. 1982. Population ecology of Rocky Mountain bighorn sheep in the upper Yellowstone River drainage, Montana/Wyoming. Ms. thesis. Montana State University. 79 pp.

Keefer, W. R. 1972. *Geologic story of Yellowstone National Park*. Geological Survey Bulletin 1347. Washington, D.C.: U.S. Govt. Printing Office. 92 pp.

Kelsall, J. P. 1968. *The migratory barren-ground caribou of Canada*. Canadian Wildlife Service. 340 pp.

–––––– and E. S. Telfer. 1974. Biogeography of moose with particular reference to western North America. *Nat. Can.* **101**:117–130.

Kendall, K. C. 1980. Food habits of Yellowstone grizzly bears, 1978 and 1979, pp. 17–23. In *Yellowstone grizzly bear investigations—report of the interagency study team*. L. J. Roop, K. R. Greer, and L. E. Oldenburg (eds.). National Park Service Report.

Kingston, N., and J. K. Morton. 1975. *Trypanosoma cervi* from elk in Wyoming. *J. Parasitol.* **6**:17–23.

Kittams, W. H. 1948–58. Northern winter range studies, Yellowstone National Park. Yellowstone files. Typewritten.

––––––. 1950b. Sagebrush on the lower Yellowstone range as an indicator of wildlife stocking. Yellowstone files. 14 pp. Mimeo.

––––––. 1953. Reproduction in Yellowstone elk. *J. Wildl. Manage.* **17**:177–184.

––––––. 1956. Bighorn sheep census, Yellowstone Park. Yellowstone files.

––––––. 1959. Future of the Yellowstone wapiti. *Naturalist* **10**:30–39.

––––––. 1963. Migration of tagged elk, northern Yellowstone herd—Yellowstone elk migration. Yellowstone files. 54 pp. Typewritten.

Knight, R. R. 1970. *The Sun River elk herd*. Wildlife Monograph No. 23. 66 pp.

Kruuk, H. 1972. *The spotted hyena—a study of predation and social behavior*. Chicago: University of Chicago Press, 335 pp.

–––––– and M. Turner. 1967. Comparative notes on predation by lion, leopard, cheetah and wild dog in the Serengeti area, East Africa. *Mammalia* **31**:1–27.

Lahren, L. A. 1971. Archeological investigations in the upper Yellowstone Valley, Montana: a preliminary synthesis and discussion, pp. 168–181. In *Aboriginal man and environments on the plateau of northwest America*. A. H. Stryd and R. A. Smith (eds.). Students Press, University of Calgary.

––––––. 1976. *The Myers-Hindman site: an exploratory study of human occupation patterns in the upper Yellowstone Valley from 7000 BC to AD 1200*. Anthropologos Researches International. 195 pp.

Lambertson, R. 1967. Notes on 1967 exclosure study. Yellowstone files. 2 pp. Handwritten.

Laycock, W. A. 1958. The initial pattern of revegetation of pocket gopher mounds. *Ecology* **39**:346–351.

Leopold, A. S., S. A. Cain, C. M. Cottam, I. N. Gabrielson, and T. L. Kimball. 1963. Wildlife management in the national parks. *Trans. North Am. Wildl. Conf.* **24**:28–45.

Lieb, J. W. 1973. Social behavior in Roosevelt elk cow groups. M.S. thesis. Humboldt State University, 82 pp.

Lincoln, G. A., R. W. Youngson, and R. V. Short. 1970. The social and sexual behaviour of the red deer stag. *J. Reprod. Fert. (Suppl.)* **11**:71–103.

Lindsley, C. A. 1916. Annual report of the superintendent, Yellowstone National Park. Yellowstone National Park library. 46 pp. Typewritten.

_____. 1917. Monthly report of superintendent, Yellowstone National Park, December 1917. Yellowstone National Park library. Typewritten.

_____. 1918a–e. Monthly reports of superintendent, January–May, 1918. Yellowstone National Park library. Typewritten.

_____. 1918f. Annual report of superintendent, Yellowstone National Park. Yellowstone National Park library. 54 pp. Typewritten.

_____. 1919a. Monthly report of acting superintendent, Yellowstone National Park, January 1919. Yellowstone National Park library. Typewritten.

_____. 1919b,c. Monthly report of acting superintendent, Yellowstone National Park, November–December, 1919. Yellowstone National Park library. Typewritten.

_____. 1920a–d. Monthly reports of acting superintendent, Jan.–Apr. 1920. Yellowstone National Park library. Typewritten.

_____ and J. W. Nelson. 1917. Special report of superintendent, Yellowstone National Park, and supervisor, Gallatin National Forest. Report on the northern elk herd as shown by census of spring, 1917. Yellowstone National Park archives.

Lindsley, E. 1897. Supplemental Report. In *Annual report of superintendent, Yellowstone National Park, 1897*. Washington, D.C.: U.S. Govt. Printing Office. 34 pp.

Linhart, S. B., and F. F. Knowlton. 1975. Determining the relative abundance of coyotes by scent station lines. *Wildl. Soc. Bull.* **3**:119–124.

Lovaas, A. L. 1970. *People and the Gallatin elk herd*. Montana Fish and Game Department. 44 pp.

Ludlow, W. 1876. *Reconnaissance from Carroll, Montana Territory on the Upper Missouri to the Yellowstone National Park and return, made in the summer of 1875*. Washington, D.C.: U.S. Govt. Printing Office. 141 pp.

Luck, R. F. 1971. An appraisal of two methods of analyzing insect life tables. *Can. Entomol.* **103**:1261–1271.

MacArthur, R. H. 1972. *Geographical ecology*. New York: Harper and Row, 269 pp.

Mackie, R. J. 1964. Montana deer weights. *Mont. Wildl.* Winter 1964, pp. 9–14.

_____. 1970. *Range ecology and relations of mule deer, elk and cattle in the Missouri River Breaks, Montana*. Wildlife Monograph No. 20, 79 pp.

_____. 1973. *Responses of four browse species to protection on big game ranges in western Montana*. Job Completion Report W-120-R-3, Montana Fish and Game Department. 30 pp.

_____, D. F. Pac, and H. E. Jorgensen. 1978. Population ecology and habitat relationships of mule deer in the Bridger Mountains, Montana. In *Montana deer studies*, pp. 83–122. Project W-120-R, Montana Fish and Game Department.

Martin, L. D., and B. M. Gilbert. 1977. A cheetah-like cat in the North American Pleistocene. *Science* **195**:981–982.

_____. 1978. Excavations at Natural Trap cave. *Nebr. Acad. Sci.* **6**:107–116.

Martinka, C. J. 1978. Ungulate populations in relation to wilderness in Glacier National Park, Montana. *Trans. North Am. Wildl. Conf.* **43**:351–357.

May. R. M. 1977. Thresholds and breakpoints in ecosystems with a multiplicity of stable states. *Nature* **269**:471–477.

_____. 1979. Arctic animals and climatic changes. *Nature* **281**:177–178.

McBee, R. H., and D. E. Worley. 1962. Physiology and parasitology of the Yellowstone Park elk. Unpublished report. Yellowstone files. 17 pp.

_____. 1964. Rumen physiology and parasitology of the northern Yellowstone elk herd. Yellowstone files. Unpublished report. 28 pp.

_____, J. L. Johnson, and M. P. Bryant. 1969. Ruminal microorganisms from elk. *J. Wildl. Manage.* **33**:181–186.

McCarty, E. C., and R. Price. 1942. *Growth and carbohydrate content of important mountain forage plants in central Utah as affected by clipping and grazing*. U.S. Department of Agriculture Technical Bulletin 818. 51 pp.

McCullough, D. R. 1969. *The tule elk—its history, behavior and ecology*. University of California Publication Zoology No. 88. 209 pp.

_____. 1978. Population dynamics of the Yellowstone grizzly bear. In *Dynamics of large mammal populations*. C. W. Fowler and T. D. Smith (ed.). New York: Wiley [In press 1978; published 1981.]

McDougall, W. B. 1943. Random remarks on the Yellowstone winter range survey. Yellowstone files. 4 pp. Typewritten.

McNaughton, S. J. 1976. Serengeti migratory wildebeest: Facilitation of energy flow by grazing. *Science* **191**:92–94.

_____. 1978. Serengeti ungulates: Feeding selectivity influences the effectiveness of plant defense guilds. *Science* **199**:806–807.

_____. 1979a. Grazing as an optimization process: grass–ungulate relationships in the Serengeti. *Am. Nat.* **113**:691–703.

_____. 1979b. Grassland herbivore dynamics, pp. 46–81. In *Serengeti—Dynamics of an ecosystem*. A. R. E. Sinclair and M. Norton-Griffiths (eds.). Chicago: University of Chicago Press.

Meagher, M. M. 1973. *The bison of Yellowstone National Park*. National Park Service Scientific Monograph Series No. 1. 161 pp.

_____. 1974. Yellowstone's bison—A unique wild heritage. *Natl. Parks Conserv. Mag.* May:9–14.

_____. 1976. *A boundary control program for Yellowstone bison*. Information Paper No. 12. Yellowstone National Park. 7 pp.

_____ and J. R. Phillips. 1980. *Restoration of natural populations of grizzly and black bears in Yellowstone National Park*. Proceedings of the International Conference on Bear Research and Management No. 5. in press.

Mealey, S. P. 1975. The natural food habits of free ranging grizzly bears in Yellowstone National Park, 1973–74. M.S. thesis. Montana State University. 158 pp.

Mech, L. D. 1966. *The wolves of Isle Royale*. Fauna of the National Parks No. 7. Washington, D.C.: U.S. Govt. Printing Office. 210 pp.

_____. 1970. *The wolf*. New York: Natural History Press/Doubleday. 384 pp.

Mereszczak, I. M. 1978. The effects of three levels of range improvements on Roosevelt elk nutrition. M.S. thesis. Oregon State University. 86 pp.

Miller, R. S. 1967. Pattern and process in competition, pp. 1–74. In *Advances in ecological research*, Vol. 4, J. B. Cragg (ed.). New York: Academic.

Mills, H. B. 1935a. Observations on the Yellowstone elk herd during the winter reduction program of 1935. Yellowstone files. 19 pp. Typewritten.

_____. 1935b. A preliminary study of the bighorn sheep of Yellowstone National Park. Yellowstone files. 9 pp. Typewritten.

_____. 1936. Observations of Yellowstone elk. *J. Mammal.* **17**:250–253.

Mitchell, B. 1963. Determinations of age in Scottish deer from growth layers in dental cement. *Nature (London)* **198**:350–351.

_____. 1967. Growth layers in dental cement for determining the age of red deer. *J. Anim. Ecol.* **36**:279–293.

_____. 1973. The reproductive performance of wild Scottish red deer, *Cervus elaphus*. *J. Reprod. Fert. (Suppl.)* **19**:271–285.

_____ and D. Brown. 1974. The effects of age and body size on fertility in female red deer (*Cervus elaphus* L.). *Proc. Int. Congr. Game Biol.* **11**:89–98.

_____, D. McCowan, and I. A. Nicholson. 1976. Annual cycles of body weight and condition in Scottish red deer, *Cervus elaphus*. *J. Zool.* (London) **180**:107–127.

_____, B. W. Staines, and D. Welch. 1977. *Ecology of red deer—a research review relevant to their management in Scotland*. Institute of Terrestrial Ecology. 74 pp.

Mitchell, J. M. 1961. Recent secular changes in global temperature. *Ann. N.Y. Acad. Sci.* **95**:235–251.

_____. 1970. A preliminary evaluation of atmospheric pollution as a cause of the global temperature fluctuation of the past century. pp. 139–155. In *Global effects of environmental pollution. AAAS Symposium*, S. F. Singer (ed.). New York: Springer-Verlag.

Morey, C. R. 1967. Final reduction report 1966–67, Yellowstone National Park. Yellowstone files. 17 pp. Mimeo.

Morgan, J. K. 1970. *Ecology of the Morgan Creek and East Fork of the Salmon River bighorn sheep herds and management of bighorn sheep in Idaho.* Idaho Fish and Game Department Project W-142-R-1. 155 pp.

Morisita, M. 1965. The fitting of the logistic equation to the rate of increase of population density. *Res. Popul. Ecol.* **7:**52–53.

Morton, M. A. 1976. Nutritional values of important mule deer winter forage plants in the Bridger Mountains, Montana. M.S. thesis. Montana State University. 103 pp.

Mould, E. D. 1980. Aspects of elk nutrition and associated analytical procedures. Ph.D. thesis. Washington State University. 72 pp.

Mueggler, W. F. 1967. Response of mountain grassland vegetation to clipping in southwestern Montana. *Ecology* **48:**942–949.

_____. 1972. *Plant development and yield on mountain grasslands in southwestern Montana.* Intermountain Forest and Range Experiment Station, USDA Forest Service INT-124. 18 pp.

_____ and C. A. Harris. 1969. Some vegetation and soil characteristics of mountain grasslands in central Idaho. *Ecology* **50:**671–678.

_____ and D. L. Bartos. 1977. *Grindstone flat and big flat exclosures—a 41-year record of changes in clearcut aspen communities.* USDA Forest Service Research Paper INT-195. 16 pp.

_____ and W. L. Stewart. 1980. *Grassland and shrubland habitat types of western Montana.* USDA Gen. Tech. Report INT-66. 154 pp.

Murie, A. 1940. *Ecology of the coyote in the Yellowstone.* Fauna of the National Parks No. 4. Washington, D.C.: U.S. Govt. Printing Office. 206 pp.

Murie, O. J. 1943. Observations on elk slaughtered in reduction program in Yellowstone National Park, January 4–13, 1943. Report to National Park Service. Yellowstone National Park library. 15 pp. Typewritten.

_____. 1951. *The elk of North America.* Harrisburg, Pa.: Stackpole. 376 pp.

Murphy, D. A. and J. A. Coates. 1966. Effects of dietary protein on deer. *Trans. North Am. Wildl. Conf.* **31:**129–138.

National Academy of Science. 1962. *Range research—basic problems and techniques.* National Academy of Science, National Research Council, Publication 870, 341 pp.

National Park Service, U.S. Department of Interior. 1920. Chief Ranger's monthly report, Yellowstone National Park, May. Yellowstone National Park library. Typewritten.

_____. 1938. Winter range data. Yellowstone National Park archive. Typewritten.

_____. 1953. Management plan for northern elk herd. Yellowstone files. 5 pp. Mimeo.

_____. 1957. Management plan for the northern elk herd, Yellowstone National Park. Yellowstone files. 9 pp. Mimeo.

_____. 1961. Management of Yellowstone's northern elk herd. Yellowstone files. 20 pp.

_____. 1964. Wildlife management background information, Yellowstone National Park. Yellowstone files. 20 pp.

_____. 1975a. The natural role of fire—A fire management plan, Yellowstone National Park. National Park Service, Yellowstone National Park. 32 pp. Mimeo.

_____. 1975b. Restoring a viable wolf population in Yellowstone National Park. Draft environmental assessment. Yellowstone Park.

Nelson, E. W. 1917. Conservation of game in the national forests and national parks. *Am. For.* March.

Nelson, J. R., and T. A. Leege. 1979. Nutritional requirements and food habits. In *Ecology and management of North American elk.* J. W. Thomas (ed.). Harrisburg, Pa.: Stackpole. [In press 1979; published 1982.]

Neter, J. and W. Wasserman. 1974. *Applied linear statistical models.* Homewood Ill.: R. D. Irwin. 842 pp.

Norris, P. W. 1877. *Annual report of the superintendent, Yellowstone National Park.* Washington, D.C.: U.S. Govt. Printing Office. 9 pp.

———. 1880. *Annual report of the superintendent, Yellowstone National Park, 1879.* Washington, D.C.: U.S. Govt. Printing Office. 31 pp.

———. 1881. *Annual report of the superintendent, Yellowstone National Park, 1880.* Washington, D.C.: U.S. Govt. Printing Office. 64 pp.

O'Gara, B. W. 1968. A study of the reproductive cycle of the female pronghorn. Ph.D. thesis. University of Montana. 161 pp.

——— and K. R. Greer. 1970. Food habits in relation to physical condition in two populations of pronghorn. *Proc. Antelope States Workshop* **4:**131–139.

Oldemeyer, J. L. 1966. Winter ecology of bighorn sheep in Yellowstone National Park. M.S. thesis. Colorado State University. 107 pp.

———, W. J. Barmore, and D. L. Gilbert. 1971. Winter ecology of bighorn sheep in Yellowstone National Park. *J. Wildl. Manage.* **35:**257–269.

Olsen, A. L. 1938. The "firing line" in the management of the northern elk herd. *Univ. Idaho Bull.* **8:**36–42.

Owensby, C. E. 1969. Effect of cages on herbage yield in true prairie vegetation. *J. Range Manage.* **22:**131–132.

Packer, P. E. 1963. Soil stability requirements for the Gallatin elk winter range. *J. Wildl. Manage.* **27:**401–410.

Palmer, W. C. 1965. *Meteorological drought.* Research Paper No. 15, U.S. Department of Commerce.

Parker, K. W. 1954. *A method for measuring trend in range condition on National Forest ranges with supplemental instructions for measurement of vigor, composition and browse.* USDA Forest Service. 37 pp.

——— and R. W. Harris. 1959. The 3-step method for measuring condition and trend of forest ranges; a résumé of its history, development and use. pp. 55–59. In *Techniques and methods of measuring understory vegetation.* Southern Forest Experiment Station. USDA Forest Service.

Parsons, T. M. 1936. A summary of the studies on bighorn mountain sheep in Yellowstone National Park. Yellowstone files. 4 pp. Typewritten.

Passey, H. B., V. K. Hugie, and E. W. Williams. 1964. Herbage production and composition fluctuations of natural plant communities as related to climate and soil taxonomic units. pp. 206–221. In *Forage plant physiology and soil range relationships.* American Society of Agronomy Special Publication No. 5.

Patten, D. T. 1968. Dynamics of a shrub continuum along the Gallatin River in Yellowstone National Park. *Ecology* **49:**1107–1112.

Pechanec, J. F., G. D. Pickford, and G. Stewart. 1937. Effects of the 1934 drought on native vegetation of the upper Snake River Plains, Idaho. *Ecology* **18:**490–505.

Peek, J. M., A. L. Lovaas, and R. A. Rouse. 1967. Population changes within the Gallatin elk herd, 1932–65. *J. Wildl. Manage.* **31:**304–315.

Pengelly, W. L. 1963. Thunder on the Yellowstone. *Naturalist* **14:**18–25.

Peterman, R. M., W. C. Clark, and C. S. Holling. 1978. The dynamics of resilience: shifting stability domains in fish and insect systems, pp. 321–341. In *Population dynamics. Proceedings British Ecological Society Symposium,* R. M. Anderson, B. D. Turner, and L. R. Taylor (eds.). London: Blackwell.

Peterson, R. O. 1977. *Wolf ecology and prey relationships on Isle Royale.* Scientific Monograph Series No. 11, U.S. National Park Service. 210 pp.

———. 1979. The role of wolf predation in a moose population decline, pp. 329–333. In *Scientific research in the National Parks.* R. M. Linn (ed.). National Park Service Proceedings Series. No. 5.

_____ and D. L. Allen. 1974. Snow conditions as a parameter in moose-wolf relationships. *Nat. Can.* **101:**481–492.

Petocz, R. G. 1973. The effect of snow cover on the social behavior of bighorn rams and mountain goats. *Can. J. Zool.* **51:**987–993.

Péwé, T. L. 1967. Mammal remains of pre-Wisconsin age in Alaska. pp. 266–271. In *The Bering land bridge*. D. M. Hopkins (ed.). Stanford University Press.

Picton, H. D. 1978. Climate and reproduction of grizzly bears in Yellowstone National Park. *Nature* **274:**888–889.

_____. 1979. A climate index and mule deer fawn survival in Montana. *Int. J. Biometeor.* **23:**115–122.

Pimlott, D. H. 1967. Wolf predation and ungulate populations. *Am. Zool.* **7:**267–278.

_____ and P. W. Joslin. 1968. The status and distribution of the red wolf. *Trans. North Am. Wildl. Conf.* **33:**373–388.

Pitcher, J. 1901. *Annual report of the superintendent, Yellowstone National Park.* Washington, D.C.: U.S. Govt. Printing Office. 21 pp.

_____. 1902. *Annual report of the superintendent, Yellowstone National Park.* Washington, D.C.: U.S. Govt. Printing Office. 22 pp.

_____. 1903. *Annual report of the superintendent, Yellowstone National Park.* Washington, D.C.: U.S. Govt. Printing Office. 17 pp.

_____. 1905. *Annual report of the superintendent, Yellowstone National Park.* Washington, D.C.: U.S. Govt. Printing Office. 27 pp.

_____. 1906. *Annual report of the superintendent, Yellowstone National Park.* Washington, D.C.: U.S. Govt. Printing Office. 22 pp.

Pollack, A. M. 1974. Seasonal changes in appetite and sexual condition in red deer stags maintained on a six-month photoperiod. *J. Physiol. (London)* **244:**95–96P.

Poore, M. E. D. 1962. The method of successive approximation in descriptive ecology, pp. 36–68. In *Advances in ecological research*, Vol. 1. J. B. Cragg (ed.). New York: Academic.

Porter, S. C., and G. H. Denton. 1967. Chronology of neoglaciation in North American cordillera. *Am. J. Sci.* **265:**177–210.

Quimby, D. C., and J. E. Gaab. 1957. Mandibular dentition as an age indicator in Rocky Mountain elk. *J. Wildl. Manage.* **21:**435–451.

_____ and D. E. Johnson. 1951. Weights and measurements of Rocky Mountain elk. *J. Wildl. Manage.* **15:**57–62.

Reppert, J. N., and R. E. Francis. 1973. *Interpretation of trend in range condition from 3-step data.* USDA Forest Service Research Paper RM-103. 15 pp.

Richmond, G. M. 1965. Glaciation of the Rocky Mountains, pp. 217–230. In *The Quaternary of the United States*. H. E. Wright and D. G. Frey (eds.). Princeton University Press.

_____. 1972. Appraisal of the future climate of the Holocene in the Rocky Mountains. *Q. Res.* **2:**315–322.

Rickard, W. H., J. D. Hedlund, and R. E. Fitzner. 1977. Elk in the shrub–steppe region of Washington: An authentic record. *Science* **196:**1009–1010.

Riggs, R. A., and J. M. Peek. 1980. Mountain sheep habitat–use patterns related to post-fire succession. *J. Wildl. Manage.* **44:**933–938.

Robbins, C. T., R. S. Padbielancik-Norman, D. L. Wilson, and E. D. Mould. 1981. Growth and nutrient consumption of elk calves compared to other species. *J. Wildl. Manage.* In press.

Robertson, J. H. 1939. A quantitative study of true prairie vegetation after three years of extreme drought. *Ecol. Monogr.* **9:**431–492.

_____ and H. P. Cords. 1957. Survival of rabbitbrush, *Chrysothamnus* spp., following chemical, burning and mechanical treatments. *J. Range Manage.* **10:**83–89.

Robinson, W. B. 1952. Some observations on coyote predation in Yellowstone National Park. *J. Mammal.* **33:**470–476.

Roemer, A. 1933. Report of type mapping and range survey. Yellowstone files. 6 pp. Typewritten.

Romme, W. H. 1979. Fire and landscape diversity in subalpine forests of Yellowstone National Park. Ph.D. thesis. University of Wyoming. 167 pp.

Rush, W. M. 1932a. *Northern Yellowstone elk study*. Montana Fish and Game Commission. 131 pp.

———. 1932b. Bang's disease in the Yellowstone National Park buffalo and elk herds. *J. Mammal.* **13**:371–372.

Sadlier, R. M. F. S. 1969. *The ecology of reproduction in wild and domestic mammals*. London: Methuen. 321 pp.

Schaller, G. B. 1972. *The Serengeti lion—a study of predator–prey relations*. Chicago: University of Chicago Press. 480 pp.

Schier, G. A. 1975. *Deterioration of aspen clones in the middle Rocky Mountains*. USDA Forest Service Research Paper INT-170. 14 pp.

Schladweiler, P. and D. R. Stevens. 1973. Weights of moose in Montana. *J. Mammal.* **54**:772–775.

Schlegel, M. 1976. Factors affecting calf elk survival in north central Idaho—a progress report. *Proc. W. Assoc. State Fish Game Comm.* **56**:342–355.

———. 1977. *Movements and population dynamics of the Lochsa elk herd*. Idaho Fish and Game Department Report. Project W-160-R4 Job No. 3.

Schoener, T. W. 1974. Resource partitioning in ecological communities. *Science* **185**:27–39.

Schullery, P., 1980. *The bears of Yellowstone*. Yellowstone Library and Museum Association. 175 pp.

Scott, J. A., N. R. French, and J. W. Leetham. 1979. Patterns of consumption in grasslands, pp. 89–105. In *Perspectives in grassland ecology*. N. R. French (ed.). New York: Springer-Verlag.

Scout diaries, 1898–1916. Yellowstone National Park archives.

Seidensticker, J. C., M. G. Hornocker, W. V. Wiles, and J. P. Messick. 1973. *Mountain lion social organization in the Idaho primitive area*. Wildlife Monograph No. 35. 60 pp.

Sellers, R. E., and D. G. Despain. 1976. Fire management in Yellowstone National Park. *Proc. Annu. Tall Timbers Fire Ecol. Conf.* **14**:99–113.

Server, F. E. 1876–77. Diary of a trip through Yellowstone Park and down the Snake River to Fort Hall. Montana State University archives, File No. 507.

Shaw, E. W., and B. W. Clark. 1920. Report on game protection and patrol of winter elk range on the Absaroka and Gallatin National Forests, 1919–1920. U.S. Forest Service Report. Copies at headquarters, Gallatin National Forest and Yellowstone National Park library. Typewritten.

Shoesmith, M. W. 1978. Social organization of wapiti and woodland caribou. Ph.D. thesis. University of Manitoba. 155 pp.

———. 1979. Seasonal movements and social behavior of elk on Mirror Plateau, Yellowstone National Park, pp. 166–176. In *North American elk: ecology, behavior and management*. M. S. Boyce and L. D. Hayden-Wing (eds.). Laramie: University of Wyoming.

Shore, W. B. 1912. An incident in the annual elk migration. *Outdoor Life*, February:125–130.

Short, H. L., E. E. Remmenga, and C. E. Boyd. 1969. Variations in rumino-reticular contents of white-tailed deer. *J. Wildl. Manage.* **33**:187–191.

Shreve, F. 1924. Soil temperature as influenced by altitude and slope exposure. *Ecology* **5**:128–156.

Simpson, A. 1916. Letter to Chief Forester, U.S. Forest Service. Yellowstone National Park archive.

——— and V. Bailey. 1915. Investigation of the elk herds in the Yellowstone Park region of Wyoming, Montana and Idaho. U.S. For. Serv. and U.S. Biol. Surv. Yellowstone National Park library. 56 pp. Typewritten.

Sinclair, A. R. E. 1975. The resource limitation of trophic levels in tropical grassland ecosystems. *J. Anim. Ecol.* **44**:497–520.

_____. 1977. *The African buffalo—A study of resource limitation of populations.* Chicago: University of Chicago Press. 355 pp.

_____. 1979. Dynamics of the Serengeti ecosystem: Process and pattern. pp. 1–30. In *Serengeti—Dynamics of an ecosystem.* A. R. E. Sinclair and M. Norton-Griffiths (eds.). Chicago: University of Chicago Press.

_____ and M. Norton-Griffiths, eds. 1979. *Serengeti-Dynamics of an ecosystem.* Chicago: University of Chicago Press. 389 pp.

Singer, F. J. 1979. Habitat partitioning and wildfire relationships of cervids in Glacier National Park, Montana. *J. Wildl. Manage.* **43**:437–444.

Skinner, C. K. 1950. Problems of surplus elk in Yellowstone National Park. Yellowstone files. 6 pp.

Skinner, M. P. 1927. The predatory and fur bearing animals of the Yellowstone National Park. *Roosevelt Wildl. Bull.* **4**:163–281.

_____. 1928. The elk situation. *J. Mammal.* **9**:309–317.

_____. 1929. White-tailed deer formerly in the Yellowstone Park. *J. Mammal.* **10**:101–115.

_____. No date–*ca.* 1935. Studies of wapiti foods in Yellowstone National Park—Aspen. Yellowstone files. 19 pp. Typewritten.

Slade, N. A. 1977. Statistical detection of density dependence from a series of sequential censuses. *Ecology* **58**:1094–1102.

Smuts, G. L. 1978. Interrelations between predators, prey, and their environment. *Bioscience* **28**:316–320.

Soil Conservation Service, U.S. Department of Agriculture. 1963. Range site and condition survey northern elk range, Yellowstone Park, June 3–14. Yellowstone files. 9 pp. Typewritten.

Southern, H. N. 1970. The natural control of a population of tawny owls (*Strix aluco*). *J. Zool. (London)* **162**:197–285.

Spinage, C. A. 1972. African ungulate life tables. *Ecology* **53**:645–652.

Stelfox, J. G. 1976. *Range ecology of Rocky Mountain bighorn sheep.* Canadian Wildlife Report Series. No. 39. 50 pp.

_____ and R. D. Taber. 1969. Big game in the northern Rocky Mountain coniferous forest. pp. 197–220. In *Coniferous forests of the northern Rocky Mountains.* R. D. Taber (ed.). University of Montana Foundation.

Stevens, D. R. 1970. Winter ecology of moose in the Gallatin Mountains, Montana. *J. Wildl. Manage.* **34**:37–46.

Stewart, G., and S. S. Hutchings. 1936. The point-observation-plot (square-foot density) method of vegetation survey. *J. Am. Soc. Agron.* **28**:714–722.

Stewart, S. T. 1975. Ecology of the West Rosebud and Stillwater bighorn sheep herds, Beartooth Mountains, Montana. M.S. thesis. Montana State University. 130 pp.

Stockton, C. W. 1973. A dendroclimatic analysis of the Yellowstone National Park Region, Wyoming-Montana. Laboratory of Tree-Ring Research, University of Arizona. 56 pp. Unpublished report.

Stoddart, L. A. 1946. *Some physical and chemical responses of* Agropyron spicatum *to herbage removal at various seasons.* Utah State Agricultural Experiment Station Bulletin 324. 24 pp.

_____ and A. D. Smith. 1943. *Range management.* New York: McGraw-Hill. 547 pp.

Strong, W. E. 1875. *A trip to the Yellowstone National Park in July, August and September, 1875.* Norman: University of Oklahoma Press. 165 pp.

Struthsaker, T. T. 1967. Behavior of elk during the rut. *Z. Tierpsychol.* **24**:80–114.

Tansley, A. G. 1935. The use and abuse of vegetational concepts and terms. *Ecology* **16**:284–307.

Telfer, E. S., and J. P. Kelsall. 1971. Morphological parameters for mammal locomotion in snow. Paper presented at 51st Annual Meeting of the American Society of Mammalogists.

_____. 1979. Studies of morphological parameters affecting ungulate locomotion in snow. *Can. J. Zool.* **57**:2153–2159.

Thorne, E. T. 1970a. *Nutritional requirements of elk for reproduction*, pp. 54–79. Job Progress Report Project FW-3-R-19, Wyoming Game and Fish Commission.

———. 1970b. *Diagnosis of diseases in wildlife*. Job Progress Report No. FW-3-R-17, Wyoming Game and Fish Commission. 32 pp.

———. 1976. *Status, mortality and response to management of Whiskey Basin Bighorn sheep*. Job Completion Report, FW-3-R-22, Wyoming Game and Fish Department.

——— and G. Butler. 1976. *Comparison of pelleted, cubed, and baled alfalfa hay as winter feed for elk*. Wildlife Technical Report No. 6, Wyoming Game and Fish Department. 38 pp.

———, R. E. Dean, and W. G. Hepworth. 1976. Nutrition during gestation in relation to successful reproduction in elk. *J. Wildl. Manage.* **40**:330–335.

———, J. K. Morton, and W. C. Ray. 1979. Brucellosis, its effect and impact on elk in western Wyoming, pp. 212–220. In *North American elk: Ecology behavior and management*. M. S. Boyce and L. D. Hayden-Wing (eds.). Laramie: University of Wyoming.

Tolhurst, F. B. 1926. Account of trip through Yellowstone. 1882. In *Scrapbook of B. Haynes Arnold*. Yellowstone Park files.

Trainer, C. E. 1971. The relationships of physical condition and fertility of female Roosevelt elk (*Cervus canadensis roosevelti*) in Oregon. M.S. thesis. Oregon State University. 93 pp.

Tweedy, F. 1886. Flora of the Yellowstone National Park. Washington, D.C.: Author. 78 pp.

USDA Forest Service. 1969. *Range environmental analysis handbook. Region 1.*

———. 1977. *Range analysis handbook. Region 1.*

U.S. Fish and Wildlife Service. 1980. *A plan for the recovery of the northern Rocky Mountain wolf*. 67 pp.

Varley, G. C., and G. R. Gradwell. 1968. Population models for the winter moth, pp. 132–141. In *Insect abundance*. T. R. E. Southwood (ed.). Oxford: Blackwell.

Verme, L. J. 1962. Mortality of white-tailed deer fawns in relation to nutrition. *Proc. Natl. Deer Dis. Symp.* **1**:15–30.

Vesey-Fitzgerald, D. F. 1960. Grazing succession among East African game animals. *J. Mammal.* **41**:161–172.

Waddington, J. F. B., and H. E. Wright. 1974. Late Quaternary vegetational changes on the east side of Yellowstone Park, Wyoming. *Q. Res.* **4**:175–184.

Wahl, E. W. 1968. A comparison of the climate of the eastern United States during the 1830s with the current normals. *Mon. Weather Rev.* **96**:73–82.

——— and T. L. Lawson. 1970. The climate of the mid-nineteenth century compared to the current normals. *Mon. Weather Rev.* **98**:259–265.

Walcheck, K. 1976. Montana wildlife 170 years ago. *Mont. Outdoors* **7**:15–30.

Waldrop, H. A., and H. J. Hyden. 1963. Landslides near Gardiner, Montana. In *Short papers in geology, hydrology and topography*. U.S. Geological Survey Professional Paper 450E. pp. E11–E14.

Walter, H. 1973. *Vegetation of the earth in relation to climate and the eco-physiological conditions*. New York: Springer-Verlag. 237 pp.

Warren, E. R. 1926. A study of the beaver in the Yancey Region of Yellowstone National Park. *Roosevelt Wildl. Ann.* **1**:1–191.

Wear, D. W. 1885. *Annual report of the superintendent, Yellowstone National Park*. Washington, D.C.: U.S. Govt. Printing Office. 5 pp.

———. 1886. *Annual report of the superintendent, Yellowstone National Park*. Washington, D.C.: U.S. Govt. Printing Office. 3 pp.

Weaver, J. E., and F. W. Albertson. 1936. Effects of the great drought on the prairies of Iowa, Nebraska and Kansas. *Ecology* **17**:567–639.

———, J. H. Robertson, and R. L. Fowler. 1940. Changes in true-prairie vegetation during drought as determined by list quadrats. *Ecology* **21**:357–362.

Weaver, J. 1978. *The wolves of Yellowstone*. Natural Resources Report No. 14, National Park Service, 38 pp.

Wedel, W. R., W. M. Husted, and J. H. Moss. 1968. Mummy cave: Prehistoric record from Rocky Mountains of Wyoming. *Science* **160:**184–186.

West, R. M. 1937. Post-mortem examinations of elk slaughtered in Yellowstone Park. Report of 1937 reduction program in the northern Yellowstone elk herd. Yellowstone files. Typewritten.

Westra, R., and R. J. Hudson, 1979. Urea recycling in wapiti, pp. 236–239. In *North American elk: Ecology, behavior and management.* M. S. Boyce and L. D. Hayden-Wing (eds.). Laramie: University of Wyoming.

Whitlock, G., and L. E. Hayes. 1935–36. Absaroka winter game studies. Unpublished report, Gallatin National Forest files.

Whittaker, R. H. 1967. Gradient analysis of vegetation. *Biol. Rev.* **42:**207–264.

Willard, E. E., and C. M. McKell. 1978. Response of shrubs to simulated browsing. *J. Wildl. Manage.* **43:**514–519.

Wolff, J. O. 1978. Burning and browsing effects on willow growth in interior Alaska. *J. Wildl. Manage.* **42:**135–140.

Woolf, A. 1968. Summer ecology of bighorn sheep in Yellowstone National Park. M.S. thesis. Colorado State University. 112 pp.

Worley, D. E. 1979. Parasites and disease of elk in the northern Rocky Mountain region: A review, pp. 206–211. In *North American elk: Ecology, behavior and management.* M. S. Boyce and L. D. Hayden-Wing (eds.). Laramie: University of Wyoming.

———— and R. E. Barrett. 1964. Studies on the parasites of the northern Yellowstone elk herd. In *Rumen physiology and parasitology of the northern Yellowstone elk.* R. J. McBee and D. E. Worley (eds.). Yellowstone files. Unpublished report.

Wright, G. M. 1934. Report upon winter range of the northern Yellowstone elk herd and a suggested program for its restoration. Yellowstone files. 14 pp. Typewritten.

———— and B. H. Thompson. 1935. *Wildlife management in the national parks.* Fauna of the National Parks No. 2. Washington, D.C.: U.S. Govt. Printing Office. 142 pp.

Young, S. B. M. 1897. *Annual report of superintendent, Yellowstone National Park.* Washington, D.C.: U.S. Govt. Printing Office. 34 pp.

————. 1907. *Annual report of the superintendent, Yellowstone National Park.* Washington, D.C.: U.S. Govt. Printing Office. 27 pp.

————. 1908. *Annual report of the superintendent, Yellowstone National Park.* Washington, D.C.: U.S. Govt. Printing Office. 19 pp.

Yount, H. 1881a. Report of gamekeeper for 1880. In *Annual report of the superintendent, Yellowstone National Park.* Washington, D.C.: U.S. Govt. Printing Office, 64 pp.

————. 1881b. Report of gamekeeper. In *Annual report of the superintendent, Yellowstone National Park, 1881.* Washington, D.C.: U.S. Govt. Printing Office. 81 pp.

INDEX

Age distributions
  changes over time, 51
  females, 49–51, 54–56
  instability of, 53
  males, 51, 54–56
  stationary, 53
ANOVA: *see* Variance, analysis of
Aspen; *see also* Vegetation, measurements
  of
  abundance, 86–87, 92
  fire relationships, 107–111, 113–115,
    127
  grazing, 125, 127, 135
  measurements of, 99, 111, 412–420

Bear
  numbers, 190–191
Bear, black
  numbers, 188–189
  predation upon elk, 64, 189, 191
Bear, grizzly
  numbers and status, 188
  predation upon elk, 64, 191
Beaver, 92
  aspen relationships, 182
  interspecific competition with elk, 183.
  numbers, 182

Behavior, social, 76–84
  agonism and food supplies, 81–84
  agonism and snow cover, 82–83
  agonistic behavior, 77–83
  associations between individuals, 77
  behavior, patterns of, 78–83
  dominance hierarchies, 77–83
  group constancy, 76–77, 83
  group size, 76
  social dominance, 77–83
Bison, 392
  brucellosis, 167, 200
  carrying capacity, 185
  chest height, 171
  foot load, 172
  grazing, semidomesticated, 119
  habitat utilization, 173–174
  herd composition, 441
  interspecific competition with elk,
    179–181
  numbers, 167
  numbers, historical, 156–157
  rate of increase, observed, 167
  relationships to elk, 442
  winter diets, 176–177
  winter feeding, 28
  winter range, 166–167

Note: Entries refer to the northern Yellowstone elk unless otherwise indicated.

BLA: *see* Boundary line area
Boundary line area, 4–5
  appearance of, 94
  effects of human activities upon, 122
  elk distribution within, 27, 29–30, 199
  elk management within, 199–200
  soils, 94, 118, 368–369
  vegetation of, 87–88, 94–95, 101, 124,
      128–129, 338–345, 364–368
Brucellosis
  in bison, 167, 200
  in elk, 193

Carnivores, 186–195
  effects of elk reduction on, 193
  elk as food for, 189–191
  predation on elk, 63–64, 193–195
Carrying capacity, 62, 66–67
  ecological, 62, 66–67, 134–136,
      152–154, 185, 193
  economic, 62, 134
Census, bias errors in, 18–19
  of elk, 13–15, 17–23
Climate, 5–8
  altithermal, 102
  drought of 1930s, 105
  glaciation, Pinedale, 102
  growing conditions, summary of, 371
  LIA: *see* Little Ice Age
  Little Ice Age, 102, 123
  neoglaciation, 102
  Palmer drought index, 370
  precipitation, trends of, 104–105
  precipitation, water year, 370–371
  temperature, trends of, 102–105
  tree-ring records of, 105, 371
  trends of, 101–107
  water runoff, 105
Competition
  interference, 81
  interspecific, 178–181, 184–185
  intraspecific, 84, 193
Condition, 72–73
  fat reserves as index, 72–73
Cougar
  numbers and status, 187
Coyote
  densities, 187
  numbers, 187, 190–191
  predation upon elk, 63, 64, 191
  predation upon deer, 160
  predation upon pronghorn, 169

Deer, mule
  carrying, capacity, 185
  chest height, 171
  foot load, 172
  habitat utilization, 173
  herd composition, 159, 434
  human predation upon, 158
  interspecific competition with elk,
      179–180
  mortality of young, 159
  numbers, 159
  numbers, historical, 157
  predation upon, 159–160
  relationships to elk, 435
  winter diets, 176–177
  winter range, 158–159
Deer, red, 69
Deer, white-tailed, 74
  interspecific competition with elk, 182
  numbers, 182
  winter range, 182
Density-dependence, 36, 67–68
Density, winter, 30–32
  and standing biomass, 67
Diseases, 191–193
Dispersal, 61, 65
  emmigration, 61
  immigration, 61

Eagles, 190–191
Early records to 1886, 10–11
  1836–86, 204–211
  1886–1910, 11–12, 212–218
  1911–20, 12–15, 219–237
  1921–29, 15–17
  1930–68, 17–21
  1969–79, 21–23
Ecology, physiological, 69–75
Ecosystems
  role of elk in dynamics, 152
Elk: *see* footnote p. 469 of Index
Erosion, 114–118
  accelerated, 114–118
  geologic, 114

Facilitation, ecological
  between species of ungulates, 184–185
Food
  daily intake of, 69
  quality of, 70
  quantity available, 151
  quantity consumed, 151–152

Food habits, 142–144
  plant parts, selection of, 143–144
Food preferences
  by forage classes, 176–177
  by less abundant ungulates, 174–176
  by plant parts, 177
  by plant species, 177
Food selection
  relationship to body size, 174–175
  and skull characteristics, 175
Forage
  availability of, 432–433
  consumption, 432–433
  ridgetops, 433
  winter, 73
Forage quality, 75, 144–146
  crude protein as index, 144–145
  grasses, 144–145
  shrubs and trees, 144–145
Forage utilization, 146–150
  grasses, 146–148
  sagebrush, 148
  willows, 148
Fire, 107–114
  and aspen, 107–115
  and big sagebrush, 107
  management of, 197–198

Goats, mountain, 83
Gophers, pocket, 90–91, 124, 154, 403
Grasshoppers, 124, 154
Growth, 71–72
  rates of, 73
Grazing systems, 134, 136

Habitat relationships, 137–155
  food supply, changes over time, 150–152
Habitat utilization
  effects of snow depth, 139–140
  effects of spring greenup on use, 140
  foraging activities, 141–142
  by less abundant ungulates, 173–174
  summer range, 142
  winter range, 137–142
Herbivores
  management of, 198–201
Herbivory, 154–155
Herd segments, 32–34
History and numbers, interpretation of, 23–25
Home range
  affinity for, 34

Human developments and activities, 118–122
  boundary line area, 122
  cultivation, 120–122
  feeding of ungulates, 119–122
  livestock grazing, 119–121
Human predation
  effects on numbers, 14, 16, 20–21, 25, 66, 77
  effects on increase rate, 23

Inanition, 75
Immune response, 75–193
Insects
  budworms, western, 155
  influence on elk distribution, 76
  management of, 201

K_c: see Carrying capacity, economic
K_I: see Carrying capacity, ecological

Lactation, 69
Life tables, 54–55
Lungworm, thread, 192–193

Man
  Euro-American, 189
    management of, 201–202
  hunter-gatherers, 189, 194
Management, 196–203
  bison, 200
  elk, 199–200
  experimental, 197
  monitoring needs for, 202
  pronghorn, 200–201
  research needs for, 202–203
  Yellowstone Park, 196–202
Moose
  carrying capacity, 185
  chest height, 171
  foot load, 172
  habitat utilization, 174
  herd composition, 169, 442
  interspecific competition with elk, 179
  numbers, 157–158, 169
  relationships to elk, 442
  winter diets, 176–177
  winter range, 169
Mortality, 46–61
  adult, 49–56, 64, 74
  calf, 48–49, 63–64, 74–75, 83–84, 241–242
    $\hat{k}$-factors, 243–245

Mortality (*cont.*)
    density dependent, 57–61, 64–65
    differential male, 47
    males, 242
        k-factors, 246–247
    k-factor analysis of, 58–61
    natural vs. human, 56–57, 64–65
    neonates, 48–49
    over winter, 49
    patterns of, 49–56, 64, 240–241
    sex ratios, 46–48
    winter, 64–65, 74, 189–190

Natality, 36–39, 62–63
National parks
    management of, 1, 196–197
National Park Service, 3, 10, 14
Northern Yellowstone elk
    definition of, 1
Northern winter range
    area of, 3, 4
    boundary line area, 4
    elevation, 5
    land ownership, 5
Nutrition, 69–71, 73–74
    fatty acids, production of, 69
    food, protein content of, 70
    plane of, 69
    rumen, fermentation rates, 69–70
    rumen, microbes, 70

Parasites, 191–193
Plant-herbivore systems, 152
Population regulation, 35, 67–68, 198
Populations, eruptions of, 12, 15
Precipitation
    distribution of, 5–8
    trends in, 104–105
Predation: *see* Carnivores
Pregnancy rates
    adults, 38–39
    relationship to elk numbers, 37–38
    two-year-olds, 38, 239
    yearlings, 36–38, 238
Pronghorn
    carrying capacity, 185
    chest height, 171
    foot load, 172
    habitat utilization, 174
    herd composition, 169, 443
    human predation of, 169
    interspecific competition with elk, 180

    mortality of young, 168
    numbers, 168, 195
        historical, 157
    predation upon, 169
    rate of increase, observed, 168
    relationship to elk, 443
    winter diets, 176–177
    winter range, 167
Protein, crude, 70

$\bar{r}$: *see* Rate of increase, observed
r_m: *see* Rate of increase, intrinsic
r_p: *see* Rate of increase, potential
Range condition; *see also* Vegetation
    narrative reports of, 100–101, 421–
        431
Range management
    concepts of, 101
Range studies: *see* Vegetation
Rate of increase, intrinsic, 62
Rate of increase, observed, 20–21, 23
Rate of increase, potential, 23
Recruitment, 44–46, 63–64, 239–240
    relationship to population size, 45–46
Refugia, ecological, 183–184
Resource division
    and body size, 170
    by geographic area, 170–173
    by habitat utilization, 173–176
    by separation in space, 170–174
    among ungulates, 169–178
Resource limitation of ungulates, 194
Resource partitioning
    among species of ungulates, 183–184

Sagebrush; *see also* Vegetation, measure-
        ments of,
    abundance, 86, 90–92, 95, 124–125
    fire relationships, 107–111, 128
    grazing 128, 148
    measurements of, 99, 415–420
Seasonal distribution, 12, 23–24
    models of, 34
    historical, 23–25
    interpretation of, 34–35
    relationships to management, 34–35
    spring, summer, and autumn, 32
    winter, 4–5, 22–31
    winter range, upper, 4–5, 35
Sex and age composition, 39–44
Sex ratios, 46–48
Sexual maturity, 73

Sheep, bighorn, 83
  aerial counts, 161–165
  carrying capacity, 185
  chest height, 171
  fire ecology and, 185
  foot load, 172
  ground counts, 161, 165
  herd composition, 166, 440–441
  habitat utilization, 173–174
  interspecific competition with elk, 165,
    179–181, 200
  numbers, 156–157, 160–166, 436–440
    temperature effects upon observability,
      163–165
  rate of increase, observed, 164
  relationships to elk, 441
  selection of plant species and parts, 177
  winter diets, 176–177
  winter range, 160
Skeleton
  measurement of, 71–72
Social organization: *see* Behavior, social

Tapeworm, fringed, 192
Tick, winter, 192

Undernutrition, 70, 73–75, 193
Ungulate-vegetation equilibria
  management of, 198–199

Variance, analysis of, 371, 376, 386–391,
    396–401, 404–407, 419
Vegetation, 85–136
  abiotic influences upon, 101–118
  BLA: *see* Boundary line area
  boundary line area, 87–88, 94–95, 101,
    124, 128–129, 338–345, 364–
    368
    sagebrush in, 95
  changes over time
    aspen, 92
    forests, 89–92
    grasslands, 90–91, 93–94
    ridgetops, 93
    sagebrush grasslands, 91–93
    spring, summer, and autumn ranges,
      89–91
    willows, 91
  characteristic, 85–88
  climax, 85–88, 125, 134
    zootic, 87–88, 93, 100, 128, 134, 148,
      361, 377, 433

  description of, 8–9
  "deterioration" of, 126–134
  effects of elk upon, 150
  grasses, longevity of, 410
  grasslands
    boundary line area, 364–368
    descriptive measurements of, 353–368
    on mudflows, 368
    ridgetops and upper slopes, 361–364
  historical photos of, 88–95
  interpretation of changes over time,
    122–136
  litter accumulation, 98
  management of, 197–198
  measurements of, 95–101, 124–126,
    353–420,
    agronomy cages, 412
    aspen, 412–420, 412–415
    belt transects, 99, 416
    chart quadrats, 98–99, 379–398
    descriptive, 99
    grasses, leaf length, 394–395
    harsh physiographic sites, 406–412
    herbaceous species, 97–99
    herbage production, 97
    line-intercept, 411–412
    meter-square quadrats, 373–376
    Parker transects, 98–99, 379–406
    photo points, 98
    photo transects, 377–379
    plant vigor, 394–395, 409
    sagebrush, 99, 415–420
    square-foot-density, 97–98, 376–377,
      406
    square-meter quadrats, 97
    square-yard quadrats, 98, 406–411
    standing crop, 371–373
    trees and shrubs, 412–420
    willows, 99, 415–420
  overgrazed, 100–101
  past
    Holocene trends, 88
    pollen profiles, 88
  plants, exotic
    management of, 198
  present, 85
  ridgetop, 87–88, 98
  spring, summer, and autumn ranges, 123,
    248–291
  succession, plant retrogressive, 100–101,
    124–125, 134
  types, 85–88

Vegetation (*cont.*)
   ungulate effects upon, 134–136, 148–151
   winter range, 292–352
      beetle effects upon, 131
      boundary line area, 94–95
      conifers, browsing of, 129
      fire suppression upon, 136
      grazing disclimax, 94
      moose browsing of, 131
      outside the park, 95, 346–351
      photo comparisons, 123–124
      ridgetops, 127–128
      sagebrush, 125, 128
      sedge meadows, 93
      ungulate effects upon, 125–126
      utilization of grasses, 394, 398, 403, 406, 410
      willows, 93, 129–135

Weights,
   birth, 71, 74
   body, 70–74

Willow; *see also* Vegetation, measurements of
   abundance, 86, 87, 93, 129–134
   fire relationships, 124, 131
   grazing, 125, 129–134, 148
   measurements of, 99, 415–420
Winter hunting of elk, 11, 199–200
Winter range, upper Yellowstone, area, 4–5
   elk distribution within, 11–12, 35
Wolf, gray, 186–187, 194–195
   introduction of, 201
Wolverine, 187, 201
Worms, nematode, 154

Yellowstone National Park, 1–2, 85, 196, 203
   administration of, 3, 14
   area of, 3
   establishment of, 3
   geology and geography of, 3
   management of, 1, 196–202